Handbook of
Budgeting
for Nonprofit
Organizations

Jae K. Shim   Joel G. Siegel
Abraham J. Simon

**Software
Included!**

For Windows™

PRENTICE HALL
Englewood Cliffs, New Jersey 07632

Library of Congress Cataloging-in-Publication Data

Shim, Jae K.
    Handbook of budgeting for nonprofit organizations / by Jae K. Shim, Joel G. Siegel,
Abraham J. Simon.
        p.   cm.
    Includes index.
    ISBN 0-13-085580-4 (cloth)
    1. Nonprofit organizations—Finance.   I. Siegel, Joel G.   II. Simon, Abraham J.
III. Title.
HG4027.65.S54   1996   95-45619
658.15—dc20   CIP

Printed in the United States of America

10 9 8 7 6 5 4 3 2

This publication is designed to provide accurate and authoritative information in regard to
the subject matter covered. It is sold with the understanding that the publisher is not
engaged in rendering legal, accounting, or other professional service. If legal advice or
other expert assistance is required, the services of a competent professional person should
be sought.
*—From the Declaration of Principles jointly adopted by a Committee of the American
Bar Association and a Committee of Publishers and Associations*

ISBN 0-13-085580-4

PRENTICE HALL
Career & Personal Development
Englewood Cliffs, NJ 07632
A Simon & Schuster Company

On the World Wide Web at http://www.phdirect.com

Prentice-Hall International (UK) Limited, *London*
Prentice-Hall of Australia Pty. Limited, *Sydney*
Prentice-Hall Canada Inc., *Toronto*
Prentice-Hall Hispanoamericana, S.A., *Mexico*
Prentice-Hall of India Private Limited, *New Delhi*
Prentice-Hall of Japan, Inc., *Tokyo*
Simon & Schuster Asia Pte. Ltd., *Singapore*
Editora Prentice-Hall do Brasil, Ltda., *Rio de Janeiro*

DEDICATION

Ellen Coleman and Eugene Brissie

outstanding editor and publisher

CONTENTS

Part III
Budgeting for Specific Types of Nonprofit Organizations 213

Part IV
Financial Analysis for the Nonprofit Organization 323

ABOUT THE AUTHORS

JAE K. SHIM, Ph.D., is President of the National Business Review Foundation, a consultant to nonprofit organizations, and Professor of Accounting and Finance at California State University, Long Beach. He earned his doctorate from the University of California at Berkeley.

Dr. Shim has 44 books to his credit and has published over 50 articles in accounting and financial journals including *Financial Management, Decision Sciences, Management Science, Long Range Planning*, and *Management Accounting*. Many of his articles have dealt with budgeting, planning, and modeling in the not-for-profit sector. He has also authored monographs on municipal accounting, budgeting, and financial management for New York City.

Dr. Shim received the Credit Research Award for his article on financial management. He is also the recipient of a Ford Foundation Award, Mellon Research Fellowship, and Arthur Andersen Research Grant.

JOEL G. SIEGEL, Ph.D., CPA, is a consultant to nonprofit organizations and Professor of Accounting and Finance at Queens College of the City University of New York. He was previously associated with Coopers and Lybrand, CPAs and Arthur Andersen, CPAs.

Dr. Siegel is the author of 47 books and approximately 200 articles on business topics including many articles in the area of budgeting. His books have been published by Prentice Hall, Richard Irwin, McGraw-Hill, HarperCollins, John Wiley, Macmillan, Probus, International Publishing, Barron's, and the American Institute of CPAs.

His articles have appeared in various business journals including *Financial Executive, Financial Analysts Journal*, and *The CPA Journal*.

In 1972, he received the Outstanding Educator of America Award. Dr. Siegel is listed in *Who's Who Among Writers* and *Who's Who in the World*.

Dr. Siegel is the chairperson of the National Oversight Board.

ABRAHAM J. SIMON, Ph.D., CPA, is Professor of Nonprofit Accounting and Reporting and Chairperson of the Department of Accounting and Information Systems at Queens College, and a consultant to nonprofit organizations including the City of New York. He earned his doctorate from the University of Pennsylvania. Dr. Simon was a finance officer in the U.S. Army. He served as Chairperson of the Government and Nonprofit Section of the American Accounting Association. Dr. Simon also served as Chairperson of the Social Science Committee of the Research Foundation of the City University of New York.

Dr. Simon's books have been published by the Council on Municipal Performance, Prentice Hall (including the *Vest-Pocket MBA*), Dow-Jones Irwin, Matthew Bender, American Management Association, and the U.S. Printing Office. His articles have appeared in many journals including *Journal of Collective Negotiations in the Public Sector, National Economic Planning*, and the *National Public Accountant*. Dr. Simon also served on the editorial board of *Research in Governmental and Nonprofit Accounting*.

ACKNOWLEDGMENTS

We thank Ellen Coleman for her input and assistance on this book. Her efforts are recognized and appreciated. We also thank Barry Richardson for developmental editing and Tom Curtin for production editing.

Thanks goes to Dr. Stephen W. Hartman for authoring Chapters 2 and 12. Dr. Hartman is a consultant to nonprofit entities and a Professor at the Graduate School of Business at New York Institute of Technology.

Anique Qureshi, Ph.D., CPA, a consultant and Assistant Professor at Queens College, coauthored Chapter 5.

Adrian Fitzsimons, Ph.D., CPA, CMA, CFA, Professor of Accounting at St. John's University and consultant to Deloitte, Touche, CPAs, coauthored Chapter 13.

Robert Fonfeder, Ph.D., CPA, of Hofstra University, and a consultant, coauthored Chapter 8.

Professor Lois Schneider, Chairperson of Library Sciences at Queens College, coauthored Chapter 11.

We wish to acknowledge the editorial research done by Carol Fitzpatrick, former graduate assistant at California State University, Long Beach, now budget analyst of Long Beach Unified School District.

We also express appreciation to Jeffrey Brauchler and Leo Kehoe, research assistants, for their assistance with Chapters 4 and 6, respectively.

Special thanks to Rene Ramelow-Porter for her excellent work in developing the user disk that accompanies this book.

WHAT THIS BOOK WILL DO FOR YOU

Sound budgeting preparation, procedures, analysis, and control will improve efficiency, productivity, and effectiveness of your nonprofit organization. Budgeting enhances your ability to plan future direction, establish objectives, and obtain input from staff members. This *Handbook* provides the practical guidance necessary to assure your success.

Effective budgeting produces many valuable benefits for nonprofit organizations, such as:

❒ Producing an integrated plan for all phases of the organization's operations. Budgeting shows department and program contributions to the overall organization and reveals how each element fits into the whole picture.

❒ Measuring and appraising performance, effectiveness, and efficiency. Examples are quotas for donor contributions and fund-raising costs.

❒ Establishing performance yardsticks and targets and variance analysis. This enables reliable evaluation of programs and responsibility units.

❒ Setting cost and operating controls.

❒ Studying alternative courses of action and their effects by using "what-if" analysis.

❒ Prioritizing programs and activities.

❒ Communicating the organization's goals to all units and employees.

❒ Gaining a better handle on fund-raising in terms of funds needed and the costs associated with raising the funds.

❒ Showing what funding is needed to pay for programs and services.

❒ Looking at cooperation among different departments to achieve the organization's goals.

❒ Creating "healthy" competition.

❒ Encouraging teamwork.

In addition, the budgeting information you'll find in this book will help you appraise and analyze political and economic conditions, competitive factors, stability, risk, constraints, pricing, service capabilities, quality of performance, trends, employee capabilities, availability and cost of physical and human resources, cost control techniques, and technological developments. You will not only see how you fit into the budget process, but, more important, how you can excel in budgeting to accomplish the best results on a day-to-day basis.

This *Handbook* offers a comprehensive and practical look at all aspects of budgeting for nonprofit organizations. Some key areas covered include:

- ❒ Proven methods of formulating accurate, realistic, and reliable estimates.

- ❒ Control and variance evaluation to appraise revenue and costs.

- ❒ Setting realistic prices for services.

- ❒ Planning and scheduling activities and associated costs.

- ❒ Spotting problems immediately and taking corrective action.

- ❒ How financial models help determine the correlation between key factors and variables.

- ❒ Using computer software, including spreadsheets, in preparing and evaluating budgets.

Step-by-step instructions and rules of thumb are given to determine what to look for, what to be on guard against, what to do, how to do it, and how to use it in carrying out daily activities and operations. Examples are given of real-life practical applications. Emerging budgeting trends are discussed so as to keep you up to date.

In addition, this book comes with a work-saving diskette featuring a number of Lotus 1-2-3 spreadsheet templates that enable you to start using these budgeting techniques right away.

Jae K. Shim, Joel G. Siegel, and Abraham J. Simon

Part I

The Nonprofit Budget

Chapter 1

Budgeting Needs of Nonprofits: An Overview

Nonprofit organizations (NPOs) range from small, community-related entities to large national and international associations. They serve the interests of many types of people and offer a diverse array of services. Nonprofit budgets are intended to provide the best possible service given resource limitations; success is in terms of how much service is provided and at what quality.

Budgeting ensures the continued life and growth of the NPO and helps establish priorities. The budget is a plan of action, a mechanism for making choices among alternative expenditures.

PREPARING THE BUDGET

Budgets may be prepared by program or function by responsibility unit, by source, and by natural object of expenditure. When preparing the budget, you should consider many factors such as the desires of donors, availability of grants and contracts, conditions in the area (e.g., health care), and changing social values and interests.

Capital budgets apply to the acquisition or sale of assets having a useful life exceeding one year. Operating budgets are prepared each year showing expected revenues and costs.

When budgeting for the nonprofit organization, you must consider what service levels to provide, what to charge for these services, how to obtain funds to support the services, and how to allocate funds among programs. You should determine the organization's revenues first on an overall basis, and then on individual revenues. This approach provides direction in budget preparation for each responsibility unit within the organization. The unit's budget report should identify revenue by type, expenses by category, output measures, and unit cost for the service. It is difficult to estimate revenues over the next year. You may want to project different revenue levels on a best case, worst case scenerio and then make plans for activity at several different levels. Once each responsibility unit receives estimates of its activity level and its anticipated revenues, it then forecasts its expenditures.

Budgets present the nature and amount of available resources, and how the resources are to be used. Budgets may be in dollars and physical amounts (e.g., service hours). Budgets show proposed programs and their expected costs and accomplishments. Does your organization have the financial ability to meet its objectives? The degree of control exercisable by donors over resources must also be specified. You can use computer spreadsheets to quickly update interrelated financial forecasts as events occur.

Budgeting output for the NPO involves results measures, process measures, and social indicators. The *results measures* will show if the organization is accomplishing its objectives and the *process measures* will indicate the quantity of work. The *social indicators* are not control measures per se, but they may be used for strategic planning during the budgeting process. Both quantity and quality measures should be devised, even though measures of the quality of service are highly subjective.

The budget should not only be used as a planning mechanism but also as a way of both identifying needs for change and making those changes in a timely fashion.

A long-term plan should be based on short-term goals. You must analyze programs to determine if they should be retained or disbanded based on service accomplishments and costs. New programs should be established, if warranted. The activities in the planning stage are defining major objectives, specifying strategies to accomplish goals, and initiating the program planning process. Long-term planning starts with a mission statement that reflects the NPO's purpose, objectives, and strategies. There should be flexibility built into the system as the need arises. Alternatives should be assessed. Those people who have responsibilities for conducting an activity should have responsibility for the budgetary planning related to that operation.

HOW TO SOLVE SPECIAL BUDGETING PROBLEMS

The sources of financing for nonprofit organizations are limited requiring careful budgeting of cash inflows. Further, many NPOs do not have strong balance sheets and lose money, so it is not easy for them to borrow. You can minimize this problem through sound budgeting control over spending.

Gifts, grants, and other income can be difficult to estimate when planning for the coming year's activities. Funding comes from a variety of sources and may be narrowly focused (restricted by the donor). An economic downturn or unforeseen circumstances may result in a severe curtailment of funds (e.g., government contracts) that are urgently needed to cover operating costs. One way to improve the budgeting of income is to use computerized and quantitative models taking into account such factors as the risk of realization and timing.

Because NPOs are supposed to break even (make no profit), budgeting becomes a problem of balancing income to costs. Further, if a profit is made, a granting foundation may give less money in the future.

There is little room to increase revenues if costs exceed estimates. Therefore, a careful estimate of revenues and expenditures must be made during the budget process, and there must be stringent control during the year to make sure managers are not exceeding the estimated costs for their programs and services. Expenditure cuts may be needed to close the gap. On the other hand, if expenses are below revenue the NPO may not be delivering all the services expected. In budgeting, revenues may need to be raised and spent consistent with contracts, regulations, limitations, and restrictions. Restrictions on the use of funds or the time period involved can cause budgeting problems. Budgets may have to be presented to current and prospective donors to assure compliance with their wishes. For example, restricted funding may be given for a performance hall. Other large donations may be usable for general operating expenses or special projects. Perhaps only the income, but not the principal, of an endowment may be spent. The budget must clearly recognize any limitations.

With nonprofit organizations, there are often demands for better accountability and operational detail by outside agencies, including governing boards, standard-setting bodies, concerned citizens' groups, and funding agencies. Using the right budgeting techniques allows you to see problems before they occur so you can take steps to prevent them. The budget must satisfy the outside funding sources' requirements including cost reimbursement information. For example, some watchdog groups insist that NPOs should spend no more than 40 percent of their funds on administration and funds-raising.

The actual relationship between the costs incurred and the benefits provided may be difficult to measure. To illustrate, in a performing arts organization, the measure might be the amount of ticket sales and contributions it is able to generate with its programs. Its benefit to the community is not easily calculated. Nevertheless, if the programs produced are not valuable enough to the community, it will not generate enough revenue to cover costs, and it will have to cease operations.

Nonprofit budgeting is especially difficult because moneys may be in separate "pots"—unrestricted and restricted. Restricted fund groups may be numerous. The solution is a detailed recordkeeping system.

Budgeting variable costs is difficult because income is uncertain. Again, using computerized and financial models will help. Budgeting is also difficult when the NPO must allocate its costs between government contracts versus the public at large. The solution is to devise a cost allocation basis that logically fits the cost to the activity.

Nonprofit budgets are usually not easily adapted to changing circumstances. One reason is that many NPOs do not undergo significant variations in the service levels they provide each year. Their cost structure contains many fixed costs. Further, the longer the time period of the budget, the more uncertainty. NPOs are not accustomed to modifying budget allocations once made. The solution is to implement a flexible budgeting system.

Preparation of the budget should include community representatives, regulatory agencies, and funding sources. An NPO must respond to these external forces that often have conflicting objectives and priorities. Internal budget participants may also have different objectives. Concerns for quality of service often override cost issues. A teamwork approach is needed to resolve conflicting interests.

BUDGET PROCESS OBJECTIVES

A budget is a formal statement of expected resources and proposed expenditures. The process includes long-term planning, program/service planning, budget development, analysis, and control.

The operating objective of the NPO is to convert available resources into services. To meet its goals, the NPO needs a comprehensive plan to allocate resources and select among alternatives. The budget is a coordinated and interrelated plan segregated into areas of responsibility, indicating the amount expected to be required for definite purposes or programs and the amounts estimated to be received from specific sources. The budget may assure legal authorization of funds and efficiency in the delivery of services.

The organization's resources must be sufficient to perform needed programs. If not, the objective needs to be altered or an alternative approach used. What risks are there? How long does it take to accomplish the goal?

The budget structure follows the daily operating structure. If the NPO operates on a program basis, the budget will be a program budget. If the organization is departmental, so is the budget. A responsibility system of budgeting segregates the organization into work units, assigns individual responsibility for each operation of the units, and classifies costs as controllable or noncontrollable by the unit.

INCOME AND COSTS

Income may come from many sources including contributions, gifts, grants, contracts, membership fees, investment income, royalties, etc.

Forecasting a unit's expenditures can be difficult. Expenditures are often broad. It may be impossible to match expenses incurred in providing a program service to any specific revenue source that supports these services. Preparing a budget is easier if expenditures are grouped into separate categories.

When revenues are not related to costs, guidelines stated in nonmonetary, service-related terms may appear more useful in guiding budget preparation. In patient-oriented NPOs, budget guidelines could be based on the number of patients serviced by type of service. Other NPOs may establish budgets on the number of hours of operations and estimated traffic during these hours.

Under functional reporting used by some NPOs (e.g., voluntary health and welfare organizations), expenditures are accumulated by program purpose for which costs were incurred.

After program activities are budgeted, staffing evaluations are done to determine if enough employees are available or if recruitment efforts need to be budgeted for more staff and volunteers.

Budgets need to reveal commitments made by the NPO. For example, a grant might establish new computer training facilities at a school, but not provide for the continued maintenance cost of the program or for the teachers' salaries for instruction.

CONCLUSION

Today, funding agencies for and contributors to nonprofit organizations are most sophisticated in their own financial understanding and experience. Regular demands are made on NPOs for better accountability and operational detail by a variety of external agencies, including governing boards, standard-setting bodies, and funding agencies. Simple budgeting and planning techniques allow you to see problems before they occur and to take steps to prevent them. Budgets can be used for:

❑ setting performance standards and targets,

❑ encouraging efficiency,

❑ providing benchmarks for evaluation,

❑ indicating cash required for programs, and

❑ showing startup costs and minimum operating costs.

By taking advantage of the technological advances in computer programs, you can quickly give people the information they need to effectively monitor daily operations. Once the budgets are in place, variances from original estimates of revenues and expenditures will show you and other interested parties where to focus your correctional efforts.

Chapter 2

Gaining Control of Revenues with Nonprofit Budgeting*

There is a wide range of nonprofit organizations. Basically, the NPO includes any organization defined as 501(c)(3) and 501(c)(4) under the federal tax code for tax-exempt organizations. They consist of religious groups, performing arts, hospitals, institutions of higher education, cultural organizations, trade groups, labor unions, hobby groups, fan clubs, and others. Exhibit 1 shows Nonprofit Organizations: Number, by Type: 1980 to 1992.

While the primary purpose of a business organization is to improve the financial position of its owner(s), being profitable is irrelevant for the nonprofit organization and may actually be detrimental to its existence. The primary purpose of an NPO is to provide a service to the public or its constituents. Nonprofits rely on the public, or their members, to provide their operating income. Their objective is providing the highest level service at the lowest possible cost.

A major difference between for-profit and nonprofit organizations is that the latter are, for the most part, exempt from federal income tax on their revenues. Nonprofits often rely on private, organizational, or governmental contributions for a large portion of their revenue instead of the ser-

*This chapter was written by Stephen W. Hartman, Ph.D., a budgeting consultant and Professor at the Graduate School of Management at New York Institute of Technology. Special mention is given to Marilyn Purnell for her research on Budgeting for Nonprofit Organizations.

EXHIBIT 1
Nonprofit Organizations:
Number, By Type: 1980 to 1992

Type	Number of Institutions		Percent Change	Percent of Total
	1980	1992	1980 to 1992	1992
Trade, Business, Commercial	3,118	3,851	23.51%	17.8%
Agriculture	677	1,082	59.82%	5.3%
Scientific, Engineering, Tech.	1,039	1,365	31.38%	6.3%
Educational*	2,376	1,294	–45.54%*	6.0%
Cultural*		1,887		8.7%
Social Welfare	994	1,773	78.37%	8.2%
Health, Medical	1,413	2,290	62.07%	10.6%
Public Affairs	1,068	2,190	105.06%	10.1%
Fraternal, Foreign Interest, Nationality, Ethnic	435	561	28.97%	2.6%
Religious	797	1,175	47.43%	5.4%
Veteran, Hereditary, Patriotic	208	586	181.73%	2.7%
Hobby, Avocational	910	1,504	65.27%	6.9%
Athletic Sports	504	845	67.66%	3.9%
Labor Unions	235	249	5.96%	1.1%
Chambers of Commerce	105	168	60.00%	1.1%
Greek & non-Greek Letter Societies	318	339	6.60%	1.6%
Fan Clubs	NA	506		2.3%
Total	14,197	21,665	52.6%	100.00%

*1980 Data for cultural associations included with educational associations.
*Source: Interpolated from Table No. 1325, "National Nonprofit Associations—Number, by Type: 1980 to 1992," *Statistical Abstract of the United States*, 1993 (Washington, D.C.: GPO, 1993), p. 787.

vice fees and investment income for-profit businesses charge. The nonprofit's reliance on contributions can cause great cyclical revenue swings consistent with the state of the economy. For example, in May, 1992, the Joffrey Ballet announced that an expected one-million-dollar donation was revoked plunging them $1.2 million into debt. As a result, the company canceled its New York spring season and cut back on its Los Angeles' commitments.

Administrators in not for profit organizations must struggle with the uncertainties that go hand in hand (sic) with dependence on economic conditions and public support. The need-for-funds is perennial, and drastic reductions in public funding force not-for-profit organizations into heroic efforts to survive.[1]

BUILDING REVENUES THROUGH CONTRIBUTIONS AND GRANTS

Contributions and grants normally comprise a large portion of a nonprofit's revenues. There are four basic types of grants: foundation, private, endowment, and matching. These grants have individual specifications. Some grants may be unrestricted, allowing their use for any purpose the nonprofit deems necessary, including current operations, whereas other grants are restricted for one purpose only and require very strict accounting. Restricted grants may be given, for example, for the purpose of constructing a particular building or pursuing a particular type of research. Nonprofits having restricted grants could find themselves with a situation where one activity is extremely well funded while their operating budget is basically nonexistent. Foundation grants, for example, normally are highly restricted and can be used only for certain clearly specified purposes.

Foundation grants fund many nonprofit activities. A foundation may contribute a grant to a municipality's philharmonic association for the purpose of developing and training new musicians. The grants may be either solicited or unsolicited. In a solicited grant, the prospective grantee applies to the foundation for specific funding. For example, an organization may apply to the Ford Foundation to receive funding for a specific research activity it feels the foundation would support. In an unsolicited grant, the foundation makes an independent determination of projects it would support and then specifies the size of the grant and its purpose. For example, the MacArthur Foundation makes unsolicited grants to individuals it feels have made outstanding societal or cultural contributions, making it possible for that person to continue his or her individual activities without having to be concerned with self-sustaining economic activities. All foundation grants must be accounted for in terms of how funded activities have been achieved. Both solicited and unsolicited foundation grants have a specified time period. The terms of the grant specify if, and under what conditions, a foundation grant is renewable.

In an endowment grant the capital received must be invested to generate current income to fund the specified activity. For example, a foundation grant may be given to a university to "endow a chair," meaning that a grant has been given specifically for the purpose of creating an endowment for hiring a "distinguished professor" in a given field. The capital can never be used, but must be forever invested. This often turns out to be one of the few predictable sources of "hard money" a nonprofit organization has.

Contributions can also include non-cash items such as donated facilities and other fixed assets, donated materials and services, and volunteer labor. For accounting purposes, these are recorded as assets at fair market value. If volunteer labor is managed the same way as paid labor, it must be expensed as paid labor.

Exhibit 2 shows Corporate Philanthropy—Donations by Type of Beneficiary: 1980 to 1991.

EXHIBIT 2
Corporate Philanthropy -
Donations by Type of Beneficiary: 1980 to 1991
1987 = 100.0

Beneficiary	1980	1991	Percent Change	% of Total 1991
Health and Human Services	470	545	16.06%	27.12%
Federated Drives	237	255	7.53%	12.69%
Education	523	702	34.29%	34.90%
Employee Matching Gifts	63	127	101.44%	6.32%
Culture and Art	151	238	57.25%	11.82%
Civic, Community Activities	162	227	39.78%	11.29%
Community Improvement	65	(NA)	(NA)	(NA)
Environment; Ecology	15	20	31.19%	0.98%
Total	1,383	2,011	45.40%	100.00%

Source: Interpolated from Table No. 620, "Corporate Philanthropy—Donations, by Type of Beneficiary: 1980 to 1991," *Statistical Abstract of the United States, 1993* (Washington, D.C.: GPO, 1993), p. 388.

Exhibit 3 shows private Philanthropy Funds, by Source and Allocation, from 1980 to 1991, in billions of constant 1987 dollars.

EXHIBIT 3
Private Philanthropy Funds, by Source and Allocation:
In Billions: 1980 to 1991
1987 = 100

Sources:	1980	1991	% Change 1980 to 1991	% of Total 1991
Individuals	57	92	63.14%	82.61%
Foundations	4	7	79.41%	6.25%
Corporations	3	5	70.81%	4.89%
Charitable	4	7	73.22%	6.25%
Total Funds	68	112	65.04%	100.00%
Allocations:				
Religion	31	61	96.11%	54.17%
Health	7	9	17.87%	7.77%
Education	7	12	71.31%	10.66%
Human Service	7	9	39.32%	8.49%
Arts, Culture and Humanities	4	8	77.11%	7.05%
Public/Society	2	4	110.38%	3.93%
Environment/ Wildlife[1]	0	2	1*	2.00%
International[1]	0	2	1*	2.08%
Undesignated	9	4	−54.82%	3.77%

[1]Included in "Undesignated" in 1980.

Source: Interpolated from Table No. 617, "Private Philanthropy Funds, by Source and Allocations: 1970 to 1991," *Statistical Abstract of the United States, 1993* (Washington, D.C.: GPO, 1993), p. 387.

Overall, Exhibit 3 shows a large dollar increase in philanthropic funding from 1980 to 1991. Individuals are the biggest philanthropic contributors with the majority of their contributions being allocated to religion. However, all allocation categories showed significant percentage increases from 1980.

Another major source of nonprofit organizational resources is volunteerism. Exhibit 4 shows the Percent of Adult Population Doing Volunteer Work in 1989.

EXHIBIT 4
Volunteer Workers and Percent of Adult Population Doing Volunteer Work
1989

Volunteer Workers Number (1,000)	38,042
Percent of Population	20.40%
Percent Distribution of Volunteers, By Type of Organization	
Total	100.00%
Churches & Other Religious Organizations	37.40%
Schools & Other Educational Organizations	15.10%
Civic or Political Organizations	13.20%
Hospitals & Other Health Organizations	10.40%
Social or Welfare Organizations	9.90%
Sport or Recreational Organizations	7.80%
Other Organizations	6.30%

Source: Interpolated from Table No. 614, "Percent of Adult Population Doing Volunteer Work: 1989," *Statistical Abstract of the United States*, 1993 (Washington, D.C.: GPO, 1993), p. 386.

BEWARE OF THESE DONATION PITFALLS

Nonprofit organizations depend heavily on contributions as revenue sources. However, there are dangers in receiving certain types of contributions:

1. *Land:* A donation of land can have serious consequences if the title is not free and clear, or there are serious hazardous wastes or other environmental conditions associated with it or it is highly restricted by local zoning laws. For example, Love Canal was donated by Hooker Chemical Corporation to the unsuspecting local school board.

2. *Appreciated property:* A nonprofit organization may become the unwitting co-conspirator to a fraudulent appraisal scheme when art, jewelry, real estate, historical artifacts, or other property items are donated.

3. *Worthless property:* A nonprofit organization accepting worthless property will incur disposal costs as well as possible liability in the event the property is hazardous.

4. *Cash:* Accepting cash can materially change the purpose of a nonprofit if the terms of its transmittal seriously compromise its mission. Furthermore, the source of the cash must be investigated to determine its legitimacy.

5. *Long-term gift:* This type of gift often involves real estate. The serious question is whether the nonprofit organization can afford the long-term maintenance required with any long-term gift.

6. *Testamentary gifts:* Long delays can ensue should the estate be challenged. If the estate consists of property that needs constant maintenance, the question arises as to who will perform it while the estate is being probated. If the maintenance is not performed, the property may deteriorate to the point where it becomes an actual liability.

7. *Volunteers:* Know your volunteers. It is important to determine that unethical persons do not become "volunteers" for a nonprofit with the explicit purpose of exploiting it for their own ends.

Each type of contribution must be examined on its own merits. In some cases, it may make more sense for a nonprofit organization to refuse a donation than to assume its liabilities.

USING FUND DRIVES TO GENERATE SUPPORT

Nonprofit organizations often have fund drives. Fund drives solicit pledges of financial support. Membership and subscription fees may also be viewed as a contribution if they do not provide an economic benefit other than a tax deduction.

Another method nonprofits use to raise funds is to sponsor a performance and sell tickets. The revenue earned from the ticket sales is accounted for in the period the performance is actually given. There are two methods for selling tickets. One is to assign seats; the other is to have open seating with no guaranteed seats. In the case of assigned seating, each ticket must match an assigned seat; therefore it is not possible to sell more tickets than the seating permits. Ticket prices can vary by the seat location in the hall with the most advantageous seats having the highest prices.

In the case of open seating, it is possible to sell more tickets than there are seats. Experience will indicate what the number of seats must be as a proportion of total ticket sales. For example, it may be possible to sell 50% more tickets than there are seats simply because fewer than 50% of ticket purchasers are expected to actually materialize at the performance. However, since it is open seating, it is not possible to vary the ticket prices according to the seat location in the hall.

Nonetheless, for both assigned and unassigned seating, it is possible to charge differential rates depending on whether it is a matinee, evening, weekend performance, gala, or opening night. Nonprofits sponsoring assigned seating performances can issue season or series tickets, including a seat for every performance of the season, or for a selected set of performances either on a regular or "patron" basis. Patron tickets include a contribution on top of the ticket price as well as including some status benefits such as theater parties and admission backstage to meet the performers and director.

The risk nonprofits assume in sponsoring performances is that ticket sales will not offset the cost of the performance. A careful market analysis must be done to determine the economic feasibility of sponsoring a particular performance or performance series. Estimates must be made of the ability of a performance to "draw" a sufficient audience to offset its costs. These costs include expenses incurred from fund-raising, marketing, administration, insurance, and production expenses including the costs of hiring stagehands, musicians, the use of theater equipment, and facility rental costs if they do not own it. Extremely large and complex performances are accompanied by escalated production costs. Budgeting for these performances includes careful projections of revenues vs. costs. Large productions often have many union scale musicians, which can quickly become an economic nightmare. A marketing failure can easily lead to an unsustainable loss.

Performing companies almost never produce enough ticket revenue to offset their operational costs. They often depend heavily on contributions from "patrons" to make up the deficit. During periods of recession, ticket sales slow and "patrons" are less likely to contribute.

THE FUND-RAISING PROSPECTUS AS A MARKETING TOOL

Any fund-raising campaign needs to present a prospectus to the prospective donor as an integral part of its solicitation activity. The basic objective of the fund-raising prospectus is to acquaint potential donors, whether they are foundations, corporations, governments or individuals, about the NPO's history, purpose, potential, accomplishments, donor benefits, and financial goals.

Basically, a prospectus is a marketing tool and should be treated as such. It needs to be attractively prepared using attention-getting phrases and style. A wide variety of media, including multimedia formats, can be considered. However, cost is a major consideration in any fund-raising campaign, and the nonprofit must seek to utilize the most cost effective prospectus in terms of the market that is being sought.

The prospectus should be accompanied by an effective, professional and appealing cover letter. The cover letter needs to be written in such a way that it will attract the attention of the target donor. Prospective donors receive many such solicitations, and the cover letter must have a "hook" that will allow the prospectus to be read.

A successful prospectus will contain at least the following elements:

1. An introduction covering some of the same information as in the cover letter but more general in nature. The uniqueness of the organization in achieving its goals should be emphasized.

2. A description of the organization and its historical purpose, stressing stability, soundness, and breadth of patronage.

3. The goals of the organization as outlined in the overall budget process.

4. Near term organizational objectives.

5. What the present needs are that the organization is attempting to meet and how much progress it is making in meeting these needs.

6. A brief description of the key people in the organization.

7. Key financial information concerning the nonprofit organization. This would include the current budget, a five-year plan, and summary budgets of past performance.

8. A summary of the key things the nonprofit wants the target audience to remember. The basic appeal of the organization should be re-stated.

It is essential that the organization's ethics be above reproach when making solicitations, and the prospectus must therefore be as professional as possible. While in many cases fund-raising activities are directed to a particular cause, it must be pointed out that the contributions are going to be given to the nonprofit organization for its determination of their best use. This can avoid an ethical dilemma when contributions are used for more than one cause or crisis.

MAKING SURE GIFTS ARE TAX-DEDUCTIBLE

One of the major incentives a donor has for giving to an NPO is that the donation is tax-deductible. However, in order for the donation to be tax-deductible the U.S. Internal Revenue Service (IRS) specifies it must meet certain qualifications:

1. The donation must be an irrevocable transfer of property or cash from a donor who is of legal age and of sound mind to a nonprofit organization qualified by the IRS as tax-exempt.

2. The donor cannot maintain any control or influence over the donation after it has been received by the nonprofit.

3. If the donor receives a benefit as a result of making a contribution to a qualified nonprofit organization, only the amount of the contribution that exceeds the value of the benefit is tax-deductible.

4. The donor may not receive any benefits from any contributions after they have been made to the qualified nonprofit organization. If the

donor still derives benefit from the contribution, then it loses its tax deductibility while becoming the irretrievable property of the non-profit organization.

5. Only the amount paid by a donor to a qualified nonprofit organization in excess of the fair market value for merchandise, goods, or services is tax-deductible.

6. A contribution is "for the use of" a qualified nonprofit organization when it is held in a legally enforceable trust for the qualified organization or in a similar legal arrangement.

7. Only out-of-pocket expenses are tax-deductible when a donor serves as a volunteer for a qualified nonprofit organization.

BUDGETING FOR NONPROFIT ORGANIZATIONS

Budgeting in the nonprofit sector is a comprehensive process consisting of several functions:

❏ *Planning and Conceiving.* This is the initial step for the nonprofit organizational budgeting process. It is essential to determine the programmatic needs and resources required and available. The needs and resources are expressed in dollar amounts for the next fiscal year's operations.

❏ *Management and Coordination.* These processes are key elements in implementing the nonprofit organization's budget. Careful thought has to be given to the organizational structure and the management team.

❏ *Assessing and Reporting/Accounting.* These are necessary to determine how resources were actually used in the budgetary process.

The budgetary process by its very nature is proactive. It seeks to determine the future utilization of resources prior to a fiscal year and is therefore future oriented. On the other hand, financial management is concerned with current utilization of resources and is therefore oriented to the present. However, there is an interrelationship between the two functions. Financial management will help to determine future revenues and expenditures, and programmatic budgetary planning is essential to the formation and implementation of a budget. In point of fact, budgetary planning and financial management are parallel functions in the nonprofit sector. Both interact with each other and decisions implemented in one area define the parameters for the other. For example, when the nature of a program is determined, thought must be given to its budgetary costs with upper and lower parameters. Similarly, when financial management determines the total budgetary size of a particular function, this directly affects the parameters of programmatic planning. An essential reciprocal process is created in this manner. It is essential to have a harmonious relationship between program managers and the financial management team since each is very dependent on the other.

Financial management transformations in operational procedures can have major productivity associations that will directly affect program budgeting. Restrictions or methodological changes in using system resources can dramatically affect programmatic procedures having immediate system implications. This will directly affect programmatic budgeting and planning.

Ineffective financial management and accounting can seriously affect the most well-conceived programmatic budgeting and planning. If lackadaisical financial management allows a program to run without stringent financial controls, the program planners will see their best budgetary plans rendered ineffective.

NONPROFIT BUDGETARY POLITICS

Nonprofit budgeting is the quintessence of the nonprofit political process. The very existence of a nonprofit as well as the achievement of its basic mission depends on the securing and allocating of budgetary resources. Therefore, the budgetary process is at the heart of the considerable political dynamics occurring within all nonprofit organizations

The nature of the budgetary political process varies considerably from one nonprofit to another. Relationships existing within the nonprofit between department heads and those having the ability to approve funds are critical to determining the rules of the budgetary game. Additionally, the budgetary political process varies depending on whether or not the funds are being derived internally from the nonprofit's current revenues or from an external funding source. Nonetheless, in order to be successful in the nonprofit budgetary process, one must be familiar with the nonprofit's budgetary ploys and accomplished in performing them.

Probably the most comprehensive description of nonprofit budgeting ploys is found in Robert N. Anthony and Regina E. Herzlinger, *Management Control in Nonprofit Organizations* (Homewood, IL: Richard D. Irwin, Inc., 1980).

SIX BENEFITS OF SOUND BUDGETARY MANAGEMENT

It is essential for an NPO to maintain financial control through effective budgetary management. Strong budgetary management has several benefits for a nonprofit organization:

1. It mandates a planning and prioritizing process for all programmatic activities and support functions.

2. The budget controls spending activities while ensuring they occur within an overall revenue and spending plan, making certain the organization's programmatic and service objectives are achieved.

3. It provides central direction for all of the nonprofit's activities, preventing waste while achieving programmatic coordination and integration.

4. The forced participatory nature of the budgeting process fosters organizational teamwork.

5. The budgetary process includes measurement and control features with programmatic and service level outcome dimensions for achieving objectives. This creates resource utilization performance measures.

6. A well-developed budgetary process demonstrates credibility and responsibility to external funding sources.

BUDGET PLANNING FOR THE FISCAL YEAR

The fiscal year does not necessarily coincide with the calendar year. (For example, the Federal Fiscal year runs from October 1 to September 30.) Nonetheless, a fiscal year always lasts twelve months. Despite the fact that certain programs may last less or longer than a calendar year, their budget still conforms to the fiscal year. However, their budget calendar may differ.

Many functions are performed during the annual fiscal-year cycle. These include the conceptualization of plans and programmatic decisions, the implementation of procedures and programs, and the completion of budgetary reviews, reports and audits.

Audit procedures determining how funds were spent and revenues were allocated are also coordinated with the end of the fiscal year. Revenues and expenditures must be accounted for on a regular yearly basis.

Therefore, the annual fiscal year is important for programmatic budget planning, management control, and auditing procedures. The fiscal year is the standard unit of time for evaluating and developing programs, developing operational and budgetary policies, and completing spending programs. All the activities of the nonprofit organization are synchronized to the fiscal year.

The effect of the fiscal year is to enforce a budgetary discipline on nonprofit organizations and their programmatic activities. The nonprofit's programmatic cost effectiveness and productivity is evaluated in terms of its annual programmatic goals. The ability of the nonprofit to obtain refunding is predicated upon the fiscal year's activities.

Thus, an NPO's budgetary planning, financial management, and continued funding are synchronized with the annual fiscal-year cycle. The net effect of the fiscal year is to keep the nonprofit attuned to current societal needs and developments. This helps to maintain public accountability for the nonprofit sector as well as legitimizing and authenticating its activities. It also maintains its responsibility to its clientele as well as to the broader public.

WORKING WITHIN THE BUDGET CYCLE

The budget cycle encompasses the full programmatic range of the budgetary activities. While the fiscal year is a defined annual time period, the budget cycle encompasses all of the activities leading up to the fiscal year as well as subsequent to it.

The budget cycle covers at least five areas:

1. *Program and Budget Planning*. Here programmatic needs are assessed leading to the development of planning, cost calculating, and actual budget creation.

2. *Obtaining Budgetary Funds*. After receiving departmental fund requests, the nonprofit organization negotiates with donors to obtain funding. Consequent to the provision of fund estimates, final budget estimates are created and allocations are made.

3. *Financial Fund Management.* This includes the day-to-day management of internal funds, financial transactions, accounting, operations reporting, and cost controls.

4. *Productivity Evaluation, Budgetary, and Audit Reports.* Here the nonprofit organization is involved with closing out the end of the year including cost effectiveness, and financial and performance audit reports.

5. *Reevaluation.* Based upon the end-of-the-year evaluations, the nonprofit organization implements a program reevaluation. The purpose of the reevaluation is to evaluate actual program costs for the purpose of establishing new programmatic budget levels.

DEVELOPING A BUDGET CALENDAR

Budgeting is a sequential process of time-sensitive events. As such, budgeting must proceed on an orderly and predictable basis. Therefore, many nonprofit organizations find it essential to develop a budgetary calendar. Exhibit 5 presents an example of a nonprofit organization's Budget Calendar. It is the responsibility of the comptroller and finance department to administer the budgetary calendar, ensuring the timely completion of all functions. Individual programs also have their own budgetary calendar depending on their funding source.

EXHIBIT 5
Budget Calendar

Function	Date	Administrative Unit
Prepare Preliminary Budget Requests	April 1	All Program & Operating Department Directors
Prepare First Departmental Draft Budgets	May 1	All Program Directors and Operating Department Heads
Consolidate & Review Requests	June 1	Comptroller and Accountants
Prepare and Submit Budget	June 15	Comptroller and Accountants
Review Budget	July 1	Budget Committee
Final Budget	July 15	Budget Committee
Revise Budget	August 1	Department Directors
Final Budget Presentation	September 1	Chief Executive Officer

The budgetary calendar begins with the preparation phase of the budgetary process. Budget requests are largely proactive and are a function of the availability of funding sources. The availability of funding sources will determine the nonprofit's departmental service levels as formulated in program and budgetary planning. The comptroller and accountants review expenditure requests in terms of revenue projections and adjust the budget accordingly. It is useful to have one or more funding source representative on the budget committee to review prospective service activities in terms of current funding availability and funding source program priorities. Their presence and support become particularly critical when the Chief Executive Officer presents the final budget to the board of directors for final approval prior to the beginning of the fiscal year.

A budget calandar for a specific grant, program, or activity may be different than that of the overall organization because the grantor may have a different time period and the contract may have stipulated due dates.

FOUR TYPES OF NONPROFIT ORGANIZATIONAL BUDGETS

The NPO uses a budget as a financial plan to project revenues and expenditures for a defined fiscal period, normally a year. Nonprofit organizations have four types of budgets:

OPERATING BUDGET

This is the financial plan that exists for current operations. It includes a projection of current expenses and revenues for the fiscal year. It supports all current programs, funds and related services.

If revenues do not relate to costs, guidelines may be set in nonmonetary, service-related terms. For example, in health care, guidelines may be based on the number of patients served and the identification of type of service provided.

Exhibit 6 presents an illustrative operating budget.

EXHIBIT 6
Operating Budget

Revenue:
  Contributions

Special events
Grants
  Foundation
  Government
Membership dues
Service fees
Contractual revenue
Concession revenue
Rental income
Auxiliary activities
Investment income
Miscellaneous income
Total revenue
Expenses by object of expense
  Salaries
  Fringe benefits
  Payroll taxes
  Supplies
  Communication
  Professional fees
  Publications
  Exhibits and displays
  Conferences
  Grants and awards
  Rentals
  Insurance
  Travel and lodging
Total Expenses
Excess (deficit) on Operations

GRANT OR CONTRACT PROPOSAL BUDGET

This is a specific budget for a particular grant or program. Often, a grant specifies that a defined budget be established for grant administration purposes. A grant or contract proposal budget may have a different budget calendar than the nonprofit organization because the fiscal year of the granting agency may be different and the terms of the contract may have certain due dates.

CASH BUDGET

A cash budget differs from the operating budget in that it deals with short term cash flows covering such items as deposits, payments, loans, advances, and equipment purchases. The cash budget is normally operated in tandem with the operating budget permitting managers to plan the timing of expenses using the availability of cash flow. The cash budget indicates if anticipated cash resources are adequate to finance operations.

A cash budget identifies possible cash shortages or overages. Shortages may require borrowing. Overages may mean there is extra money to invest for a return. A cash budget helps in the planning and timing for receipts, borrowing, repaying debt, and utilizing assets. The cash budget period depends to some degree on the stability of the NPO's major operations. For example, a shorter period is suggested when activities are erratic.

Probability analysis may be used to predict cash flows. For example, if the probability of receiving a donation from Donor A is 90%, a possible donation of $6,000,000 is $5,400,000.

Exhibit 7 shows an illustrative cash budget.

CAPITAL BUDGET

This budget is used for planning major expenditures having a useful life of at least five years. It is used for the purchase of major equipment such as vehicles, and structures. Capital budgets help the nonprofit plan the timing of these purchases and financing methods. The capital budget involves the following: (1) a listing of what is needed, why, its cost, and expected income to be derived; (2) if needed for technological update; and (3) amount of total capital budget based on sources of funding (e.g., donor contributions, patient revenue).

BUDGETING REVENUE

Budgeted revenue may be based on past experience taking into account changes in the current environment and possible changes in the future.

The revenue budget depends on many variables including consistency and timing of donations, demographics, economic and political conditions, competition, professional reputation, government regulations (e.g., reimbursement policies), size of institution, fund drives, stability, changes in tax

EXHIBIT 5
Cash Budget

Cash Inflows:

Membership fees	$900,000	
Guest fees	60,000	
Rental income	200,000	
Contributions	1,000,000	
Grants	800,000	
Contracts	400,000	
Investment income	80,000	
Loan proceeds	150,000	
Sale of assets	50,000	
Total cash inflows		$3,640,000

Cash Outflows:

Salaries	$350,000	
Rent	220,000	
Supplies	160,000	
Insurance	40,000	
Utilities	80,000	
Telephone	30,000	
Maintenance	20,000	
Accounting and legal fees	190,000	
Travel	60,000	
Payment of debt	300,000	
Purchase of fixed assets	500,000	
Total cash outflows		1,950,000

Net cash inflows	$1,690,000
Beginning cash balance	230,000
Ending cash balance	$1,920,000

law, social conditions, community relationships, and new services to be provided. For example, it is difficult to estimate gifts, contributions, and endowments. Such income sources can drastically decline when an economic downturn occurs or unforseen circumstances happen. Government contract revenue may fall off with changing political attitudes.

Revenue planning considers activities and service levels to perform, what price to charge, how to raise funds to support services, and how to allocate the funds among programs. The NPO may project revenue levels under alternative assumptions such as best-case, worst-case, and normal case.

Primary sources of revenue provide most of the NPO's revenue such as patient care services in a health care facility received directly from patients and insurance carriers. *Secondary sources* of revenue include interest income, dividend income, and royalties. A religious institution's major revenue source is its weekly offerings from members. A college's primary revenue source includes tuition, alumni grants, and admission fees. A trade association's major revenue source is membership fees. Sometimes revenue falls below that which is based on fair market value. For example, a health care facility may be underpaid from Medicaid.

Some income is easy to budget (e.g., membership fees) while other income is difficult to forecast (e.g., donations). Financial models are helpful in this regard using computer software.

Gross revenue equals the number of service units times the estimated price or rate per unit.

EXAMPLE 1

A child care center is licensed to care for up to 30 children. The expected number of students is 80%. Thus, 24 children are actually expected on average. The center operates 50 weeks a year. It is open 35 hours a week. The hourly rate charged is $6.

Gross revenue = 24 children × 50 weeks × 35 hours × $6 = $252,000

In estimating revenue, a simple-average and a weighted-average (over a five year period) may be calculated. A simple-average equals:

$$\frac{\text{Total revenue for 5 years}}{5 \text{ years}}$$

A weighted-average is more desirable because it gives more weight to the most recent years, reflecting higher current fees or prices. If a five year weighted-average is used, the current year is given a weight of 5 while the first year is assigned a weight of 1.

EXAMPLE 2

A charity is estimating its donations for 19X6. The donations over the last five years were:

Year	Donation
19X5	$15 million
19X4	12 million
19X3	11 million
19X2	9 million
19X1	10 million
Total	$57 million

If the donation for 19X6 is budgeted based on a simple-average, it would equal:

Simple-average = $\dfrac{\text{Total for 5 years}}{\text{5 years}}$ = $\dfrac{\$57 \text{ million}}{\text{5 years}}$ = $11.4 million

If the donation for 19X6 is estimated using a weighted-average, it would equal:

Year	Donation	x	Weight	=	Total
19X5	$15 million	x	5	=	$75 million
19X4	12	x	4	=	48
19X3	11	x	3	=	33
19X2	9	x	2	=	18
19X1	10	x	1	=	10
Total	$57 million		15		$184 million

Weighted-average = $\dfrac{\text{Total Weighted Amount}}{15}$ = $12.3 million (rounded)

BREAKING DOWN THE COST CLASSIFICATIONS

All nonprofit organizational budgets have fixed and variable costs. Fixed costs include rent, utilities, and insurance. The largest variable element an NPO has is the salary associated with the number of employees necessary to provide services. Additional challenges arise in estimating expenses associated with achieving various programmatic objectives. This is particularly true if the nonprofit organization has little or no prior experience in a particular program.

Estimating salary costs becomes particularly difficult if various types of workers are used at different stages of a project and only for a specified period of time. For example, certain seasonal activities have peak periods followed by a long lull. Performances require the work of many different people including those who construct sets, performers, and union scale musicians.

For ongoing activities, it is important to know the breakdown between variable and fixed costs. This makes it possible to estimate the unit cost of providing services to certain populations and how much it would cost to achieve service increases to larger populations. Exhibit 8 shows an activity's hypothetical fixed and variable cost breakdowns with a projected 30% increase in services. As can be seen, only the variable costs would increase by $7,500 while the fixed costs remain the same. Thus, the total projected cost of a 30% service increase would be $107,500 compared to $100,000.

EXHIBIT 8
Projecting Fixed and Variable Costs
in Dollars

Cost Category	Present Costs	30% Increment	Projected Cost
Variable Costs	25,000	7,500	32,500
Fixed Costs	75,000		75,000
Total	100,000		107,500

However, life is not that simple. The reality is that fixed costs are variable when their utilization exceeds their planned capacity. For example, a sports arena can only seat so many people. Beyond that capacity, either the arena must be expanded or replaced.

Fixed costs also have variable components. For example, telephone charges have both a fixed monthly fee and a utilization fee. Thus, the more the telephone is used, the more it is going to cost. This is an example of a mixed cost factor having both fixed and variable cost elements.

Thus, in projecting nonprofit organizational budgets, fixed, variable, and mixed costs must be considered. Variable costs are based on unit utilization, while fixed costs may face adjustments due to excess utilization. The mixed costs contain both variable and fixed cost calculations.[2]

Nonprofit organizations also have direct and indirect costs. Direct costs occur as a straightforward result of a particular activity. For example, if a nonprofit sponsors a performance, the cost of hiring employees for that performance is a direct cost. Indirect costs are costs related to the administration of the organization, although a portion of these activities may be related to supervising the performance.

Nonprofits also have common and joint costs. The cost of rendering two or more services may have several overlapping and shared costs. For example, advertising in a nonprofit journal shares common distribution and printing costs. If a nonprofit derives income from sponsoring performances and advertises those performances in its journal, then a common cost of the performance is the cost of advertising both the performance and the nonprofit organization. The challenge for nonprofit budgeting is properly allocating common and joint costs between various aspects of the same function.

Exhibit 9 illustrates a hypothetical operating budget of a nonprofit organization where costs are allocated between the broad functions of management and fund-raising. Exhibit 9 demonstrates the apportionment of expenses among functions.

EXHIBIT 9
Operating Budget for a Hypothetical Nonprofit
in Dollars

Expense Categories	General Administration	Fund Raising	Total
Salaries	94,286	34,586	128,872
Payroll Taxes and Benefits	34,886	12,797	47,683
Consulting Fees	18,243	7,450	25,693
Professional Fees	41,750	7,256	49,006
Supplies	1,542	1,683	3,225
Telephone	1,345	1,893	3,238
Postage	1,543	2,254	3,797
Office Rental Cost	32,430	23,541	55,971
Equipment Rental	2,450	2,650	5,100
Printing	5,240	7,560	12,800
Professional Travel	2,840	2,340	5,180
Insurance	8,250	2,200	10,450
Miscellaneous	2,150	1,850	4,000
Total Expenditures	246,955	108,060	355,015

PRESENTING BUDGET REPORTS

Budget reports are internal working documents intended to provide management ongoing financial information. The two basic budget reports are expenditure and revenue. Budget reports depend on the type of budgetary system in place within the organization as well as management priorities. Separate expenditure and revenue budget reports can be developed or they can be combined.

The method used for presenting budget reports depends on the purposes management wants them to serve. They may provide year-to-year comparisons, revenues as a percentage of expenditures, expenditures and revenues as a percentage of budgeted amounts, or any of several variations.

REVENUE REPORTS

Revenue reports are intended to update management on the current status of revenue receipts in relation to budgeted totals. Revenue reports are retrieved from current revenue fund accounts. For a summary revenue report, amounts can be totalled by source. Exhibit 10 shows a sample Revenue Report for a hypothetical nonprofit's general fund.

EXHIBIT 10
A Nonprofit's Revenue Report in Dollars
July 1, 1994

Revenue Account #	Revenue Source	Budget Amount	Received to Date	Balance	Percentage Received
04	State Grant	240,000	145,000	95,000	60.42
12	Federal Grant	525,000	375,000	150,000	71.43
32	Rotary Club Grant	15,000	6,000	9,000	40
	Total	780,000	526,000	254,000	67.44

EXPENDITURE REPORTS

Expenditure reports are very useful for management. The report should be customized for the needs of the particular manager. It should provide the manager with information regarding the department or departments he or she is monitoring. Comparisons can be done between the current and previous fiscal years, percentage breakdowns, amounts spent to date, etc. Basic information to be included is retrieved from current expenditure accounts and should include the names of the budget category, amounts budgeted, encumbrances on the current budget, actual expenditures, and the balance in the current budget. Encumbrances represent financial claims against the account.

Exhibit 11 shows a sample expenditure report for a hypothetical nonprofit organization.

EXHIBIT 11
Nonprofit Expenditure Report in Dollars
July 1, 1994

Budget Unit	Budget Amount	Encumbrances	Actual Expenditure	Balance
Administration	125,780	7,234	63,554	54,992
Mailing Department	25,000	3,553	11,552	9,895
Human Resources	48,240	2,412	21,598	24,230
Fund Raising Dept.	125,690	1,569	62,200	61,921
Telephone	15,000	553	7,240	7,207
Services Department	450,329	25,678	224,000	200,651
Visitation Department	314,961	5,489	152,500	156,972
Totals	1,105,000	46,488	542,644	515,868

The manager must compare the revenue report with the expenditure report. Comparing the Revenue Report in Exhibit 10 with the Expenditure Report in Exhibit 11 shows that $526,000 revenues were received while the nonprofit spent $542,644 with encumbrances of $46,488 for a total of $589,132. Thus, revenues fell short of expenditures, including encumbrances, and managers have a problem.

It can be seen that revenue and expenditure reports are essential in managing the budgetary process for a nonprofit. It makes the whole process a great deal easier to conceptualize.[3]

Notes to Chapter 2

1. Robert D. Vinter and Rhea K. Kish, *Budgeting for Not-For-Profit Organizations* (New York: The Free Press, 1984), p. 1.

2. For a more complete discussion of flexible nonprofit budgeting and cost behavior, see Arnold J. and Philip R. Olenick, *A Nonprofit Organizational Operating Manual* (New York: The Foundation Center, 1991), pp. 101–111.

3. The topic of budget reports is covered in detail in C. William Garner, *Accounting and Budgeting in Public and Nonprofit Organizations* (San Francisco: JosseyBass Publishers, 1991), pp. 78–83.

Chapter 3

Setting Goals and Determining Priorities

The primary objective during the strategic-planning process is to set the goals for operations during the next business cycle and to effectively distribute the available resources to accomplish those purposes. A budget is vitally important as a managing tool for the activities of the nonprofit organization. But to be meaningful, the NPO must know where it is currently headed; it must formulate goals and objectives to help realize its mission. Priorities can change quickly, just as the people and environments of the organization change. This means there are many people who should be involved in the budget preparation and approval process to produce a budget that will be fully supported.

SEVEN STEPS TO STRATEGIC PLANNING

There are generally seven steps that take place during the strategic-planning process. They are:

1. Identifying and defining the mission

2. Determining goals and objectives

3. Performing an external audit

4. Conducting an internal audit

5. Formulating strategies and setting program priorities

6. Allocating resources (budget) to accomplish goals

7. Evaluating operations during the year

If a plan is being prepared for the first time, obtain information from similar NPO's, foundations, donors, government funding agencies, and consultants.

While this overall process is the same in both the for-profit and nonprofit worlds, there are some significant differences that will be reviewed and discussed. One key difference is the emphasis given to the first step in the seven-step process.

DEFINING THE MISSION

The definition of the mission becomes the cornerstone for the rest of the nonprofit organizational structure. A clear and concise definition of the NPO's mission, or strategic plan, is vital if the rest of the process is to proceed effectively because the nonprofit's "product" is not a concrete object that can be held up for inspection; the "product" is serving the needs of the nonprofit's community. The entire planning and budgeting process will be easier if the strategic mission is clearly defined. A distinct and concise mission statement expedites the setting of budgeting priorities for programs and services. Once the mission is agreed upon, then the organization's goals and objectives are formulated.

SETTING GOALS AND OBJECTIVES

During this phase in the strategic-planning and budgeting process, goals and objectives should be formulated for the next business cycle (usually one year) and for long-range planning. Long-range could be two to three years or up to ten years in the future. The important consideration in establishing goals is consider how successful current programs have been in helping to realize the organization's mission and what the organization should be doing each year, in particular, what things should be done differently because of environmental changes or changes in the defined mission of the organization. Goals can start out in broad general terms, but then should be further specified and defined. This will help in the design of programs and activities and resource allocation later in the process. The organization must decide what its goals and objectives are before it starts worrying about the costs involved.

PERFORMING THE EXTERNAL AUDIT

To help set priorities for the activities and programs, the next step in the budgeting process is to perform an external audit to determine the opportunities and threats critical to the organization. This can be done using marketing research studies, or general observation and knowledge of the community. This review should answer questions such as: What type of community does the organization serve? Does the donor constituency reflect the community culture? What types of programs and fund-raising activities will be successful? For example, will a black-tie dinner dance or western rodeo better fit the community profile? Are there segments of the community that are not being targeted by the organization's fund-raising efforts that should be? What is the fund-raising competition like? What other organizations are competing for the same dollars we are? How successful have they been and why have they been successful?

There are also three primary sources of external demands and constraints that influence the budgeting and program planning process: the parent agency, the funder, and governmental regulations. A program will not be instituted that runs counter to the policies and regulations of these bodies. Contributors, or funders, may impose many of their own constraints, and may include such things as dollar ceilings on program support, forms of funding, length of funding, application forms and formats, program performance tracking, and line-item cost. Government regulations provide NPOs with many procedural headaches. Among other things, there are rules regarding financial accountability, employer fairness, and environmental responsibility.

CONDUCTING THE INTERNAL AUDIT

The internal audit, to determine the strengths and weaknesses of the organization, is the next step in the planning process. The organization must possess adequate strengths to be successful. This review should answer questions such as: Is leadership in place for our volunteers? Does the organization have competent staff? Have procedures and systems been established to bring the organization's message and service to the community and to thank and recognize donors in an appropriate and timely fashion? Does the organization have the necessary technological equipment and trained personnel to provide support for the assessment of the activities?

The accounting and finance functions play critical roles in the effective management of the firm. The data provided by these departments allow managers and administrators to monitor their performance during the year using budget to actual comparisons. While the nonprofit organization does not compete so ruthlessly with its competitors as for-profit organizations, the rivalry is still there as similar organizations try to meet the needs of the community. A successful organization will be rewarded with community support and sufficient resources to continue its existence.

Another important internal consideration is the organizational culture and leadership. These are important influences on the total performance, but they are difficult to quantify, examine, and explain. Different environments and different organizations appropriately display various styles of leadership. Some cultural areas to consider when evaluating possible changes in management are the motivation provided to employees (both monetary and nonmonetary), the creativity encouraged by management as the organization tries to solve problems, and the capacity of the organization to adapt and evolve as environmental changes occur.

SETTING PROGRAM PRIORITIES

Once the goals and objectives are defined, and the external and internal evaluations are done, then the planning proceeds to setting program priorities and the actual allocation of resources. This is another area in which the natural differences between for-profit and nonprofit organizations come into focus.

A for-profit organization's goals relate to producing the tangible product that is for sale, but the NPO may have members who disagree on whether offering a certain program will more effectively meet the needs of the community than offering an alternative program. This is one of the main areas of contention in the nonprofit world; determining just what activities should take place to best meet the needs of the community and which programs will attract the most support and most generous amounts of needed resources, or contributions, to keep the organization in existence. For example, should the country club stage a masquerade dinner dance with silent auction for fund-raising, or should a carnival and bake sale be planned? Should the staff hire a private fundraiser or should members assume the responsibility? Should dues be increased to help pay for needed building repairs?

Programs and activities must be decided upon and priorities set before management can begin the job of allocating resources. The main aspects of programs, their scopes, and the general volume of the programs should be identified before the resource requirements can be estimated for budgeting purposes. One exception to this is when a budget ceiling has been established prior to the program, thus requiring the program to be designed around the existing budget constraint. In either case, it is crucial to have program managers intimately involved with the agency's administrators when the budget is being developed because of the reciprocity between the program plan and the budget. A major decision in either area will affect the other. To illustrate this, a significant change in the program scope or activities will likely have a significant budget impact. Similarly, a decision to alter the budget can drastically affect the program.

ALLOCATING RESOURCES

After setting priorities for accomplishing goals and objectives, the resources needed for each program are evaluated. When a program is developed, the most decisive step in budgeting for nonprofit organizations is performed: the determination of resource needs for the program, and at what level each resource is needed. Every program will have certain unique resource needs resulting from its particular service, customers, or scope. However, there are certain demand relations that are universal to all service programs.

Most of the service programs depend heavily on personnel, and this personnel will also require some kind of space and/or physical facilities in which to carry out its tasks. Another consideration is that some programs will require certain supporting services or assistance from the parent agency.

The program plan should contain more detailed information of the resource requirements and identify the types of staff competencies needed. It should also detail any distinctive non-personnel resources necessary for program operations. *Note:* This information will be important if budget reduction steps are necessary in the future.

After management has established priorities for its programs and activities, total resources are estimated for the next business cycle. For-profit businesses usually begin by estimating gross sales for their products, but because nonprofit companies generally do not produce products from raw materials like manufacturing firms do, they must estimate donor contributions or tax revenues appropriated by a governmental unit, or in the case of a small nonprofit, funds raised by ticket sales. These estimates are usually based on historical data and information gained by the external and internal audits.

When the total resources available during the next business cycle are calculated, management begins the job of allocating to the various programs and activities. Non-profit organizations will allocate differently than for-profit businesses. For example, churches do not prepare a production budget or a direct materials budget. The allocation process itself can be quite cumbersome, and will depend on the time available and the amount of collaboration management has decided to allow.

EVALUATING OPERATIONS

The entire strategic-planning process is not a one-time activity; it is ongoing. However, it will not remain an effective planning and control tool unless it is constantly revised to reflect current company policies and changing costs. The first step for formulating each year's budget must be a review of the organization's goals. If any of these have changed, the budget must be revised accordingly. Also, actual cost data and variance analysis reports from the previous year must be examined to determine any appropriate cost modifications.

Careful planning and preparation of the strategic budget will benefit a nonprofit organization in many ways. It will force management to estimate its future program costs and plan ways of meeting them. Moreover, it will require them to consider the entity's external economic environment and will give them advance warning of any problems they might face such as cash shortages. Most importantly, the budget will coordinate the activities of all departments and give management a base against which to measure and evaluate their actual performance levels.

PROS AND CONS OF NONPROFIT BUDGET PROCESSES

There are various types of budget processes that can be used by the administrative staff, employees of the organization, and the consumers in the community. Some examples of these procedures and their individual handicaps and benefits are discussed below.

Imposed

In some for-profit businesses, the budget is imposed by top management with little, or no, consultation with lower management or people working in the field. An imposed budget is generally resented by those working towards the bottom of the organization as too unrealistic and not sensitive to the needs of employees. The most serious disadvantage of this type of budget is the motivational implications to line management and operating personnel.

There are, however, some advantages to imposed budgets. They may be more sensitive to general economic trends and their effects on the NPO as a whole. Also, top management can address any internal developments such as new applications, new services, or changes in strategic plans. Finally, there is the speed with which these budgets can be prepared and any necessary changes or adjustments can easily be made.

Imposed budgeting does work for some nonprofit organizations, like churches and condominium boards, but not for others such as schools. In a democratic nation, members of the community would not allow a budget to be imposed on them, with no vote or expression of whether the program is serving their needs, especially if the resources to operate the program come from their taxes.

Consultative

In nonprofit businesses, budgets are usually either consultative or participatory. A consultative budget originates from top management after a thorough discussion with lower management and some key line personnel. This process is usually done through committees. One of the disadvantages with the consultative budget is the amount of time it takes. A committee of six or seven people will seldom agree on anything in a short period of time! Nevertheless, the committee can be a means of sharing responsibility. The agreement made in most group settings does not guarantee the best overall, or most cost effective, solution, but the decision is shared by all and is considered "safe" since the blame, or acclaim, is divided among all members.

The key advantage is that this process brings together a wide variety of different points of view, and the pooling of diverse opinions naturally leads to the participants' understanding of each other's problems and helps to foster better cooperation.

Participatory

The participatory budget originates from the lowest area of responsibility. While this is the most closely aligned to human motivation, it also has disadvantages. There is the problem of who is allowed to participate and to what degree. Should *all* personnel and members of the community participate? The advantages of this procedure are considerable for motivating people because when the end product is produced, everyone feels like their wants and needs have been considered.

To illustrate, in the winter of 1993, California's Long Beach Unified School District, which serves over 75,000 students, implemented a participatory budgeting process. Representatives from the community, employee bargaining units, and concerned parents were invited to help the school board and management find areas of the budget where expenses could be cut back. The targeted amount needed was about $9 million. Most of the participants only saw their narrow end of the operation and voiced their opinion with no regard for other departments or the overall operation. However, after many committee meetings, a list combining the best suggestions from all of the concerned participants was approved by the board. While some individuals were disappointed their own suggestions were not used, there was an overall feeling that all areas had been examined and the cutback list was the "best" solution to a difficult problem. Like the consultative budget, this budget process is also very time consuming and cumbersome. It works well in small organizations or when there is plenty of time to enact a complete participatory process.

Once the budget is established, it becomes the criterion to evaluate operations. The allocations become the standards to measure activity against throughout the year. Variance reports will alert management to the problem areas where they need to focus their efforts. For example, if expected revenues are not being received as planned, then program cutbacks may have to be considered. Similarly, if expenditures are exceeding forecasted amounts, then management can discuss the options of cutbacks or additional fund-raising efforts that may need to be implemented.

Legislative/Incremental

In nonprofit organizations, the legislative budget is a request for funds by interested parties and the only purpose is to convince the legislature that the NPO needs the funds. The budget is prepared not as a wish list, but as a reasonable estimate of funds needed in the light of expected resources. Once a program is established, it is expected to continue. This leads to the fact that the largest determining factor of the size and content of a current budget is usually the previous budget.

Management

Once the legislative budget is approved, it becomes known as the management budget. This budget is the plan showing the amount of spending that is authorized for each area (department). Ideally, the budget should fine tune the stated organizational policy and strategic mission as defined earlier. These allocations in government are referred to as appropriations. Once appropriated, these are the funds that can be legally spent throughout the year. It is typical of departments to "find" excess monies near the end of a fiscal year, and at this time there is a general feeling that funds need to be spent or the money will be lost. If the department doesn't use all of the money that is appropriated, there is a concern that the new budget will be less because budget allocators will feel the department really didn't need all of its budget. Unfortunately, most of the year-end spending is done in haste and there are a lot of wasted dollars on items that were not really necessary. To guard against this year-end spending practice, a program should be implemented that rewards excess funds that a department has left at year-end. That department is able to keep the funds to supplement its budget the following fiscal year.

Line-Item

This type of budget simply lists the sources of revenue and categories of costs. Each line refers to a specific expense (e.g., salaries, rent). It is done by organizational unit rather than by program. Like all forms of budgeting, this type of budget attempts to project and control expenditures. Historical amounts may be adjusted at a predetermined rate (e.g., considering inflation). Projected increases are referred to as *increments*. Usually cost categories are established for recording all expenditures and, at the end of the budget year, a variance analysis is done to show the difference between projected and actual expenditures. Line-item budgeting relies specifically on the organization's accounting system and skill level. It answers the questions: Where did the money come from? How much? Where did it go? How much was spent? It does not ask the more important question, "Was the money well spent for necessary items?"

Performance

Performance budgeting considers work proposed, work actually initiated, and work completed. The concept is that work programs of several departments can be coordinated and that the funds may be expended in the most economical manner possible. Overlapping and duplication of effort are minimized. "Is the public getting its money's worth?"

With performance budgeting, the NPO is able to tell the public how much public service was delivered. Satisfying the community is the focus of performance budgeting. Results mean a larger budget, and when a department shows performance, it is able to maintain or increase its budget. Before this approach, results were secondary and the focus was on the size of the department's budget and the size of its staff.

Performance budgeting stresses the budget process as a tool for work measurement and efficiency analysis. A problem with this budget technique is objectively measuring the quality and quantity of the performance.

Planning-Programming

The Planning-Programming-Budget System (PPBS) attempts to stretch budgeting into the allocation of funds among various competing departments and programs to try to inject greater rationality into the budgeting process. PPBS is defined as a full process of (1) planning goals and objectives, (2) developing programs to achieve these goals, and (3) budgeting for projects within each program. Ideally, it was intended to include a classification of the cost by programs with common goals, the development of qualitative and quantitative measures of program outputs, a projection of anticipated program cost inputs and related service outputs over a period of time, the identification of special problem areas and the use of analytical techniques to appraise various possible solutions, and an integration of this information into the budgetary process.[1]

In many respects, PPBS techniques used in budgeting are similar to capital budgeting techniques used in for-profit companies. PPBS seeks to relate anticipated benefits to the anticipated costs of providing those benefits. With limited resources available, it is also used to establish new program priorities, so that the program that appears to provide the largest excess of benefits over costs would be implemented first. It is also used to help management choose among possible alternative courses of action by indicating what course would be cheapest.

Where departmental domains are less quantifiable, goals and objectives do not translate easily into dollar values for programs and projects.

The shorter the budget time period, the less time lag before corrective action may be implemented.

CONTROLLING COSTS WITH FLEXIBLE BUDGETING

There is one type of budgeting process that results in the construction of a flexible (variable) budget that will fluctuate depending upon the demand for services. An example of a nonprofit organization that uses this type of budget is a hospital. In a hospital, activity is measured in terms of revenues and expenses and is contingent on the number of clients, or patients, that are served. The flexible budget is an approved plan that facilitates budgetary control and operational examinations at various service levels rather than being a form of appropriations.

A flexible budget is an extremely useful tool for controlling costs. In contrast to a static budget, the flexible budget is characterized as follows:

1. It is geared toward a range of activity rather than a single level of activity.

2. It is dynamic in nature rather than static. By using the cost-volume formula (or flexible budget formula), a series of budgets can be easily developed for various levels of activity.

The static (fixed) budget is geared for only one level of activity and there are problems with cost control. Flexible budgeting distinguishes between fixed and variable costs, thus allowing for a budget that can be automatically adjusted (via changes in variable cost totals) to the particular level of activity actually attained. Thus, variances between actual costs and budgeted costs are adjusted for volume ups and downs before differences due to price and quantity factors are computed.

The primary use of the flexible budget is to accurately measure performance by comparing actual costs for a given output with the budgeted costs for the same level of output. It requires the departmental costs to be separated into fixed and variable elements.

Figure 1 illustrates the underlying concept of flexible budgeting and variance analysis for performance evaluation.

FIGURE 1

JOHN JAY HOSPITAL
FLEXIBLE BUDGET FOR DEPARTMENT 1

LEVEL OF OPERATIONS (RELATED TO CAPACITY)	70%	85%	90%	100%
DIRECT EXPENSES (VARIABLE)	$262,500	$318,750	$337,500	$375,000
DIRECT EXPENSES (FIXED)	$100,000	100,000	100,000	100,000
ALLOCATED GEN. EXPENSES (FIXED)	80,000	80,000	80,000	80,000
ALLOCATED SVC. DEPT EXPENSES				
DEPT. 5 (FIXED)	100,000	100,000	100,000	100,000
DEPT. 6 (FIXED)	20,000	20,000	20,000	20,000
DEPT. 7 (SEMIVARIABLE)	55,000	62,500	65,000	70,000
TOTAL EXPENSES	$617,500	$681,250	$702,500	$745,000
BILLING UNITS	57,750	70,125	74,250	82,500
COST PER UNIT OF SERVICE	$10.69	$9.71	$9.46	$9.03

FLEXIBLE BUDGET VARIANCE ANALYSIS FOR DEPARTMENT 1

	ACTUAL EXPENSES	FLEXIBLE BUDGET	VARIANCES
LEVEL OF OPERATIONS (RELATED TO CAPACITY)	85%	85%	
DIRECT EXPENSES (VARIABLE)	$320,000	$318,750	($1,250)--UNFAVORABLE
DIRECT EXPENSES (FIXED)	101000	100,000	(1,000)--UNFAVORABLE
ALLOCATED GEN. EXPENSES (FIXED)	78000	80,000	2,000--FAVORABLE
ALLOCATED SVC. DEPT EXPENSES			
DEPT. 5 (FIXED)	100,500	100,000	(500)--UNFAVORABLE
DEPT. 6 (FIXED)	22,500	20,000	(2,500)--UNFAVORABLE
DEPT. 7 (SEMIVARIABLE)	64,000	62,500	(1,500)--UNFAVORABLE
TOTALS	$686,000	$681,250	($4,750)--UNFAVORABLE

NOTE: (1) DIRECT VARIABLE EXPENSE VARIANCE PROBABLY RESULTED IN THE DEPARTMENT'S LACK OF ABILITY TO CONTROL VARIABLE COSTS.

(2) DIRECT FIXED EXPENSE VARIANCE SUGGESTS THAT THE DEPARTMENTAL SUPERVISOR "OVERSPENT" HIS ALLOCATED FIXED EXPENSES.

(3) DEPARTMENTS 5 AND 6 VARIANCES PROBABLY CAUSED BY INADEQUATE METHODS OF COST CONTROL

(4) DEPARTMENT 7 VARIANCE COULD HAVE BEEN CAUSED BY HAVING TOO MANY EMPLOYEES OR THE INABILITY TO CONTROL COSTS.

There is one feature of the flexible budget: certain costs are not proportional to a level of activity. For example, a country club cannot have less than one bartender. In preparing a flexible budget, it must be kept in mind that sometimes the relationships developed will not be simple percentage ones. Reports on budget variances can be costly to prepare. One type of report is a narrative summary of the reasons for budget deviations for major income and expense categories only. This would serve to focus the attention of the Board on areas that need prompt attention. If detailed explanations were needed, the Board could request additional information.

The primary billing unit for many hospitals is a day of room occupancy, and the overall level of operations in hospitals is typically expressed in the rate of room occupancy. The flexible budgets setting out the anticipated operating costs at various room occupancy levels becomes an important tool in planning future operations and for establishing billing rates based on the anticipated costs of providing services. Flexible budgets for specific revenue-producing departments, such as radiology, should also be formulated and related to various operation levels.

If a flexible budget system is used, it is customary to segregate the budgetary accounts and to keep them separate from the accounting system of the hospital. However, if a fixed budget is used because of legal requirements or preference, it then is most effective to integrate the budget into the accounting system. The accrual basis of accounting used to record the organization's actual transactions should be the same as the basis used to prepare the budget.

BREAK-EVEN AND COST-VOLUME-REVENUE ANALYSIS

Break-even and Cost-volume-profit (CVP) analysis is not limited to profit firms. CVP is appropriately called *cost-volume-revenue (CVR) analysis*, as it pertains to non-profit organizations. The CVR model not only calculates the break-even service level, but helps answer a variety of "what-if" decision questions.

EXAMPLE 1

A social service center has a $1,200,000 lump sum annual budget appropriation to help rehabilitate mentally ill clients. On top of this, the center charges each patient $600 a month for board and care. All of the appropriation and revenue must be spent. The variable costs for rehabilitation activity average $700 per patient per month. The annual fixed costs are $800,000. The manager wishes to know how many clients can be served.

Let x = number of clients to be served.
Revenue = Total expenses
Revenue = Variable expenses + Fixed expenses
Lump sum appropriation + $600 (12) x = $700 (12) + $800,000
$1,200,000 + $7,200 x = $8,400 x + $800,000
($7,200 - $8,400)x = $800,000 - $1,200,000
- $1,200 x = -$400,000
x = $400,000/$1,200
x = 333 clients

We will investigate the following two "what-if" scenarios:

(1) Suppose the manager is concerned that the total budget for the coming year will be cut by 10% to a new amount of $1,080,000. All other things remain unchanged. The manager wants to know how this budget cut affects the next year's service level.

$1,080,000 + $7,200 x = $8,400 x + $800,000
($7,200 - $8,400)x = $800,000 - $1,080,000
- $1,200 x = -$280,000
x = $280,000/$1,200
x = 233 clients

(2) The manager does not reduce the number of clients served despite a budget cut of 10%. All other things remain unchanged. How much more does he/she have to charge his/her clients for board and care?

In this case, x = board and care charge per year.

$1,080, 000 + 333 x = $8,400 (333) + $800,000
333x = $2,797,200 + $800,000 - $1,080,000
333x = $2,517,200
x = $2,517,200/333 clients
x = $7,559

Thus, the monthly board and care charge must be increased to $630 ($7,559/12 months).

NOTE TO CHAPTER 3

1. Enke, Ernest L. "The Accounting Preconditions of PPB," *Readings in Governmental and Nonprofit Accounting* (Wadsworth Publishing Co., 1977).

Chapter 4

Potential Problems in Nonprofit Budgeting

A large fraction of the costs of an NPO are discretionary; that is, there are costs for which the optimum amount is not known and many times not knowable. How much should it cost to provide meals for the homeless? Or to provide fire services for a community? This is in contrast to the engineered costs in a for-profit organization. For example, in estimating the cost of making a car, well-informed people have a good idea of the cost of operations; raw materials, direct labor, and indirect costs can be reliably estimated. With NPOs, there are several potential problem areas in the planning and budget preparation procedures that need to be addressed. If administrators are aware of these possible pitfalls, they will more easily recognize them and take steps to alleviate or eliminate them during the budgeting process.

IDENTIFYING THE PEOPLE FACTOR IN BUDGETING

A nonprofit organization, just like most for-profit companies, needs to consider people in every aspect of its business planning, including budgeting. Some managers try to ignore the behavioral aspects involved in the budgetary process, but "it is now becoming clear that budgets represent extremely powerful behavioral forces."[1] When participation is limited due to time constraints or administrative decisions, fixed budget groups will be given the authority to formulate the budget. These people often consider themselves to be the organization's watchdogs whose principal function is to be constantly looking for deviations from the budget and reporting these to top management.

From a behavioral viewpoint, it will help provide a challenge and sense of responsibility if managers and line personnel are allowed to participate in the budget process. Widespread employee participation will also increase the probability that the goals of the budget will be accepted by the people actually doing the work to meet the goals. Individuals will be more likely to try to gain self-esteem and self-actualization by "meeting the budget" or finishing the project "within the budget."

Sometimes the budget amounts for a program can be determined through a negotiation process between a supervisor and his/her managers. Each manager is then competing for a share of limited resources in order to successfully provide services to the organization's clients. There are also important carryover consequences from year to year. Each party develops judgments about the ability, integrity, and forthrightness of the other party and this will affect their attitude during negotiations. The attitude of professionals toward their area of concern also becomes an important factor.

The budget process is most effective when negotiating parties trust each other. The supervisors trust their subordinates and assume they are competent, that they possess goodwill and honesty. The administrators have enough confidence in their managers' abilities that they do not impose their own solutions to problems. The supervisors do not hide information in order to gain leverage over their managers, and they do not force goals onto subordinates. Managers must also trust their superiors. The budget is based on assumptions about the external world, and these can often prove wrong. If managers do not trust their supervisors to recognize this fact, they will be reluctant to make estimates. They may be afraid of their bosses and find their negotiations to be more of an interrogation than a collaboration. This negotiation process will lead to some of the internal budget games discussed below.

HOW TO AVOID BEING MANIPULATED BY INTERNAL BUDGET GAMES

The budget process may be endangered by individuals who engage in underhanded tactics and schemes to manipulate the budget toward outcomes that will advance their own personal agendas. In order to play the "budget game" effectively, administrators and managers should be aware of the tactics used in two different arenas:

- ❐ Within the organization

- ❐ Outside the organization (These are tactics used between the board that authorizes funds or the legislative unit and the head of the organization.)

Since the maneuvers that take place within the organization can be particularly damaging to effective program planning and budgeting, they will be reviewed in greater detail. They are divided into the following four categories:

1. New program schemes

2. Maintaining or increasing ongoing programs

3. Resisting budget cuts

4. Tactics used by supervisors

The next section gives some specific definitions and examples of maneuvers commonly used by managers in different situations. It is important to emphasize that the strategies chosen depend on each manager's moral character, the size of the NPO, and whether the income for the organization is generated by contributions, grants, or a combination of revenue sources. Some simple procedures for controlling these difficult situations are suggested.[2]

RECOGNIZING NEW PROGRAM SCHEMES

"Foot in the Door"

Because new programs must prove they are deserving of funding in comparison to established programs, this tactic is used by managers to sell a new program by intentionally underestimating and concealing the real magnitude of the program until it has built a constituency. This scheme needs to be detected and denied when proposed, and the manager must be held to the initial decision to limit the spending to the original cost estimate.

"Bait and Switch"

The manager first requests an inexpensive program, but then increases the scope and cost estimates after the initial approval. Again, the manager must be held to the original decision and the spending must be limited to the original estimate.

"Hidden Pea"

The manager conceals the nature of a politically unattractive program by hiding it within an attractive program. It is necessary to break down the initial program proposal to make *all* features—attractive and unattractive—apparent to the decision-makers.

"Divide and Conquer"

The manager seeks approval of a program budget from more than one supervisor. This can be avoided if responsibility lines are clearly defined. New ideas can be extremely difficult to evaluate. If authority is divided, this lessens the chance that a good idea will be rejected.

"Digression"

The manager bases a specific request, for example, funds for facilities replacement, on the premise that an overall program for public works has been approved, when this is not the case. To expose this ploy, ask the manager to specify who approved the public works program, maintain an overall knowledge of approved programs, or take time to investigate alleged approvals.

"Shell Game"

The manager uses statistics to mislead supervisors about the true state of affairs. In the example presented, the manager wanted funds to be used for community volunteer street patrols, but he knew his superiors were more interested in drug suppression. He drew up the chart, as shown in Figure 1, and emphasized to the community group that over half the funds were intended for drug suppression. The catch was that the source of "OTHER" funds was not known, and there were no plans for obtaining such funds.

A careful analysis is required to detect this strategy.

"It's Free"

The manager will argue that someone else will pay for the project, so the organization might as well approve it. For example, a private school district applied for a $6 million grant to set up special instructional programs on

FIGURE 1

Funding Source			
Purpose	Federal	Other	Total
Street Patrols	2,000,000	50,000	2,050,000
Drug Suppression	500,000	3,000,000	3,500,000
			5,550,000

computers at all of the high schools. The school administrators overlooked the fact that once the initial funding provided equipment and personnel, the district was required to reconstruct classrooms to provide proper networking capabilities and it would need to continue to fund the program, including all of the maintenance costs for 300 new computers. All long-term project costs should be carefully reviewed to guard against this stratagem.

"Implied Top-Level Support"

The manager implies that someone higher up in the organization asked for the item to be included in the budget. The manager hopes that the supervisor will not take the time to bring the third party into the discussion. All documentation must be examined thoroughly, and if it is found to be ambiguous or unjustified, the alleged sponsor should be contacted for verification of support.

"You Are to Blame"

This tactic implies that the supervisor is at fault and that defects in the budget submission therefore should be overlooked. For example, if the supervisor is delayed in requesting the budget submission, the manager claims there was not sufficient time to properly justify requests and any flaws or shortcomings are the fault of the supervisor. A qualified response to this argument is to hold the budget to the original guidelines.

"We Must Be Up to Date"

The manager insists the organization must be a leader and adopt the newest technology. This is usually used in budgeting for computers and related equipment, or for hospital and lab equipment. The manager should be required to show the benefit of purchase will exceed the initial cost of the equipment and continued upkeep.

"Nothing Too Good for Our Valued Employees"

This ploy is often used to justify items for personal comfort and safety, especially in military budgets, new hospital equipment, and various school and university budgets. To respond to this maneuver, try to shift the discussion from emotional grounds to logical grounds. Analyze the recommendation to see if the benefits are connected to the cost. Stress the message that in a world of scarce resources, not everybody can get all that they deserve.

"A Rose Smells Sweeter"

Sometimes managers will call their budget proposals by misleading, but attractive, labels. If a volunteer fire department cannot get approval to build new facilities, it may propose building an annex or wing. However, if the proposal is analyzed, an astute supervisor will see that the wing will be twice as large as the original building.

"Expert Opinions"

Managers want to hire "unbiased" experts from outside the organization to support its request, either in the print media or at formal hearings. A supervisor's response is to show that these experts are biased because of their connection with the program or because they are likely to benefit if the request is approved.

MAINTAINING OR INCREASING ONGOING PROGRAMS

"Show of Strength"

The manager will demonstrate, or threaten to demonstrate, support for his/her request with such things as a work slowdown or strike. It is necessary to have fair criteria for program selection and to have the conviction to stand by the decision that is made in order to counter this maneuver.

"Reverence for the Past"

The manager will insist that whatever was spent on last year's program must have been necessary in order to carry out the goals and objectives, therefore the only matter to be negotiated is the proposed increase above the "base." Administrators often find they must accept this premise because of time constraints in the budget process. For selected programs, however, a zero-based budget review can be applied.

RESISTING BUDGET CUTS

"Make a Study"

Often a manager will say cuts should not be made until the consequences are studied. The answer is to implement a review of the program in question.

"End Run"

This occurs when the manager goes outside normal channels to obtain a reversal of a decision. If the end run is made to a powerful body, and the decision is reversed, administrators have to live with the decision. Managers who attempt an end run should be reprimanded for going outside proper channels.

TACTICS USED BY SUPERVISORS

"I Only Work Here"

The supervisor tells the manager that the request is beyond the scope of the ground rules set for the department by higher administrators. One solution to this problem is for the issue to be decided by the higher authority.

"Arbitrary Cuts"

The supervisor reduces the budget for certain discretionary items by randomly chosen percentages, but gives the impression of knowledgeable authority. One solution to this problem is for administrators to challenge the rationality of the supervisor's decisions.

STEERING THROUGH CHANGING ENVIRONMENTS: INTERNAL AND EXTERNAL

The dynamic environments in the world of the nonprofit organization present several possible problem areas for budget formulators and administrators. The internal and external environmental factors must be continually observed and evaluated because of their potential significant budget impacts. Some of the areas that should be reviewed as part of the internal and external audits during the budget process include the following:

Changes in Program Recipients

New activities or programs may be required in this situation. For example, in a hospital program for leukemia patients, the number of adult patients has increased significantly over the last ten years compared to the number of children. This may require hospital administrators to consider the implementation of new treatment procedures and a reallocation of budget funds.

Staff Composition and Expertise

An example of this is that the staff for one program, tax advisory services for low-income people, is now composed of trained professionals, instead of the volunteers who ran the program in the beginning. The ramifications are that the salary and benefit budgets will need to be increased during the next budget planning cycle in order to retain these professionals, while the scope of the program also needs to be expanded as the community demands for the more professional level of services have increased.

Funding Constraints and Commitments

Various funding agencies put constraints on restricted revenues and grant programs, including the condition that the nonprofit must continue a program once the initial start-up funding is granted. During the budget planning process, these ongoing commitments need to be reviewed and included in the allocation of resources. Other constraints may include requirements mandating things such as dollar ceilings on program support or overhead charges, forms of funding, length of funding, application forms and formats, program performance tracking and demands, line-item cost specificity, reimbursement rates, and financial reporting procedures. Agencies applying to receive funds from these sources should inquire about these constraints before applying.

Government regulation provides another major source of restrictions. Other than those that deal with taxation, NPOs must also fulfill these requirements. There are separate regulations dealing with their tax-exempt status that detail such things as financial accountability, environmental responsibility, employer fairness, and other areas. The agency has a responsibility to know and understand all governmental restrictions and statutory laws that affect it, even if these requirements are not specifically mentioned in award notices. Moreover, an agency should thoroughly investigate all governmental restrictions and requirements when expanding into different service areas.

Social and Economic Conditions

For an NPO, a continuing recession in the community can cause a serious shortfall of any estimated contribution income. Cultural nonprofit organizations, such as opera companies, may find it more difficult to sell tickets to performances.

Social unrest can have both a good and bad impact on program planning. There are many new opportunities to provide services that are urgently needed, yet the community may not be able to support the cost of those programs. Beneficial activities, such as drug or gang suppression education, that are designed to alleviate some dangerous neighborhood conditions, may need to be curtailed or stopped altogether if revenues from other sources are not immediately forthcoming.

Demographic Trends

A community shift in age categories or ethnic group distributions can affect the types of services required or demanded by the neighborhood served by the NPO. These should be monitored regularly by decision-makers.

Policies, Rules and Regulations

Nonprofit organizations are subject to statutes enacted by governmental authorities and any changes that affect the organization should be considered during the budget-planning process. Moreover, existing agency standards and procedures may also determine such budget items as personnel hierarchies and salary rates, benefit packages, workload and performance measures, cost factors for indirect overhead, and payment schedules.

Research and Development Advances

Technological improvements can mean either that resources need to be allocated to buy new equipment or supplies to better serve the agency's customers, or they can mean that the cost of a program can be lower because service efficiency has been improved. Both of these events will be considerations during the next budget process.

NOTES TO CHAPTER 4

1. Caplan, Edwin H. *Management Accounting & Behavioral Science* (Addison-Wesley Publishing Co., 1971).

2. Adapted from Karapetian, Mette B. *A Study of Budgeting for Nonprofit Organizations*, unpublished master's thesis (California State University at Long Beach, 1992) and Anthony, R. and D. Young, *Management Control in Nonprofit Organizations*, 3rd Edition (Richard D. Irwin, Inc., 1988).

Part II

Preparing, Analyzing, and Evaluating the Nonprofit Budget

Chapter 5

How Financial Modeling and Computers Make Budgeting Easier*

Due to technological advances in computers (such as spreadsheets, financial modeling languages, graphics, data base management systems, and networking), more nonprofit organizations are using financial modeling to develop their budgets.

A financial model, narrowly called a budgeting model, is a system of mathematical equations, logic, and data that describes the relationships among financial and operating variables. A financial model can be viewed as a subset of broadly defined planning models or a stand-alone functional system that attempts to answer a certain financial planning problem.

When financial modeling is used:

1. one or more financial variables appear (revenues, expenditures, investment, cash flow, etc.);

2. you can manipulate (set and alter) the value of one or more financial variables; and

3. the model influences strategic decisions by revealing to the decision-maker the implications of alternative values of these financial variables.

---

*Anique Qureshi, Ph.D., CPA, consultant and Assistant Professor at Queens College, coauthored this chapter.

Financial models fall into two types: simulation (better known as "what-if" models) and optimization models. "What-if" models attempt to simulate the effects of alternative policies and assumptions about the organization's external environment. They are basically a tool for management's laboratory. Optimization models are used to maximize or minimize an objective such as present value of revenue or cost. Experiments are being done with multi-objective techniques, such as goal programming.

Models can be deterministic or probabilistic. Deterministic models do not include any random or probabilistic variables whereas probabilistic models incorporate random numbers and/or one or more probability distributions for variables such as revenues, costs, etc. Financial models can be solved and manipulated computationally to derive the current and projected future implications and consequences. COMSHARE's *One-up*™ is a good example of a financial model that integrates all the latest software in a networking environment.

WIDE-RANGING APPLICATIONS OF FINANCIAL MODELS

Basically, a financial model is used to build a comprehensive budget (that is, projected financial statements, such as the revenue/expenditure statement, fund statement of financial position, and cash flow statement). Such a model can be called a budgeting model, since you are essentially developing a master budget with such a model. Applications and uses of the model, however, go beyond developing a budget. They include:

- ❒ Financial statement reporting
- ❒ Financial forecasting and analysis
- ❒ Variance analysis
- ❒ Merger and acquisition analysis
- ❒ Project investment analysis
- ❒ Employee benefit analysis
- ❒ Capacity planning
- ❒ Break-even and cost-volume-revenue analysis
- ❒ Activity revenues and expenditures projections

- ❏ Lease/purchase evaluation
- ❏ Appraisal of performance by segments
- ❏ Socioeconomic impact analysis
- ❏ Development of long-term strategy
- ❏ Enrollment projections
- ❏ Planning financial requirements
- ❏ Risk analysis
- ❏ Cash flow analysis
- ❏ Cost and price projections

HOW FINANCIAL MODELING IS BEING USED

The use of computer-based financial modeling is rapidly growing, due to the increasing need for improved and quicker support for management decisions as a decision support system (DSS) and wide and easy availability of computer hardware and software.

Some of the functions being served by financial models are:

- ❏ Projecting financial results under a given set of assumptions; evaluating the financial impact of various assumptions and alternative strategies; and preparing long range financial forecasts.

- ❏ Computing surplus/deficit, cash flow, and ratios for five years by months, as well as revenue, power generation requirements, operating expenses, manual or automatic financing, and rate structure analysis.

- ❏ Providing answers and insights into "what-if" questions, and generating financial scheduling information.

- ❏ Forecasting fund and revenue/expenditure statements with emphasis on alternatives for the investment securities portfolio.

- ❏ Projecting operating results and various financing needs, such as equipment levels and financing requirements.

- ❏ Generating performance (variance) reports for various segments and responsibility units.

❏ Projecting financial implications of capital investment programs.

❏ Showing the effect of various volume and activity levels on budget and cash flow.

❏ Evaluating the alternatives of leasing or buying computer equipment.

Supported by the expanded capabilities provided by models, many nonprofit entities are increasingly successful in including long-term strategic considerations in their plans, thus enabling them to investigate the possible impact of their current decisions on the future welfare of the organization.

SPEEDING UP THE BUDGETING PROCESS WITH COMPUTERS

Budgeting models are used to generate pro forma financial statements and financial ratios, the basic tools for budgeting and planning. In addition, financial models can be used for risk analysis and "what-if" experiments. They also help with the day-to-day operational and tactical decisions necessary for immediate planning problems. For all these purposes, the use of computers is essential.

As conditions change and events occur in the ever-dynamic nonprofit environment, financial planning and budget preparation and revision procedures can become both tedious and burdensome. Decision-makers demand that new information be incorporated quickly and efficiently into the accounting and budgeting system, yet time and resource constraints previously worked against this.

In recent years, however, spreadsheet software and computer-based financial modeling software have been developed and used in an effort to speed up the budgeting process and allow managers to investigate the effects of changes in budget assumptions and scenarios. Budgeting, financial forecasting, and planning can also be done using spreadsheet templates or add-in programs. More and more nonprofit organizations are developing computer-based models for planning and budgeting, using powerful, yet easy-to-use, English-like modeling languages such as COMSHARE's *IFPS (Interactive Financial Planning System)*™. Other well-known system packages include *SIMPLAN*™, *EXPRESS*™, *Encore! Plus*™, *Venture*™, and *MicroFCS*™. They not only help build a budget for planning and control but answer a variety of "what-if" scenarios. The resulting calculations provide a basis for choosing among alternatives under conditions of uncertainty.

USING A SPREADSHEET PROGRAM FOR MODELING AND BUDGETING

In this section we will discuss how you can use spreadsheet programs such as *Lotus 1-2-3*™ and a stand-alone package such as *IFPS/Plus*™ to develop a budgeting model. In what follows, we will show how to develop a projected statement of income and expenses for Seaside Country Club.

EXAMPLE 1

1. Income for 1st month:

Annual dues	$ 15,000
Initiation fees	1,000
Greens fees	2,000
Restaurant	30,000
Other	2,000
Total	$ 50,000

2. Operating expenses follow:

Maintenance of greens, grounds, and clubhouse	$ 5,000 + 13% of sales
Golf activities	12% of sales
General and administrative	6,000 + 5% of sales
Payroll taxes	6% of sales
Restaurant-related expenses	17,500 + 10% of sales
Other expenses	1,500 + 1% of sales
	$30,000 + 47% of sales

3. Income increases by 5% each month

1. Based on this information, we will create a spreadsheet for the projected statement of income and expenses for the next 12 months and in total.

2. We will do the same in 1. assuming that income increases by 7.5% and operating expenses = $30,000 plus 49% of sales. This is an example of "what-if" analysis. (See Figure 1.)

TAKING A LOOK AT BUDGETING SOFTWARE PACKAGES

The following discusses IFPS/Plus™ in great depth, with illustrations. Such other popular stand-alone software as *SIMPLAN™*, *Express™*, and *Encore! Plus™* are also briefly discussed.

IFPS/PLUS

IFPS/Plus is a multipurpose, interactive financial modeling system, often called a *decision support system (DSS)*, which facilitates building, solving, and asking "what-if" questions of financial models. The output from an IFPS/Plus model is in the format of a spreadsheet, that is, a matrix or table in which:

❐ The rows represent user-specified variables such as market share, revenue, growth in revenue, unit price, variable cost, contribution margin, fixed cost, surplus/deficit, net present value, and internal rate of return.

❐ The columns designate a sequence of user-specified time periods such as month, quarter, year, total, percentages, or departments.

❐ The entries in the body of the table display the values taken by the model variable over time or by segments of the entity such as divisions, service lines, regional territories, and departments.

IFPS/Plus offers the following key features:

❐ Like other special purpose modeling languages, IFPS/Plus provides an English-like modeling language. That means without an extensive knowledge of computer programming, the budgeting manager can build budgeting models of his/her own, and use them for "what-if" scenarios and managerial decisions.

❐ IFPS/Plus has a collection of built-in financial functions that perform calculations such as net present value (NPV), internal rate of return (IRR), loan amortization schedules, and depreciation alternatives.

FIGURE 1

SEASIDE COUNTRY CLUB
PROJECTED STATEMENT OF INCOME AND EXPENSES
For the 12 Months and in Total

	1	2	3	4	5	6	7	8	9	10	11	12	TOTAL
Income:													
Annual dues	$15,000	$15,750	$16,538	$17,364	$18,233	$19,144	$20,101	$21,107	$22,162	$23,270	$24,433	$25,655	$238,757
Initiation fee	$1,000	$1,050	$1,103	$1,158	$1,216	$1,276	$1,340	$1,407	$1,477	$1,551	$1,629	$1,710	$15,917
Greens fees	$2,000	$2,100	$2,205	$2,315	$2,431	$2,553	$2,680	$2,814	$2,955	$3,103	$3,258	$3,421	$31,834
Restaurant	$30,000	$31,500	$33,075	$34,729	$36,465	$38,288	$40,203	$42,213	$44,324	$46,540	$48,867	$51,310	$477,514
Other	$2,000	$2,100	$2,205	$2,315	$2,431	$2,553	$2,680	$2,814	$2,955	$3,103	$3,258	$3,421	$31,834
Total	$50,000	$52,500	$55,125	$57,881	$60,775	$63,814	$67,005	$70,355	$73,873	$77,566	$81,445	$85,517	$795,856
Expenses:													
Variable exp.	$23,500	$24,675	$25,909	$27,204	$28,564	$29,993	$31,492	$33,067	$34,720	$36,456	$38,279	$40,193	$374,052
Fixed exp.	$30,000	$30,000	$30,000	$30,000	$30,000	$30,000	$30,000	$30,000	$30,000	$30,000	$30,000	$30,000	$360,000
Total	$53,500	$54,675	$55,909	$57,204	$58,564	$59,993	$61,492	$63,067	$64,720	$66,456	$68,279	$70,193	$734,052
Surplus/Deficit	($3,500)	($2,175)	($784)	$677	$2,211	$3,821	5,513	$7,288	$9,153	$11,110	$13,166	$15,324	$61,804

SEASIDE COUNTRY CLUB
PROJECTED STATEMENT OF INCOME AND EXPENSES
For the 12 Months and in Total

	1	2	3	4	5	6	7	8	9	10	11	12	TOTAL
Income:													
Annual dues	$15,000	$16,125	$17,334	$18,634	$20,032	$21,534	#23,150	$24,886	$26,752	$28,759	$30,915	$33,234	$276,356
Initiation fee	$1,000	$1,075	$1,156	$1,242	$1,335	$1,436	$1,543	$1,659	$1,783	$1,917	$2,061	$2,216	$18,424
Greens fees	$2,000	$2,150	$2,311	$2,485	$2,671	$2,871	$3,087	$3,318	$3,567	$3,834	$4,122	$4,431	$36,847
Restaurant	$30,000	$32,250	$34,669	$37,269	$40,064	$43,069	$46,229	$49,771	$53,504	$57,517	$61,831	$66,468	$552,712
Other	$2,000	$2,150	$2,311	$2,485	$2,671	$2,871	$3,087	$3,318	$3,567	$3,834	$4,122	$4,431	$36,847
Total	$50,000	$53,750	$57,781	$62,115	$66,773	$71,781	$77,165	$82,952	$89,174	$95,862	$103,052	$110,780	$921,186
Expenses:													
Variable exp.	$24,500	$26,338	$28,313	$30,436	$32,719	$35,173	$37,811	$40,647	$43,695	$46,972	$50,495	$54,282	$451,381
Fixed exp.	$30,000	$30,000	$30,000	$30,000	$30,000	$30,000	$30,000	$30,000	$30,000	$30,000	$30,000	$30,000	$360,000
Total	$54,500	$56,338	$58,313	$60,436	$62,719	$65,173	$67,811	$70,647	$73,695	$76,972	$80,495	$84,282	$811,381
Surplus/Deficit	($4,500)	($2,588)	($532)	$1,679	$4,054	$6,609	$9,354	$12,306	$15,479	$18,890	$22,556	$26,498	$109,805

❑ IFPS/Plus also has a collection of built-in mathematical and statistical functions such as linear regression, linear interpolation, polynomial autocorrelation, and moving average.

❑ IFPS/Plus supports use of leading and/or lagged variables that are commonly used in budgeting.

❑ IFPS/Plus also supports deterministic and probabilistic modeling. It offers a variety of functions for sampling from probability distributions such as uniform, normal, bivariate normal, and user-described empirical distributions.

❑ IFPS/Plus is non-procedural in nature. This means that the relationships, logic, and data used to calculate the various values in the output do not have to be arranged in any particular top-to-bottom order in an IFPS/Plus model. IFPS/Plus automatically detects and solves a system of two or more linear or nonlinear equations.

❑ IFPS/Plus has extensive editing capabilities that include adding statements to and deleting statements from a model, making changes in existing statements, and making copies of parts or all of a model.

❑ IFPS/Plus supports sensitivity analysis by providing the following solution options:

(a) WHAT-IF

❑ The IFPS/Plus lets you specify one or more changes in the relationships, logic, data, and/or parameter values, in the existing model and recalculates the model to show the impact of these changes on the performance measures.

(b) GOAL-SEEKING

❑ In the GOAL-SEEKING mode, IFPS/Plus can determine what change would have to take place in the value of a specified variable in a particular time period to achieve a specified value for another variable. For example, the manager can ask the system to answer the question, "How much tuition should be imposed on new students to achieve a balanced budget for the next year?"

(c) SENSITIVITY

❐ This particular command is employed to determine the effect of a specified variable on one or more other variables. The SENSITIVITY command is similar to the WHAT-IF command but it produces a convenient, model-produced tabular summary for each new alternative value of the specified variable.

(d) ANALYZE

❐ The ANALYZE command examines in detail those variables and their values that have contributed to the value of a specified variable.

(e) IMPACT

❐ The IMPACT command is used to determine the effect on a specified variable of a series of percentage changes in one or more variables.

(f) IFPS/OPTIMUM

❐ The IFPS/OPTIMUM routine is employed to answer questions of "What is the best?" type rather than "What-if."

(g) OTHER FEATURES OF IFPS/PLUS INCLUDE:

• Routine graphic output

• Interactive color graphics

• Data files that contain both data and relationships

• A consolidation capability that lets the manager produce composite reports from two or more models.

• Extraction of data from existing non-IFPS/Plus data files and placing them in IFPS/Plus-compatible data files.

In the following section, we present, step by step, how to build a model using IFPS/Plus. (The following example was adapted from COMSHARE, *Comprehensive Fundamentals of IFPS*, 1984, pp.3-1 through 3-10, with permission.)

EXAMPLE 2

The Computer Services Department of a local university must prepare a model to project revenues- and expenses-related computer repairs and consulting services offered to clients who purchase their computer system. Data on variables such as wages, service and repair rates, unit sales, miscellaneous expenses, and number of hours worked are defined in the model. Figures 2 and 3 show how to input the model and various IFPS/Plus output for next year's quarterly budgeted statement of income and expenses.

FIGURE 2
Entering the Model

```
? MODEL SERVICE
BEGIN ENTERING NEW MODEL
? AUTO
1 ? *
2 ? *
3 ? *     YEAR QUARTERLY BUDGETED REVENUES AND EXPENSES
4 ? *          SERVICES DEPARTMENT
5 ? *
6 ? COLUMNS Q1, Q2, Q3, Q4
7 ? *
8 ? * REVENUE
9 ? REPAIR REVENUE = REPAIR HOURS * REPAIR SERVICE RATE
10 ? CONSULTING REVENUE = CONSULTING HOURS * CONSULTING RATE PER HOUR
11 ?     TOTAL SERVICE INCOME = L9 + L10
12 ? *
13 ? *EXPENSES
14 ? REPAIR SALARIES = REPAIR HOURS * HOURLY REPAIR WAGE
15 ? CONSULTING SALARIES = CONSULTANTS WAGE * NUMBER OF CONSULTANTS
16 ? OTHER SALARIES = 1000 FOR 4
17 ? MISC EXPENSES = 500
18 ?     SALARIES AND EXPENSES = SUM (L14 THRU L17)
19 ? *
20 ? NET INCOME = TOTAL SERVICE INCOME – SALARIES AND EXPENSES
21 ? *
22 ? *
23 ? *
24 ? * REPAIR WORK
25 ? ACCUMULATED UNIT SALES = UNIT SALES + PREVIOUS
26 ? UNIT REPAIR PER QTR = 5% * ACCUMULATED UNIT SALES
27 ? AVG REPAIR HOURS PER UNIT = 2.8
28 ? REPAIR HOURS = UNIT REPAIR PER QTR * '
29 ?                    AVG REPAIR HOURS PER UNIT
30 ? REPAIR SERVICE RATE = 20.70 FOR 4
31 ? HOURLY REPAIR WAGE = 10.90 FOR 4
32 ? *
33 ? *
34 ? * CONSULTING
35 ? CONSULTING HOURS = 350 FOR 3, 400
36 ? CONSULTING RATE PER HOUR = 70
37 ? NUMBER OF CONSULTANTS = 5
38 ? CONSULTANTS WAGE = 5600 FOR 4
39 ? *
40 ? * .
41 ? UNIT SALES = 200, 350, 350, 500
42 ? END
READY FOR EDIT
```

FIGURE 3
IFPS Output

? SAVE

MODELS AND REPORTS SAVED ON FILE MRFBUD
? SOLVE
MODEL SERVICE VERSION OF 09/24/94 11:04 -- 8 COLUMNS 20 VARIABLES
ENTER SOLVE OPTIONS
? WIDTH 70 30 10 2
? L1 THRU L37

	Q1	Q2	Q3	Q4
2 -YEAR QUARTERLY BUDGETED REVENUES AND EXPENSES				
SERVICES DEPARTMENT				
REVENUE				
REPAIR REVENUE	579.60	1593.90	2608.20	4057.20
CONSULTING REVENUE	24500.00	24500.00	24500.00	28000.00
TOTAL SERVICE INCOME	25079.60	26093.90	27108.20	32057.20
EXPENSES				
REPAIR SALARIES	305.20	839.30	1373.40	2136.40
CONSULTING SALARIES	28000.00	28000.00	28000.00	28000.00
OTHER SALARIES	1000.00	1000.00	1000.00	1000.00
MISC EXPENSES	500.00	500.00	500.00	500.00
SALARIES AND EXPENSES	29805.20	30339.30	30873.40	31636.40
NET INCOME	−4725.60	−4245.40	−3765.20	420.80
REPAIR WORK				
ACCUMULATED UNIT SALES	200.00	550.00	900.00	1400.00
UNIT REPAIR PER QTR	10.00	27.50	45.00	70.00
AVG REPAIR HOURS PER UNIT	2.80	2.80	2.80	2.80
REPAIR HOURS	28.00	77.00	126.00	196.00
REPAIR SERVICE RATE	20.70	20.70	20.70	20.70
HOURLY REPAIR WAGE	10.90	10.90	10.90	10.90
CONSULTING				
CONSULTING HOURS	350.00	350.00	350.00	400.00
CONSULTING RATE PER HOUR	70.00	70.00	70.00	70.00
NUMBER OF CONSULTANTS	5.00	5.00	5.00	5.00

WHAT-IF

After reviewing the results shown in Figure 3, the department decides to consider the effect of changes.

Case 1: What if the consulting rate per hour changes to $80 and consultants' wages decrease by 5%?

Case 2: What if unit repair per quarter decreases by 10%?

To test these possibilities, the WHAT-IF command will be used and produces the output shown in Figure 4.

FIGURE 4
What-If Analysis Output

```
? MODEL SERVICE
READY FOR EDIT, LAST LINE IS 41
? SOLVE
MODEL SERVICE VERSION OF 09/24/94 11:04 -- 8 COLUMNS 20 VARIABLES
ENTER SOLVE OPTIONS
? WHAT IF
WHAT IF CASE 1
ENTER STATEMENTS
? CONSULTING RATE PER HOUR = 80
? CONSULTANTS WAGE  =  CONSULTANTS WAGE * 1.05
? SOLVE
ENTER SOLVE OPTIONS
? WIDTH 70 30 10 2
? REPAIR REVENUE, CONSULTING REVENUE, CONSULTING SALARIES, NET INCOME
```

```
***** WHAT IF CASE 1 *****
2 WHAT IF STATEMENTS PROCESSED
```

	Q1	Q2	Q3	Q4
REPAIR REVENUE	579.60	1593.90	2608.20	4057.20
CONSULTING REVENUE	28000.00	28000.00	28000.00	32000.00
CONSULTING SALARIES	29400.00	29400.00	29400.00	29400.00
NET INCOME	−2625.60	−2145.40	−1665.20	−3020.80

```
? WHAT IF
WHAT IF CASE 2
ENTER STATEMENTS
? L26 = L26 * .90
? SOLVE
ENTER SOLVE OPTIONS
? REPAIR REVENUE, REPAIR SALARIES, NET INCOME
```

```
***** WHAT IF CASE 2 *****
1 WHAT IF STATEMENT PROCESSED
```

	Q1	Q2	Q3	Q4
REPAIR REVENUE	521.64	1434.51	2347.38	3651.48
REPAIR SALARIES	274.68	755.37	1236.06	1922.76
NET INCOME	−4753.04	−4320.86	−3888.68	228.72

GOAL SEEKING

The GOAL SEEKING capability allows "backwards" solution of a model, i.e., the user is able to set a goal on a variable such as surplus/deficit, and adjust another variable, say, sales, to achieve the goal.

Case 1: What consulting rate per hour is required to generate consulting revenue of $30,000 for the first 3 quarters and $33,000 for the 4th quarter?

Case 2: If unit repair per quarter decreases by 10%, what repair service rate per hour is required to generate repair revenue for $700, $1,700, $2,800, and $4,500, respectively, for the next 4 quarters?

The output is shown in Figure 5.

FIGURE 5
Goal Seeking Output

```
? BASE MODEL
? GOAL SEEKING
GOAL SEEKING CASE 1
ENTER NAME OF VARIABLE(S) TO BE ADJUSTED TO ACHIEVE PERFORMANCE
? CONSULTING RATE PER HOUR
ENTER 1 COMPUTATIONAL STATEMENT(S) FOR PERFORMANCE
? CONSULTING REVENUE = 30000 FOR 3, 33000


***** GOAL SEEKING CASE 1 *****
```

	Q1	Q2	Q3	Q4
CONSULTING RATE PER HOUR	85.71	85.71	85.71	82.50

```
? WHAT IF
WHAT IF CASE 1
ENTER STATEMENTS
? UNIT REPAIR PER QTR = UNIT REPAIR PER QTR * .90
? GOAL SEEKING
GOAL SEEKING CASE 2
ENTER NAME OF VARIABLE(S) TO BE ADJUSTED TO ACHIEVE PERFORMANCE
? REPAIR SERVICE RATE
ENTER 1 COMPUTATIONAL STATEMENT(S) FOR PERFORMANCE
? REPAIR REVENUE = 700, 1700, 2800, 4500


***** WHAT IF CASE 1 *****
1 WHAT IF STATEMENT PROCESSED


***** GOAL SEEKING CASE 2 *****
```

	Q1	Q2	Q3	Q4
REPAIR SERVICE RATE	27.78	24.53	24.69	25.51

Prospective users of IFPS/Plus are encouraged to refer to the following sources from COMSHARE (3001 S. State Street, Ann Arbor, MI 48108):

❒ COMSHARE, IFPS Cases and Models, 1979.

❒ COMSHARE, IFPS Tutorial, 1980.

❒ COMSHARE, IFPS User's Manual, 1984.

❒ COMSHARE, IFPS/Personal User's Manual, 1984.

❒ COMSHARE, IFPS University Seminar, 1984.

❒ COMSHARE, Comprehensive Fundamentals of IFPS, 1984.

❒ COMSHARE, Papers available from the COMSHARE University Support Programs, 1986.

SIMPLAN: A PLANNING AND MODELING SYSTEM

SIMPLAN is more than a financial modeling package; it is an integrated, multipurpose planning, budgeting, and modeling system. In addition to a general financial modeling function, the system has the capability to perform (1) revenue forecasting and time series analysis and (2) econometric modeling. Thus, sophisticated users can really take advantage of the package. For forecasting revenue, interest rates, material supplies, factor input prices, and other key variables, SIMPLAN offers a variety of time series forecasting models. These include time trends, exponential smoothing, and adaptive forecasting. Forecasts developed by any of these methods may be incorporated directly into SIMPLAN models and reports.

As for econometric modeling capability, SIMPLAN offers models for sales, market share and industry that can, with SIMPLAN, be specified, estimated, validated, simulated, and linked directly to division financial and production models or the entire nonprofit organization's financial models.

SIMPLAN can be used to estimate single-equation and simultaneous-equation linear and non-linear models to simulate the effects of alternative operating strategies and economic conditions on market share and industry demand. Direct access from SIMPLAN to all series of the National Business and Economic Research (NBER) macroeconomic database is available on several time-sharing networks.

With SIMPLAN, 16 major functions are integrated into a single planning and modeling system. These functions include:

❏ Database creation

❏ Database manipulation

❏ Consolidation

❏ Model specification

❏ Model changes

❏ Report formulation

❏ Report changes

❏ Statistical analysis

❏ Forecasting

❏ Econometrics

❏ Model solution

❏ Validation

❏ Policy simulation

❏ Report generation

❏ Security

❏ Graphical display

EXPRESS

EXPRESS provides the standard set of financial planning and analysis features, including the generation of pro forma financial statements, budgeting, analysis, projections, target analysis, and consolidations. One of the special modeling features of the system is risk analysis (including Monte Carlo simulation).

EXPRESS contains a variety of analytical and statistical features. Besides the standard mathematical capabilities, the system has the following automatic built-in calculations: sorting, percent difference, lags and leads, maximum/minimum of a set of numbers, year-to-date, and rounding. The statistical features include a number of time series analysis and forecasting routines such as exponential smoothing, linear extrapolation, deseasonalization, multiple regression, cluster analysis, and factor analysis.

EXPRESS contains the report generator and display features for the system. All the display capabilities are integrated with the system's data management, analysis, and modeling routine. The system has full graphic display capabilities.

ENCORE! PLUS

The analytical functions are similar to IFPS/Plus, but Encore has more model building capability. For example, it is stronger in its risk analysis than IFPS/Plus, and even includes a Monte Carlo Simulator. Since Encore! Plus is more powerful at the application development level than, say, IFPS/Plus, it requires a higher level of programming ability.

A QUICK LOOK AT OTHER BUDGETING AND DECISION SUPPORT SOFTWARE PACKAGES

In addition to specialized budgeting and financial modeling software discussed above, there are a variety of computer software designed specifically for budgeting and DSS software. Some are *stand-alone* packages, others are *templates*, and still others are spreadsheet *add-ins*.

BUDGET EXPRESS

Budget Express is a Lotus 1-2-3 spreadsheet add-in package designed to aid users in budgeting and financial planning. It offers enhancements like multiple-level worksheet outlining features, which lets users hide rows and columns containing detail, and several budget analysis, consolidation and goal-setting tools. Budget Express "understands" the structure of financial worksheets and concepts such as months, quarters, years, totals, and subtotals, speeding up budget and forecast preparation. The program creates column headers for months, automatically totals columns and rows, and calculates quarterly and yearly summaries. And for sophisticated what-if analyses, just specify your goal and Budget Express displays your current and target values as you make changes. (*Add-in*)

PROPLANS

ProPlans creates your financial plan automatically and accurately—and slices months from your annual planning and reporting process. You just enter your forecast data and assumptions into easy-to-follow, comprehensive data-entry screens, and ProPlans automatically creates the detailed financials you need to run your NPO for the next year—your statement of activities, balance sheet, cash flow statement, and ratio reports. (*Template*)

COMPETE

Compete is a hybrid spreadsheet that permits users to define and explore the relationships between different sets of data, examine the ramifications of a variable change, and analyze which components need to be changed to reach a desired goal. (*Add-in*)

PROFIT PLANNER

Profit Planner provides titles and amounts for revenues, expenses, assets, liabilities, and fund balance in a ready-to-use 1-2-3 template. Financial tables are automatically generated on screen. It presents results in 13 different table formats, including a pro forma activities statement, balance sheet, and cash flow statement. Profit Planner even compares your activity statement, balance sheet, and ratios against industry averages, so you're not working in a vacuum. (*Template*)

UP YOUR CASH FLOW

This program generates cash flow and revenue and expense forecasts; detailed revenue by service line and payroll by employee forecasts; monthly balance sheets; bar graphs; ratio and break-even analyses, and more. (*Stand-alone*)

CASH COLLECTOR

Cash collector assists you in reviewing and aging receivables. You always know who owes what; nothing "falls through the cracks." When collection action is required, simply click through menu-driven screens to automatically generate letters and other professionally written collection documents (all included) that are proven to pull in the payments. (*Stand-alone*)

BUDGET SOLUTIONS

Budget Solutions is very useful for performing proportional resource allocations from within a worksheet while accounting for time constraints imposed anywhere within a budget's account hierarchy. (Add-in)

CASH FLOW ANALYSIS

This software provides projections of cash inflow and cash outflow. You input data into categories: revenues, fund raising costs, general and administrative expenses, long-term debt, other cash receipts, supplies inventory build-up/reduction, and capital expenditures (acquisition of long-term assets such as furniture). The program allows changes in assumptions and scenarios and provides a complete array of reports. (*Stand-alone*)

QUICKEN

This program is a fast, easy-to-use, inexpensive accounting and budgeting program that can help you manage your NPO by helping you manage your cash flow. You record bills as postdated transactions when they arrive; the program's *Billminder* feature automatically reminds you when bills are due. Then, you can print checks for due bills with a few keystrokes. Similarly, you can record invoices and track aged receivables. Together, these features help you to maximize cash on hand. (*Stand-alone*)

CapPLANS

CapPLANS evaluates return based on net present value (NPV), internal rate of return (IRR), and payout period. Choose among five depreciation methods, including straight line. Run up to four sensitivity analyses; and project profitability over a 15-year horizon. In addition to a complete report of your analysis, CapPLANS generates a concise executive summary—great for expediting approval. Add ready-made graphs to illustrate profitability clearly, at a glance. (*Template*)

PROJECT EVALUATION TOOLKIT

This template calculates the dollar value of your project based on six valuation methods, including discounted cash flow and impact on the balance sheet. Assess intangibles such as impact on strategy or labor relations. And use scenario planning to show the effects of changing start dates, revenue forecasts, and other critical variables. (*Template*)

@RISK

How will a new competitor affect your market share? @RISK calculates the likelihood of changes and events that affect your bottom line. First use @Risk's familiar @ functions to define the risk in your worksheet. Then let @Risk run thousands of what-if tests using one of two proven statistical sampling techniques—Monte Carlo or Latin Hypercube. You get a clear, colorful graph that tells you the likelihood of every possible bottom-line value. At a glance you'll know if your risk is acceptable, or if you need to make a contingency plan. (*Add-in*)

CFO SPREADSHEET APPLICATIONS

These ready-to-use spreadsheet templates offer easy ways to make many financial decisions. They are divided into four modules: cash management, operating strategies, capital budgeting, and advanced topics. (*Template*)

INVENTORY ANALYST

Inventory Analyst tells precisely how much supplies inventory to order and when to order it. Choose from four carefully explained ordering methods: economic order quantity (EOQ), fixed order quantity, fixed months requirements, and level load by work days. Inventory Analyst ensures that you'll always have enough stock to get you through your ordering period.

Just load up to 48 months' worth of inventory history, and Inventory Analyst makes the forecast based on one of three forecasting methods: time series, exponential smoothing, or moving averages; it explains which method is best. Inventory Analyst will adjust your forecast for seasonality, too. (*Template*)

WHAT'S BEST!

If you have limited resources—for example, people, equipment, supplies, time, or cash—then *What's Best!* can tell you how to allocate these resources in order to maximize or minimize a given objective, such as profit or cost. *What's Best!* uses a proven method—linear programming—to help you achieve your goals. This product can solve a variety of business problems that cut across every industry at every level of decision-making. (*Add-in*)

WHAT-IF SOLVER

What-If Solver is an optimization software that solves linear and non-linear constrained optimization problems. (*Add-in*)

Chapter 6

How Capital Budgeting Helps Nonprofit Organizations

Capital budgeting is the selection of the best alternative long-term invest-ment opportunity. It includes programming and financing the acquisition of or additions to long-term assets. Strategic capital budgeting decisions are extremely important to nonprofits. As an NPO grows, problems regarding long-range investment proposals become more essential. Capital budgeting tools are used in planning new projects and in making major revisions of projects already underway.

The types of scarce resources that may be committed to a project include cash, manpower, and square footage of space. When predicting costs for a project, the allocation of scarce resources must be expressed in financial terms.

There are two general types of capital budgeting decisions—*screening* and *preference*. Screening looks at whether a proposed project meets an approval standard. For example, there may be a policy of accepting cost reduction projects only if they furnish a return of, say, 12 percent. Preference decisions relate to selecting from competing courses of action.

The basic kinds of capital investment decisions are choosing between proposed projects and replacement decisions. Selection requires judgments regarding future events of which you lack direct knowledge. Timing and risk have to be taken into account. Your task is to reduce the possibility of mak-ing a wrong decision. To help you deal with the uncertainty, consider using the risk-return trade-off. Discounted cash flow methods are more realistic than methods not taking into account the time value of money in evaluating investments. The time value of money is a crucial consideration during inflationary periods.

Planning for capital expenditures requires you to determine the best proposal, the amount of money involved, and how long it will take to complete. You must make an analysis of current programs, study new proposals, and coordinate interrelated proposals. In project planning, consider the interaction of cost, time, and quality. Budgeted cost and time should be compared to actual cost and time for control purposes.

MAKING THE RIGHT DECISION

You must consider your cash status, financing strategy, and growth rate when making capital budgeting decisions. Will the project generate a return above the long-range expected return? Projects must be tied into the nonprofit's long-range planning, weighing the entity's strengths and weaknesses. The objectives and the extent to which they depend on outside factors (e.g., inflation, interest rate) must be taken into account. Further, the capital budget may need to be modified after considering economic, financial, and political variables. But consideration also should be given to fixed costs that are difficult to modify after the initial decision has been made.

Cost-benefit analysis is helpful. Is there excessive effort for the proposal? Can it be conducted internally or must it be performed externally? Is there a better and less expensive way to achieve the final result? Problem areas need to be identified, such as when long-term borrowed funds are used to finance a project where adequate cash inflows will not be available to pay debt when due.

Cash flows of a project should be measured using different possible variations (e.g., change in price of a new service). By modifying the assumptions and evaluating the results you can see the sensitivity of cash flows to relevant factors. An advantage is the analysis of risk in proposals based on alternative assumptions. Higher risk requires higher return.

"What if" questions are critical and difficult when formulating a capital budget. Assumptions and estimates must be sound. Spreadsheets can be used to evaluate the cash flow effects of buying long-term assets.

After the goals to be accomplished are set forth, the cost of each goal should be determined. The income to be generated must also be determined. Of course, goals must be realistic.

For example, rising health care costs have forced hospitals and medical practices to carefully appraise the attractiveness of new medical and laboratory equipment. Therefore, capital budgeting analysis must be properly undertaken to assure the medical facility is getting the best value for the dollar. This is especially crucial now that the federal and state governments are looking for ways to reduce health care costs.

Once an investment proposal is approved, controls should be implemented over expenditures. The project's status should be reported. Expenditures should be tied to the project and controls in place assuring the expenditures conform with the accepted investment proposal. The project's progress should be monitored at crucial stages.

Factors to take into account in determining capital expenditures include risk, liquidity, competition, return rate, dollar amounts, budget ceiling, likelihood of success, time value of money, forecasting errors, and long-term strategy.

The types of capital budgeting decisions include refinancing debt, nonprofit investments such as safety and health, obtaining new facilities or expanding current ones, facility replacement, cost control, fund-raising, merger evaluation, and new and current service appraisal.

Exhibit 1 presents a typical project application form, Exhibit 2 shows an advice of project change, and Exhibit 3 is a typical appropriation request.

This chapter presents the capital budgeting techniques including accounting rate of return, payback, discounted payback, net present value, profitability index, and internal rate of return. Consideration is given to contingent proposals, capital rationing, and nondiscretionary projects. Risk is also taken into account.

Net present value, internal rate of return, and profitability index are effective in selecting sound investment proposals. The payback method is inadequate for this purpose because it does not take into account the time value of money. In the case of mutually exclusive proposals, net present value, internal rate of return, and profitability index methods are not always able to rank projects in the same order; it is possible to derive different rankings under each approach. Risk should be considered in the capital budgeting process using probabilities, simulation, and decision trees.

EXHIBIT 1
Project Application

DEPARTMENT NAME				APPLICATION NO.	
DEPARTMENT CODE _____				OFFENSIVE ❏	
FUNCTION CODE _____				DEFENSIVE ❏	
PROJECT TITLE					
DESCRIPTION/OBJECTIVES					

EXPENDITURES AMOUNTS

FISCAL YEAR	1st Qtr.	2nd Qtr.	3rd Qtr.	4th Qtr.	TOTAL
19					
19					
19					
19					
19					
TOTAL					

DATE	SUBMITTED BY
COMMENTS	

For The Department

EXHIBIT 2
Advice of Project Change

DEPARTMENT NAME	DATE
DEPARTMENT CODE	APPROPRIATION REQUEST NO.
PROJECT TITLE	

EXPENDITURE AMOUNTS

	ORIGINAL AUTHORIZED	LATEST ESTIMATE	INCREASE (DECREASE)
CAPITAL			
EXPENSE			
TOTAL			

AMOUNT SPENT TO DATE $_____ AMOUNT COMMITTED TO DATE $_____

WHY IS THIS NEW AMOUNT BEING REQUESTED?

_____   _____
PROJECT SPONSOR   DEPARTMENT/AREA SUPERVISOR

PROJECT TO BE CONTINUED ☐
REVISED REQUEST REQUIRED ☐
SEE COMMENT ON REVERSE
SIDE ☐

FINAL APPROVER_____
DATE_____

EXHIBIT 3
Appropriation Request

ORIG. DEPT. NAME		DEPT. CODE	APPROPRIATION NO.
BUDGET CAPITALIZED☐ EXPENSE☐		PROJECT APPLIC. NO.	
ACCOUNTING CODE		PROJECT APPL. TOT. EXP.$	APPROPRIATION TOTAL $
DESCRIPTION			
PURPOSE			
CURRENT FACILITIES			
PROPOSED FACILITIES			
COST JUSTIFICATION (SAVINGS/BENEFITS)			
PROPOSED EXPENDITURES	APPROVALS		DATE

CHOOSING A DISCOUNT RATE CAN BE CRITICAL

The major problem in using capital budgeting in the nonprofit sector is deciding what discount rate to use. Some NPOs use the interest rate associated with a special bond issue, such as when a school is built. Other nonprofit entities use the interest rate that could be earned by depositing funds in an endowment fund rather than spending it on capital improvements. Still other nonprofits employ discount rates arbitrarily selected by their governing boards.

You must be careful not to use an unrealistically low discount rate because projects may be accepted even though they are not profitable.

Certain NPOs, such as hospitals and schools, use as the discount rate the average return rate on private sector investments. The average discount rate provides more useful results than that associated with a specific interest rate on a special bond issue or the return rate on an endowment fund.

A lower required rate of return may be used by nonprofit entities than commercial businesses because they do not pay taxes.

ACCOUNTING (SIMPLE) RATE OF RETURN

Accounting rate of return (ARR) measures profitability from the accounting point of view by comparing the initial (or average) investment to future annual profits.

Rule of thumb: Choose the proposal with the highest ARR.

EXAMPLE 1   Initial investment $8,000
Life   15 years
Cash inflows per year $1,300

$$\text{Depreciation} = \frac{\text{Cost} - \text{Salvage value}}{\text{Life}} = \frac{\$8,000 - 0}{15} = \$533$$

$$\text{ARR} = \frac{\text{Cash inflows per year} - \text{Depreciation}}{\text{Initial investment}}$$

$$\frac{\$1,300 - \$533}{\$8,000} = \frac{\$767}{\$8,000} = 9.6\%$$

If you use average investment, ARR is

$$\text{ARR} = \frac{\$767}{\$8,000/2} = \frac{\$767}{\$4,000} = 19.2\%$$

Note: When average investment is used instead of the initial investment, Accounting Rate of Return is doubled.

The advantages of ARR are that:

❐ it is easy to compute and understand,

❐ profitability is taken into account.

❐ the numbers apply to financial statement presentation, and

❐ full useful life is considered.

The disadvantages of ARR are that it:

❐ ignores time value of money, and

❐ uses income rather than cash flow information.

USING PAYBACK PERIOD TO ASSESS CAPITAL PROJECTS

Payback is the number of years it takes to get back your initial investment. Payback helps in appraising a project's risk and liquidity, and rate of return. An advantage of payback is that it allows nonprofit organizations with a cash problem to analyze the turnover of scarce resources in order to recover earlier those funds invested. Further, there is likely to be less possibility of loss from changes in economic conditions, obsolescence, and other unavoidable risks.

The payback period is good to use where preliminary screening is more important than precise figures, in cases where a poor credit position is a principal factor, and when investment funds are particularly scarce. Some believe that payback should be used in unstable situations because the future is so unpredictable that it is useless to forecast cash flows more than two years in advance.

An NPO may set a limit on the payback period beyond which an investment will not be made. Another nonprofit may use payback to select one of several investments, choosing the one with the least payback period.

The benefits of the payback period are that it:

❏ considers investment risk,

❏ can be used to supplement other measures,

❏ is simple to comprehend and use, and

❏ is recommended when there is a cash flow problem.

The drawbacks of the payback period are that it:

❏ does not measure earnings,

❏ does not take into account cash flows received after the payback period,

❏ ignores the time value of money,

❏ does not specify how long the maximum payback period should be, and

❏ penalizes projects that result in small cash flows in their early years and high cash flows in their later years.

Do not select a project only because the payback calculation points to acceptance. You still have to use the present value and internal rate of return methods.

If cash inflows differ each year, compute the payback period by adding up the annual cash inflows to arrive at the amount of the cash outlay. The result is the length of time to recover your investment.

You are considering a new product. It will initially cost $250,000. Expected cash inflows are $80,000 for the next five years. You want your money back in four years.

$$\text{Payback period} = \frac{\text{Initial Investment}}{\text{Annual cash inflow}} = \frac{\$250,000}{\$80,000} = 3.125$$

Because the payback period (3.125) is less than the cutoff payback period (4), you should accept the proposal.

EXAMPLE 3   You invest $40,000 and receive the following cash inflows:

Year 1	$15,000
Year 2	20,000
Year 3	28,000

$$\text{Payback period} = \frac{\$40,000}{\underbrace{\$15,000 + \$20,000}_{\$35,000} + \underbrace{\$5,000}_{\$28,000}} = 2.18 \text{ years}$$

$$\quad\quad\quad\quad\quad\quad 2 \text{ years} \quad + \quad .18$$

PAYBACK RECIPROCAL ALLOWS QUICK ESTIMATES

The reciprocal of the payback period provides a fast, reliable estimate of the internal rate of return (IRR) on an investment when the project life exceeds twice the payback period and the cash inflows are equal each period.

EXAMPLE 4

ABC Charity is considering three projects, each of which requires an initial investment of $10,000, and each of which is expected to produce a cash inflow of $2,000 yearly. The payback period is five years ($10,000/$2,000), and the payback reciprocal is 1/5, or 20 percent. The table of the present value of an annuity of $1 shows that the factor of 5 applies to the following lives and internal return rates:

Life (in years)	IRR
10	15%
15	18
20	19

The payback reciprocal is 20 percent relative to the IRR of 18 percent when the life is 15 years, and 20 percent relative to the IRR of 19 percent when the life is 20 years. This reveals that the payback reciprocal gives a reasonable approximation of the IRR if the useful life of the project is at least twice the payback period.

DISCOUNTED PAYBACK PERIOD

Before considering discounted cash flow methods, it should be noted that there is less accuracy with a discounted cash flow analysis if there is future uncertainty, the environment is changing, and cash flows are difficult to predict.

You can take into account the time value of money by using the discounted payback method. The payback period will be longer with the discounted method because money has less value over time.

EXAMPLE 5   Assume the same facts as in Example 3 and a cost of capital of 10 percent.

$$\text{Discounted payback} = \frac{\text{Initial cash outlay}}{\text{Discounted annual cash inflows}}$$

	$40,000	
Year 1	Year 2	Year 3
$15,000 +	$20,000 +	$28,000
× .9091 ×	.8264 ×	.7513
$13,637 +	$16,528 +	$21,036
$30,165	+	$ 9,835
		$21,036
2 years	+	.47 = 2.47 years

NET PRESENT VALUE

The present value method compares the present value of future cash flows anticipated from a proposal to the initial cash outlay for the investment. Net cash flow is the difference between the expected cash inflow received and the expected cash outflow of the investment. The discount rate used should be the minimum return rate earned on the money. In general, a return of 10–13 percent is reasonable.

An advantage of net present value is that it considers the time value of money. A drawback is the subjectivity in estimating annual cash inflows and the expected benefit period.

If a proposal is to generate a return, invest in it only if it gives a positive net present value. If two proposals are mutually exclusive (acceptance of one prevents the acceptance of another), then accept the proposal with the highest present value.

The net present value method usually gives more accurate indications than other methods. By using net present value and the best estimates of reinvestment rates, the most advantageous project may be chosen.

EXAMPLE 6   You are considering replacing Executive 1 with Executive 2. Executive 2 requires a payment upon contract signing of $200,000. He will receive an annual salary of $330,000. Executive 1's current annual salary is $140,000. Because Executive 2 is superior in talent, you expect an increase in annual cash flows from operations (ignoring salary) of $350,000 for each of the next ten years. The cost of capital is 12 percent.

As indicated in the following calculations, since there is a positive net present value, Executive 1 should be replaced with Executive 2.

Year	Explanation	Amount	×	Factor	=	Present Value
0	Contract signing bonus	$-200,000	×	1		$-200,000
1–10	Increased salary					
	($300,000 – $140,000)	–160,000	×	5.6502[a]		-904,032
1–10	Increase in annual cash					
	flow from operations	+350,000	×	5.6502[a]		1,977,570
	Net present value					$873,538

[a]Present value of an ordinary annuity factor for 10 years and an interest rate of 12 percent.

EXAMPLE 7

You are thinking of replacing an old computer system with a new one. The old system has a book value of $800,000 and a remaining life of ten years. The expected salvage value of the old machine is $50,000, but if you sold it now, you would obtain $700,000. The new computer system costs $2,000,000 and has a residual value of $250,000. The new computer system will result in annual savings of $400,000. The minimum rate of return is 14 percent. Straight-line depreciation is used. You have to ascertain if the computer system should be replaced.

	Profit	Cash Flow
	$400,000	$400,000

Annual savings
Less: Additional depreciation
New machine:

$$\frac{\$2,000,000 - \$250,000}{10} = \$175,000$$

Old machine:

$$\frac{\$800,000 - \$50,000}{10} = \$\ 75,000 \qquad \$100,000$$

Income	$300,000	
Net cash inflow		$400,000

The net present value follows:

Year	Explanation	Amount × Factor = Present Value	
0	Cost of computer	$–2,000,000 × 1.0 =	$–2,000,000
0	Sale of old computer	700,000 × 1.0 =	700,000
1-10	Annual increase in cash flows	400,000 × 5.216 =	2,086,400
10	Incremental salvage	200,000 × .270 =	54,000
			$840,400

The replacement of the old computer system with a new one is recommended because of the positive net present value.

THE PROFITABILITY INDEX HELPS RANK PROJECTS

The profitability (ranking) index is a net rather than an aggregate index and is used to differentiate the initial cash investment from subsequent cash inflows. If there is a budget limitation, proposals of different dollar amounts can be ranked on a relative basis. Use the index as a means to rank projects in descending order of attractiveness.

A proposal should be accepted when the profitability index equals or exceeds 1.

The internal rate of return and the net present value methods may give conflicting conclusions when competing projects have different times. The profitability index provides the correct decision, however, and is the best under these circumstances.

Capital rationing takes place when a nonprofit organization is unable to invest in projects with a net present value of zero or more. The nonprofit entity sets an upper limit to its capital budget based on budgetary limitations.

When capital rationing exists, the project with the highest ranking index instead of net present value should be chosen. Exhibit 4 presents the capital rationing steps.

EXHIBIT 4

CAPITAL RATIONING DECISION PROCESS

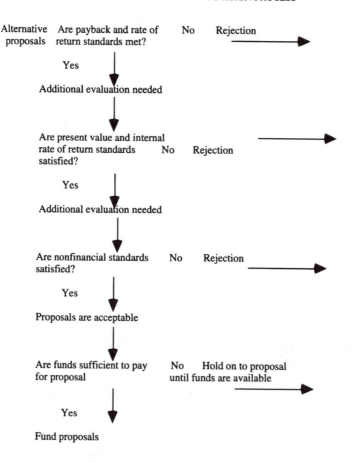

EXAMPLE 8

Assume the following data for two proposals:

	Proposal X	Proposal Y
Initial investment	$100,000	$10,000
Present value of cash inflows	500,000	90,000

The net present value of proposal X is $400,000 and that of proposal Y is $80,000. Using the present value approach, proposal X is superior. However, this is erroneous when there is a budget limitation. In this case, proposal Y's ranking index of 9 exceeds proposal X's index of 5. Therefore, the ranking index should be employed in appraising proposals when budget limitations exist. The net effect is that proposal Y should be chosen.

EXAMPLE 9

Projects	Investment	Present Value	Profitability Index	Ranking
A	$ 70,000	$112,000	1.6	1
B	100,000	145,000	1.45	2
C	110,000	126,500	1.15	5
D	60,000	79,000	1.32	3
E	40,000	38,000	.95	6
F	80,000	95,000	1.19	4

The budget constraint is $250,000. You should select projects A, B, and D revealed by the following computations:

Projects	Investment	Present Value
A	$70,000	$112,000
B	100,000	145,000
D	60,000	79,000
	$230,000	$336,000

where

Net present value = $336,000 − $230,000 = $106,000

However, the ranking index has some deficiencies. It breaks down whenever more than one resource is rationed.

A general approach to solve capital rationing situations is the use of <u>mathematical</u> programming. The goal is to choose the project mix that maximizes the net present value subject to a budget limitation.

EXAMPLE 10

Using the information in Example 9, we can set up the problem as a mathematical programming one. First, we label project A as X_1, B as X_2, and so on; the problem can be stated as follows:

Maximize NPV = $42,000X_1$ + $45,000X_2$ + $16,500X_3$
$$+ \$19,000X_4 - \$2,000X_5 + \$15,000X_6$$

subject to

$70,000X_1$ + $100,000X_2$ + $110,000X_3$ + $60,000X_4$ + $40,000X_5$
$$+ \$80,000X_6 \leq \$250,000$$

$$X_1 = 0, 1, (i = 1, 2, \ldots 6)$$

Using the mathematical program, solution routine, the solution to this problem is

$$X_1 = 1, X_2 = 1, X_4 = 1$$

and the net present value is $106,000. Thus, projects A, B, and D should be approved.

CONTINGENT PROPOSALS

A contingent proposal requires acceptance of another related one. Thus, the proposals must be examined together. You compute a profitability index for the group.

EXAMPLE 11

Proposal	Present Value of Cash Outflow	Present Value of Cash Inflow
A	$160,000	$210,000
B	60,000	40,000
Total	$220,000	$250,000

$$\text{Profitability index} = \frac{\$250,000}{\$220,000} = 1.14$$

INTERNAL RATE OF RETURN (TIME-ADJUSTED RATE OF RETURN)

The internal return rate is the return earned on a given proposal. It is the discount rate equating the net present value of cash inflows to the net present value of cash outflows to zero. The internal return rate assumes cash inflows are reinvested at the internal rate. This approach involves trial-and-error computations. However, the use of a computer or calculator simplifies the internal rate-of-return process. The internal return rate can be compared with the required rate of return (cutoff rate).

If the internal rate of return equals or exceeds the required rate, the project is approved.

The advantages of IRR are that it:

☐ is more realistic and accurate than the accounting rate of return, and takes into account the time value of money.

The disadvantages of IRR are that:

☐ when multiple reversals in cash flow occur the project could result in more than one IRR,

☐ it does not take into account the varying size of investment in competing projects and their respective profitabilities, and it is difficult and time consuming to calculate especially when there are uneven cash flows.

To solve for the internal return rate when uneven cash inflows exist, use the trial-and-error approach while working through the present value tables.

There are several guidelines to follow when using the IRR method:

1. Calculate net present value at the cost of financing, expressed as r_1.

2. Determine if net present value is positive or negative.

3. If the net present value is positive, use a higher rate (r_2) than r_1. If it is negative, use a lower rate (r_2) than r_1. The exact IRR at which net present value equals zero lies between the two rates.

4. Compute net present value using r_2.

5. Use interpolation to obtain the exact rate.

EXAMPLE 12

A project costing $100,000 is anticipated to result in the following cash inflows:

YEAR	
1	$50,000
2	30,000
3	20,000
4	40,000

Using trial and error, you can compute the internal rate as follows;

Year	10%	*Present Value*	16%	*Present Value*	18%	*Present Value*
1	.909	$45,450	.862	$43,100	.847	$42,350
2	.826	24,780	.743	22,290	.718	21,540
3	.751	15,020	.641	12,820	.609	12,180
4	.683	27,320	.552	22,080	.516	20,640
		$ +112,570		$+100,290		$ +96,710
Investment		-100,000		-100,000		-100,000
Net present value		$ +12,570		$ +290		$ -3,290

The internal rate of return on the project is a little more than 16 percent because at that rate the net present value of the investment is approximately zero.

If the return on the investment is expected to be in one lump sum after a period of two years, you can use the Present Value of $1 table to find the internal rate.

EXAMPLE 13

You are considering two mutually exclusive investment proposals. The cost of financing is 10 percent. Expected cash flows follow:

Project	Investment	Year 1	Year 6
A	$10,000	$12,000	
B	10,000		$20,000

Internal rates of return are

$$\text{Project A} : \frac{\$10,000}{\$12,000} = .8333$$

Looking across one year on the table, .8333 corresponds to internal rate of 20 percent.

$$\text{Projects B} : \frac{\$10,000}{\$20,000} = .5000$$

Looking across six years on the table, .5000 corresponds to an internal rate of 12 percent. Project A should be selected because it has a higher internal rate of return than project B.

If the cash inflows each years, are equal, the internal rate of return is computed first by determinung a factor (which happens to be the same as the payback period) and then looking up the rate of return on the Present Value of an Annuity of $1 table.

EXAMPLE 14

You invest $100,000 in a proposal that will generate annual cash inflows of $15,000 a year for the next 20 years.

$$\text{Factor} = \frac{\$100,000}{\$15,000} = 6.6667$$

Refer to the Present Value of an Annuity of $1 table. Looking across 20 years, the factor closest to 6.6667 is 6.6231 in the 14 percent column. Hence the internal rate is about 14 percent.

EXAMPLE 15

Initial investment	$12,950
Estimated life	10 years
Annual cash inflows	$3,000
Cost of capital	12%

The internal rate of return computation follows, including interpolation to arrive at the exact rate.

$$\text{PV of annuity factor} = \frac{\$12,950}{\$3,000} = 4.317$$

The value 4.317 is somewhere between 18 percent and 20 percent in the 10-year line of the Present Value of annuity table. Using interpolation you get

	Present Value of Annuity Factor	
18%	4.494	4.494
IRR		4.317
20%	4.192	
Difference	.302	.177

Therefore,

$$\text{IRR} = 18\% + \frac{.177}{.302}(20\% - 18\%)$$

$$= 18\% + .586(2\%) = 18\% + 1.17\% = 19.17\%$$

Because the internal rate of return (19.17 percent) exceeds the cost of financing (12 percent), the project should be accepted.

COMPENSATING FOR LOSSES ON NONDISCRETIONARY PROJECTS

Some investments are made out of necessity instead of profitability (e.g., safety devices). Here you will have a negative cash flow. Thus, your discretionary projects must earn a return rate in excess of the cost of financing to compensate for the losses on nondiscretionary projects.

EXAMPLE 16

A nonprofit entity's cost of financing is 14 percent and $30 million of projects, 25 percent of which are nondiscretionary projects. It thus must earn $4.2 million per year (14% × $30 million). The $22.5 million of discretionary projects ($30 million − 25%) must earn 18.7 percent ($4.2 million / $22.5 million) rather than 14 percent to achieve the overall goal of $4.2 million.

COMPARING THE VARIOUS METHODS

The discounting cash flow approaches (net present value, internal rate of return, and profitability index) generally arrive at the same conclusions for competing proposals. However, these methods have different rankings to mutually exclusive proposals in some situations. Any one of the following conditions can result in contradictory rankings:

❏ The trend in cash flow of one project is the reverse of another.

❏ A higher cost for one project than another.

❏ Different project lives.

One of the following characteristics of the organization may also result in conflicting rankings:

❏ Capital rationing exists in which there is a maximum funding amount for capital investments.

❏ Future investment opportunities are anticipated to be different than at present.

The prime reason for different rankings of alternative projects under the present value and internal return rate methods applies to the varying assumptions of the reinvestment rate used for discounting cash flows. The net present value method assumes cash flows are reinvested at the cost of financing rate. The internal return rate method assumes cash flows are reinvested at the internal rate.

The net present value method usually results in a correct ranking because the cost of financing is a more realistic reinvestment rate.

Which method is best depends upon which reinvestment rate is closest to the rate the NPO earns on future cash flows from a project.

The minimum return rate required for a proposal may be waived in a case where the proposal has substantial future benefit, relates to a necessity program (e.g., safety requirement), and has qualitative benefit (e.g., service quality).

EXAMPLE 17

Assume the following:

	Cash Flows					
Project	0	1	2	3	4	5
A	$(100)	$120				
B	(100)					$201.14

Computing Internal Rate of Return and Net Present Value at 10 percent gives the different rankings as follows:

	Internal Rate of Return	Net Present Value
A	20%[a]	9.09
B	15%	24.90

[a]From present value of $1 table, the IRR for a factor of

$.8333 \left(\dfrac{\$1000}{\$120} \right)$ is 20 percent.

The general rule is to use the Net Present Value ranking. Hence, project B would be selected over project A.

TAKING A CLOSER LOOK AT THE CAPITAL BUDGETING PROCESS

The following questions should be answered in the capital budgeting process:

❑ What is the project's quality?

❑ Are there unusual projects?

❑ Is risk versus return taken into account in selecting projects?

❑ How is uncertainty considered in the analysis?

❑ Do you know which proposals and services are most profitable?

❑ In appraising a proposal, are both money and time accounted for?

❑ Do you periodically track the performance of programs in terms of initial expectations?

❑ Is the proposal consistent with the nonprofit's financial position?

❏ Are you risk prone or risk averse?

❏ How is the expected life arrived at?

❏ Does the proposal conform with long-term objectives?

❏ Is there a cost-benefit analysis for each project?

❏ How are probable cash flows computed?

❏ Before making a final decision, are all the results of the capital budgeting approach considered and integrated?

❏ Are qualitative factors considered (e.g., political and economic environment)?

❏ Is the discounted payback method employed?

Diagram 1 shows the capital budgeting process.

```
┌─────────────────────────────────────────────────────────────────┐
│ Diagram 1: The process of Capital Budgeting                       │
│                                                                   │
│                                                                   │
│  Planning--------------------------Programming-----Financing      │
│     (1)        (2)        (3)        (4)       (5)       (6)       (7)   │
│      ┬          ┬          ┬          ┬         ┬         ┬         ┬    │
│    Goals      Cost      Income    Analysis   Proposal  Amended    Used  │
│                                                                   │
│      ├--------- Steps in Creating a Capital Budget -------------├------ B -------├------ A ------┤ │
└─────────────────────────────────────────────────────────────────┘
```

Diagram 1 illustrates the order of the steps used in creating a capital budget for a nonprofit organization. Steps 1–5 are self-explanatory. Point "B" signifies the final stages of creating a capital budget. Step 6 represents the capital budget that has been formed. It is at this point that we see how the nonprofit organization (such as a hospital) uses a capital budget.

The resources of a hospital consist of contributions, gifts, pledges, and grants. After a hospital has its capital budget, the resources that will be used (for acquisition or additions) are placed in a fund, consisting of a set of accounts that are used for specific activities or in achieving certain goals. Hospitals use the plant replacement and expansion fund to account for the acquisition of fixed assets (such as property, plant, and equipment). The resources in the plant replacement and expansion fund are given to the hospital by donors. These funds are "restricted" because they have a have a specific purpose. The plant replacement and expansion fund is decreased when expenditures are made (due to specifications that are made by the donor). This decrease in the fund will occur between point "B" and point "A."

CONSIDERING THE EFFECT OF INFLATION ON CAPITAL BUDGETING

The accuracy of capital budgeting decisions rests partly upon the reliability of the information about cash inflows and outflows. For example, the failure to take into account price-level changes because of inflation in capital budgeting situations can cause errors in projecting cash flows and thus lead to incorrect conclusions.

There are two alternatives for dealing with a capital budgeting situation with inflation:

1. adjust the cash flows in nominal terms and discount them at a nominal cost of financing (minimum required return rate), or

2. adjust both the cash flows and cost of financing in constant terms and discount the constant cash flows at a constant cost of financing.

The two approaches basically yield similar results.

REVIEWING THE PROJECT

The postcompletion project review is another aspect of studying project performance. A comparison is made of the actual cash flow from operations of the project with the estimated cash flow used to justify the project.

There are several reasons why this review is useful. First, managers recommending projects will be more careful. Second, it identifies those managers who are consistently optimistic or pessimistic with regard to cash flow projections. How reliable are the proposals submitted and approved? Top administration will be more equipped to evaluate the bias that may be anticipated when a manager proposes a project.

The post completion review provides a chance to:

❐ Strengthen or salvage projects having difficulties.

❐ Reinforce successful projects.

❐ Improve the overall quality of future proposals.

❐ Terminate unsuccessful projects before there are excessive losses.

EXAMPLE 18

A nonprofit organization has the following expected cash flows estimated in real terms:

Real Cash Flows (000s)

Period	0	1	2	3
	−100	35	50	30

The nominal cost of financing is 15 percent. Inflation is estimated at 10 percent per annum. Then the first cash flow for year 1, which is $35,000 in current dollars, will be $35,000 × 1.10 = $38,500 in year 1 dollars. Similarly the cash flow for year 2 will be $50,000 × (1.10)^2 = $60,500 in year 2 dollars, etc. By discounting these nominal cash flows at the 15 percent nominal cost of financing, you arrive at the following net present value:

Period	Cash Flows	Present Value Factors	Present Values
0	−100	1.000	-100
1	38.5	.870	33.50
2	60.5	.756	45.74
3	39.9	.658	26.25
			Net present value = 5.49 or $5,490

Rather than converting the cash flow projections into nominal terms, we could convert the cost of financing into real terms by using the following formula:

$$\text{Real cost of financing} = \frac{1 + \text{nominal cost of financing}}{1 + \text{inflation rate}} - 1$$

This financing equals:

$$\text{Real cost of financing} = \frac{(1 + .15)}{(1 + .10)}$$

$$= \frac{1.15}{1.10} = 0.045 \text{ or } 4.5 \text{ percent.}$$

You will obtain the same answer except for rounding errors ($5,490 versus $5,580).

Period	Cash Flows	Present Value Factor = $1/(1+.045)n$	Present Values
0	−100	1.000	−100
1	35	$\frac{1}{1(1 + .045)} = .957$	33.50
2	50	$\frac{1}{1(1.045)^2} = .916$	45.80
3	30	$\frac{1}{1(1.045)^3} = .876$	26.28
			Net present value = 5.58 or $5,580

In reviewing a project's status, use the same approach employed in the initial approval process for consistency. For example, if a project was approved using present value analysis, use the identical procedures in the postaudit review.

As per the management-by-exception principle, the managers responsible for the initial estimates should be asked to provide a full explanation of any major differences between estimates and actual experience.

For control, project performance evaluation should not be performed by the group that proposed the project. A review report should be issued. In general, only projects above a minimum dollar amount require review, periodic appraisal, or both.

EVALUATING RISK IN CAPITAL BUDGETING

Risk analysis is crucial in making capital investment decisions due to the large capital involved and the long-term nature of the investments. The higher the risk of a proposed project, the greater must be the return to compensate for that risk. The interrelation of risk among all investments must be taken into account. Diversification may lead to the best combination of expected net present value and risk.

Do not automatically disregard a high-risk project. For example, a new service line with much risk may be accepted if there is a likelihood of a major breakthrough. The NPO may be able to afford a few unsuccessful new services if a highly successful one eventually develops.

Probabilities can be assigned to projected cash flows based on risk. The probabilities are multiplied by the monetary values to arrive at the expected monetary value of the investment. A probability distribution can be produced by computer.

The tighter the probability distribution of projected future returns, the lower is the risk of the project.

There are several ways to incorporate risk into capital budgeting, including:

❏ Risk-adjusted discount rate,

❏ Standard deviation and coefficient of variation,

❏ Certainty equivalent,

❏ Semivariance,

❐ Simulation,

❐ Sensitivity analysis,

❐ Decision (probability) trees.

Other ways to adjust for uncertainty include:

❐ Reducing the expected life of an investment,

❐ Using pessimistic cash flow projections, and

❐ Comparing the results of optimistic, pessimistic, and best-guess estimates of cash flows.

RISK-ADJUSTED DISCOUNT RATE

Risk can be incorporated in capital budgeting by calculating probable cash flows based on probabilities and assigning a discount rate based on the uncertainty of alternative proposals.

Using this technique, an investment's value is computed by discounting the expected cash flow at a rate allowing for the time value of money and for the risk applicable to the cash flow. The cost of financing (discount rate) is adjusted for a project's risk. A profitable investment is indicated by a positive net present value. With this approach, you judge the risk class of the proposed capital investment and the risk-adjusted discount rate suitable for that class.

STANDARD DEVIATION AND COEFFICIENT OF VARIATION

Risk measures the dispersion around a probability distribution. It is the variability of cash flow around the expected value. Risk can be measured in either absolute or relative terms. First, the expected value, $\overline{A}$, is

$$\overline{A} = \sum_{n=1}^{n} A_i p_i$$

where A_i = the value of the ith possible outcome

p_i = the probability that the ith outcome will occur

n = the number of possible outcomes.

Then, the absolute risk is computed by the standard deviation

$$\sigma = \sqrt{\sum_{i=1}^{n} (A_i - \overline{A})^2 p_i}$$

EXAMPLE 19

You are appraising whether to approve proposal X or Y. Each proposal requires an initial cash outlay of $12,000 and has a three-year life. Annual net cash flows along with expected probabilities follow:

Proposal X	
Expected Annual Cash Inflow	*Probability*
$5,800	.4
6,400	.5
7,000	.1
Proposal Y	
Expected Annual Cash Inflow	*Probability*
$3,400	.3
8,000	.5
11,000	.2

The inflation rate and interest rate are estimated at 10 percent. Proposal X has a lower risk because its cash flows show greater stability than those of proposal Y. Because proposal X has less risk, it is assigned a discount rate of 8 percent, but proposal Y is assigned a 10 percent discount rate due to greater risk.

Proposal X

Cash Inflow	*Probability*	*Probable Cash Flow*
$5,800	.4	$2,320
6,400	.5	3,200
7,000	.1	700
Expected annual cash inflow		$6,220

Proposal Y

Cash Flow	*Probability*	*Probable Cash Flow*
$3,400	.3	$1,020
8,000	.5	4,000
11,000	.2	2,200
Expected annual cash inflow		$7,220

Proposal X

Year	*Explanation*	*Amount*	×	*Factor*	=	*Present Value*
0	Initial investment	$-12,000	×	1		$-12,000
1-3	Annual cash flow	+6,220	×	2.5771[a]		+16.030
	Net present value					$ +4,030

Proposal Y

Year	*Explanation*	*Amount*	×	*Factor*	=	*Present Val*
0	Initial investment	$-12,000	×	1		$-12,000
1-3	Annual cash flow	+7,220	×	2.4869[b]		+17.955
	Net present value					$+5,955

[a] Using an 8 percent discount rate.

^b Using a 10 percent discount rate.

Even though project Y has greater risk, it has a higher risk-adjusted net present value. Proposal Y should be chosen.

The relative risk is expressed by the coefficient of variation:

$$\frac{\sigma}{\bar{A}}$$

CASE STUDY: LIBRARY

The following is a list of the steps in which a library will go through in order to make up a capital budget.

Step 1: Planning

The library will make an assessment of the community's needs. After this assessment, the library board will formulate goals to meet those needs. The objective is to provide better services. Therefore, by finding out what the community needs, the library will be better able to serve them. For instance, if a library has assessed that a community desires a faster way of locating material, the board may decide that (1) the library needs computers or (2) if the library already has computers, then they may need to acquire more advanced computer programs. The goal would be to acquire computer programs which is more up-to-date. (3) Maybe the computers have become obsolete. In this case, the library's goal is to obtain new computers.

Step 2: Programming

Now that the board has made their long-term and/or short-term goals they should sort these goals in priority order. Assume the library has three goals with goal 1 being the most important, goal 2 is the second most important, and goal 3 is the least important. Listing these goals in terms of priority will result in goals 1, 2, and 3. A priority order enable the library to focus on what is essential. After the goals have been listed in priority, there should be an estimate of the cost of each goal and the expected income the library will attain. The cost and income are evaluated to see if the objectives of the library can be met. If the cost exceeds the income, then the board will have to chose an alternative goal.

Step 3: Financing

When steps 1 and 2 have been completed a capital budget is proposed and amended. After the capital budget has been decided upon, it must be financed. Capital investment techniques are used to ascertain the best proposals. Nonprofit organizations use capital investment techniques to attain the most from their limited resources of funds (cash). In a library, there are three capital investment techniques commonly used consisting of return on investment, payback period, and internal rate of return.

As an example of the capital budgeting process for library X, assume a project will result in $8000 annual savings from an initial investment of $12,000.

$$\text{ROI} = \frac{\text{Annual Savings}}{\text{Investment}} = \frac{\$8,000}{\$12,000} = 66.6\%$$

$$\text{Payback Period} = \frac{\text{Investment}}{\text{Annual savings}} = \frac{\$12,000}{\$8,000} = 1.5 \text{ years}$$

Assume instead that the initial investment of $12,000 resulted in the following cash flows:

Year	Cash Flow
1	$5000

2	$4000
3	$3000
4	$2000
Total	$14000

Using the internal rate of return method based on trial-and-error yields an IRR of about 17%.

Year	Cash Flow	1+i	$(1+i)^n$	Total
1	5,000.00	1+.1665	11665	4,286.33
2	4,000.00	1+.1665	1.1665	3,429.06
3	3,000.00	1+.1665	1.1665	2,571.80
4	2,000.00	1+.1665	1.1665	1,714.53
Total				12,001.71
Initial Investment				12,000.00
NPV				1.71

EXAMPLE 20

You are decided whether to invest in one of two projects. Depending on economic conditions, the projects provide the following cash inflows in each of the next five years:

Economic Condition	Probability	Proposal	Proposal
Recession	.3	$1,000	$ 500
Normal	.4	2,000	2,000
Boom	.3	3,000	5,000

We now compute the expected value ($\overline{A}$), the standard deviation (σ) and the coefficient of variation ($\sigma/\overline{A}$).

Proposal X :

A_i	p_i	$A_i p_i$	$(A_i - \overline{A})$	$(A_i - \overline{A})^2$
$1,000	.3	$300	-$1,000	$1,000,000
2,000	.4	800	0	0
3,000	.3	900	1,000	1,000,000
		$\overline{A} = \$2,000$		$\sigma^2 = \$2,000,000$

Because $\sigma^2 = \$2,000,000$, $\sigma = \$1,414$. Thus,

$$\frac{\sigma}{\overline{A}} = \frac{\$1,414}{\$2,000} = .71$$

Proposal Y:

A_i	p_i	$A_i p_i$	$(A_i - \overline{A})$	$(A_i - \overline{A})^2$
$ 500	.3	$ 150	$-1,950	$ 3,802,500
2,000	.4	800	450	202,500
5,000	.3	1,500	2,550	6,502,500
		$\overline{A} = \$2,450$		$\sigma^2 = \$10,507,500$

Since, $\sigma^2 = \$10,507,500$, $\sigma = \$3,242$. Thus,

$$\frac{\sigma}{\overline{A}} = \frac{\$3,242}{\$2,450} = 1.32$$

Proposal A is less risky than proposal B, as determined by the coefficient of variation.

CERTAINTY EQUIVALENT

The certainty equivalent method applies to utility theory. You specify at what point the nonprofit entity is indifferent to the selection between a certain sum of dollars and the expected value of a risky sum. The certainty equivalent is multiplied by the original cash flow to derive the equivalent certain cash flow. You then use the usual capital budgeting. The risk-free return rate is used as the discount rate under the net present value method and as the cutoff rate under the internal rate of return method.

SEMIVARIANCE

Semivariance is the expected value of the squared negative deviations of the possible outcomes from an arbitrarily selected point of reference. Semivariance evaluates risk related to different distributions by referring to a fixed point designated by you. In calculating semivariance, positive and negative deviations contribute differently to risk, whereas in computing variance, a positive and negative deviation of the same magnitude contribute equally to risk.

Since there is an opportunity cost of tying up funds, the investment risk is measured mostly by the prospect of failure to earn the return.

SIMULATION

You obtain probability distributions for a number of variables (e.g., investment outlays) when doing a simulation. Selecting these variables from the distributions at random results in an estimated net present value. A computer is used to obtain many results using random numbers.

SENSITIVITY ANALYSIS

Forecasts of many calculated net present values and internal return rates under alternatives are compared to identify how sensitive net present value or internal rate of return is to changing conditions. You determine whether one or more than one variable affects net present value once that variable is changed. If net present value is significant, you are dealing with a much riskier asset than was initially expected. Sensitivity analysis provides an immediate financial measure of possible errors in forecasts. It stresses decisions that may be sensitive.

Sensitivity analysis provides administrations with an idea of the extent to which unfavorable developments such as decreased volumes, shorter useful lives, or higher costs are apt to affect the success of a project. It is used because of the uncertainty in real-life situations.

DECISION TREES

A decision (probability) tree graphically depicts the sequence of possible outcomes. The capital budgeting tree shows cash flows and net present value of the project under alternative circumstances.

The advantages of decision trees are that they:

❏ Make you aware of adverse eventualities,

❏ Show the conditional nature of future cash flows, and

❏ Reflect possible outcomes of the project.

The drawback of using decision trees is that many problems are too involved to permit yearly depiction. A three-year project having three possible outcomes following each year has 27 paths.

CORRELATING CASH FLOWS OVER TIME

When cash inflows are independent from year to year, it is easy to measure the overall risk of an investment proposal. In some instances, however, particularly with the introduction of a new service, the cash flows experienced in early years affect future years' cash flows. This is referred to as time dependence of cash flows, and it has the effect of increasing the risk of the project.

NORMAL DISTRIBUTION AND NPV ANALYSIS: STANDARDIZING THE DISPERSION

With the assumption of independence of cash flows over time, the expected NPV would be:

$$NPV = PV - I$$
$$= \sum_{t=1}^{n} \frac{\overline{A}_t}{(1+r)^t} - I$$

The standard deviation of NPVs is

$$\sigma = \sqrt{\sum_{t=1}^{n} \frac{\sigma_t^2}{(1+r)^{2t}}}$$

EXAMPLE 21

You want to introduce one of two services. The probabilities and present values of expected cash inflows are

Service	Investment	Present Value of Cash inflows	Probability
A	$225,000		
		$450,000	.4
		200,000	.5
		−100,000	.1
B	80,000		
		320,000	.2
		100,000	.6
		−150,000	.2

	Initial Investment (1)	Probability (2)	P/V of Cash Inflows (3)	P/V of Cash Inflows (2)×(3) = (4)
		.40	$450,000	$180,000
		.50	200,000	100,000
Service A	$225,000	.10	−100,000	−10,000
				$270,000
or				
		.20	$320,000	$64,000
		.60	100,000	60,000
Servce B	$80,000	.20	−150,000	−30,000
				$94,000

Net present value:

Service A : $270,000 − $225,000 = $45,000

Service B : $ 94,000 − $ 80,000 = $14,000

Service A is superior to service B by $31,000.

EXAMPLE 22

XYZ Charity's cash inflows are time dependent, so that year 1 results ($ATCI_1$) affect the cash flows in year 2 ($ATCI_2$) as follows:

If $ATCI_1$ is $8,000 with a 40 percent probability, the distribution for $ATCI_2$ is

0.3	$5,000
0.5	10,000
0.2	15,000

If $ATCI_1$ is 15,000 with a 50 percent probability, the distribution for $ATCI_2$ is

0.3	$10,000
0.6	20,000
0.1	30,000

If $ATCI_1$ is $20,000 with a 10 percent chance, the distribution for $ATCI_2$ is

0.1	$15,000
0.8	40,000
0.1	50,000

The project requires an initial investment of $20,000, and the risk-free rate is 10 percent.

The charity uses the expected net present value from decision tree analysis to determine whether the project should be accepted. The analysis follows:

Time 0	Time 1		Time 2	NPV at 10%	Joint Probability	Expected NPV
		.3	$5,000	$-8,595[a]	.12[b]	$-1,031
	$8,000 ⟨.5		10,000	-4,463	.20	-893
.4		.2	15,000	-331	.08	-26
/		.3	$10,000	$1,901	.15	285
$-20,000 ⟨.5	$15,000 ⟨.6		20,000	10,165	.30	3,050
.1		.1	30,000	18,429	.05	921
		.1	$15,000	$10,576	.01	106
	$20,000 ⟨.8		40,000	21,238	.08	2,499
		.1	50,000	39,502	.01	395
					1.00	$5,306

[a] $NPV = PV - 1 = \$8,000\ PVIF_{10.1} + \$5,000\ PVIF_{10.2} - \$20,000$
$$= \$8,000(.9091) + \$5,000(.8264) - \$20,000$$
$$= \$-8,595$$

[b] Joint probability of the first path = $(.4)(.3) = .12$

Since the NPV is positive ($5,306), the charity should accept the project.

The expected value (A) and the standard deviation σ provide much information by which to evaluate the risk of an investment project. In a normal probability distribution, some probability statement regarding the project's NPV can be made.

Example: The probability of a project's NPV providing an NPV of less than or exceeding zero can be calculated by standardizing the normal variable x as follows:

$$z = x - NPV$$

$$o$$

where x = outcome to be found

NPV = expected NPV

z = standardized normal variable whose probability value can be found in Exhibit 5.

EXAMPLE 23 Assume an investment with the following data:

	Period 1	Period 2	Period 3
Expected cash inflow ($\bar{A}$)	$5,000	$4,000	$3,000
Standard deviation (σ)	1.140	1.140	1.140

Assume the cost of financing is 8 percent and the initial investment is $9,000. Then the expected NPV is

$$
\begin{aligned}
\text{NPV} &= \text{PV} - I \\
&= \frac{\$5,000}{(1+.08)} + \frac{\$4,000}{(1+.08)^2} + \frac{\$3,000}{(1+.08)^3} - \$9,000 \\
&= \$5,000(\text{PVIF}_{8.1}) + \$4,000(\text{PVIF}_{8.2}) + \$3,000(\text{PVIF}_{8.3}) - \$9,000 \\
&= \$5000(.9259) + \$4,000(.8573) + \$3,000(.7938) - \$9,000 \\
&= \$4,630 + \$3,429 + \$2,381 - \$9,000 = \$1,440
\end{aligned}
$$

The standard deviation about the expected NPV is

$$
\begin{aligned}
\sigma &= \sqrt{\sum_{t=1}^{n} \frac{\sigma_t^2}{(1+r)^{2t}}} \\
&= \sqrt{\frac{\$1,140^2}{(1+.08)^2} + \frac{\$1,140^2}{(1+.08)^4} + \frac{\$1,140^2}{(1+.08)^6}} \\
&= \sqrt{\$2,888,411} = \$1,670
\end{aligned}
$$

The probability that the NPV is less than zero is then

$$
z = \frac{x - \text{NPV}}{\sigma} = \frac{0 - \$1,440}{\$1,670} = -.862
$$

The area of normal distribution that is z standard deviation to the left or right of the mean may be found in Exhibit 5. A value of z equal to $-.862$ falls in the area between 0.1949 and 0.1922. There is approximately a 19 percent chance that the project's NPV will be zero or less. Looking another way, there is a 19 percent probability that the internal rate of return of the project will below the risk-free rate.

EXHIBIT 5   Normal Probability Distribution Table

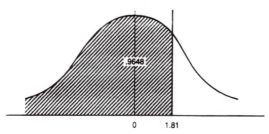

0   1.81

Areas Under the Normal Curve

Z	0	1	2	3	4	5	6	7	8	9
.0	.5000	.5040	.5080	.5120	.5160	.5199	.5239	.5279	.5319	.5359
.1	.5398	.5438	.5478	.5517	.5557	.5596	.5636	.5675	.5714	.5753
.2	.5793	.5832	.5871	.5910	.5948	.5987	.6026	.6064	.6103	.6141
.3	.6179	.6217	.6255	.6293	.6331	.6368	.6406	.6443	.6480	.6517
.4	.6554	.6591	.6628	.6664	.6700	.6736	.6772	.6808	.6844	.6879
.5	.6915	.6950	.6985	.7019	.7054	.7088	.7123	.7157	.7190	.7224
.6	.7257	.7291	.7324	.7357	.7389	.7422	.7454	.7486	.7517	.7549
.7	.7580	.7611	.7642	.7673	.7703	.7734	.7764	.7794	.7823	.7852
.8	.7881	.7910	.7939	.7967	.7995	.8023	.8051	.8078	.8106	.8133
.9	.8159	.8186	.8212	.8238	.8264	.8289	.8315	.8340	.8365	.8389
1.0	.8413	.8438	.8461	.8485	.8508	.8531	.8554	.8577	.8599	.8621
1.1	.8643	.8665	.8686	.8708	.8729	.8749	.8770	.8790	.8810	.8830
1.2	.8849	.8869	.8888	.8907	.8925	.8944	.8962	.8980	.8997	.9015
1.3	.9032	.9049	.9066	.9082	.9099	.9115	.9131	.9147	.9162	.9177
1.4	.9192	.9207	.9222	.9236	.9251	.9265	.9278	.9292	.9306	.9319
1.5	.9332	.9345	.9357	.9370	.9382	.9394	.9406	.9418	.9430	.9441
1.6	.9452	.9463	.9474	.9484	.9495	.9505	.9515	.9525	.9535	.9545
1.7	.9554	.9564	.9573	.9582	.9591	.9599	.9608	.9616	.9625	.9633
1.8	.9641	.9648	.9656	.9664	.9671	.9678	.9686	.9693	.9700	.9706
1.9	.9713	.9719	.9726	.9732	.9738	.9744	.9750	.9756	.9762	.9767
2.0	.9772	.9778	.9783	.9788	.9793	.9798	.9803	.9808	.9812	.9817
2.1	.9821	.9826	.9830	.9834	.9838	.9842	.9846	.9850	.9854	.9857
2.2	.9861	.9864	.9868	.9871	.9874	.9878	.9881	.9884	.9887	.9890
2.3	.9893	.9896	.9898	.9901	.9904	.9906	.9909	.9911	.9913	.9916
2.4	.9918	.9920	.9922	.9925	.9927	.9929	.9931	.9932	.9934	.9936
2.5	.9938	.9940	.9941	.9943	.9945	.9946	.9948	.9949	.9951	.9952
2.6	.9953	.9955	.9956	.9957	.9959	.9960	.9961	.9962	.9963	.9964
2.7	.9965	.9966	.9967	.9968	.9969	.9970	.9971	.9972	.9973	.9974
2.8	.9974	.9975	.9976	.9977	.9977	.9978	.9979	.9979	.9980	.9981
2.9	.9981	.9982	.9982	.9983	.9984	.9984	.9985	.9985	.9986	.9986
3.0	.9987	.9990	.9993	.9995	.9997	.9998	.9998	.9999	.9999	1.000

BIBLIOGRAPHY FOR CHAPTER 6

Freeman, Robert, Craig Shoulder, and Edward Lynn. *Governmental and Nonprofit Accounting* (Prentice-Hall, 1988).

Gross, Malvern, William Warshauer, and Richard Larkin. *Financial and Accounting Guide for Not-for-Profit Organizations* (John Wiley, 1995).

Hay, Leon. *Accounting for Governmental and Nonprofit Entities* (Library of Congress Cataloging in Publication Data, 1989).

Henke, Emerson. *Introduction to Nonprofit Organization Accounting* (Kent, 1988).

Herbert, Leo. *Accounting and Control for Governmental and Other Nonbusiness Organizations* (McGraw-Hill, 1987).

Inez, L. and Jackson Ramsey. *Library Planning and Budgeting* (Library of Congress Cataloging in Publication Data, 1986).

Kamath, Ravindra. "Capital Budgeting Practices of Large Hospitals," (*Engineering Economist*, Spring 1992, pp. 203–231).

Smith, Stevenson. *Accounting for Librarians and Other Not-for-Profit Managers* (Library of Congress Cataloging in Publication Data, 1983).

Chapter 7

Examining Illustrative Budgets for Typical Nonprofit Organizations

There are many budget methodologies, techniques, and formats that may be used by nonprofit organizations. One type of budget format—the cash budget—focuses on future cash inflows and outflows for the budgetary period. An alternative budget format focuses on future flows-of-financial-resources. The flows-of-financial-resources format comes in two styles. The first version emphasizes inflows-of-financial-resources in the form of support and revenues, and outflows-of-financial-resources in terms of expenditures. The second version restricts expenditure outflows to expenses and does not include expenditure outflows for other purposes.

Remember that budgets are about future transactions. Flows-of-financial-resources budgets, in contrast to cash budgets, do not focus on future cash transactions, but rather on future transactions that emanate from future contractual performance. Such contractual performance may or may not coincide with future flows of cash associated with these same contracts. Generally, flows-of-financial-resources result from sellers who will be executing their side of a contract prior to the receipt of cash payment from buyers.

Another important distinction to understand for budgeting purposes is between transactions resulting from an entity's normal operations and transactions that result from other activities. The former would be considered "operating transactions" while the latter, "nonoperating transactions." Cash budgets typically encompass not only operating transactions, but also nonoperating ones. In a similar vein, flows-of-financial-resource budgets can include both operating and nonoperating transactions. The two types of flow-of-financial-resources budget, however, do not include the same types of nonoperating transactions.

The flows-of-financial-resources budget that emphasizes "total flows" differs from the flows-of-financial-resources budget that emphasizes "expenses." The former budget could be called the "total financial resource flows" budget. The latter budget could be dubbed the "expenses" flows-of-financial-resources budget.

The "total financial resource flows" budget type covers nonoperating transactions that include expenditure transactions involving: (a) the acquisition of noncash assets and (b) the retirement of debt. The "total financial resource flows" budget also includes expenditures that result from incurring expenses. Expenses arise mostly from operating activities so they are considered the result of operating transactions. However, there are some expenses, such as interest expense related to nonoperating assets or nonoperating activities, that are considered the result of nonoperating transactions.

The "expenses" budget type covers expenditures that result from incurring expenses, but does not cover expenditures that result from the acquisition of assets or the retirement of debt.

The "total financial resource flows" budget and the "expenses" type budget have both inflows of resources as well as outflows. The outflows cannot continue without adequate inflows-of-financial-resources. For the "total financial resource flows" budget type, inflows arise from:

❐ disposals of noncash assets,

❐ the retirement of debt,

❐ operating revenues,

❐ operating support (usually in the form of contributions for operating activities), and

❐ nonoperating revenues.

For the "expenses" flows-of-financial-resources type budget, inflows are included only from operating revenue, operating support, and nonoperating revenue.

Exhibits 1, 2, and 3 illustrate respectively a "cash flows" budget and two versions of the "total financial resource flows" budget. On the outflows side, we have expenditures that result from: acquisition of assets and retire-ment of debt, and expenses of both the operating and nonoperating variety. **Exhibits 1, 2, and 3** also illustrate the inflows-of-financial-resources side. Inflows result from: (a) disposition of assets, (b) retirement of debt, (c) operating and nonoperating revenue, (d) public support from contributions expected from the public, and (e) nonoperating revenue.

    Exhibit 1 illustrates a "cash flows budget." Moving from a "cash flows" budget to the "total financial flows" budgets (**Exhibits 2 and 3**) or to an "expenses" budget (**Exhibits 2-14**) involves, in an accounting sense, chang-ing the accounting basis. In the next section, there is a discussion of the rela-tion between the cash basis and the accrual basis.[1] The objective of this expo-sition is to clarify how a budget should be structured to fit into an NPO's accounting system.

    The illustrative budgets in all of the exhibits (excluding **Exhibits 1, 2, and 3**) stress a programmatic approach to the expense side of the "expense" type budget. The use of this expense format follows from the current trend in recommended financial management practice to concentrate on reporting activities in a programmatic way. This approach can be compared with orga-nizing the expense side by the nature or object of an expense. Exhibit 1 illus-trates the "cash flows" format using the "object of expense" approach to organizing expenses. The programmatic format is referred to as a function expense budget, whereas the object of expense method of disclosing expens-es can be termed the object-of-expense, total expenditure type budget.

HOW TO DETERMINE THE BASIS OF ACCOUNTING FOR THE ILLUSTRATIVE BUDGETS

The two accounting bases most commonly used are the cash basis and the accrual basis. There are also various combinations of the two of them such as the modified accrual method.[1] No one-to-one relationship exists between an accounting basis and a particular type of budget. However, most small nonprofit organizations prepare a cash-oriented budget. In general, only at fiscal year-end, if needed, is the cash-basis budget adjusted to an accrual basis.

    The cash basis recognizes and records both operating and nonoperat-ing transactions only when cash is involved. The accrual method recognizes operating and nonoperating transactions not only when cash is involved but when the entity also receives or extends credit. A cash budget is on the cash basis except that the budget deals not with actual transactions, but with expected or planned cash transactions. A total expenditure type budget and an "expense" type budget are typically some version of accrual-basis accounting.

Expenses should be accounted for on the accrual basis whether you are referring to actual expenses or budgeted expenses. However, many nonprofit entities prepare their budgets on the cash basis and therefore estimate their expenses accordingly. Similarly, on the inflow-of-resources side of the budget, these organizations estimate support and revenues on the cash basis.

The rationale for using the cash-basis budget is that it is preferable to underestimate resource inflows rather than overestimate them and find oneself short when actual resource inflows fall below the estimate. However, although underestimating resource inflows might be logical if not carried to excess, underestimating resource outflows is definitely not prudent. In any event, there can be imprudent cash-basis estimates as well as prudent accrual-basis ones. Given the advantages of the latter, the prudent approach most likely is to estimate both cash-basis and accrual-basis budgets.

Cash-basis budgets include certain items that would be excluded from an accrual-basis one, and vice versa. For example, contributions pledged last year but not collected until this year would be included in the cash-basis budget for the current year, but excluded from the accrual-basis budget. On the contrary, contributions pledged this year but not expected to be collected until next year would be excluded from the cash-basis budget but included in the accrual-basis one. Similarly, materials bought and received in the prior year but paid for this year would be included in the cash-basis budget for the current year, but excluded from the accrual-basis budget. In contrast, materials bought and received this year but not to be paid for until next year would be included in this year's accrual-basis budget but excluded from the cash-basis budget.

The aforementioned differences between the cash basis and the accrual basis are examples of *timing* differences. Whether an item appears in the cash-basis budget or the accrual-basis budget is a timing concern. However, timing is not unimportant where there is a concern over the likelihood of overspending during the reporting period. Generally speaking, the accrual basis makes the budget a superior device for the purposes of both monitoring and controlling spending.

Permanent differences also exist between cash-basis and accrual-basis budgets. Contributions of nonmonetary items such as donated materials, donated equipment, volunteer services, or donated space give rise to permanent differences between cash-basis and accrual-basis budgets.

These permanent differences in the form of nonmonetary contributions show up, where applicable, in accrual-basis budgets, but are excluded from cash-basis budgets. However, some nonprofits include such nonmonetary items in their budgets when the monetary items are on the cash basis. The result is a budget that is partly cash basis and partly accrual basis. This is one version (of many) of what could be referred to as an "impure" or "modified" cash-basis budget in contrast to a "pure" cash-basis budget. A modified cash-basis budget is more detailed and practical for planning than a pure cash-basis one. Nevertheless, it still does not offer the advantages of control and monitoring provided by a "full" accrual-basis budget.

It should be noted that expenditures are not synonymous with expenses. Although there is some overlap, each concept covers items that the other does not. An accrual-basis expenditure constitutes the using up of financial resources during a specific time period for the acquisition of goods, services, or other financial resources. The goods, services, or other financial resources may be bought either for operating or nonoperating purposes. An expense represents the using up or consumption of goods or services during the fiscal period for operating purposes. Operating purposes are the basic objectives for which the nonprofit organization is organized and carries out its activities.

Normally, expenses represent the using up of real resources in the production process. In the nonprofit sector, one encounters expenditures of financial resources being treated as expenses. For example, in the case of pledges to give money, one has a financial expenditure that from the point of view of the giving entity is treated as an expense. Strictly speaking, there is no using up of a real resource; rather, what has occurred is a transfer of a financial asset from one party to another. This is similar to the sale of a real asset, such as inventory, being treated by the seller as an expense in terms of cost of goods sold. A real resource was not consumed, it was merely transferred from one party to another.

The illustrative budgets stress estimated accrued expenses instead of estimated accrued expenditures, except for **Exhibits 1, 2, and 3**, which show both. This conforms with current recommended practice, which is to report in terms of a functional expense and programmatic format.

EVALUATING TRANSACTIONS WITH A CHART OF ACCOUNTS

A chart of accounts is a framework for evaluating and classifying transactions. The illustrative budgets cannot furnish useful information in a consistent and comparable manner without using a chart of accounts which has been tailored to satisfy current and future needs of the nonprofit organization. There are several sources for charts of accounts in the not-for-profit area including:

- ❏ American Institute of Certified Public Accountants,

- ❏ American Hospital Association,

- ❏ American Association of Museums,

- ❏ National Association of College and University Business Officers,

- ❏ National Association of Independent Schools,

- ❏ United Way of America,

- ❏ Club Managers Association of America,

- ❏ and National Health Council, National Assembly of National Voluntary Health and Social Welfare Organizations.[2]

This list is not all-inclusive.

Note that some of the above sources used for guides to budgetary and accounting categories for internal managerial use are no longer considered the primary sources of financial reporting standards for external financial reporting, what is commonly called GAAP. The Financial Accounting Standards Board (FASB) has issued several pronouncements that are the primary sources of GAAP for external financial reporting.[3] However, the FASB pronouncements are not intended to apply to internal budgeting and accounting. Of course, the internal information systems do have to provide the necessary information for external reporting, but their prime function must be providing managers with useful information for decision-making.

The accounts making up the chart of accounts are analytical categories into which financial information is accumulated and summarized. The transaction inflows and outflows must be described in terms of certain characteristics for accumulation in the accounts.

Resource inflows must be classified:

❏ as to entity affected;

❏ as estimated or actual;

❏ as restricted or unrestricted, in order to assign to the proper fund;

❏ as to accounting basis, cash or accrual;

❏ as to source, such as contribution, grant, sale, and loan;

❏ as operating or nonoperating;

❏ as monetary or nonmonetary;

❏ as to temporal character, such as current, or noncurrent, prepaid or deferred, or recurring or nonrecurring;

❏ as to intraentity responsibility center.

Resource outflows should be classified in terms of all of the above characteristics used for the resource inflow side, except for source. Further, where applicable, outflows should be classified by object of expenditure or expense and program or activity.

The illustrative budgets presented could not have been prepared without drawing upon some preconceived chart of accounts for the Illustrative nonprofit organization or the other hypothetical nonprofits. The hypothetical accounts that make up the chart of accounts reflect in one way or another many of the classification characteristics noted above. The issue of restricted versus unrestricted resources will be covered when "budgeting and fund accounting" is discussed.

HOW TO APPLY FUND ACCOUNTING TO THE ILLUSTRATIVE BUDGETS

Contributions received by an a nonprofit organization to be used in the general support of those basic activities for which it was organized are deemed unrestricted resources. Contributions that are obtained from donors with those donors' stipulations or understandings that the contributions are to be used solely for explicitly stated purposes, that are more narrowly defined than simply the general support of the NPO, are considered restricted resources.

Restricted resources can be accounted for in two ways: in their own special accounts or in their own restricted funds. Funds are simply a more elaborate accounting device used for the accounting of restricted resources. A fund is an accounting entity (it may also be a legal entity) with its own self-balancing set of accounts, including its own ledgers, journals, etc.

If restricted resources are of no real consequence in the life of a particular NPO, then specific accounts instead of specific funds would be the manner in which an NPO would account for restricted resources received. However, if restricted resources are a normal, recurring, and important financing source for the NPO, then it would use funds and fund accounting to account for these resources. The NPO would account for unrestricted resources in a general, operating, or unrestricted fund. Such a fund also could be called a *current fund*. The NPO would account for restricted resources through funds specifically designated for that purpose, that is, through restricted funds.

Budgets typically cover both unrestricted resource inflows expected to be available and restricted resource inflows expected to become available on an unrestricted basis during the budget period. When fund accounting is in use for a particular type of NPO, these two types of resource inflows would be accounted for in the current fund. Hence, the budget that covers both types of resources also would represent the budget for the current fund.

The current fund usually does not account for purchases of major capital facilities. When fund accounting is used, the acquisition of major capital assets may be accounted for through a separate noncurrent fund that could be called a plant and equipment fund. A separate capital budget may account for the acquisition of the major capital items. The separation of the capital budget from the current operating budget makes sense where fund-raising activities for the capital facilities are in addition to normal fund-raising functions. The capital budget could then represent the budget for the noncurrent fund to account for the major capital facilities.

The current fund is used to account for the purchase of fixed assets other than of nonrecurring major capital facilities. However, even the purchase of major capital facilities may be accounted for through the same fund in which assets other than fixed assets are accounted for. Current assets may also be accounted for in this fund. When this is the practice, the nonprofit organization uses an unrestricted fund, instead of a current fund, and does not specify it as current or noncurrent. The unrestricted fund accounts for both current and long-term assets and liabilities. The budget covering this fund would then be comprised of both an operating budget and a capital budget in the form of an annual budget.

Thus far, we have assumed that each fund has its own budget and there is a one-to-one correspondence between budgets and funds. This need not be the case. Although a fund normally is not associated with more than one budget, a budget can refer to more than one fund. A particular NPO could have its annual budget constructed so that it encompasses both its normal operating functions and the acquisition of all fixed assets including major facilities. At the same time, it could account for operations through a current fund and the purchase of major capital facilities through a plant and equipment fund. In that instance, the annual budget would cover the fiscal activities of both the current fund and the plant and equipment fund.

The budget presented in **Exhibit 1** is an annual budget that covers both current operations as well as the acquisition of fixed assets. However, the figure does not contain the kinds of details that a full capital budget would show. Therefore, this figure basically shows budgeted operating activities and certain budgeted nonoperating transactions. Further, the figure does not refer to any of the funds that the illustrative not-for-profit organization might be using to account for its activities. If the illustrative NPO uses one unrestricted fund to account for its activities, the budget shown in **Exhibit 1** can be assumed to cover the budgeting side of the activities of this fund.

Remember that a fund is an accounting device that can track actual receipts and expenditures on the cash basis or it can track actual revenues, contributions, and expenses (or expenditures) on the accrual basis. The budget shows not actual, but anticipated (planned) receipts and expenditures on the cash basis or it can present expected (planned) contributions, revenues and expenses (or expenditures) on the accrual basis. In general, budgets are not formally incorporated into the accounting records of an NPO whether or not it uses fund accounting. This is why **Exhibit 1** does not explicitly tie the budget being illustrated to a particular fund or funds that may be used in the accounting system for the illustrative not-for-profit organization.

The budgets illustrated in the remaining exhibits are organized on a functional basis; that is, these budgets focus on planned expenses instead of expenditures, and therefore are operating budgets. Such budgets may apply to current fund or unrestricted fund activities, whichever is used by the NPO in its accounting system.

If an NPO does not use fund accounting, the budgets will not cover any funds. Rather, their relationship to the accounting system will be in terms of the relationship between the actual amounts being tracked in the accounting systems and the budgeted amounts shown in the budget.

COMPARING THE ILLUSTRATIVE BUDGETS AND THE FINANCIAL STATEMENTS

Budgets present how an entity plans to use its resources to accomplish its goals. Financial statements reveal how an entity actually used its resources. Budgets are primarily for internal use. However, financial statements are prepared for use internally by management and externally by people or organizations who are not directly responsible for the operation of a nonprofit organization, but are concerned with knowing how well it is performing its activities to achieve its objectives.

Financial statements may contain data on budgeted amounts as well as actual amounts. The financial statements of a private sector NPO typically report only how monies were actually received and spent and not how the NPO planned for its receipts and expenditures. This is because budgeting is an art rather than a science. The best estimates of future receipts and expenditures can go astray. Events beyond management control can easily disturb the best-laid plans.

However, budgets are not only planning documents, but, also control mechanisms. Management's failure to budget adequately and live within its resource limits is useful information to outside users concerned with accountability. Contributors and other resource providers may insist on receiving budget figures before making a contribution. They may also insist on receiving comparisons between planned and actual performance after making their contributions.

These comparisons often are presented not only in specialized reports to the contributors, but also in the general financial statements provided external users. Generally accepted accounting principles for private sector NPOs do not require the inclusion in their financial statements of historical information on the budget for the fiscal period.

Although in general, private sector NPOs do not include budgeting information in their financial statements, there are important exceptions. Some NPOs include budgetary information and make comparisons between budget and actual figures in their statements. Such a presentation is strongly recommended as providing highly useful information. When the financial statements contain comparisons between budgeted and actual amounts, both sets of figures must use the same accounting basis for consistency. For example, if actual figures are on the cash basis, the budgeted figures also must be on the cash basis. If actual figures are on the accrual basis, budgeted figures must be on the same basis for a meaningful comparison. The comparison of actual to budgeted is important for internal management control. Even though there is no consensus on the need for budgetary disclosure for private sector NPOs in their financial statements prepared for external users, the same position does not apply to public sector NPOs.[4]

EXPLAINING THE ILLUSTRATIVE BUDGETS

The following exhibits present a series of illustrative budgets for different types of nonprofit organizations. **Exhibits 1, 2 and 3** show a comprehensive, cash-basis budget, and alternative total flows of resources budgets for the illustrative NPO using an object-of-expense format. The different categories of contributions, revenues, expenses, and expenditures are generally more than are required by specific nonprofits providing particular types of services. Thus, one would select from **Exhibit 1** those revenue or expense or other categories that one expects to use. The remaining exhibits, **Exhibits 2-14**, cover operating budgets for particular types of NPOs using a functional and programmatic expense format. You should use the budget format suitable to your organization. In some cases, you may have to combine elements from different budget types to work up an appropriate and useful format for your particular budget. The exhibits are not intended to cover all possible types of NPOs.

BUDGET LOCATOR

To facilitate the use of the illustrative budgets, they are listed below by figure number and type of NPO.

Exhibit	*Type of Not-for-Profit Organization*
1	Illustrative Not-for-Profit Organization (Cash Basis)
2	Illustrative Not-for-Profit Organization—Alternative A (Accrual Basis Including Depreciation, Total Flows of Financial Resources)

3 Illustrative Not-for-Profit Organization—Alternative B (Accrual Basis Including Depreciation, Total Flows of Financial Resources, Segregation of Nonoperating Items)

4 Foundations

5 Religious Organizations

6 Social Service Organizations

7 Professional or Trade Associations

8 Scientific and Research Organizations

9 Clubs and Leisure Activities Organizations

10 Museums

11 Independent Schools

12 Labor Unions

13 Performing Arts Centers

14 Libraries

ILLUSTRATIVE NONPROFIT ORGANIZATION

The first illustrative budget shown is Exhibit 1 for the Illustrative Not-for-Profit Organization. This is an all-inclusive budget that brings together a relatively comprehensive set of budget categories. Following Exhibit 1 is a discussion of each of the budgetary categories, in order, presented in the illustrative budget. Most, but not all, of the categories are discussed.[5]

EXHIBIT 1

Illustrative Not-for-Profit
Budget
for the Year Ended, June 30, 19X1
(Cash Basis)

	Budget
Public support and revenue	
Public contributions	$ 402,797
Special events	51,439
Legacies and bequests	34,002
Total direct support	$ 488,238

Indirect contributions	$ 81,954
Foundation grants	43,593
Government grants	39,233
Total public support	$ 164,780
Membership dues	$ 77,072
Fees for services	130,778
Sales	73,236
Contractual revenue	29,643
Concession income	9,590
Rental income	8,370
Auxiliary activities	26,156
Investment income	38,362
Miscellaneous income	8,719
Total revenue	$ 401,926
Total public support, grants, and revenue	$ 1,054,944

Expenses by object of expense

Employee payroll	$ 370,050
Employee benefits	40,706
Payroll taxes, etc.	24,644
Temporary help	26,354
Materials and supplies	52,348
Exhibits and displays	6,977
Professional fees	17,490
Prizes	17,629
Communication	12,212
Conferences	26,139
Travel and lodging	26,167
Publications	24,073
Printing and promotion	19,341
Equipment rental	5,248
Equipment maintenance	3,872
Occupancy	38,325
Insurance	3,471
Licenses	4,070
Royalties	18,783
Benevolences	20,053

Specific aid to people	43,593
Dues to affiliates	16,565
Awards and grants	87,186
Contingencies	15,000
Interest expense	4,087
Miscellaneous	9,337
Depreciation (Not shown on cash basis)	
Total expenses	$ 933,720
Excess (deficit) on operations and the annual budget	$ 121,224

Public Support and Revenue

All budget items are forecasts of future activity. Public support and revenue represent forecasted inflows of resources. Public support constitutes resource inflows without any quid pro quo outflows of goods and services from the organization to the resource provider. Revenue, on the other hand, represents inflows of resources in exchange, in general, for outflows of goods and services from the organization to the resource provider.

You should distinguish between budgetary and accounting categories. Expected inflows of public support should be described as "estimated public support" while inflows of actual public support should be described simply as "public support." "Estimated public support" would be the budgetary category while "public support" would be the accounting category. Similarly, expected inflows of revenue should be described as "estimated revenue" and actual inflows of revenue should be described simply as "revenue."

In **Exhibit 1**, the budget categories of "estimated public support" and "estimated revenue" are described as "public support" and "revenue" under the column headed "budget." This simplification is useful to compare budgeted amounts and actual amounts. The budgeted amount for estimated public support and estimated revenue would appear in a column headed "budget" and the actual dollar amount for public support and revenue appears in a column headed "actual."

Public Contributions

These are contributions that the entity obtains directly from the public without formal or contracted-for intervention of some fund-raising intermediary. Such contributions are either in the form of cash or a pledge to pay cash at some future date. Public contributions are one type of public support.

One should distinguish between budgetary and accounting categories for public contributions. The budget category would be "estimated public contributions" while the accounting category would be simply "public contributions." In **Exhibit 1**, the budgetary category "estimated public contributions" is shown simply as "public contributions" with the dollar amount appearing in the column headed "budget."

Special Events

Public contributions raised from special funding events are different from public contributions obtained from general fund-raising activities. A name for this category would be "estimated public contributions from special fund-raising events." In **Exhibit 1**, the name is simplified to "special events" with the estimated dollar amount shown in the column headed "budget."

The special fund-raising event generally offers some quid pro quo in the form of a good or service to the contributor, such as entertainment, food, or recreation, for which the contributor would have had to pay separately were it not a part of the fund-raising event. The direct costs of fund-raising events are netted against the contributions received from such events and only the excess of the contributions over the direct costs are included in the budget as estimated public contributions from special events.

When the contributions are obtained via television or radio in the form of shows, such shows are typically not treated as special fund-raising events. There is an exception to this general rule. If contributors benefit directly from the fund-raising television or radio show, their contributions can be treated as arising from a special fund-raising event. Contributions from the general public who were simply viewers or listeners to the show are treated as public contributions from general fund-raising activities.

Advertisers who promote their products on the fund-raising show and contribute toward covering all or part of the cost of the show can be considered typical examples of contributors benefiting directly from the event. Such advertiser-contributors are receiving a quid pro quo service for which they would have had to pay separately.

If the advertiser-contributors' contributions cover only part of the costs of the show, the covered costs are netted against the contributions, with no excess included in the budget. The uncovered costs of the show are included in the budget as part of general fund-raising expenses. If the advertiser-contributors' contributions exceed the total cost of the show, then the costs are netted against such contributions, and any excess contributions form the advertiser-contributor are shown in the budget as additional public support from special fund-raising events. Contributions from listeners or viewers are treated as noted above.

The netting of certain types of costs against the resource inflows they help generate is an accepted accounting practice for purposes of showing the actual financial results of an organization's operations to outside parties. However, whether certain types of budgeted costs are reported to outsiders as netted against estimated resource inflows has no bearing on the fact that such costs should be estimated separately from the corresponding resource inflows.

Thus, the budgeted direct costs of special fund-raising events that are reported as netted against estimated resource inflows from such activities, nevertheless, should be estimated separately from the resource inflows. This allows the accounting treatment for budgeted items to be similar to that of actual items so that the budgeted can be meaningfully compared with actual for external reporting purposes.

Legacies and Bequests

On the cash basis, legacies and bequests are recorded when the proceeds are received. On the accrual basis, they are recorded when the recipient organization has a firm legal basis to obtain a legacy or bequest during the budget period, even though no proceeds are anticipated to be received until future periods.

Nonmonetary Contributions

These typically include donations of: (a) the volunteer services of people; (b) materials and supplies; (c) the use of factory, automotive, and office equipment; (d) factory or office space in a building; (e) the use of intangible assets such as patents or copyrights; (f) advertising time or space; and (g) similar goods or services.

Volunteer services typically are accounted for as nonmonetary contributions only if they satisfy certain criteria as follows:

1. The duties conducted by volunteers must be so essential and necessary that the organization would have paid to obtain these services if volunteers had not been available.

2. The volunteer activities must be under control similar to that exercised over an employee performing the services.

3. There must be an objective way of measuring and valuing the services.

4. The not-for-profit organization must not be operated primarily for the benefit of its membership.

These conditions tend to rule out certain types of volunteer activities. Thus, fraternal organizations, labor unions, religious institutions, political parties, professional and trade organizations, and country and social clubs usually do not record volunteer services. Further, periodic fund-raising activities of volunteers are not recorded because typically they do not meet one of the four criteria. When volunteers provide services that are not usually provided by the entity, these services should not be deemed nonmonetary contributions, since the duties are not considered an essential part of the organization's activities.[6]

For external reporting purposes, the FASB has set out specific criteria for recognizing contributions of services. In *Statement of Financial Accounting Standards* No. 116, the FASB provides that:

> Contributions of services shall be recognized if the services (a) create or enhance nonfinancial assets or (b) require specialized skills, are provided by individuals possessing those skills, and would typically need to be purchased if not provided by donation.[7]

Valuation of nonmonetary contributions would be normally at the monetary equivalent that the organization would have had to give up to obtain the goods or services. This assumes that the goods or services are of such a nature that there is an objective basis for valuation. (Nonmonetary contributions are *not* shown in **Exhibit 1** because it has been prepared on the cash basis. Nonmonetary services will be included in **Exhibit 2** and **Exhibit 3**.)

Total Direct Support

The first three items in **Exhibit 1** appearing under the categories of "public support and revenue" represent estimates of "public support" expected directly from the public. The composition of such support will vary among nonprofit entities.

Indirect Contributions

These represent contributions from other private sector nonprofit organizations except for foundations. These other private sector nonprofit organizations may or may not be affiliated with the illustrative nonprofit organizations. The separation of direct from indirect contributions is useful for those nonprofit organizations having both types of contributions because such a separation helps to appraise the effectiveness of fund-raising activities.

Foundation Grants

For some types of NPOs, foundation grants are an important source of indirect contributions so they must be tracked separately from other indirect contributions.

Government Grants

This indirect contribution is an important source of support for certain types of NPOs.

TOTAL PUBLIC SUPPORT

Total direct and indirect support from the public, fund-raising intermediaries, and from the public (government) sector are brought together in one total amount. Six of the seven types of support presented so far in **Exhibit 1** constitute sources of resources that do not arise from the quid pro quo provision of services that are sold in order to raise funds. The seventh type—direct contributions from special events—does involve the sale of goods or services to raise the contributions, but only the excess portion (over the cost of the goods or services provided) of the monies raised is treated as support.

For some NPOs, these types of support represent the major sources of resource inflows. However, other types of NPOs rely on other resource sources, which are now discussed.

Membership Dues

Dues that are contributions are to be distinguished from membership dues, in that the latter are payments by an individual in return for services received by that individual. Simply belonging to an organization and making payments does not constitute paying dues, as that term is used here. The payment has to be in exchange for services. That is, services must be available for use by the member over and above simple membership or even participation in the governance of the organization.

Fees for Services

These represent payments by the public for the services provided by programs that fulfill the objectives for which the NPO was organized. These fees are payments in return for services received. They are distinguished from membership dues, although both are quid pro quo payments, in that members normally participate in organization governance in some way. In general, certain types of NPOs stress services rendered to their members, while other types of NPOs are not organized primarily to render benefits to their members but to the public at large.

Sales

Nonprofit organizations may sell services, literature, and other materials to members, the public at large, other nonprofits, and so on. Revenues from these sources, if significant, should be segregated.

The distinction between fees for services and sales of services is conventional and depends on usage for a particular class of entities. For example, you do not usually speak of a fee for services when you buy a ticket for a theatrical performance, even though a performing arts company sells tickets to its performance which represent services rendered. A performing arts group can be thought of as selling services. On the other hand, you would normally think of obtaining services for a fee from a social service organization that charges for its family counseling services.

Contractual Revenues

Some NPOs render services on a contractual basis with clients.

Rental Income

This revenue source arises from the rental by the NPO of equipment or space to others.

Concession Income

Under certain circumstances, some NPOs, such as performing arts groups, make facilities available to concessionaires who provide goods on a commercial basis.

Auxiliary Activities

These activities are conducted for the benefit of employees, members, or public clientele, but are not the major activities for which the NPO was formed. For example, a research organization might have a cafeteria for employee convenience. Such a function is clearly not the primary purpose for which this type of NPO was organized. Thus, it is considered an auxiliary activity. In **Exhibit 1**, the income from auxiliary activities is net of the costs of operating the activities.

Investment Income

This includes earnings from investments in both equity and debt securities in the form of dividends and interest. It also includes interest on savings accounts.

Miscellaneous Revenue

This represents the residual revenue that does not fit into any other revenue class. It includes insignificant revenue not justifying a separate classification. However, an immaterial revenue source today may become significant at a later date. In such a case, it should be reclassified from miscellaneous revenue to its own account when it becomes significant in amount.

TOTAL REVENUE

This is the sum of the various revenue categories. In **Exhibit 1**, the revenue categories begin with membership dues and end with miscellaneous revenue.

TOTAL PUBLIC SUPPORT, GRANTS, AND REVENUES

Most NPOs total their estimated support, grants, and revenues to arrive at an amount such as that shown in **Exhibit 1**. However, this is not always true.

Certain NPOs are concerned with appraising the degree to which their activities are being supported on the basis of revenue generated. Therefore, NPOs, such as performing arts companies, will first deduct their expenses from revenue in order to determine a figure that represents a surplus (deficit) from services provided to their members or to the public.

BUDGETED EXPENSES

In **Exhibit 1** expenses are organized in an "object of expense" format instead of a "functional expense" format. Expenses rather than expenditures are stressed in this format. Recall that expenditures, on the accrual basis, represent the use of financial resources for the purchase of goods or services or other financial resources, during the fiscal period for operating or nonoperating activities, either for cash or on account. An expense represents the using up or consumption for operating purposes of goods or services. An expense can also represent a using up of financial resources for operating purposes that does not result in the acquisition of goods, services, or other financial resources.[8]

The goods, services, or financial resources that are used up or consumed may have been acquired during the current reporting period. If so, the expenditure and the expense are the same. However, the goods, services, or financial resources that are used up may have been acquired during a prior reporting period. In that case, the expenditure was recognized in a previous period and the expense recognized during the current period. The expenditure and the expense are no longer synonymous. Goods, services, and financial services may be purchased or paid for during the current period and consumed in the operations of a future period. Again, the expenditure and the expense are not synonymous. The expenditure would be recognized in the current period and the expense would be recognized in a future period.

The object-of-expense format stresses the objects, goods and services, i.e., real or financial resources, estimated as used up or consumed during the current fiscal period. This format emphasizes the input instead of the output side of the organization's activities. Objects of expense are represented by the costs of the goods, services, and financial resources consumed or used up.

Employee Payroll, Benefits, and Payroll Taxes

In Exhibit 1, this is the budgeted cost of employee services expected to be consumed during the budget period. These budget and accounting categories cover the major expenses for permanent employees that are represented by such costs as salaries, fringe benefits, and payroll taxes, etc.

Materials and Supplies

In Exhibit 1, this is the budgeted cost of materials and supplies expected to be consumed in the operations for the fiscal period. The cost of materials and supplies expected to be used in a future period would not be shown in the current period's budget.

Temporary Help

It is useful to separate the cost of permanent employee services from the cost of temporary, short-term personnel. A distinctive budgetary expense category is established to accumulate and monitor such costs.

Professional Fees

This category includes the expenses of professional consultants.

Communication

This category covers such expenses as telephone, telegraph, and similar items.

Conferences

The budgeted cost of conferences, conventions, and meetings should include only the extra cost associated with holding them. Any costs that would have been incurred whether or not a conference occurred should be classified to some other expense category.

Occupancy

This category covers such costs as rentals of facilities, maintenance expenses of owned facilities, and utility bills (e.g., electricity, heating). Interest on a mortgage and insurance on the property would also be included. Expenses normally classified in other categories would not be included. For example, depreciation on building and equipment is typically shown in another category.

Insurance

This category covers insurance not classified elsewhere.

Benevolences

These represent budgeted spending by religious organizations in the form of contributions or donations to other causes beyond aiding local or immediate congregations. Benevolences represent the using up of financial resources for operating purposes.

Specific Aid to Persons

This category covers the budgeted cost of goods or services expected to be consumed by a client or patient of a social service NPO and paid for by the NPO.

Goods and services purchased and used by an NPO in its own activities are not treated as "specific aid to persons." An example of "specific aid to persons" is the payment for medical services for a client of an NPO that is not itself a medical organization.

Dues to Affiliates

This category encompasses budgeted payments by the NPO to an affiliated NPO for an exchange of services. An example is the payment from a local organization to a national affiliate for services rendered by the latter.

Awards and Grants

This category covers such items as grants by foundations as well as scholarships awarded by performing arts companies, and similar items.

Nonmonetary Contributions

These include contributed volunteer services, and materials. This category represents the kind of nonmonetary contributions that were discussed earlier as one of the categories of public support. Monetary contributions on the resource inflow side represent contributions that the NPO expects to receive. However, nonmonetary contributions on the expense side represent contributed services, materials, and so on that the NPO expects to use in its operations. It is possible for the amount that the NPO expects to receive to differ from the amount that it anticipates to use in contributed materials.

(Nonmonetary contributions as an expense are *not* shown in Exhibit 1 because the cash basis is assumed. Nonmonetary contribution will be included in Exhibit 2 and Exhibit 3.)

Miscellaneous Expenses

This category is defined for the expense side in a manner similar to miscellaneous revenue for the revenue side.

Contingencies

Some NPOs estimate contingent expenses that may or may not occur.

Depreciation

Depreciation expense represents the allocation of the original cost of a capital asset into expense over the period benefitted. It is a nonmonetary expense, and therefore does not appear in a cash-basis or flows-of-financial-resources budget. Cash-basis and flows-of-financial-resources budgets show the expected purchase or disposition of capital assets but not the depreciation on these assets.

In accrual-basis budgets for commercial entities, depreciation may be included and then compared to actual at the end of the period. If the budget does not include a depreciation provision but the actual does include the amount, the actual will have to be adjusted before the user can make meaningful comparisons. According to generally accepted accounting principles, depreciation expense should be included in the financial statements of NPOs.

The category of estimated depreciation expense has been provided for in the object of expense format of **Exhibit 1**, but no amount has been assumed for this expense.

In accounting for depreciation, some NPOs recommend that it be segregated from other expenses and that two total expense amounts be accumulated, one without depreciation and one with depreciation. The usefulness of including depreciation for a particular NPO may be determined best by those who have to prepare and use the budget for planning and control.

The one area where including depreciation is definitely recommended is for budgets prepared to support grants to NPOs, when such grants allow for the recovery of some or all of the depreciation allocable to the project that the grant is funding. Even here there are allocation problems because of inherent arbitrary estimates. Further, it should be noted that recoveries based on historical costs do not compensate for the opportunity cost of capital facilities during inflationary periods. However, this is a general weakness with historical cost-based depreciation for budgeting use.[9]

TOTAL EXPENSES

The expense categories start at employee payroll and end with depreciation to obtain total operating expenses.

NONOPERATING EXPENDITURES

The next two categories cover expenditures that do not represent expenses. As previously mentioned, expenditures involve the use of financial resources. Some expenditures are simultaneously considered expenses. Neither of the next two categories are considered expenses. Neither category results in increasing or decreasing the fund balance of the NPO because they arise from nonoperating transactions.

ACQUISITION OF ASSETS

This category applies to the budgeted acquisition of capital assets that can be capitalized initially and subsequently charged as an operating expense through depreciation. The budgetary format used in **Exhibit 1** segregates nonoperating expenditures from expenses. In order to avoid a duplication of expenses and expenditures, no amount is assumed for depreciation but an amount is assumed for expenditures on the acquisition of assets. If amounts were shown both for expenditures for the acquisition of depreciable capital assets and for depreciation on these same capital assets, we would have a partial double counting. An example is if we included in the budget an expenditure of $30,000 for the purchase of equipment and at the same time included $6,000 of the $30,000 as depreciation expense.

RETIREMENT OF DEBT

This category is not an expense category; therefore, it is shown under nonoperating expenditures.

ILLUSTRATIVE NONPROFIT ORGANIZATION— ALTERNATIVE A

In **Exhibit 2**, the financial information shown for the Illustrative NPO is modified from the cash basis to the accrual basis to reflect "total flows-of-financial-resources" rather than only cash flows. The cash basis must be modified to reflect both the accrual basis and flows-of-financial-resources.

EXHIBIT 2

Illustrative Not-for-Profit—Alternative A
Budget
For the Year Ended, June 30, 19X1
(Flows of Financial Resources, Including Depreciation)

	Budget
Total public support, grants, and revenue (cash basis)	$1,054,944
Adjustment for the accrual basis due to permanent differences (nonmonetary contributions)	122,060
Total public support, grants, and revenue (cash basis plus nonmonetary contributions)	$1,177,004
Adjustment for the accrual basis and flows-of-financial-resources due to timing differences	557,822
Total public support, grants, and revenue (accrual basis and flows-of-financial-resources)	$1,734,826
Total expenses (cash basis)	$ 933,720
Adjustment for the accrual basis due to permanent differences (nonmonetary contributions)	122,060
Total expenses (cash basis plus nonmonetary contributions)	$1,055,780

Adjustment for the accrual basis and flows-of-financial-resources	193,218
Total expenses (accrual basis and flows-of-financial-resources	$1,248,998
Excess (deficit) on operations before depreciation	485,828
Depreciation	19,378
Excess (deficit) on operations after depreciation	$ 466,450

From **Exhibit 2**, you can see that the cash basis is adjusted both on the inflow and outflow side. On the inflow side, cash inflows are modified to financial inflows by including accruals for such items of support as pledges to be collected, which are recorded as pledges receivable. Accruals can result in financial inflows from support items being greater than cash inflows from such items if pledges receivable are expected to increase during the budget period. Revenue items also are accrued as a result of such items as sales to be collected, which are recorded in the form of accounts receivable. Again, the financial inflow from financial resources such as accounts receivable will be greater than the cash inflow if accounts receivable are expected to increase during the budget period. Thus, the accrual basis will reflect the effect of such financial resources as pledges and accounts receivable. The rise and fall in such financial assets is not reflected on the pure cash basis.

The accrual basis also reflects nonmonetary contributions which were discussed above. Nonmonetary contributions by their very nature would not be considered a financial resource; however, NPOs record such inflows if the conditions described earlier are met. The types of items that qualify as nonmonetary contributions and the assumed breakdown between services and goods assumed for **Exhibit 2** is as follows:

❏ Estimated volunteer services $60,400

❏ Estimated donated materials $25,625

❏ Estimated donated rental value of equipment $7,950

❏ Estimated donated rental value of office facilities $19,225

❏ Estimated donated advertising time $8,860

The five nonmonetary items together add up to a total of $122,060 for the estimated nonmonetary contributions shown in **Exhibit 2**.

On the outflow side, similar adjustments must be made between the cash basis and the accrual basis as for the inflow side. Accrual of liabilities for unpaid purchases of expense-type items as well as capital-type items are necessary for the accrual basis. Thus, accrual-based expenses will exceed cash basis expenses if, e.g., there has been an increase in accounts payable. Of course, the pure cash basis would not recognize any liabilities whether they be of the short-term or long-term variety.

Once nonmonetary contributions of services and supplies are recognized as inflows, they must be simultaneously recognized on the outflow side. This is shown in **Exhibit 2**.

The accrual basis also recognizes depreciation. This is a noncash expense that nevertheless, as was the case for the nonmonetary contributions, is reported in the budget shown in **Exhibit 2**.

ILLUSTRATIVE NONPROFIT ORGANIZATION— ALTERNATIVE B

Exhibit 3 is also on the accrual basis and reflects flows-of-financial-resources. Thus, **Exhibit 3** includes the same adjustments as did **Exhibit 2** to modify the cash basis to the accrual basis. **Exhibit 3** goes a step beyond **Exhibit** 2 by segregating nonoperating items from operating items. This separate disclosure of nonoperating items is reflected both on the inflow and outflow sides in **Exhibit 3**.

EXHIBIT 3

Illustrative Not-for-Profit—Alternative B
Budget for the Year Ended, June 30, 19X1
(Flows of Financial Resources, Including Depreciation)
(Nonoperating Items Segregated)

	Budget
Total public support, grants, and revenue (cash basis)	$1,054,944
Adjustment for nonoperating items (cash basis)	81,607

Total public support, grants, and revenue (cash basis)	$ 973,337
Adjustment for the accrual basis due to permanent differences (nonmonetary contributions)	122,060
Total public support, grants, and revenue (cash basis plus nonmonetary contributions)	$ 1,095,397
Adjustment for the accrual basis and flows-of-financial-resources	557,822
Total public support, grants, and revenue (accrual basis and flows-of-financial-resources)	$ 1,653,219
Total expenses (cash basis)	933,720
Adjustment for nonoperating items (cash basis)	13,424
Total expenses (cash basis)	$ 920,296
Adjustment for the accrual basis due to permanent differences (nonmonetary contributions)	122,060
Total expenses (cash basis plus nonmonetary contributions)	$ 1,042,356
Adjustment for the accrual basis and flows-of-financial-resources	193,218
Total expenses (accrual basis and flows-of-financial-resources)	$ 1,235,574
Excess (deficit) on operations before depreciation	$ 4,176,454
Depreciation	19,378
Excess (deficit) on operations after depreciation	$ 398,267
Nonoperating revenue	
Rental income	$ 8,370
Auxiliary activities	26,156

Investment income	38,362
Miscellaneous income	8,719
Nonoperating expenses	
Interest expense (on Nonoperating Assets)	4,087
Miscellaneous	9,337
Nonoperating revenue net of nonoperating expenses	68,183
Excess (deficit) on the annual budget	$ 466,450

Typical nonoperating items on the inflow side are: (1) income from rental, (2) auxiliary activities, (3) investment income, and (4) miscellaneous revenue. This list is not exhaustive. Nor are each of the items shown, with the exception of auxiliary activities, necessarily nonoperating items for every NPO. What is a nonoperating item for any NPO is basically determined by what the normal services are that a particular NPO was organized for according to its bylaws. If an NPO is organized to provide subsidized rental housing for the needy, the income from rentals would not be a nonoperating item. However, if the normal operating activities and services of an NPO do not involve rentals, then such income from rental would be a nonoperating item. The line of demarcation between operating and nonoperating items is dependent on the normal services provided by a NPO.

The same approach applies to the outflow side. On the outflow side, interest expense and miscellaneous expense are shown as nonoperating items. They both could also be operating items if they are necessary expenses arising from the NPO's normal operating activities and services. Interest expense incurred with respect to nonoperating assets or activities is clearly a nonoperating expense. However, interest incurred on day-to-day operating transactions could be considered an operating expense. For example, a temporary delay in collection of pledges might force an NPO to rely on short-term borrowing as a bridge to fund its services and to prevent an interruption of such services to its normal clientele.

SHOWING BUDGETED EXPENSES BY PROGRAM AND FUNCTION

In **Exhibit 1**, budgeted expenses are shown by an "object of expense" format. In **Exhibit 4** and subsequent exhibits, the expense format is by program and function. This is known as the programmatic format or the functional expense format.

Programs are the manner in which an NPO organizes its activities to carry out its goals. The functional expense format separates expenses into program and support. Program expenses are the incremental costs associated with the operation of a particular program. These are the costs that would cease if the program were terminated. Support expenses are composed typically of general and administrative expenses associated with the overall management of the operations of the NPO and of fund-raising expenses that generate resource inflows to finance its activities.

Illustrative financial statements using the functional expense format for different types of NPOs can be found in *Statement of Position 78-10*. These financial statements contain illustrative accounting categories that have been used as guides for the budgetary categories in **Exhibits 4 through 14**. Consistency between the budgetary and accounting categories permits appropriate comparisons to be made between budget and actual for planning and control purposes.

In the case of **Exhibit 1**, we have already discussed most of the budget categories. However, for the other exhibits we only discuss a few of the major budget categories for background purposes.

Exhibits 1, 2 and 3 are identified as simply a budget. However, the remaining exhibits in this chapter are identified as operating budgets. The reason for this distinction is that **Exhibits 1, 2, and 3** cover a more comprehensive budget than the other exhibits. The budgets of **Exhibits 1, 2, and 3** include such items as repayment of debt and the acquisition of major capital assets. The other exhibits are restricted to transactions resulting from day to day operating activities. If the budget is only for day-to-day operating items, it should be identified as an operating budget. If the budget includes such items as debt repayment and acquisition of major capital assets, it should be referred to simply as the budget.

All of the budgets presented in the exhibits following **Exhibits 1, 2, and 3** cover unrestricted resources. However, some are identified as unrestricted operating budgets, while the other budgets are identified as operating budgets. The difference between the two types of identification is to forewarn the user that certain types of NPOs use significant amounts of restricted resources while others do not. For those NPOs that receive significant amounts of restricted resources, such resources are not available for operating purposes until the restrictions are met. At the time that the restrictions are met, the resources become unrestricted and are part of the "unrestricted operating budget." If the NPO does not use significant amounts of restricted resources, its budget is identified as an "unrestricted operating budget."

FOUNDATIONS

EXHIBIT 4

Private Foundation
Unrestricted Operating Budget
for the Year Ended, June 30, 19Xl

	Budget
Public support and revenue	
Public contributions	$ 19,584
Legacies and bequests	26,078
Total support	$ 45,662
Endowment and investment income	$ 2,292,131
Total support and revenue	$ 2,337,793
Budgeted expenses by program and function	
Program grants	
Education	$ 369,676
Energy research	427,175
Environment protection	340,615
Health	184,244
Total program expenses	$ 1,321,710
Supporting services	
Management and general	$ 366,196
Federal excise taxes	69,749
Total supporting services	$ 435,944
Total operating expenses	$ 1,757,654
Excess (deficit) on the operating budget	$ 580,138

Public Contributions, Legacies, and Bequests

Exhibit 4 presents the unrestricted operating budget for a private foundation. In this budget, public contributions, legacies, and bequests are assumed to be of the unrestricted variety and therefore could be included as part of the resource inflows of the unrestricted operating budget.

Endowment and Investment Income

This revenue category includes interest on debt securities and dividends on equity investments. Such income is subject to federal excise tax. The federal excise tax is shown separately as a budgeted expense under the supporting services expenses in **Exhibit 4**.

RELIGIOUS ORGANIZATIONS

EXHIBIT 5

Religious Organization
Unrestricted Operating Budget
for the Year Ended, June 30, 19X1

	Budget
Public support and revenue:	
Public support:	
Public contributions	$ 27,082
Membership contributions	
Pledged offerings	290,701
Weekly offerings	183,479
Special events	123,819
Legacies and bequests	43,567
Total support	$ 668,648
Estimated revenue:	
Revenue from educational activities	$ 35,453
Other revenue generating activities	244,515
Investment income	176,902
Miscellaneous revenue	9,615
Auxiliary enterprises	26,850
Total support and revenue	$ 1,161,982
Budgeted expenses by program and function	

Program services

Pastoral	$ 265,053
Missionary and benevolences	149,969
Education	95,914
Health care	61,039
Social services	62,783
Burial and cemetery services	78,433
Environment protection	59,878
Religious personnel development	44,748
Auxiliary enterprises	20,336
Total program expenses	$ 838,151

Supporting services

General and administrative	$ 113,358
Fund raising	26,156
Total supporting services	$ 139,514
Total operating expenses	$ 977,665
Excess (deficit) on the operating budget	$ 184,317

Special Events

Revenue raised from special events is assumed to be gross of deducting the costs of running these events. The costs have not been subtracted, instead, they are included in fund-raising expenses. This is different from the procedure followed in **Exhibit 1**; however, it is the same as the approach used in **Exhibit 10**.

Legacies and Bequests

These are assumed to be of the unrestricted variety.

Other Revenue Generating Activities

The revenue expected to be realized from "other revenue generating activities" is presented net of the expenses of operating these other activities.

Auxiliary Activities

Revenue from auxiliary activities is presented separately from the expenses for these functions. Therefore, the revenue is shown gross, not net.

Benevolences

Review the discussion for this category in **Exhibit 1**.

SOCIAL SERVICE GROUPS

EXHIBIT 6

Social Services Organization
Unrestricted Operating Budget
for the Year Ended, June 30, 19X1

	Budget
Public support and revenue	
Public support:	
Public contributions	$ 402,797
Special events	51,439
Legacies and bequests	34,002
Nonmonetary contributions	122,060
Total direct support	$ 610,299
Indirect support:	
Indirect contributions	$ 81,954
Foundation grants	43,593
Government grants	39,233
Total indirect support	$ 164,781
Revenues:	
Fees for services	$ 130,778
Sales of educational and informational materials	73,236
Auxiliary activities	26,156
Investment income	39,233

Miscellaneous revenue	8,719
Total revenue	278,122
Total support, grants and revenue	$ 1,053,201
Budgeted expenses by program and function	
Program services	
Drug treatment	$ 261,557
Family counseling	247,607
Mental health	310,380
Total program expenses	$ 819,544
Supporting services	
Fund raising	$ 52,317
General and administrative	139,497
Total supporting services	$ 191,814
Total operating expenses	$ 1,011,358
Excess (deficit) on the operating budget	$ 41,843

Special Events

Revenue from special events, in **Exhibit 6**, is assumed to be net of the costs of running them. This is the approach followed in **Exhibit 1**. However, it differs from the approach in **Exhibits 5 and 10**. Either approach should be acceptable in a budgeting framework provided it is clearly disclosed, and a budget user can convert from one approach to the other. In **Exhibit 6**, the costs of running special events is $51,439. If the method used in **Exhibits 5 and 10** are practiced, gross revenue from special events would be $68,800. If revenue from special events are shown gross, the expenses would have to be presented separately.

Legacies and Bequests

These are assumed to be of the unrestricted variety.

Nonmonetary Contributions

Those contributions expected to be received are shown separately at $122,060. Nonmonetary contributions expected to be used are assumed to be equal in amount to nonmonetary contributions expected to be received. Nonmonetary contributions expected to be used are assumed to be distributed throughout the functional expense categories.

Auxiliary Activities

Income from auxiliary activities is shown net of costs in **Exhibit 6**. The costs of auxiliary activities are expected to amount to $34,850.

PROFESSIONAL OR TRADE ASSOCIATIONS

EXHIBIT 7

Professional or Trade Association
Unrestricted Operating Budget
for the Year Ended, June 30, 19X1

	Budget
Estimated revenues	
Membership dues	$ 418,496
Special assessments	191,815
Conferences and meetings	810,825
Advertising and sales of publications	226,689
Investment income	31,387
Miscellaneous income	8,511
Total revenue	$ 1,687,723
Budgeted expenses by program and function	
Program services	
Technical services	$ 496,957
Education	78,467
Conferences and meetings	397,566
Membership services	95,904
Publications	113,341
Communications	61,030
Total program expenses	$ 1,243,265

Supporting services

Membership development	$ 348,948
General and administrative	78,427
Total supporting services	$ 427,375
Total operating expenses	$ 1,670,640
Excess (deficit) on the operating budget	$ 17,083

Special Assessments

This revenue category appears in **Exhibit 7**, and covers a special type of membership dues. These dues are separate from regular membership dues that are for standard amounts of a recurring nature. Special assessments are of the nonrecurring variety and for nonstandard amounts. Because these are of the nonrecurring and nonstandard type, they should be budgeted and accounted for separately. Separation pinpoints the areas in which budget estimates are most likely to go astray and therefore aids in current and future budget preparation.

SCIENTIFIC AND RESEARCH ORGANIZATIONS

EXHIBIT 8

Scientific and Research Organization Unrestricted Operating Budget for the Year Ended, June 30, 19X1

	Budget
Estimated revenues	
Contractual revenue	
Government	$2,493,505
Private Sector companies	610,299
Foundation grants	95,910
Other grants	34,875
Investment income	25,670
Miscellaneous income	9,105
Total revenue	$3,269,364

Budgeted expenses by program and function

Program services

Energy research	$ 744,564
Environmental research	671,328
Medical research	700,971
National defense	636,454
Total program expenses	$2,753,318

Supporting services

Procurement of contracts and grants	$ 43,582
Management and general	357,461
Total supporting services	$ 401,043
Total operating expenses	$3,154,361
Excess (deficit) on the operating budget	$ 115,003

CONTRACTUAL REVENUE

This is a distinctive revenue category for NPOs of the scientific and research type. These contracts generally result in the various program expenses presented in Exhibit 8. A useful budget format would be one that evaluates the expected profitability of the organization's activities on a contract-by-contract basis.

CLUBS AND LEISURE ACTIVITIES ORGANIZATIONS

EXHIBIT 9

Leisure Activities Club
Unrestricted Operating Budget
for the Year Ended, June 30, 19X1

	Budget
Estimated revenues	
Membership dues	$ 873,599
Special assessments	90,673
Initiation fees	80,211

Outdoor sports

Golf	151,703
Tennis	95,904
Swimming	61,620
Minor sports	18,025

Hotel or clubhouse facilities

Room rental charges	191,808
Room service—food, beverages, etc.	43,978
Baths and swimming pool	43,587
Gymnasium and athletics	52,504
Telephone	5,235
Billiards	4,361
Card rooms	6,007
Bowling	31,389
Newsstand and sundries	69,944
Barber shop	54,055
Valet	43,593
Restaurant and bar	351,066
Sports shop	61,029
Garage	43,785
Investment income	26,545
Miscellaneous income	8,433
Total revenue	$2,409,055

Budgeted expenses by program and function

Program services

  Outdoor sports

Golf	$ 177,858
Tennis	69,754
Swimming	43,598
Minor sports	26,155

  Hotel or clubhouse facilities

Room supplies and servicing of rooms	43,604
Room service—food, beverages, etc.	34,888
Baths and swimming pool	33,113
Gymnasium and athletics	35,082
Telephone	3,317
Billiards	1,748
Card rooms	3,502
Bowling	17,442
Newsstand and sundries	52,314
Barber shop	35,076
Valet	26,165
Restaurant and bar	200,533
Sports shop	43,598
Garage	29,645
Total program expenses	$ 877,392
Supporting services	
Entertainment expense	524,857
Maintenance of grounds and buildings	191,808
General and administrative	786,413
Total supporting services	$1,503,078
Total operating expenses	$2,380,470
Excess (deficit) on the operating budget	$ 28,585

Special Assessments and Initiation Fees

In **Exhibit 9**, as in **Exhibit 7**, the dues from the membership are segregated between normal, recurring, and other types. Again, there are special assessments. These may be levied to eliminate a past deficit. Initiation fees charged to new members cover the benefits of joining an already operating organization because normal dues alone are not considered by themselves sufficient to cover the costs of such benefits.

It could be argued that normal recurring dues should cover the present value of future benefits. However, the presence of new members might result in incremental costs justifying initiation fees. Such fees also have been used to maintain the exclusiveness of the membership on an economic basis, which may be less uncomfortable socially than having to discriminate on some other basis.

MUSEUMS

EXHIBIT 10

Art Museum
Unrestricted Operating Budget
for the Year Ended, June 30, 19X1

	Budget
Public support and revenue	
Direct support:	
Public contributions	$ 165,652
Special events	88,929
Legacies and bequests	43,791
Nonmonetary contributions	34,869
Total direct support	$ 333,241
Indirect support:	
Indirect contributions	$ 43,411
Foundation grants	262,134
Government grants	61,425
Total indirect support	$ 366,970
Revenue:	
Membership dues	$ 87,768
Admission charges	262,428
Auxiliary activities	384,488
Investment income	864,008
Miscellaneous revenue	9,493
Total revenue	$1,608,185
Total public support, grants and revenue	$2,308,396

Budgeted expenses by program and function

Program services

Maintenance of collection and curatorial	$ 959,912
Exhibitions	68,877
Education	38,362
Research	26,164
Fellowships	78,476
Community services	32,259
Public information	34,883
Net additions to the collection	730,623
Total program expenses	$1,969,555

Supporting services

Management administrative	$ 105,494
Fund raising	27,028
Total supporting services	$ 132,522
Cost of sales and expenses of auxiliary activities	198,793
Total operating expenses	$2,300,871
Excess (deficit) on the operating budget	$ 7,525

Special Events

Revenue from special events is assumed to be gross of the costs to run them. Such costs have not been subtracted, but rather are included in fund-raising costs. This differs from the procedure in **Exhibit 1**.

Legacies and Bequests

These are assumed to be of the unrestricted type.

Nonmonetary Contributions

Contributions expected to be received are presented separately from those expected to be used. Nonmonetary contributions expected to be used are included in the expenses of two programs at $17,434 in each program. The programs are the "maintenance of the collection" and "exhibitions."

Auxiliary Activities

Revenue from such activities is shown separately from expenses.

INDEPENDENT SCHOOLS

EXHIBIT 11

Private School
Unrestricted Operating Budget
for the Year Ended, June 30, 19X1

	Budget
Public support and revenue	
Direct support:	
Public contributions	$ 244,817
Legacies and bequests	87,387
Special alumni giving	419,645
Total direct support	$ 751,849
Indirect support:	
Indirect contributions	$ 87,768
Foundation grants	122,447
Government grants	88,343
Total indirect support and grants	$ 298,558
Revenue:	
Tuition and fees	$3,390,470
Summer school and other educational programs	288,584
Auxiliary activities	71,297
Endowment and other Investment income	62,578
Miscellaneous revenue	10,267
Total revenue	$3,823,196
Total support, grants and revenue	$4,873,602

Budgeted expenses by program and function

Program services

Instruction	$3,054,108
Library	296,605
Student activities	104,623
Scholarship and financial aid	210,020
Summer school and other educational programs	314,836
Auxiliary activities	53,067
Total program expenses	$4,033,259

Supporting services

Administrative and general	$ 421,202
Fund raising	61,611
Total supporting services	$ 482,813
Total operating expenses	$4,516,072
Excess (deficit) on the operating budget	$ 357,530

Legacies, Bequests, and Special Alumni Giving

These revenue categories are assumed to be of the unrestricted type so that these expected resource inflows would be included in the unrestricted operating budget.

Auxiliary Activities

The income from such activities is shown in Exhibit 1 net of expenses to run them. However, in Exhibit 11 these expenses are presented as part of the program expenses in the expenses section of the budget. This means that the auxiliary activities in the revenue section of the budget are not shown net of expenses, but show gross revenues from such activities. Whenever a budget shows expenses of auxiliary activities separate from the revenues, it is understood that such revenues are on a gross basis rather than a net basis.

LABOR UNIONS

EXHIBIT 12

Labor Union
Unrestricted Operating Budget
for the Year Ended, June 30, 19X1

	Budget
Estimated revenues	
Check-off membership dues	$2,596,123
Direct dues	24,801
Agency fees in lieu of dues	768,395
Allocations from affiliated unions	454,333
Administrative charges apprenticeship training	42,622
Sale of union informational materials	57,529
Miscellaneous revenue	9,534
Total revenue	$3,953,337
Budgeted expenses by program and function	
Program services	
Dues allocated to affiliated unions	$1,223,115
Organizing activities	263,891
Negotiation activities	994,110
Grievance activities	523,676
Allocations to strike fund	87,360
Total program expenses	$3,092,152
Supporting services	
Administrative and general	$ 610,647
Total supporting services	$ 610,647
Total operating expenses	$3,702,799
Excess (deficit) on the operating budget	$ 250,538

Membership Dues: Check-off, Direct, and Agency Fees

There are several categories of membership dues for a labor union for which brief explanations would be helpful. Check-off membership dues refer to an arrangement, whereby an employer automatically subtracts union dues from the employees' paychecks involved. Agency fees in lieu of dues apply to a set of circumstances known as the agency shop whereby not all employees who are eligible to join a union must do so.

The agency shop is different from the union shop, whereby a worker eligible to join a union must become a member after a probationary period has elapsed. In the agency shop, those employees eligible to join the union and who do so, pay union dues. If a check-off arrangement is collectively negotiated, membership dues become check-off dues. Eligible employees do not have to join a union under an agency shop. They may nevertheless find that under a particular collectively bargained agency shop they have to make payments in lieu of union dues.

Payments in lieu of taxes are justified to take care of the "free rider" problem which arises in connection with public goods and external economies.[10]

Some workers who are not required to join the union, nevertheless, pay the equivalent of dues directly to the union for benefits they receive.

PERFORMING ARTS CENTERS

EXHIBIT 13

Performing Arts Center
Unrestricted Operating Budget
for the Year Ended, June 30, 19X1

	Budget
Estimated revenues	
Membership dues	$ 175,339
Admissions:	
Subscriptions	1,676,092
Groups	681,093
Students	358,332
Individuals	213,692
Specials	105,010

Other	37,200
Tuition	560,507
Concessions	261,553
Investment income	68,877
Miscellaneous revenue	10,449
Donated materials, services and facilities	229,204
Total revenue	$4,377,347

Budgeted expenses by program and function

Program services

Direct production costs	$1,979,111
Other production expenses	1,583,289
Drama school	349,716
Mobile productions for the local community	800,363
Administrative and general expenses	793,388
Donated materials, services and facilities	229,204
Total operating expenses	$5,735,070
Excess (deficit) from operations	$(1,357,723)

Public support

Estimated contributions and support	$1,117,718
Excess of donated materials received over those consumed	43,769
Total direct support	$1,161,487
Less: fund-raising expenses	44,561
Total direct support net of fund-raising expenses	$1,116,926
Foundation grants	262,428
Government grants	88,162
Total nonoperating support and grants net of fund-rasing expenses	$1,467,516
Excess (deficit) on the operating budget	$ 109,793

Concessions

Estimated income from concessions is presented net of the related estimated expenses.

Donated Materials, Services, and Facilities

Those nonmonetary contributions expected to be received are estimated at $229,204 plus $43,769, whereas the amount expected to be used during the current budget period is only $229,204. The difference of $43,769 is shown after the calculation of the balance on the operating budget and therefore does not affect this balance. However, the overall balance on the budget is affected so that a surplus of $109,793 is reduced significantly to a smaller surplus of $66,024 without the excess nonmonetary contributions of unused donated materials.

LIBRARIES

EXHIBIT 14

Library
Unrestricted Operating Budget
for the Year Ended, June 30, 19X1

	Budget
Public support and revenue	
Direct support:	
Public contributions	$ 20,053
Legacies and bequests	63,733
Nonmonetary contributions received	55,410
Total direct support	$ 139,196
Indirect support:	
Foundation grants	$ 19,578
Municipal government support	1,396,712
State government support	247,024
Federal government grants	69,556
Total indirect support and grants	$1,732,870

Estimated revenues

Fees for services to individuals	$ 54,829
Fees for services to government entities	90,672
Book, record, art, and other rentals, photocopy fees, and fines	266,090
Sales of educational materials	39,521
Rental of facilities	28,482
Investment income	21,511
Miscellaneous revenue	12,040
Total revenue	$ 513,145
Total support, grants and revenue	$2,385,211

Budgeted expenses by program and function

Program services

Circulating library	$ 878,830
Research library	162,165
Interlibrary services	62,774
Library services for the handicapped	106,366
Educational services	42,721
Community adult services	102,007
Community children's services	77,595
Total program expenses	$1,432,458

Supporting services

General and administration	$ 838,725
Fund-raising	10,811
Total supporting services	$ 849,536
Total operating expenses	$2,281,993
Excess (deficit) on the operating budget	$ 103,218

Funding.   Funding may be received from government, business, and individuals. Library funds may have to be transferred between library categories.

Nonmonetary Contributions

These are expected to be received during the budget period and are shown separately as part of the inflow of resources from public support. However, nonmonetary contributions expected to be used during the budget period have been included in the "circulating library" program.

Physical Measures

Libraries should use physical measures in budgeting such as labor hours in services—cataloging, acquisition and bindery, and reference work.

Expenses

Expenses include salaries, rent, books, periodicals, utilities, insurance, supplies, and exhibition costs. Costs should be allocated among responsibility units such as reference, circulation, and online services. Expenses may be categorized by services rendered such as requisitioning and processing publications, cataloging, library tours, handling exhibitions, and security.

Formula Budgeting

Formula budgeting is unique to libraries. Funds are allocated based on a predetermined standard. Examples of standards are student enrollment, number of faculty, number of courses, or library circulation. Formula budgeting is used to insure the equitable distribution of resources. Formula budgeting has gained popularity because it is easy to prepare, is simple, requires minimal justification, not costly to use, and requires few planning and budgeting skills. Further, formula budgeting is defensible. However, there are drawbacks. There is often little justification for the numbers which are part of the formula's set of standards. Further, a false relationship may exist between the quantity and the quality of the outcome. Finally, there is not much professional judgement or consideration of unique programs or local environmental factors.

Program Budgeting

Program budgeting concentrates on the library's activities and allocates funds based on the services rendered in satisfying user needs and the library's objectives. This budgeting approach looks at alternative ways of rendering services at varying funding and priority levels. Such a budget may be segregated into major programs and under each program, the budget is further subdivided into groupings such as staff, training, cataloging, collection, and supplies. For instance, a library's information service program budget may be divided into budgets for serving in-library users, the elderly, and the handicapped. Each of those budgets is further itemized by personnel, supplies, and so on. It is easy for the administrative librarian to know the total budget for each program, such as service to the aging, but it is not as easy to obtain an immediate total of item expenditures such as staff salaries for the total library program. The total library personnel cost has to be derived from budgets of all library programs.

Exhibit 15 presents an actual library budget.

EXHIBIT 15

ABC LIBRARY BUDGET (94/95 Approved April 6, 1994)

EXPENDITURES	1993/1994	1993/1994	% Increase 93/94 to 94/95	94/95 % of Total Budget
SALARIES				
Professional	936,504	991,179		
Clerical, Full Time	572,443	568,165		
Clerical, Part Time	275,500	270,000		
Custodial	85.375	88.212		
	1,869,822	1,917,556	2.6	56.7
EQUIPMENT & BUILDING				
Equipment	40,000	40,000		
Building Alterations	40.000	40.000		
	80,000	80,000	0.0	2.4
LIBRARY MATERIALS				
Library Books	240,000	250,000		
DataBase Searches	1,500	3,000		
Recordings & Cassettes	20,000	20,000		
Periodicals & Pamphlets	35,000	40,000		
Microfilms	70,000	70,000		
Visual Materials	1,000	1,000		
Bookbinding	4,000	3,000		
Audio Visual Materials	45.000	48.000		
	416,500	435,000	4.6	12.9
SUPPLIES				
Office & Library Supplies	50,000	50,000		
Supplies, Gaylord	8,000	10,000		
Maintenance & Custodial Supplies	14.000	12.000		
	72,000	72,000	0.0	2.1
FUELS & UTILITIES				
Electricity	115,000	120,000		
Fuel Oil	17,000	15,000		
Water	800	800		
	132,800	135,800	2.3	4.0
CONTRACT OPERATIONS & MAINTENANCE				
Cartage & Refuse	4,000	3,500		
Processing	1,000	500		
Professional & Technical Services	1 0,000	10,000		
Membership Dues	500	500		
Office Equipment Repair & Maintenance	24,000	22,000		
Upkeep - PAC	60,000	65,000		
Upkeep - Gaylord	72,000	72,000		
Bus Services	1,000	1,000		
Protective Services	22,000	21,000		
Cleaning & Exterminating Services	2.000	2.000		
	196,500	197,500	0.05	5.8
OTHER EXPENSES				
Conferences	14,000	14,000		
Telephone	14,000	14,000		
Postage	9,000	9,000		
Printing & Publicity	4,000	5,500		
Travel	2,500	2,500		
Other Miscellaneous	3,000	4,000		
Programs	25,000	25,000		
Insurance	50,000	50,000		
Truck	1,000	1,000		
	122,500	125,000	2.1	3.7
SPECIAL OBJECTS OF EXPENSE				
New York State Retirement	65,000	65,000		
Social Security	143,041	146,693		
Worker's Compensation	18,000	18,000		
Life Insurance	9,000	9,000		
Health Insurance	165,520	169,161		
Disability Insurance	4,000	4,000		
Dental Insurance	6,000	6,000		
Unemployment Insurance	1,000	3,000		
Medicare	500	500		
	412,061	421,354	2.3	12.5
TOTAL EXPENSES	**3,302,183**	**3,384,210**	**2.5**	
INCOME				
Library Service Incentive Aid	4,000	4,000		
Interest	6,500	8,000		
Fines & Photocopy	60,000	63,000		
Tax Levy	3,231,683	3,309,210	2.4	97.8
TOTAL INCOME	**3,302,183**	**3,384,210**	**2.5**	

NOTES FOR CHAPTER 7

1. A discussion of accounting bases in a managerial accounting context in the area of local government finance can be found in Lennox L. Moak and Albert Hillhouse, *Concepts and Practices in Local Government Finance* (Chicago, IL: Government (formerly, Municipal) Finance Officers Association, 1975, pp. 346–352).

2. Publications that contain charts of accounts or their elements are as follows:

   William H. Daughtrey and Malvern J. Gross, Jr., *Museum Accounting Handbook*, (Washington, D.C.: American Association of Museums, 1978);

   American Hospital Association, *Chart of Accounts for Hospitals* (Chicago: American Hospital Association, 1976);

   American Institute of Certified Public Accountants (AICPA), *Audits of Certain Nonprofit Organizations*, as of December 31, 1990, AICPA Audit and Accounting Guide (Chicago: Commerce Clearing House, 1991);

   American Institute of Certified Public Accountants, *Audits of Voluntary Health and Welfare Organizations* (New York: AICPA, 1974);

   American Institute of Certified Public Accountants, *Statement of Position 78-10: Accounting Principles and Reporting Practices for Certain Nonprofit Organizations* (New York: AICPA, 1979);

   Club Managers Association of America, *Uniform System of Accounts for Clubs*, 2nd revised edition (Washington, D.C.: Club Managers Association of America, 1967);

   Government Finance Officer Association of the United States and Canada (GFOA) (formerly, Municipal Finance Officers Association), *Government Accounting, Auditing, and Financial Reporting* (Chicago: GFOA, 1988);

   National Association of College and University Business Officers (NACUBO), *College and University Business Administration*, 4th edition (Washington, D.C.: NACUBO, 1982);

National Association of Independent Schools (NAIS), *Accounting for Independent Schools*, 2nd edition (Boston: NAIS, 1977);

National Assembly of National Voluntary Health and Social Welfare Organizations, Inc.; National Health Council, Inc.; and United Way of America, *Standards of Accounting and Financial Reporting for Voluntary Health and Welfare Organizations*, 3rd edition (New York: Authors, 1988);

United Way of America, *Accounting and Financial Reporting: A Guide for United Ways and Not-for-Profit Human Service Organizations* (Alexandria, VA: United Way of America, 1974).

3. The relevant pronouncements issued by the Financial Accounting Standards Board (FASB) that are addressed specifically to financial reporting issues applicable to the nonprofit sector are as follows:

Statement of Financial Accounting Standards No. 93, "Recognition of Depreciation by Not-for-Profit Organizations" (Norwalk, CT: FASB, 1987);

Statement of Financial Accounting Standards No. 116, "Accounting for Contributions Received and Contributions Made" (Norwalk, CT: FASB, 1993);

Statement of Financial Accounting Standards No. 117, "Financial Statements of Not-for-Profit Organizations" (Norwalk, CT: FASB, 1993).

4. The importance of budgetary information for external users in the public sector is discussed, for example, in a study by A. J. Simon, "Conceptual Problems in the FANO Study by the FASB with Respect to Public Sector Accounting and Disclosure," *Proceedings of the American Accounting Association's Mid-Atlantic Regional Meeting, April 5–7, 1979* (College Park, MD: The University of Maryland for the Mid-Atlantic Region of the American Accounting Association, 1979), pp. 42–54. The "FANO Study by the FASB" refers to a study by Robert N. Anthony, *Financial Accounting in Nonbusiness Organizations: An Exploratory Study*, A Research Report for the Financial Accounting Standards Board (Stamford, CT: Financial Accounting Standards Board, 1978).

5. The discussion of the various budgetary categories is based, in part, on such sources as *Accounting and Financial Reporting: A Guide for United Ways and Not-for-Profit Human Service Organizations, Audits of Voluntary Health and Welfare Organizations, Standards of Accounting and Financial Reporting for Voluntary Health and Welfare Organizations*, and *Statement of Position 78-10: Accounting Principles and Reporting Practices for Certain Nonprofit Organizations*.

6. Nonmonetary activities are a significant component of economic activity. Accounting for nonmonetary activities is discussed in A. J. Simon, "An Economic and Macroaccounting Framework for Household Nonmarket Production and Its Uses: The Output Side," *The International Journal of Accounting Education and Research*, Vol. 12, No. 2 (Spring 1977), pp. 143–168.

7. In *Statement of Financial Accounting Standards No. 116* (p. 3), the FASB goes on to give examples of specialized skills:

   Services requiring specialized skills are provided by accountants, architects, carpenters, doctors, electricians, lawyers, nurses, plumbers, and other professionals and craftsmen. Contributed services and promises to give services that do not meet the above criteria shall not be recognized.

8. For example, a private foundation can expend certain of its financial resources directly for operating purposes. It is a major operating purpose of a foundation to provide grants, based on certain criteria, to third parties. The use of financial resources in the form of grants can simultaneously be expenditures and expenses for the foundation.

9. The weaknesses of basing depreciation on historical cost for budgeting purposes stems from the fact that budgets are future-oriented rather than backward-looking. The relevant costs for a budget are expected costs. Historical cost, if it has any use at all in budgeting, may be useful as an aid in predicting future cost. This is the standard approach to the relationship between historical cost and budgeting.

10. A discussion of the free rider problem in a labor union context can be found in G. Cassidy and A. J. Simon, "A Public Goods Approach to the Analysis of Public and Private Sector Unions," *Journal of Collective Negotiations in the Public Sector*, Vol. 6, No. 4 (1977), pp. 325–332.

Chapter 8

*Monitoring the Nonprofit Budget by Using Variance Analysis**

Budget cost is a predetermined future cost of rendering a service, based on present and anticipated future conditions. The norm depends upon quantitative and qualitative measurements. Budgets may be based on engineering studies examining time and motion. The budget preparer should work closely with employees to assure that the formulated figures are realistic and accurate, and useful for control.

Budgets are established at the beginning of the period. They may be expressed in physical amounts or dollars. Budgets aid in measuring and evaluating effectiveness and efficiency. Examples are quotas for donor contributions, salaries, and fund-raising expenses. Variances are interrelated, so an unfavorable variance in one responsibility area may cause a favorable one in another segment.

Variance analysis compares budget to actual performance. It may be performed by program, cost center, or department. When more than one department is involved, individual budgets should be formulated for each department in order to assign accountability to department administrators. Variances may be as thorough as needed, taking into account the cost-benefit. An analysis of variances may be conducted yearly, quarterly, monthly,

---

*Robert Fonfeder, Ph.D, CPA, Professor of Accounting at Hofstra University and consultant, coauthored this chapter.

daily, or hourly, depending upon the importance of highlighting a problem quickly.

Since actual figures (e.g. hours spent) are not known until period-end, variances can only be computed at that time. A significant variance requires identifying the responsible party and implementing corrective steps. Insignificant variances need not be considered further unless they recur repeatedly and/or indicate potential difficulty. In general, a variance should be studied when the inquiry will likely result in improvements such as cost reduction. Supplemental schedules should be prepared, providing more detail on large variances for control purposes.

When a program is of a long-term nature, variances figured at the time the program is finished may be too late for prompt corrective steps to be implemented. In this instance, evaluation may be performed at key points during the stage of the program. This allows for labor inefficiency, and other costs associated with problems to be recognized before the program is completed.

One measure of materiality is to divide the variance by the budgeted cost. A variance below 5 percent may be considered immaterial. A 10 percent deviation may be more acceptable to a nonprofit entity using tight standards relative to a 5 percent variation to a nonprofit entity having loose standards. In some instances, materiality is considered in terms of dollar amount or service volume. For example, you may have a policy examining any variance exceeding $50,000 or 10,000 service units, whichever is less. Materiality guidelines depend upon the nature of the element as it affects performance and decision-making. For example, where the item is crucial to future functioning, materiality limits should be encouraged. Additionally, statistical techniques can be used to determine the significance of cost and revenue variances.

The budget preparer must set acceptable tolerance ranges (e.g., percent). Even if a variance never exceeds a minimum allowable percentage or minimum dollar amount, the budget preparer may wish to bring it to the administrator's attention if the variance is always near the prescribed limit. Perhaps this may indicate the budget is out-of-date and an adjustment to current levels is needed to improve the planning process. It could also mean cost controls are lacking.

Because of the critical nature of costs, such as repairs and advertising, materiality guidelines are more stringent. Often the variance may be due to outdated standards or deficient budget planning. Therefore, it may not be due to actual performance. By questioning the variances and trying to uncover the answers, the administrator can make the operation more efficient and less costly. It must be understood, however, that quality should be maintained. If a variance is out of the administrator's control, follow-up action by the administrator is suggested. An example is utility rates that are not controllable internally.

Budgets should be evaluated on a periodic basis, and when budgeted figures are no longer realistic, they should be adjusted. Budgets may become unrealistic because of internal occurrences (e.g., program updating) or external factors such as competition. Budgets should be modified when labor conditions and methodologies change to such an extent that the budgets are not useful indicators or measures. Changes in methods, technology, organization, and functions may require changes in activities.

Favorable variances should also be studied and should be taken advantage of further. Those responsible for good performance should be rewarded.

The accuracy of budgets depends on the ability of the method to measure the relationship between expense incurrence and output results. Regression analysis may furnish reliable association. In the case of automated facilities, budget-cost data can be integrated with the computer that directs activities. Variances can then be identified and reported by the computer system and adjustments made as the operations proceed.

In evaluating variances, be sure to consider the information that has been omitted from the reports. Have there been changes in the processes that have not been incorporated in the reports? Have new services and programs increased setup times that require changes in budget standards?

KEY ADVANTAGES OF VARIANCE ANALYSIS

Budgets and variance analyses are important in financial analysis and decision making. The main benefits they offer are:

- ❏ Establishing service prices based on what costs should be
- ❏ Motivating staff to achieve predetermined goals
- ❏ Causing departments to focus on common goals
- ❏ Establishing and appraising objectives

❏ Assisting in costing and decision-making

❏ Setting bid prices on contracts

❏ Identifying problem areas in accordance with the "management-by-exception" approach

❏ Encouraging communication within the organization, such as between top administrators and supervisors

❏ Aiding in planning by forecasting needs (e. g., cash retirements)

❏ Allowing cost control and performance appraisal by comparing actual to budget amounts (Cost control is intended to result in the least possible cost based on predetermined quality standards)

❏ Simplifying recordkeeping by keeping items at budgeted amounts

❏ Identifying who is accountable for poor performance so that corrective steps may be made (Variances in product and service activities [cost, quantity, quality] are usually the administrator's responsibility. Variances in prices and methods of deliveries are also relevant. Profit variances typically relate to overall operations.)

Budget costing is not without some disadvantages. Examples are biases in formulating standards and the dysfunctional impact of setting improper norms.

When there are multiple reasons for a variance, each cause should be identified.

SETTING STANDARDS AS BUDGET GUIDELINES

Budget standards should be established. Depending upon the nature of the cost item, computerized models can be employed to corroborate what the budgeted costs should be. Budgets may be established through test runs or mathematical and technological analyses.

Standards are based on the situation being evaluated. Some examples are:

Situation	*Standard*
Pricing service	Realistic
Cost reduction	Tight
High-quality items	Perfection

Capacity may be stated in units, weight, size, dollars, price, working hours, etc. It may be expressed in different time periods (e.g., yearly, quarterly, monthly, weekly).

The types of standards follow:

❑ *Basic.* These are not altered from year to year and are used in the same manner as an index number. They are the basis to which subsequent period performance is compared. However, no consideration is given to a change in the environment.

❑ *Maximum efficiency.* These are perfect standards assuming ideal conditions, allowing for no losses, even those considered unavoidable. They will always result in unfavorable variances. Ideal standards cannot be used in forecasting and planning because they do not provide for normal inefficiencies.

❑ *Currently attainable (practical).* These apply to the service output possible if a nonprofit entity facility operated continuously, but allowing for normal losses such as holidays, vacations, and repairs. The standards presume efficient activity. They are possible but hard to achieve. Considered are normal events such as expected asset failure. Practial standards should be set high enough for motivation purposes and low enough to allow for normal interruptions. Besides pointing to abnormal deviations in costs, practical standards may be used in predicting cash flows and in planning. Attainable standards are usually used in practice.

❑ *Expected.* These are anticipated amounts based on foreseeable operating conditions and costs. They come very close to actual figures.

Budgets should be established at a realistic level. Those affected by the standards should participate in formalizing them so there will be internalization of goals. When reasonable standards exist, employees usually become aware of costs and attempt to achieve the maximum results at the lowest cost. Tight standards will discourage worker performance. On the other hand, loose standards result in inefficiency. If workers get bonuses for exceeding normal standards, such standards may be even more effective motivators.

A standard is not absolute and precise; it represents a range of possible acceptable results. Thus, variances can occur within a normal upper-lower limit. In determining tolerance limits, relative magnitudes are more important than absolute values. For example, if the budgeted cost for an activity is $300,000 a plus or minus range of $5,000 may be tolerable.

PLANNING VARIANCE

Planning variances occur when anticipated variables do not materialize. For instance, on January 1, the revenue projection may be based on considering the supply/demand relationship. However, because of actual conditions, the actual revenue may be considerably lower. This revenue volume variance may then be considered a planning error, and not a performance problem.

REVENUE VARIANCES

Revenue standards may be set to control and measure the effectiveness of marketing, as well as other relevant purposes such as stimulating sales, reallocating resources, and providing incentive awards. Sales quotas may be established. While the revenue quota is usually expressed in dollars, it may also be stated in volume. Other types of standards that may be established to evaluate revenue efforts are number of calls, new donors attracted, funds raised, number of regular donors retained, grants obtained, and contracts signed.

The revenue price variance reveals if the service is being rendered at a premium or discount. Revenue price variances may arise from uncontrollable conditions.

The analysis of revenue volume includes consideration of budgets, standards, plans, and costs. Costs must be compared to revenue. An unfavorable revenue volume variance may arise from deficient marketing or price reductions. If the unfavorable volume variance is coupled with a favorable price variance, the NPO may have lost revenue by raising its prices.

The revenue volume variance may be caused by unpredictable demand, lack of demand, or from poor revenue projections.

An unfavorable total revenue variance may point to a problem with promoting the nonprofit organization's message. Another possible reason for an unfavorable revenue situation may be a lack of quality control, substitution of poorer quality components and elements, or poor program structure.

The revenue variances (price and volume) may be prepared for revenue reporting overall and by segment.

An electronic worksheet can be used to compute revenue variances (refer to the July 1985 issue of *LOTUS*, pp. 46–48.)

COST VARIANCES

When a service is rendered, you must compute the following measures:

1. Actual cost equals actual price times actual quantity, where actual quantity equals actual quantity per unit of work times actual units of work performed.

2. Standard cost equals standard price times standard quantity, where standard quantity equals standard quantity per unit of work times actual units of work performed.

3. Total (control) variance equals actual cost less standard cost.

   Total (control) variance has the following components:

   ❏ Price (rate, cost) variance (Standard price versus actual price) × actual quantity

   ❏ Quantity (usage, efficiency) variance (Standard quantity versus actual quantity) × standard price

   Price variance and quantity variance are determined for both supplies and labor.

   A variance is favorable when actual cost is less than budgeted cost, and vice versa.

SUPPLIES VARIANCES

Quantity and delivery standards must be set before a standard price per unit can be determined. Supplies price standards must be established. The nonprofit organization should increase the initial standard price per unit to a standard weighted-average price per unit to incorporate anticipated price increases. The standard price should reflect the total cost of purchasing supplies, which includes the basic price minus discounts plus transportation, handling, and receiving. The standard price must coincide with the specific quality of supplies. In establishing the supplies price standard, the price should take into account the most economical order size and/or frequency of ordering. It is also assumed that buying, shipping, and warehousing will occur on favorable terms. Special bargain prices are ignored unless they are readily available. The supplies price standard should consider normal spoilage.

The supplies quantity variance is the responsibility of the supervisor. Supplies quantity standards are basically determined from specifications based on design and need. The standard quantity should be based on the most economical size and quality. It should incorporate spoilage and obsolescence considerations. The standard should take into account previous experience for the same or similar activity. Supplies standards may be assisted by evaluating prior experiences using descriptive statistics. Physical standards for supplies are based on determinations of type, quality, and quantity specifications. When many different kinds of supplies are required, the types and standard quantities of each supply type are itemized.

You cannot control supplies price variances when higher prices arise from inflation or shortages, or when there are rush orders.

If the supplies price variance is favorable, you would anticipate higher quality supplies being bought. Therefore, a favorable usage variance should arise. If it is not, an inconsistency exists. A favorable supplies price variance may occur due to other reasons, such as when actual price is below budgeted price due to excess supply of the item.

The controllable portion of a price variance should be highlighted from the uncontrollable in reports.

The responsible individual and reasons for an unfavorable supplies variance follow:

Purchasing manager

Failure to take discounts, failure to buy enough supplies of a certain class, emergency purchase required, overstated price, inadequate quantities, uneconomical size of purchase orders, misguided specifications, poor quality bought, and purchase at an irregular time.

Supervisor

Inadequately trained workers, deficient scheduling, and unanticipated volume changes.

Traffic management

Excessive transportation charges or too small an amount purchased.

Financial

Inadequate quantity purchased due to insufficient funds.

Budgeting

Inaccurate standard price.

Receiving

Inability to identify defective supplies.

LABOR VARIANCES

Standard labor rates may be based on the current rates adjusted for future changes in the following variables:

- ❒ Union contracts
- ❒ Changes in the mix of labor
- ❒ Changes in the operating environment
- ❒ Average experience of workers

The wage system affects the budgeted cost rates. Wage incentives can be tied to a standard cost system after standards have been formulated.

Direct labor quantities may be obtained from administrators by observing and timing workers. When salary rates are set by union contract, the labor rate variance will typically be minimal. The rate standard should be the average rate anticipated to occur during the planning period. Labor rates for the same activity may change because of seniority or union contract.

Labor time standards should include only the elements controllable by the employee or work center. If the prime purpose of a cost system is control, there should be a tight labor time standard. If costing or pricing is the major objective of the cost system, looser labor standards are required. Labor efficiency standards must also be estimated. The standard time may include allowances for normal breaks and personal needs.

Labor variances are computed in a way similar to that in which supplies variances are calculated.

POSSIBLE CAUSES OF UNFAVORABLE LABOR VARIANCES

For a labor price (rate) variance:

❐ Poor scheduling resulting in overtime work.

❐ Use of workers getting higher hourly rates than budgeted.

❐ Increase in wages.

For a labor efficiency (quantity) variance:

❐ Employee unrest.

❐ Poor supervision.

❐ Use of poor quality resources.

❐ Improperly trained workers.

❐ Power failures.

❐ Use of unskilled workers paid lower rates or the incorrect mixture of labor for a given task.

The possible causes for a labor price variance and the who or what is responsible follow:

Personnel: poor description of job or excessive salaries

Union agreement: use of overpaid or too many workers

Planning: overtime and inadequate scheduling

If there is a lack of skilled workers, an unfavorable labor price variance may not be avoidable.

Price variances arising from outside factors are beyond the administrator's control (e.g., a new minimum wage set by the government).

The responsible party and reason for an unfavorable efficiency variance follows:

Maintenance: inadequate functioning of equipment

Purchasing: poor quality resources

Personnel: employee unrest and inadequately trained workers

Supervisor: improper supervision, incorrect mixture of labor and idle time

A monthly labor report should be prepared. An unfavorable labor efficiency variance may reveal that better physical resources are required, improved operating methods are needed, and better employee training and development are called for.

If there is a permanent change in labor needed or in the labor wage rate, the administrator may want to switch to more capital assets than labor.

A favorable labor efficiency variance combined with an unfavorable labor rate variance may indicate that more skilled labor was used than needed. However, the supervisor would be justified in doing this if a rush order occurred in which the price was going to be upwardly adjusted.

Exhibit 1 presents a daily labor mix report.

EXHIBIT 1

Daily Labor Mix Report

Department Level	Skill	Actual Hours	Actual Hours in Standard Proportions	Output Variance
A				
B				
C				

Comparisons should be made between budgeted and actual operations for the current year or between actual operations for the prior year and those for the current year. Deviations between budget and actual may be examined for the entire nonprofit organization or by service category.

SERVICE VARIANCES

Standards may be used for office personnel doing clerical work, and a standard unit expense for processing a form (e.g., welfare application). The variance between the actual cost of processing a form and the standard cost can be evaluated by administrative staff and corrective action taken. The number of payroll checks prepared should be a reliable measure of the payroll department's activity. The number of invoices or vouchers apply to billing and accounts payable. In these two instances, a standard cost per unit could be based on the variable costs.

Variances of time spent and charitable donations received may be used to appraise fund-raising activities.

Variances may also be expressed in physical, rather than dollar, measures. Examples of physical measures are number of welfare recipients serviced and turnover rate in social workers.

Cost variances may be reported to administrators in special reports. For example, the variance in time and cost to process payments to retirees may be appraised. Exhibit 2 presents an illustrative format for a variance analysis report for a service activity.

EXHIBIT 2

Variance Analysis Report for a Service Activity

Function	Time Variance	Cost Variance
Processing orders		
Processing reports		
Processing invoices		
Preparing checks		
Filing paid vouchers and supporting documentation		

Variances for these activities are useful only for large nonprofit organizations where activity volume permits the arrangement and evaluation of repetitive tasks.

USING VARIANCES TO EVALUATE MARKETING EFFORTS

Before establishing a standard in a given territory, you should evaluate prior, current and projected conditions for the nonprofit entity itself and that given geographical area. Standards vary depending upon geographical location.

Some fund-raising costs can be standardized, such as presentations for which a standard time per call can be set. Direct efforts should be related to distance traveled, call frequency, etc. If percentages are based on charitable contributions generated, standards can be based on a percentage of net contributions.

Time and motion studies are usually a better means to establish standards than previous performance, because the past may include inefficiencies.

Cost variances for promotion activities may apply to the territory, service, or personnel.

Actual funds raised may not be the best measure of fund-raisers' performance because they don't consider differing territory potentials. Further, a high volume fund-raiser may have to absorb a high promotion cost. The evaluation of fund-raisers based on the trend in funds generated over the years shows signs of improvement.

Travel expense standards are often formulated based on distance traveled and the frequency of potential calls. Standards for fund-raisers' automobile expenses may be expressed in cost per mile traveled and cost per day. The standard might apply to cost per donor or cost per dollar of funds obtained. The standards also do not consider volume mix.

Consideration of fixed versus variable cost for an activity is essential in cost control and in deciding if a service line should be dropped or added.

You should evaluate fund-raisers' effectiveness within a territory, including hours spent and expenses incurred.

The control variance is segregated into fund-raiser's days and fund-raiser's costs.

Variance in days equals:
(Actual days versus standard days) times standard rate per day

Variance in costs equals:
(Actual rate versus standard rate) times actual days

Total variance equals:
Actual calls × actual amount raised
Standard calls × standard amount raised

The elements of the total variance above equal:

Variance in calls:
(Actual calls versus standard calls) × standard sale

Variance in funds raised:
(Actual sale versus standard sale) × standard calls

Joint variance: (Actual calls versus standard calls) × (Actual sale versus standard sale)

Additional performance measures of fund-raiser's effectiveness include meeting quotas, number of donor contributions from existing and new donors, and the relationship between costs and dollar donations obtained.

Are fund-raising expenses realistic considering the contributions generated? Are expenses beyond limitations pointing to possible mismanagement and violation of controls?

Standards that may be used in administrative activities follow:

Administrative Activity	*Standard of Measurement*
Personnel	Number of employees
Clerical	Number of items handled
Orders	Number of orders handled
Check writing	Number of checks written
Billing	Number of invoices

Performance measures may be of a nonmonetary nature, such as the number of files processed, the number of calls taken, and the number of forms prepared. Variances between the dollar and nondollar variables can be determined and evaluated.

CONTROLLING CAPITAL EXPENDITURES

Variance reports are helpful in controlling capital expenditures by evaluating the actual versus budgeted costs, as well as actual versus budgeted times for proposals at each stage of activity. Such reports enable administrators to take corrective cost-saving steps, such as modifying schedules. The project's director is accountable for the costs and time budget. Component elements within the project are appraised. Variances help to measure operational results and budgeting efficiency. Further, estimated cash flows of the project should be compared with actual cash flows.

Exhibits 3, 4, and 5 present capital expenditure budgets.

EXHIBIT 3

Year-to-Date Comparisons of Actual to Budget Capital
Expenditures

Type	Budgeted Projects	Projects Not Budgeted	Total	Amount Budgeted	Actual Expenditures	Over (Under) Budget

EXHIBIT 4

Capital Expenditure Performance Report (Actual vs. Estimated)

Item	Authorized Amount	Actual Amount to Date	Variance	Percent	Analysis
1	$10,000	$10,200	$200	.02	Higher prices for component services
2	6,000	6,300	300	.05	Delay due to strike

EXHIBIT 5

Capital Expenditure Progress Report

Item Number	Description	Amount Approved	Expected Date of Completion	Expend-itures to Date	Amount Needed for Completion	Total	Budget	Variance	Remark

Exhibits 6 and 7 present project status reports.

EXHIBIT 6

Project Budget Report

Number	Name	Hours	Professional Salaries	Clerical Salaries	Consultant Salaries	Other Expenses	Total	Commit- ments	Estimated Cost to Complete	Total Cost	Project Budget	Under or Over Budget

EXHIBIT 7

Project Status Report

Project Identifier	Month			Cumulative to Date			Estimate Cost to Complete			Project Budget	Cost (Over) or Under
	Manhours	Salaries	Other Expense	Total	Manhours	Amount	Purchase Commitments	Manhours	Amount	Total Cost		
Project A												
Project B												
Project C												
Total												

EVALUATING PERFORMANCE WITH VARIANCE ANALYSIS REPORTS

Performance reports may be prepared examining the difference between budgeted and actual figures for: (1) cost, quantity, and quality; (2) revenue; (3) asset turnover; and (4) growth rate.

Variance reports pose questions instead of answering them. For example, revenue volume may be down due to deficiencies in fund-raising efforts. Variance analysis reports may be stated not only in dollars, but also in ratios, graphs, percentages, and narrative.

Performance reports are designed to motivate administrators and workers to alter their activities and plans when variances exist. They should be brief and should emphasize potential difficulties and opportunities. A section for comments should be provided so that explanations may be given for variances.

The timeliness of performance reports and detail provided depends upon the level the report is directed to and the nature of the costs whose performance is being measured. One administrator may need weekly information while another may require monthly information. As you become more distant from the actual activity, the time interval for performance appraisal lengthens. Further, as you climb the ladder in the nonprofit organization, performance reports contain information in summarized form.

Performance reports should include analytical information. To obtain this, you should appraise such source data as requisitions, labor cards, and work orders. Reasons for inefficiency and excessive costs should be noted, such as those due to malfunctions and low quality.

For labor, the productivity measurement ratio of volume ouput per labor hour should be calculated. Additionally, the output of the individual should be compared to the "normal" output specified at the beginning of the reporting period. Operating efficiency can thus be measured. A labor efficiency ratio can also be calculated which is the deviation between actual hours incurred and budgeted hours.

Revenue and cost information should be provided by service line, case, patient, and geographic area. Analysis in terms of strengths and weaknesses should be made. Effectiveness measures should be employed for fund raisers by donation generated, call frequency, incentives, personnel costs, and dollar value of contributions generated per hours spent.

Cost control is initiated when such costs are assigned to functional groups such as geographic location and service line. Budgeted costs and rates should be provided and comparisons made between budgeted costs and actual costs at the end of the reporting period.

Exhibits 8 and 9 present variance analysis reports.

EXHIBIT 8 Budget Report

	Current Month			*Year-to-Date*		
Project	*Budget*	*Actual*	*Variance*	*Budget*	*Actual*	*Variance*

EXHIBIT 9 Budget Report

	Current Month			Cumulative		
	Actual	Budget	Variance	Actual	Budget	Variance
Number of staff						
Expenses						
Salaries						
Fringe benefits						
Dues						
Rent						
Insurance						
Depreciation						
Supplies						
Promotion and entertainment						
Travel						
Total expenses						
Percentage of net sales						

STUDYING POSSIBILITIES WITH "WHAT-IF" BUDGETING

Spreadsheet programs should be used in preparing budgets based on "what-if" scenarios. The effect of changes in one or more budget assumptions or related budgeted figures are quickly and clearly shown. This allows for consideration of various possibilities. For example, the effect of a change in the expected amount of contributions on related financial items, such as costs, can easily be seen.

With the increased use of the computer in financial modeling and budgeting, managers are developing the ability to compare actual activity to planned future conditions. They can quickly retrieve historic data and analyze many alternatives to the initial budget. They can ask such questions as:

❐ "What if revenues increase 20% with more innovative fund-raising techniques?"

❐ "What if a larger budget is allowed to accommodate a revised promotion program?"

❐ "What if wages were increased 5% in order to attract more qualified employees?"

The questions usually raised during the "what-if" analysis are narrower in scope than those raised during the long-term planning process and represent more of a fine-tuning and balancing process.

TRIMMING THE BUDGET WITH THE LEAST HARMFUL RESULTS

When a nonprofit entity has financial problems or the state of the economy is poor, it may be forced to trim the budget. The budget cuts should be in the least important areas. Further, some costs may be reduced because they are least essential to satisfying the goals and objectives of the nonprofit organization. A thorough analysis is needed of which programs and costs may be reduced without serious consequences.

During a mid-year review of operations, it may become necessary to modify the budget because more up-to-date information has been received by the organization. Actual income estimates may now be lower or cost estimates may be higher, but in either case the budget needs to be revised.

As line items are appraised, attention should be given to items where the number of service units can be reduced without significantly detracting from service quality. Attention may be given to items that can be deferred until the next funding period: however, the postponement of routine maintenance for extended time periods can be costly and potentially catastrophic. Some programs may be downgraded, where the same service level or comparable results are sought by pursuing less expensive means. These changes will undoubtedly have an affect on operations, but they should not affect the program's basic scope, character, quality, patients, or result levels.

If it becomes apparent that further budget reductions are required, there may be very significant program changes. This is a typical situation in periods of declining resources. It then becomes necessary to review all program plans in conjunction with the resource requirements developed for budgeting purposes.

Additional planning and administrative approvals will be needed to reduce the scope, volume, quality, client base, or character of the program. Community members may be invited into the planning process to provide their input into program cutbacks. Program effects will include deleting a component or a particular service, decreasing an area served, establishing stringent program admission requirements, or reducing service hours. The feasible program modifications should be taken into account and evaluated from the view of the remaining program value and cost. This will be an easy process if the budget line items have been separated into three groups based on priority, as discussed below.

The first group contains all items that provide the most immediate and direct benefits to the intended users of the program. Personnel salaries will probably fit into this group since most services are labor intensive. Other items are those without which the program cannot perform its function; for example, telephones for a call-in help service or textbooks for a school room.

The second category contains all items that are indirectly related or the most distant from the benefits provided to the users. Indirect overhead is included. Office equipment would fit as well, unless it is vital for the service. For example, a computer terminal for an on-line doctor referral service would belong in the first category. The second group may make the operation run more smoothly, comfortably, or efficiently, but their absence does not disable the program.

The third category consists of anything that does not belong in the first two groups. Some secretarial and support costs may be assigned here, as well as the costs for some operating supplies.

STUDYING VARIANCES HELPS FUTURE BUDGETING

Variance analysis is important in the nonprofit organization to evaluate all aspects of operations. Variances should be studied if the benefits outweigh the costs of appraising and correcting the source of the variance. Variance analysis reports should be in dollars and percentages.

Significant unfavorable variances must be studied to determine whether they are controllable internally or uncontrollable because they relate solely to outside factors. When controllable, immediate corrective action must be undertaken to handle the problem. The administrator should provide his/her recommendations. If a variance is favorable, an examination should be made of the reasons for it so that the entity's policy may include the positive aspects found. Further, the responsible unit for a favorable variance should be recognized and rewarded.

Different degrees of significance of variances may exist including:

❒ The decision model was inappropriate taking into account the goal to be achieved and thus a more appropriate model should be formulated.

❒ The variance is intolerable and thus either performance must be improved or new standards developed considering the present environment.

❒ The variance is tolerable and within a normal range and thus no remedial action is needed.

Reports on operating performance should reveal where performance varies from standard, the trend of performance, and the causes for the variances.

Reporting systems differ among nonprofit organizations regarding the frequency and timeliness of reports, details provided, data arrangement, employee distribution, and amount of variances requiring follow-up. Variances can be appraised by division, department, and responsibility unit. Variance evaluation should be made to the point that additional savings from cost control justify the additional cost of analysis and reporting. If responsibility for a variance is joint, corrective steps should also be joint. If correction of an unfavorable variance involves a conflict with an organization policy, the policy should be reappraised and perhaps altered. If the policy is not changed, the variance should be deemed uncontrollable.

Even if a variance is below a cut-off percent or dollar figure, administrators may want to study it if the variance is repeatedly unfavorable because it may indicate a problem (e.g., wasteful practice, poor supervision). The cumulative effect of a repeated minor unfavorable variance may be just as harmful as an occasional one.

Common reasons why budget and actual figures differ are the failure to consider organizational changes, cost classification, consolidation, new policies, and different revenue or expense recognition methods being used for budget versus accounting purposes.

Variances must be evaluated because they furnish useful information to administrators as a foundation for budgeting in the future. A variance can be caused by poorly prepared forecasts such as incomplete or imperfect ones. For example, a nonprofit organization that establishes a budget based on last year's budget with no adjustment for inflation or activity-level changes will undoubtedly report several variances. By using the personal computer, administrators are not only receiving variance reports, they are also taking things one step further and asking many "what if" questions.

Chapter 9

Zero-Base Budgeting for Optimum Project Planning

Zero-base budgeting (ZBB), also called priority-based budgeting, is a review of activities, programs, or operations with a view toward improving cost efficiency. It involves appraising competing alternative programs, choosing discretionary funding levels, evaluating effectiveness, and examining priorities. Unit objectives should be linked to overall targets.

Under ZBB, budgeted figures for functions or activities are expressed at minimum funding levels. The survival level is the service level and funding below which the decision unit might be eliminated. Anything above the minimum level has to be justified. Under ZBB, the administrator must justify all activities as if they were being looked upon for the first time. For example, if a manager wants to render service x, he/she must be able to justify it. If he/she cannot do so, that service will not be supported. ZBB begins fresh each year, ignoring what took place in prior years. The emphasis is on the current and future practicality of the item. An objective of ZBB is to prevent previously approved, but currently unnecessary or inefficient, activities to continue.

ZBB results in the efficient allocation of resources. An important aspect to ZBB is evaluating the input-output relationship. However, do not devote too much time to projects not likely to be funded. There are several questions that need to be answered:

❑ What are the objectives of the function?

❏ Are objectives being accomplished and measured?

❏ What are the consequences of not funding the operation?

❏ How will an alternative affect the quality of service?

❏ How will the alternative affect other costs and activities?

The typical budgeting approach involves adding or subtracting a percentage increase or decrease to the previous period's budget to derive a new budget. The prior period's costs are considered basic and emphasis is usually on what modifications are required for the coming year. Adjustments may be made for losses, inflation, etc. Have there been any economic and political changes that will bear upon the activity to be conducted? The traditional method concentrates on inputs rather than outputs applicable to goal achievement and thus does not require the appraisal of the nonprofit organization's operations from a cost/benefit perspective. Exhibit 1 highlights the differences between traditional and zero-base budgeting.

EXHIBIT 1
Traditional vs. Zero-Base Budgeting

Traditional	*Zero-Base Budgeting*
1. Begins from existing base.	1. Begins with zero base.
2. Evaluates cost/benefit for new activities.	2. Evaluates cost/benefit for all activities.
3. Results in a nonalternative budget.	3. Results in choosing several service and cost levels.
4. Begins with dollars.	4. Begins with objectives and activities.
5. Does not take into account new operating approaches as important elements in the process.	5. Explicitly looks to new approaches.

UNDERSTANDING THE ZERO-BASE BUDGETING PROCESS

The ZBB process begins with formulating the nonprofit's objectives and assumptions. Assumptions must be made of increases in wages and fringe benefits, inflation rates, etc. ZBB should be "phased in" gradually, testing it in one department or responsibility center before adopting it throughout the organization. Some nonprofits initially apply ZBB to only about 30-percent of their budgets until they gather adequate experience. There should be flexibility to adjust the levels at which packages are developed, the review and ranking process, the planning assumptions, and time limitations.

ZBB mandates that each supervisor justify his/her budget request in detail from a zero base, and thus requires an evaluation of the output from each operation or function of a particular cost/responsibility center. The consequences of rejecting a proposed project must also be taken into account.

The activities of the segment or center are expressed as *decision packages* that are to be appraised and ranked in priority order at various levels. Structured information is ultimately gathered that helps allocate funds to those activities that will achieve the greatest good. Exhibit 2 enumerates the process in formulating and implementing ZBB.

EXHIBIT 2 ZBB Process

1. Planning assumptions

2. Ranking proposals

3. Appraising and controlling

4. Preparing the budget

5. Identifying decision units

6. Evaluating decision units

A typical zero-base budget is presented in Exhibit 3.

EXHIBIT 3

Children's Playhouse
Nonprofit Performing Arts
Sample Zero-Base Budget
For the Year Ending December 31, 19XX

	Carnival	Candy Drive	Cake and Dessert Auction	Recycling Program	Yearly Skit Program	Total
Revenues:						
Sales	$8,000.00	$3,500.00	$2,000.00	$1,000.00	$1,000.00	$15,500.00
Expenditures:						
Equipment rental	2,000.00	0.00	0.00	0.00	0.00	2,000.00
Facilities rental	1,000.00	0.00	450.00	0.00	350.00	1,800.00
Security	100.00	0.00	100.00	0.00	100.00	300.00
Total expenses	3,100.00	0.00	550.00	0.00	450.00	4,100.00
Excess Revenue Over Expenditures	$4,900.00	$3,500.00	$1,450.00	$1,000.00	$550.00	$11,400.00

DEVELOPING DECISION PACKAGES FOR EXISTING AND NEW PROGRAMS

In the beginning step of ZBB, decision packages are formulated. The decision package includes a description, specific measures, and responsible individuals. Each decision package indicates the supervisor's recommended way of achieving a service in cost and time. Alternative ways of providing the service in dollars and time are also specified. For example, reducing quality will lower cost. Shortening the time may increase costs because of overtime. Consideration should be given to the track records of the decision packages. Have any shown poor results in previous years? The information should be arranged in a standardized format sheet. Administrators will analyze these decision packages for approval or disapproval. A decision package contains the following information:

❐ Description of the activity and reasons to conduct it

❐ Statement of objectives and benefits of the program

❐ The agenda to achieve the objective

❐ The priority of the program

❐ Costs to be incurred and time needed, including analysis

❐ Expected benefits from the program. The manager should ask "What am I getting from this expenditure?"

❏ Alternative methods to achieve the activity in time and cost

❏ Outcome measures

❏ Resources needed

❏ Support required by decision units

❏ Staff and support required to carry out the activity

❏ Relevant information such as legal implications, technical and operational feasibility, and uncertainties

❏ Consequences of not conducting an activity

The following decision packages arise as a result of the formulation stage:

❏ A decision package in which an activity is kept "as is." It is status quo in that the current level and activity method is presented in decision package format.

❏ A decision package for new operations or programs.

❏ A decision package consisting of a base level plus incremental amounts of activity for ongoing programs. Alternatives are presented.

Realistic objectives must be set for each decision package. A computer should be employed to track decision packages so that financial data may easily be obtained and proper comparisons can be conducted. An internal audit should be made to ascertain whether the NPO has chosen the "right" decision packages. Actual results are compared to budgeted amounts, and the causes for any deviations determined.

Decision packages can be either mutually exclusive or incremental. The former are alternative packages, meaning that the acceptance of one prevents the acceptance of another. Incremental packages relate to different effort levels. For example, one package may require 500 labor hours per month while another may need 700 hours for that same time period.

Some packages apply to the long-term while others to the near-term. Will there be immediate and tangible results? Resources are matched with objectives. Resources are directed to higher payout areas.

Be careful that decision packages are complete and not lumped together. A problem may exist when decision packages cross functional and organizational lines.

BREAKING THE BUDGET DOWN INTO ACTIVITY UNITS

The activity unit is the basic cost element of ZBB. It is the lowest unit within the nonprofit organization for which the budget is prepared. It may be a program, activity, function, line item, or organization unit. An administrator is responsible for this unit's performance. The unit is evaluated to assure it is achieving the objectives. Examples of decision units are research and development, legal services, quality control, and computer services. Activities fixed by statute, government practice, or other constraints are given priority. In some instances, an activity may be required to improve morale.

Decision units must be at a high organizational level so that the responsible administrator has effective control over the operations. Decision units should typically be chosen to parallel the flow of responsibility for budgetary decision making. Comparisons may be made for decision units that are similar in size in personnel and dollars. The definition of the activity units should be specific so as to minimize complications resulting from a multiplicity of activities in a decision unit.

APPRAISING DECISION UNITS FOR BEST RESULTS

Once the activity objectives have been specified, the decision administrator describes how his/her department currently operates and how the resources may be used (personnel and dollars). The description of operations cannot be excessively detailed, but should include the important activities, and is usually organized to define the work flow.

Productivity and effectiveness measures are required. In making decisions, financial information, performance standards, and work load must be taken into account for an activity. Examples of measurement performances include:

- ❐ *Internal audit*—audits should be conducted of information provided by each reporting unit.

- ❐ *Quality control*—number of problems.

ZBB requires that alternative ways be taken into account. After evaluating both the current and alternative operating methods, the administrators and managers select the best method. Alternative operating modes include decentralizing the function, centralizing the activity, combining functions, eliminating the operation, and contracting the activity.

ZBB must be controlled by using measures such as the following:

❐ Quarterly plan and budget modifications for the organization and decision units based on changing circumstances and data.

❐ Quarterly evaluation using pre-established performance standards.

❐ Monthly financial review of each decision unit based on a comparison of actual costs to budgeted costs, and actual receipts to budgeted receipts.

RANKING PROPOSALS FOR BUDGET CONSIDERATION

Ranking is based on input from decision unit managers and staff. Consideration should be given to quantitative and qualitative variables. Cost/benefit analysis is performed for each decision unit.

Decision packages are ranked in the order of decreasing benefit. Ranking determines the advantages to be obtained at each expenditure level and identifies the implications of rejecting those decision packages ranked below that particular expenditure level.

In ranking, the manager determines what is the most important service of his/her unit. The highest priority is assigned to the minimum increment of service, which is the amount of service the organization must engage in to render useful service. Additional service increments are then provided in priority order.

Senior administrators should conduct the final ranking of decision packages prepared by managers in the various segments and responsibility units. The initial rankings should be performed at the lower levels where the packages are initially developed. The intermediate rankings should be conducted at the middle managerial levels after the packages are studied, giving consideration to lower level recommendations. When the lower level recommendation is rejected, the reasons should be communicated to those involved. To avoid overwhelming higher managerial levels with excessive detail, the ranked decision packages may be combined into the major candidates for review and ranking.

A cutoff must be set for programs and activities at each of the approved levels. For example, a 60-percent cutoff line may be established for middle management while an 80-percent cutoff line may be established for upper management. The 60-percent middle management cutoff line would require the manager to remove the highest ranked packages until the expenditures represented for the removed packages equal 60-percent of last year's budget. These packages are then studied for reasonableness. Those remaining decision packages would then be carefully evaluated.

A ranking table is prepared for the decision packages of each responsibility center. This table assists in deciding which proposals will be financed. However, you should also rank nonfunded packages so that they may be added to the budget if additional dollars become available. Additionally, lower priority items now may later become higher priority items. Adjustments should be made to the priority listing depending upon changing events.

Various ranking approaches may be employed, including single standard, voting, and major category. *Single standard* is an approach most appropriate for similar packages. All packages are evaluated based on only one aspect such as cost/benefit ratio, return on investment, net present value, profit, or dollar savings. This method is not good for dissimilar packages because it may omit an essential program like health and safety.

In the *voting approach*, a voting committee is formed. Each committee member appraises the decision packages. The packages are then discussed at the committee meeting. A committee vote determines the ranking. In any case, the committee does approve legally required programs. Further, it gives special attention to projects involving minimum requirements to the organization.

The *major category system* segregates decision packages into categories. A ranking is then performed of decision packages by category. Some categories are more essential than others. Therefore, budgets vary depending on the category. For example, a category having substantial growth potential may be funded four times more than one having questionable prospects. Therefore, the former category will likely have a greater percentage of its decision packages funded. This approach is sound because increased emphasis is given to the "key" categories.

After allocation decisions, detailed budgets are prepared. These budgets are usually prepared based on incremental activities shown on the ranking table.

EXAMPLE 1

An administrator prepares a decision package for each service to be performed in a unit. Assuming 300 possible services (old and new), there will be 300 decision packages.

A representative decision package for service A to be rendered in Department X is shown in the diagram.

Service A - Decision Package   Cost   Time

```
┌─────────────────────────────┐  Alternative A
│                             │
├─────────────────────────────┤  Recommended way
│                             │
└─────────────────────────────┘  Alternative B
```

Each of the decision packages for all 300 services is then submitted to upper administrators. They then appraise the decision packages from all the units including that of Department X. A budget ceiling places a dollar cutoff on how many services may be funded. A priority ranking is given to all the packages. Those above the budget cutoff will be funded in some way. In this example, the decision package for service X may be rejected because it does not pass the cutoff. If it is accepted, upper management will give permission to the department administrator to perform the service either as recommended or in an alternative manner. An alternative approach may be chosen because it is less costly or requires less time.

PROS AND CONS OF ZERO-BASE BUDGETING

The advantages of ZBB are that it:

- ❑ Improves efficiency and effectiveness.
- ❑ Aids in formulating priorities and standards to be achieved.
- ❑ Matches service levels to resources. Resources should be used to achieve the best results.

❑ Makes the budgeting process more logical and less political.

❑ Improves planning and communication, such as among upper, middle, and lower management. All organizational levels are involved. Subordinates should participate because they have on-the-job experience that can be of assistance to supervisors. Creativity is encouraged by participants.

❑ Allows senior administrators to define service levels required for each responsibility or activity unit.

❑ Encourages the reorganization of activities to achieve overall objectives and enhance performance.

❑ Identifies and controls resources. The enumeration of alternatives may result in innovative and improved ways to perform.

❑ Assists in cost control.

❑ Allows for alternative courses of action.

❑ Results in sound planning.

The disadvantages of ZBB are that:

❑ Much paperwork and forms are involved.

❑ Employees may consider ZBB as a threat.

❑ It is difficult to determine performance levels.

❑ Competition instead of cooperation may arise.

❑ ZBB takes much time to implement because line managers are starting at minimal funding amounts. Line managers may not have sufficient time to spend.

❑ Upper administrators may not support the process and disregard ZBB data and implications.

❑ ZBB is expensive to implement. Benefits may not justify substantial cost outlays.

❑ Ranking may be a problem because of the interrelationship among decision packages.

❏ Resistance arises because employees are reluctant to change their ways. For instance, lower levels may consider the process a waste of time, and are being forced by higher levels to do it. Stress may be created.

Because of the problems of cost and time, it may be best to use ZBB over several years (e.g., three years) instead of one year. To conduct it annually may not be cost beneficial.

ZERO-BASE BUDGETING PRESENTS DIFFERENT CHOICES

In zero-base budgeting, administrators identify different levels of effort to performing each activity. They must identify a minimum spending level—often about 75 percent of their current operating level—and then identify in separate decision packages the costs and benefits of additional spending levels for that activity. This analysis forces every administrator to consider and appraise a spending level lower than the current operating level; gives management the alternative of eliminating an activity or selecting from several effort levels; and allows trade-offs and shifts in expenditure levels among organizational units.

Zero-base budgeting provides to administrators detailed information concerning money needed to accomplish desired ends. It spotlights redundancies and duplication of efforts among departments, focuses on dollars needed for programs instead of on the percentage increase (or decrease) from the prior year, specifies priorities within and among departments, allows comparisons across organizational lines as to the respective priorities funded, and allows a performance audit to determine whether each activity or operation was performed efficiently.

As a budgeting process, ZBB is a planning and control tool and includes the elements of objective setting, operational decision making, and evaluation. Its method is characterized as a bottom-to-top communication process. Discrete activities for decision units are evaluated and developed in the form of decision packages within the context of a minimum effort level. Further, any additional activity for a decision unit can be formulated in an independent series of incremental decision packages—each one having a specified dollar cost. In addition to the requested dollar funding, all of the narrative explaining why the expenditure is needed, consequences of not performing an activity, alternative procedures for accomplishing the goals, cross-impact analysis with other decision units, and cost/benefit analysis are included in the decision package documentation. There is no theoretical limit to the number of decision units identified or the number of decision packages developed within each decision unit.

THE VALUE OF ZERO-BASE BUDGETING

ZBB is employed to describe the operations or activities of the NPO. It achieves many benefits at different funding levels via priority ranking. It enumerates alternative service options to be achieved that best meet the budgetary requirements of the organization. ZBB enables administrators to consider the value of the units relative to the whole organization. However, unexpected eventualities may mandate immediate revision to decision packages. It is a continual process. Some nonprofit organizations have used ZBB procedures to establish a systematic plan for reviewing all programs over a period of years rather than each time a budget plan is formulated. A system of reevaluation such as ZBB can be cumbersome if used for every budgetary development cycle, but if used over a period of time, it can aid administrators in eliminating programs that no longer satisfy the needs of the people the organization serves.

Ideally, the ZBB process eliminates duplicate and overlapping programs and will require administrative boards to more effectively establish priorities and allocate their resources. Moreover, the careful examination of programs results in reduced expenditures and increased efficiency, and will provide middle management with useful information not previously available.

ESTABLISHING PROJECT BUDGETS TO MEET GOALS

Project or program budgeting should be integrated into the financial and managerial systems. Programs may be by division, department, or segment within the department. The program budget is the projected cost of conducting outputs including operations, activities, or services. Programming is structuring the methods to achieve a desired result. For example, a program budget may assign financial resources to a specific organization function such as crime prevention and traffic management.

Goals are identified and the program to achieve that goal is set. Determine for each program benefits to be achieved, activity costs, funding, personnel requirements, risks, and time needed to achieve. There is an evaluation of alternatives to determine the most efficient and least costly way to achieve program objectives. The steps to accomplish the goal should be enumerated. Scarce resources are optimally allocated to projects and programs. Program budgeting requires a detailed schedule to accomplish steps.

Program budgeting accumulates and evaluates detailed plans. It includes a combination of resources (capital, labor, raw materials, machinery, facilities, manpower) to achieve a goal within the planning period. Alternatives are appraised. The budget implements the long-term plan, and decision-making moves progressively downward. The emphasis is on output goals of services instead of input goals. Program budgeting is future-oriented, looking at the effect on the future of present decisions and choices. It involves allocating resources and emphasizing operations to achieve program objectives.

Program budgets are established for projects or programs of a one-time, long-term nature involving substantial cash outlays. Problems should be anticipated. Responsibility should be assigned for specific activities. Project costs should be appraised for reasonableness. There may have to be adjustments to the plan.

A cost/benefit analysis for programs should be performed. Programs should be prioritized. The interrelationship between programs must be specified.

Costs may be traced to individual projects as well as to individuals generating those costs. This is achieved by giving each project a number and requiring employees to key in code numbers when requisitioning supplies, filling-out expense reimbursement forms, and for wages directly applicable to the project.

An objective is to maximize the program's output subject to budget limitations. A budget ceiling may be set based on previous year's sales, desired growth rate, competition, and future expectations. Program activities include public relations, training, research and development, engineering, and maintenance.

Recurring programs should be periodically reviewed. Older programs may be out-of-date or have lost community interest. Should a program be restructured or merged to better achieve goals and improve efficiency?

Project benefits are used for capital assets and research and development programs. Examples are planning and budgeting for a new product line, capital facilities, and a government contract. The project should be segregated into major tasks or activities, which should then be subdivided into sub-activities. Program budgeting examines the tasks to complete the program, the manpower needed, and how long each operation takes. Work packages have to be approved by cost centers. A representative work-authorization form is shown in Exhibit 4.

EXHIBIT 4

Work Authorization Form

Project:						
Work-package number:						
Issue date:						
Revision date:						
Revision number:						
Work	Cost	Labor	Beginning	Ending		
Description		*Center*	*Materials*	*Hours*	*Date*	*Date*

A time sheet should be prepared for project activities. The progress in meeting time deadlines should be noted. A time schedule should be established for each stage of the project. The schedule should be seperately stated for the planning phases, budgeting, and programming. A bar chart may be used to chart activity times. Activities may be scheduled using the Program Evaluation and Review Technique (PERT). Quality of work should be inspected at key points.

BIBLIOGRAPHY

Becwar, Gregory E. and Armitage, Jack L.. "Zero-Base Budgeting: Is It Really Dead?" *Ohio CPA Journal* (Winter 1989), pp. 52-54.

Bergeron, P.M. "Zero-Base Budgeting: A Methodology for Linking Action Plans to Program Goals" *Cost and Management* (March/April, 1979), pp. 11-17.

Cheek, Logan M. *Zero-Base Budgeting Comes of Age*. New York: Amacon, 1977.

Fogarty, Andrew B. and Turnbull, Augustus B. III. "Legislative Oversight Through a Rotation Zero-Base Budget" *State and Local Government Review* (January 1987), pp. 18-22.

Foskett, D.J. and Brindley, Lynne. "Zero-Base Budgeting: The Aston Experience" *Library Management* (1991), pp. 25-33.

Herzlinger, Regina E. "Zero-Base Budgeting in the Federal Government: A Case Study" *Sloan Management Review* (Winter 1989), pp. 3-14.

Phyrr, Peter A. *Zero-Base Budgeting*. John Wiley and Sons. 1973.

Shinn, Linda J. and Sturgeon, M. Sue. "Budgeting from Ground Zero." *Association Management* (September 1990), pp. 45-48.

Stonich, Paul J. *Zero-Base Planning and Budgeting*. Homewood: Dow Jones-Irwin, 1977.

Williams, John J. "Zero-Base Budgeting and Traditional Budgeting in Perspective." *Cost and Management* (1990), pp. 245-255.

Wise, David. "Better Budgeting for Better Results: The Role of Zero-Base Budgets" *Management Accounting* (May 1988), pp. 35-36.

Part III

Budgeting for Specific Types of Nonprofit Organizations

Chapter 10

Budgeting for Hospitals and the Health Care Industry

The hospital industry has faced many challenges in recent years. In particular, cost accounting methods in hospitals have come under intense scrutiny due to a variety of factors such as increased government legislation, strong competition, pressure by third party payers, rising public demand for quality care at reasonable cost, and concern by hospitals themselves for the constant need to keep up with the rapid expansion in medical technology. An aging population of baby-boomers is creating additional strain on resources, and the current recession with the loss of jobs and medical benefits has intensified the argument for national health insurance and the reformation of the health care industry.

The majority of hospitals in the United States enjoy tax-exempt status and are operating on a break-even operating basis with a modest one or two percent overall gain per year in funding. These nonprofit care centers are under expanding pressure, their mission is seen as questionable, and their community services perceived as inadequate given the tax breaks they receive. At the federal level, it's clear that with the size of the federal deficit and the decrease in Medicare and Medicaid reimbursements, the government will not bail out the hospitals if they should be unable to meet financial obligations. In fact, the current proposed reformations in the health care industry may make things worse.[1]

At the present time, taxing authorities at all levels of government are taking another look at exemptions for not-for-profit charitable hospitals.

The pressure is increasing at the state and local levels due to their own need to generate revenues from any source. This means that there exists a very real potential for new tax liabilities for the already financially troubled hospitals.

When the Medicare/Medicaid program was instituted in 1965, the legislation included a provision that reimbursed hospitals for reasonable operating costs. The United States prospered at that time, and so did the health care industry. Competition existed, but the focus was primarily on being the first to acquire the latest technology. Challenges from health maintenance organizations (HMOs) and preferred provider organizations (PPOs) did not become serious until the 1980s. Cost benefit analyses and cost effective decisions were given little attention; hospitals were favorably perceived by the public, profits were de-emphasized, and retained earnings were used for capital investment and expansion.

In 1983, the government changed its Medicare policy from cost reimbursement to a price-per-case basis. Under the diagnostic related group plan (DRG), payment was allocated according to the diagnosed illness. Medical institutions began to look for ways to recover their losses and, with a surplus of hospital beds, some opted to become HMOs or PPOs offering discounted prices to maintain occupancy. With reduced Medicare revenues, hospitals began to shift their unreimbursed costs to the private sector.

BUDGETING FOR NONPROFIT HOSPITALS

A nonprofit hospital has a public service mission, no private ownership, is organized as a not-for-profit corporation exempt from federal taxes, and is legally able to accept tax deductible gifts. Voluntary health care entities are usually exempt from federal and state income taxes if they are operated exclusively for religious, charitable, scientific, or educational purposes, and if no part of their net earnings goes to the benefit of any private individual. However, the IRS has begun and will continue to audit large hospital organizations to determine if they are still charitable organizations as of the date of their IRS tax-exempt determination letter, or if they have turned into businesses that no longer deserve tax-exempt status. This has become an issue not only because of the state and local governments' needs for revenue resources, but also due to the concern Congress has for uninsured citizens. With an estimated 30 million Americans lacking any health insurance,

Congress questions whether or not hospitals are doing their share of charity care since the tax-exempt status of hospitals is based in part upon the idea that the hospital is responsive to the community's needs.

SETTING UP A SOCIAL ACCOUNTABILITY BUDGET

Because of this increasing governmental pressure to justify their tax-exempt status, many hospitals are beginning to reassess their priorities and reaffirm their mission within their communities. According to a General Accounting Office (GAO) report, 57 percent of the not-for-profit hospitals in five states provide charity care that amounted to less than the value of the federal taxes from which they were exempt. Therefore, it is judicious for hospitals to budget and maintain documentation related to their community service activities. With the largest community service being charity care this is usually done through a fairly new document called the social accountability budget.

The social accountability budget is a portion of the operational budget and was developed by the Catholic Health Association and the health policy firm Lewin/ICF in order to respond to the increasing challenges from tax authorities. It helps hospitals to:

1. Document in detail any community benefits they provide to the needy in their community and the broader communities.

2. Examine any policies and procedures that support or take away from community service.

3. Assess if there were unmet health care needs in their community.

4. Incorporate any pressing community needs in their strategic plans and budgets by determining what they can and should do to respond to these needs.

5. Ensure that their community and others (especially auditors) are aware of the benefits they provide.

Other examples of items found in the social accountability budget include donations to community free health clinics that are providing education to the community, sponsorship of walk-a-thons for AIDS Los Angeles or other charity organizations, etc.

Some hospitals confuse charity care with bad debts. In order for a service to qualify as charity care, by the IRS definition, the patient must be identified as charity care prior to or shortly after services are performed. In other words, a hospital cannot perform services to a patient, be unsuccessful in collecting the revenue and then report it as charity care.

There are other budget and financial issues besides charity care that are considered when tax-exempt status is granted to a hospital. The government has also been looking at the unrelated business income that "may be subject to income tax when it is derived from activities not related to exempt purposes." There are some significant exclusions from this tax; they include (a) an annual specific deduction for certain limited activities, (b) income from activities where substantially all work is performed by unpaid volunteers, (c) dividends, interest, annuities, royalties, capital gains and losses, and rents from real property except if received from a taxable entity or from proceeds of tax-exempt debt financing for another purpose, and (d) income from activities carried on for the convenience of the entity's patients, visitors, officers, or employees. Many hospitals are using investment income to supplement other income. Moreover, it is very common for hospitals to operate gift shops, parking garages, and cafeterias during the year. As long as the hospital does not encourage the general public to use these facilities, they are considered exempt from unrelated business income taxation.

PLANNING THE REVENUE BUDGET

The revenue budget is often determined by looking at activity for the prior year. The administrator examines the revenue trends and prepares projections based on factors considered important to the organization. Also, the administrators discuss with the doctors their expected case load and patient mix to help in estimating the hospital census for the year. Administrators can plan the number and types of procedures to be performed based on the census provided by the doctors. Revenues are then calculated based on the level of the census.

Budget planners should also estimate a level of surplus. A hospital needs funds for capital investments, replacement of assets, and financial survival during difficult times. A variance in the demand for services, or an increase in the percent of Medicare patients can impact income, so setting the level of desired surplus is a complex task for nonprofit CEOs and board members. Budgeting for surplus depends on the size and stability of the institution, the predictability of yearly income, the consistency of donations, and competition. Other factors that affect nonprofit institutions are government regulations regarding donations and tax-exemptions, patient expectations, and reputation. Nonprofit hospitals also depend on philanthropy. The financial and economic conditions in their immediate environment often determine the level of donations they get, and the amount of debt they might have to carry. Donations are usually estimated by looking at past experience and the types of fund drives planned for the year.

There are several other considerations when planning the hospital's revenue budget. Is there a new service to be provided this year? What is the capacity of the hospital? What are the current economic conditions in the community? Once total revenues are forecasted, the capital budget can then be planned.

ESTIMATING THE CAPITAL BUDGET

Before the operational budgets can be formulated, the capital budget must be estimated. This budget is important for several reasons: (a) the dollar value of the total capital budget is very significant, (b) it is used to approve expenditures, (c) it is used to record expenditures in applicable cost centers, and (d) the capital budget is used to calculate depreciation expense and record it at the cost center level.

The capital budget process consists of a "bottom-up" approach in formulation, and the following steps are used:

1. The Board of Directors, with input from the Executive Budget committee, will determine the amount of the total capital budget. This is most often based on the amount the hospital can afford to spend from fund-raising activities.

2. The budget requests are sent out to the departments/divisions for detail listing of all items requested, the cost, the revenue enhancement, and/or increase in efficiency.

3. The Financial Planning Department receives the list and sorts three different ways: based on cost, based on revenue enhancement, and based on the increase in efficiency.

4. These sorts are given to the vice presidents for the areas under their responsibility. They decide which items should be approved for the current year and which others approved for the following year based on the total capital budget.

The capital budget process must be complete before the operational budget process is started because if a capital item is not approved, but is necessary, it may need to be budgeted as leased equipment. Once the capital budgeting is completed, it is time to focus on the operating budget.

DETERMINING THE OPERATING BUDGET

Factors that influence hospital costs include the price of inputs such as materials, labor and overhead, patient age, acuity level of illness, and the consumption of services. Before 1983, the price charged for services was based on total costs + desired profits; but this is no longer possible. Diagnostic related groups (DRGs) have brought radical changes to pricing methods. The industry has followed in the government's footsteps, and the popularity of HMOs has increased almost overnight, forcing others to revise their pricing methods in order to bid competitively. Costs continue to rise while profits decline.

Pricing decisions must be based on sound knowledge of costs at various volume levels. Services are price sensitive if a substitute is available, and the corresponding option is to price at or below the level of the substitute. Price sensitivity is reduced when the quality of the substitute is perceived as low. This was applicable to HMOs several years ago, but the rising costs of care have reduced the perceived gap between quality and cost. Critical care, trauma, and intensive care are perceived at high value, so are programs with outstanding quality and services with high visibility. Given a favorable competitive market, pricing on the high side for the above services would improve the contribution margin (revenue less variable costs).

Price is usually not sensitive when the cost of care is reimbursed by insurance. Employers are quite aware of this and are shifting the burden of cost to employees in the form of higher deductibles and increased premium payments. Employees are reacting by selecting less costly alternatives such as HMO and PPO plans.

In order to survive, nonprofit hospitals have been forced to engage in ancillary for-profit activities in order to support declining margins. Return on investment (ROI) is not the first priority in nonprofit hospitals, and subsidies such as contributions and investment income usually are needed to help cover expenses.

There are three approaches used for planning the operations budget. The first is *zero-base budgeting (ZBB),* which requires managers to fully justify each budget line item. The second approach is *incremental budgeting* where a percentage is added to the current year budget or actual financial statements. A "top-down" process is used for the formulation of the incremental operating budget, as described in the following steps:

1. The Board of Directors, with input from the Executive Budget Committee, will determine the amount of the total operating budget. Usually the operating budget amount is based on a variance analysis of the prior year's actual and budgeted amount. The Executive Budget Committee looks at each line item and selects the lesser of the actual or the budget amount from the prior year.

2. While the Board of Directors and Executive Budget Committee are determining the total budget amount, the Financial Planning Department is working with the various departments/divisions to determine the budgeted volume per cost center.

3. Once the Board of Directors approves the final budget amount, the Financial Planning Department computes the budget per unit of service based upon the relative usage value. The relative usage value is computed based upon the standard cost per each unit.

4. The Financial Planning Department then "pushes" the budget amount down to each cost center based upon the estimated volume and relative usage value for the current year.

5. This preliminary budget is then sent to the departments/divisions for review and adjustments are made between cost centers and/or department/divisions. This is called balancing the budget because the total operating budget cannot be changed. Balancing the budget often takes longer than the first four steps, due to the political games played by the physicians and the administrators.

FLEXIBLE BUDGETING

The third approach for planning the operations budget is called *flexible budgeting*. Flexible budgeting is used to determine the impact of planned activities on cash flow and the financial statements. Overall activity will fluctuate depending upon the demand for services by the patients. Even if several budgets, including the ones discussed above, are prepared, the budget ultimately used as a comparison with actual results should be based on the actual, not the anticipated level of activity. You don't want to compare apples and oranges. The preparation of the budget based on actual activity is possible, because the flexible budgeting approach can be expressed in terms of the *cost-volume formula*:

Total Expenses = Fixed Expenses + Variable Expenses, or, in an equation form,

$$Y = a + b\,X$$

$$\text{where } Y = \text{Total expenses}$$

$$X = \text{Activity level}$$

$$a = \text{Fixed expenses}$$

$$b = \text{Variable expense per unit of } X$$

The following example illustrates the problem that a hospital unit can face with a static (or fixed) budget in evaluating its performance and how the problem can be corrected with a flexible budget.

TABLE 1
X-Ray Unit
Medical Service Corporation
Performance Report - Static Budget
May 19X4

	Master budget	Actual	Variance	
Units	2,000	1,200	800	
Sales revenue	$60,000	$36,000	$24,000	*
Variable costs:				
Film	16,000	11,500	4,500	+
Other material	4,000	3,000	1,000	+
Technician	3,000	2,500	500	+
Other labor	900	600	300	+
Other variable	26,300	19,600	400	+
Total variable	2,400	2,000	6,700	+
Contribution margin	33,700	16,400	17,300	*
Fixed costs:				
Rent	800	800	0	
Depreciation	400	400	0	
Supervision	2,000	2,000	0	
Other fixed	3,500	3,300	200	+
Total fixed	6,700	6,500	200	+
Operating income	27,000	9,900	17,100	*

*Unfavorable .
+Favorable .

TABLE 2
X-Ray Unit
Medical Service Corporation
Flexible Budget
May 19X4

	Budgeted Per unit	Number of x-rays per month				
		1000	1200	1400	1800	2000
Sales revenue	$30.00	$30,000	$36,000	$42,000	$54,000	$60,000
Variable costs:						
Film	8.00	$8,000	$9,600	$11,200	$14,400	16,000
Other material	2.00	$2,000	2,400	$2,800	$3,600	$4,000
Technician	1.50	$1,500	$1,800	$2,100	$2,700	$3,000
Other labor	0.45	$450	$540	$630	$810	$900
Other variable	1.20	$1,200	$1,440	$1,680	$2,160	$2,400
Total variable	13.15	$13,150	$15,780	$18,410	$23,670	$26,300
Contribution margin	16.85	$16,850	$20,220	$23,590	$30,330	$33,700
Fixed costs:						
Rent		800	800	800	800	800
Depreciation		400	400	400	400	400
Supervision		2,000	2,000	2,000	2,000	2,000
Other fixed		3,500	3,500	3,500	3,500	3,500
Total fixed costs		6,700	6,700	6,700	6,700	6,700
Operating income		10,150	13,520	16,890	23,630	27,000

TABLE 3
X-Ray Unit
Medical Service Corporation
Performance Report - Flexible Budget
May 19X4

Units	Costs incurred	Flexible budget	Variance explanation	
Units	1,200	1,200	0	
Sales revenue	$36,000	$36,000	0	
Variable cost:				
Film	11,500	9,600	1,900	*
Other material	3,000	2,400	600	*
Technician	2,500	1,800	700	*
Other labor	600	540	60	*
Other variable	2,000	1,440	560	*
Total variable	19,600	15,780	3,820	*
Contribution margin	16,400	20,220	3,820	*
Fixed costs:				
Rent	800	800	0	
Depreciation	400	400	0	
Supervision	2,000	2,000	0	
Other fixed	3,300	3,500	200	+
Total fixed cost	6,500	6,700	200	+
Operating income	9,900	13,520	3,620	*

*Unfavorable
+Favorable

Table 1, which shows a fixed (static) budget, clearly indicates that responsibility center managers are liable to be rewarded, or penalized, for reasons beyond their control. For example, the X-ray unit may show low profits due to reduced numbers of patients utilizing the facility, which is outside its control. Also, cost variances are useless, in that they are comparing oranges with apples. The problem is that the budget costs are based on an activity level of 2,000 patients, whereas the actual costs were incurred at an activity level below this (1,200 patients). From a control standpoint, it makes no sense to try to compare costs at one activity level with costs at a different activity level. Such comparisons would make the manager look good as long as the actual service level is less than the budgeted level.

The flexible budget is designed to overcome this deficiency. Table 2 illustrates the underlying concept. In this budget, costs are separated into variable and fixed costs, using the cost-volume formula. The budget is generated, based on the 1,200 actual number of patients. The variable cost that changes with the level of output is subtracted from the revenue to arrive at the *contribution margin* realized at each level of activity. Operating income for each specified level of output is then obtained by deducting fixed costs from each budgeted contribution margin. The unit manager is thus freed from forces beyond his/her control, in this example the number of patients served. The manager is only held accountable for profits that are attainable with the number of patients he/she was actually called upon to serve, not the expected number. Table 3 presents the performance report using a flexible budgeting system. Virtually all costs variances are unfavorable, which calls for management's attention and need to be investigated.

A flexible budget, unlike the adoption of a fixed budget, is not considered a form of appropriations, but rather serves as an approved plan that can facilitate budgetary control and operational evaluations. It only seeks to judge the manager solely on his/her performance and not reward or penalize for influences upon which he/she has no control.

When a flexible budget system is used, it is not appropriate to integrate it into the hospital's accounting system. However, if a fixed budget is used due to preference or a legal requirement, it may be effective to consolidate the budgetary accounts into the accounting system. The basis of accounting used to prepare a budget for the hospital should be accrual, the same as the basis used to record the organization's actual transactions.

In the hospital's budget, the direct labor portion of the budget is similar to regular industry. Direct labor standards help administrators estimate the staffing needs for nursing, custodians, and other staff members based on the census estimation for the next year. The personnel director will also have to determine if the hospital has adequate staffing or if additional personnel need to be recruited. Outside services can also be used, but the rates can be higher than the internal wages. The salary expense for doctors will be a semi-variable expense since most doctors get a salary and a percentage of the revenue of the patients they attract to the hospital. The fixed portion of the expense will be easy to estimate based on the contracts on file for the individual doctors. The variable expense will then be based on the estimates made during the revenue budget process.

The materials, or supplies, budget is also part of the operations budget, and is usually based on prior experience at certain levels of activity. While not so defined as some manufacturing direct materials budgets, the hospital's supplies budget can be estimated based on the level of activity expected. One computerized budgeting program used for hospitals is programmed to recognize the level of supplies that are used at a certain activity level and budgets the line items accordingly. This system does need some adjustment for factors not considered in the program; however, it gives a good first estimate for hospital managers as they proceed through the budgeting process.

Some of the additional factors to consider in the operations budget include the overhead rate. This will also be based on the level of activity in the hospital. Market forces have pushed some hospitals into modernizing their cost accounting methods, but progress has been slow. A 1988 survey conducted five years after the implementation of DRGs showed that the majority of institutions surveyed still relied on the ratio of cost to charges, and they did not know the value of inputs for a specific procedure. This puts hospitals at a disadvantage for cost control, planning, discounted contracts, and budgeting. In contrast to hospitals, government, insurance companies and third-party payers have a competitive advantage because their data base, accumulated over time, allows them to compare prices among all providers. The dual systems of reimbursement, one for government at a discounted rate and one for the private sector at an inflated level, have exposed pricing disparities. There is an increasing outcry about the inequity of a plan that allows cost shifting from hospitals to the public sector.

COSTING HOSPITAL SERVICES

Hospitals use several methods for costing their services, and the methods vary in sophistication. The most prevalent being used is the ratio of cost to charges (RCCs). This top-down method first estimates the ratio of departmental costs to charges, then applies this ratio to individual procedures. RCC might not reflect the actual cost of a procedure because the data is based on aggregate information, and the relationship between charge and cost is not always constant. Using RCC for pricing purposes might distort the true dollar value of some procedures.

Other alternatives for costing out services include actual costing, relative value units (RVUs), and standard costing, which is considered to be the most advanced method.

Actual costing tracks labor, material, and overhead costs at the procedure level. This is precise, but requires time and effort. On the negative side, direct costing fails to provide information on what costs should be.

The RVU method has two steps. Once labor, material and overhead costs are determined for a departmental service, they are assigned to components required to perform a given procedure. The most recognized RVUs are CAP units used by pathology departments and designed by the College of American Pathologists. This method resembles process costing used in manufacturing where costs are collected along the way and assigned to one product. One deficiency of RVUs is the practice of using them for labor measurement only. Pricing accuracy requires that all cost components, including overhead, be measured. When used correctly, this method is an improvement over RCC.

Standard costing also allocates costs to labor, material, and overhead based on established standards for the output level, quality, and resource utilization, but it goes one step beyond with a variance analysis that compares actual performance with standards. There are analyses of price and quantity variances for materials, labor rate and labor efficiency variances, and overhead spending and efficiency variances.

Some hospitals depend on DRG standards to price all their services. This is a form of job order costing with a fixed predetermined allocation of funds given a certain diagnosis under certain conditions. No information is gained on individual operating efficiency when such a system is used, so an in-house system should be developed to measure performance.

Hospitals with sophisticated automation systems use a combination of methods, and the most advanced have implemented standard costing. For smaller institutions, the costs of acquiring and maintaining a standard system may be greater than the benefits it generates. Variables influencing costing systems include the degree of financial pressure on the hospital, the intensity of the competition, and the efficiency level of the current method. A new cost accounting system may require six months to two years to be totally integrated into hospital administrative procedures.

Activity-based costing (ABC) is designed to trace costs to activities, and to assign them to products by using a cost-and-effect relationship. This method has been successfully used in manufacturing, but is not so well known in the medical sector. The admissions and records departments are good examples of services that do not contribute any revenues, yet their operating costs must be distributed to activities that are related to these services. Medical records can be traced back to patients by using a cost driver such as length of stay. This system can also be used to study costs by patient, by physician, or by payment plan. The implementation of ABC is time and effort intensive, requires an overhaul of the cost accounting system, and should be done in stages to facilitate the change.

Lease and depreciation expenses are other items that will be included in the budget. Managers must see if there are any planned purchases for new equipment and whether there is any equipment that will be fully depreciated during the year as these actions may affect depreciation expense.

BUDGETING FOR SPECIAL OR RESTRICTED FUNDS

Special funds are funds obtained from outside agencies and are restricted for use in clinical research, education, or patient care. The use of special funds must be documented accurately and in detail. Many outside agencies giving hospitals these funds perform detail audits of how each dollar is budgeted and spent.

The budget for special funds is based on the prior year's expense. There is little discrepancy from one year to another from most funding agencies. With the current economy, many agencies are not granting large amounts of funds and the hospital must decide if it wants to continue the program, and if it does, it must determine how to fund it.

ANALYZING THE CASH BUDGET

The cash budget is very important for a hospital, as with all nonprofit agencies. Collections are a major source of revenue. To accurately estimate collections, you must look at the payer classifications. In a hospital, different payers remit different percentages of charges. For example, different amounts of payments for the same service might be received from private uninsured patients, Health Incorporated Plan (HIP) patients, Medicare patients, and Medicaid patients. Other sources of revenues include donations, which may be classified as restricted cash, investment income, cafeteria income, and, in the case of a hospital in California, bonds issued by the California Health Services Authority.

An analysis of the cash budget should begin with the expense budgets previously discussed. Typically, the expense budgets will identify the major cash needs of the organization, and will include salaries, utilities, supplies, equipment, and other items. Payments on accounts payable and debt must also be considered in the formulation of a cash budget.

The ability to raise funds, the timing of contributions, board member involvement, and personal financial contributions are all important issues that have a major impact on budgeting for hospitals. Some hospitals ask prominent retired businesspeople to act as trustees. The experience they bring from the business community raises the ability of the board to deal with increasingly complex financial issues. The board's role as administrator is important and should provide sound financial leadership as well as dedication to the mission of the organization. A well-articulated mission serves as ammunition for critics who see no value in the existence of nonprofit health care facilities. The risk factor for medical institutions is very high, and future changes in government reimbursements could wreck even the most carefully prepared plans. Although difficult to determine at this time, the nonprofit hospitals also need to prepare for the changes that federal health care revisions will impose on their industry.

EXAMPLE I: AMERICAN RED CROSS[2]

The following case study involves the budgeting process for the Los Angeles Chapter of the American Red Cross. (See Figure 1 for Organization Chart.) The size of the Los Angeles Chapter is comparable to a large private company; its budget is in the millions of dollars. (See Figures 2 and 3 for comparative financial statements.)

One of the factors to consider in managing the Red Cross is that operations can change almost overnight. According to Nancy Kindelan, CEO of the Chapter, there have been times when a person has willed all his/her assets to the Red Cross, giving the chapter an unforeseen revenue windfall, or a natural disaster, such as an earthquake, will result in a sudden demand for services.

The following are some of her remarks on how the organization goes through its budget process:

> In January of each year, we look at our financial position, the cash in the banks, and how much we'll pay in expenses, with close attention to salaries up until the end of the fiscal year, which is June 30th. We try to estimate, to the best of our ability and knowledge, our expected cash in-flows, revenue and other kinds of support from our local community. The Red Cross calls that a "mid-year budget revenue forecast." Our budget is strictly nourished by

FIGURE 1

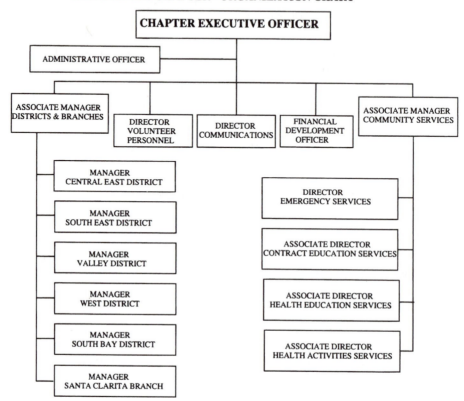

LOS ANGELES CHAPTER - ORGANIZATION CHART

FIGURE 2

AMERICAN RED CROSS
LOS ANGELES CHAPTER

STATEMENT OF NET ASSETS
JUNE 30, 1991, WITH COMPARATIVE TOTALS FOR 1990
(Dollars in Thousands)

	Notes	Unrestricted Current Operations	Land, Buildings, and Equipment	Endowment, Restricted and Board-Designated	·······Totals······· 1991	1990
ASSETS						
CASH AND CASH EQUIVALENTS		$ 374		$ 1,409	$ 1,783	$ 2,830
RECEIVABLES:						
United Way campaign	1	$3,872			$ 3,872	$ 4,277
American National Red Cross and other Red Cross offices		250			250	400
American Red Cross Los Angeles/Orange Counties Regional Blood Services	6	829			829	
Building campaign (net of allowance for uncollectible pledges of $138,000)			$ 801		801	1,231
Other		538		$ 142	680	373
Total receivables		5,489	801	142	6,432	6,281
INVENTORY AND OTHER ASSETS		694	23		717	742
LAND, BUILDINGS, AND EQUIPMENT - Net	2		7,254		7,254	7,584
DUE FROM OTHER FUNDS		753		626	*	*
LONG-TERM INVESTMENTS	1			9,252	9,252	8,655
TOTAL ASSETS		$7,310	$8,078	$11,429	$25,438	$26,092

FIGURE 2, continued

LIABILITIES

Trade payables		$ 676	$ 2		$ 678	$ 650
Accrued liabilities		631			631	588
Deferred revenue - grants		166	801	$ 136	1,103	1,497
American National Red Cross and other Red Cross offices						
Due to other funds	6	312			312	248
		626	611	142	*	*
TOTAL LIABILITIES		$2,411	$1,414	$ 278	$ 2,724	$ 2,983
NET ASSETS		$4,899	$6,664	$11,151	$22,714	$23,109
NET ASSETS - As follows:						
Endowment	4			$ 560	$ 560	$ 490
Restricted	4			504	504	502
Board-designated capital replacement fund	4			10,087	10,087	8,716
Land, buildings, and equipment			$6,664		6,664	6,658
Fund balance available for operations		$4,899			4,899	6,743
NET ASSETS - As above		$4,899	$6,664	$11,151	$22,714	$23,109

See accompanying notes to financial statements.

* Interfund borrowings eliminated in combination of funds.

FIGURE 3

AMERICAN RED CROSS
LOS ANGELES CHAPTER

STATEMENT OF PUBLIC SUPPORT, REVENUE, EXPENSES,
AND CHANGES IN NET ASSETS
YEAR ENDED JUNE 30, 1991, WITH COMPARATIVE TOTALS FOR 1990
(Dollars in Thousands)

	Notes	Unrestricted Current Operations	Land, Buildings, and Equipment	Endowment, Restricted and Board-Designated (See Note 4)	Totals 1991	Totals 1990
PUBLIC SUPPORT AND REVENUE						
Public support:						
United Way campaign contributions	1	$ 5,945			$ 5,945	$ 6,579
Membership contributions	1	2,130			2,130	2,265
Building campaign			$ 389		389	653
Special events and other contributions		187		$ 5	192	973
Legacies and bequests		1,991			1,991	2,206
Total public support		10,253	389	5	10,647	12,676
Revenue:						
Interest and dividend income		654		80	734	681
Contract education sales		981			981	941
Other		50		276	326	7
Total revenue		1,685		356	2,041	1,629
TOTAL		$11,938	$ 389	$ 361	$ 12,688	$ 14,305

FIGURE 3, continued

EXPENSES

Program services:					
Service to military families	$ 3,011	$ 80	$ 121	$ 3,212	$ 1,863
Disaster services	3,569	111	1	3,681	2,386
Health and education services	2,731	91	82	2,904	2,569
Volunteer and youth services	713	36	1	750	683
Blood services 6		97		97	66
Total program services	10,024	415	205	10,644	7,567
Supporting services:					
Financial development	1,138	9		1,147	1,017
Management and general	1,014	266		1,280	579
Total supporting services	2,152	275		2,427	1,596
TOTAL	12,176	690	205	13,071	9,163
(Deficit) excess of public support and revenue over expenses before property and equipment acquisitions and other transfers	(238)	(301)	156	(383)	5,142
Property nad equipment purchased with current funds, net of proceeds from sales of property and equipment	(307)	307			
Other transfers of current funds, primarily to the board-designated capital replacement fund	(1,299)		1,287	(12)	
NET (DEFICIT) EXCESS OF PUBLIC SUPPORT AND REVENUE OVER EXPENSES AND TRANSFERS	(1,844)	6	1,443	(395)	5,142
NET ASSETS, BEGINNING OF YEAR	6,743	6,658	9,708	23,109	17,967
NET ASSETS, END OF YEAR	$ 4,899	$ 6,664	$11,151	$22,714	$23,109

See accompanying notes to financial statements.

our community, and Washington, D.C. does not contribute anything to us . . . quite the opposite, we are the ones that contribute
to Washington; an amount of $3 million every year.

Ms. Kindelan explained that this amount is on a straight basis, determined by the national administrative body in Washington, D.C. and is based
on the geographical region or area in which the chapter operates. The statistical information regarding the mean, or average, income of a resident in
southern California, as well as the other general attributes of the region, like
the number of people living in the region, is put together in a report, along
with expected cash outflows and inflows, and the latest financial statements.

As the budget formulation process begins, Ms. Kindelan described the
procedures followed by the Los Angeles chapter. They closely follow the
following typical budget preparation cycle:[3]

Program and Budget Planning
a. Needs assessment and feasibility study
b. Program planning
c. Cost estimating
d. Budget development

Funds Procurement
a. Budget request submission
b. Negotiation with funder
c. Rebudgeting and resubmission
d. Award and acceptance

Fiscal Management
a. Designation of cost and responsibility center
b. Internal funds allocation and rebudgeting
c. Establishment of restricted accounts
d. Financial transactions, recording, and accounting
e. Operations monitoring and reporting
f. Cost control and containment

Performance Assessment, Financial Reports, Audits
a. End-of-year financial statements
b. Financial audit
c. Performance audit
d. Cost analysis

Recycle
a. Program replanning
b. Continuation budgeting
c. Cost finding and rate setting

Top managers in the Red Cross examine the needs, estimate the costs of operations, and plan accordingly in order to raise the required capital. All costs and revenues are traced to their centers in order to clearly identify and rank the various divisions and subdivisions of the chapter. Moreover, this identification helps determine which subdivision can be set free and on its own as far as raising funds is concerned instead of having to appropriate money for its operations from larger divisions. Follow-up, replanning and fine-tuning are ongoing activities, not only for control, but for preparing budgets for subsequent years as well.

During the funds procurement phase, the negotiated management approach is used, in contrast to the top-down or bottom-up styles. The lower divisions prepare and submit budgets; rarely, however, do they fully receive what they ask for. Negotiations, common points, deals and narrowing of demand by lower divisions, and increasing appropriations by higher authorities become typical procedures in the negotiations and resubmission of the budget.

The Los Angeles chapter of the Red Cross assesses its needs for the coming fiscal year, turns these assessments into quantitative formats for each of its cost centers, and submits the related schedules to the top governing body for approval. If during the year, a gap begins to develop between revenues and expenditures, the organization may be forced to cut down its workforce, or cut back on services.

EXAMPLE II: PREFERRED PROVIDER ORGANIZATION[4]

In this section, we will briefly examine the procedures used to develop the operating budget for a Preferred Provider Organization (PPO). The objectives are twofold:

1. Understand what a Preferred Provider Organization is and how it affects the managed health care service industry.

2. Become familiar with the special considerations in the budgeting of revenue for a PPO.

WHAT IS A PREFERRED PROVIDER ORGANIZATION?

The PPO was born out of the need for the public to have more personalized health care than is offered by traditional Health Maintenance Organizations (HMOs) while receiving the rates afforded members of HMOs. The objective of the PPO is to provide quality medical care at reduced rates. It is a network of physicians and hospitals (also known as "providers") that has contracted with the PPO to provide health care services at a *reduced rate* to subscribers (company employees) and the insurance companies who insure these employees. (Figure 4 shows the relationship between the patient, employer, health care provider, PPO, and insurance company.)

The PPO approach to managed health care has several advantages. First, the patient can choose from among several thousand private practice physicians and from among several hundred hospitals. These physicians have developed well-established practices and offer the prospect of a long-term relationship instead of the short-term nonpersonalized relationship common to HMOs. The patient can also change physicians or hospitals as often as desired. A further advantage to the patient is the reduced cost of receiving service from a network physician or hospital, which minimizes the patient's share of any incurred costs. The cost to the patient is slightly higher than that of an HMO. The advantage to the physicians and hospitals is increased patient volume. Employers benefit from offering a PPO through reduced health care premiums resulting from the reduced rates charged by the providers. Finally, the underwriting insurance companies benefit from PPOs because they involve less cost.

Growth in a typical PPO is realized through expansion of the physician and hospital networks. An expanding PPO network is attractive to patients, physicians, hospitals, employers, and health insurance companies. A larger network results in an increased claims volume that translates into increased revenue. Therefore, a large well-established physician/hospital network is the most important asset to the PPO. The operating budget must be developed with the goal of expanding the network.

CONSIDERATIONS IN BUDGETING PPO REVENUES

In this example, we will limit our discussion to two major types of revenue in a PPO: the administration service fee and the provider billing fee. The first is a monthly charge to insurance companies for allowing insured employees access to the physician/hospital network. The provider billing fee

FIGURE 4

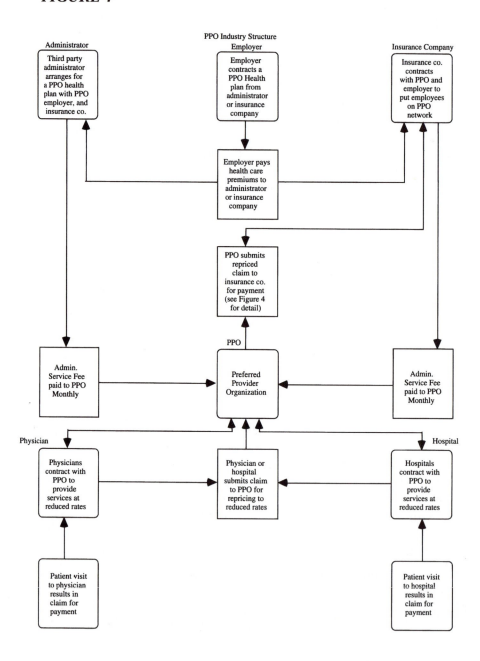

is a charge on most claims processed by the PPO on behalf of member physicians/hospitals. Certain PPOs also have a billing arrangement with insurance companies whereby the provider billing fee is not charged on processed claims, but is instead a flat percentage of the total savings the insurance company realizes by processing claims through the network.

The sales volume and mix must be forecasted in order to accurately budget revenue streams. This is the most difficult part of developing budgets for PPOs since it involves the budgeting of Enrolled Employees (EE). An EE is a single employee who is listed as a subscriber on the PPO network. The EE is the basic sales unit in the industry and the measurement that determines the relative size and prestige of PPOs in the industry. For example, a PPO with 200,000 EEs means that there are 200,000 employees working for various companies who subscribe to the PPO network through the various insurance companies offering health plans to employers. These employees are authorized to use the networked physicians and hospitals.

In most businesses, a customer orders the product or service and a bill is generated which is used as the basis for recording revenue; the sales volume is fixed and known at the time of sale. For PPOs, the exact number of EEs for a given month is not known for at least thirty days after the time of each monthly sale (the first of each month) and often not until sixty days after the sale takes place. This lag occurs because of the billing cycle in the medical insurance industry. There is no way to completely compensate for this time lag because the insurance companies themselves do not know the number of EEs on which medical premiums are collected until the tenth of each month, and this is after the cut-off of PPO billings to the various administrators of insurance companies. Once the insurance companies fix the final EE count for the month, they remit the administrative service fee to the PPO. Therefore, the PPO has no direct information system to determine the actual number of employees working for employers at any given time, and consequently must estimate the EE count based on the latest information.

To compensate for the difference between sales revenue and sales receipts, a factor for a margin of error must be built into budgeted revenue. The sales invoices are designed to allow the remitting insurance company or administrator to complete the new updated EE count information. On a monthly basis, the sales receipts actually remitted are compared to the sales volume invoiced. The variance is tracked on a six-month moving average. Historically, the invoiced volume is accurate to a plus or minus five-percent variance. For example, if 200,000 EEs are invoiced in the month of June, the actual number of units remitted will range from 190,000 to 210,000. This must be considered when budgeting income.

BASIC BUDGETING PRACTICES BASED ON SURVEY RESULTS[5]

In order to gain more familiarity, we developed a questionnaire encompassing basic budgeting issues, as shown in Figure 5. Presented are two cases summarizing the results based on the questionnaire.

FIGURE 5

QUESTIONNAIRE

Name of Organization _____

1. Is the budget made annually or every 5 years?

2. Who is responsible for the operating budget—a board of directors or a single individual?

3. Is the organization fully nonprofit via contributions?

4. Is there any operating income? Which kind? How large of a percentage of the total budget is it?

5. Which budgeting method is utilized? Zero-base budgeting? Responsibility budgeting?

6. What budgeting steps/procedures are in place?

7. What kind of government statutes and regulations are in place that nonprofit organizations have to take into account when budgeting?

8. What are the restrictions on funds raised/funds granted to the program?

9. What is the program or subprogram?

10. What is the procedure when new programs/old programs clash?

11. What budget documentation is required?

12. Does the documentation requirement look different in-house versus what is given to the prospective funders?

13. Do the funders only fund after a budget/operating blueprint has been submitted or is the program funded with "X" amount based on which the budget will be established?

14. Is the internal budgeting done per line item or based on larger areas/functions?

15. Is the budget fixed or flexible?

16. Is the budgeting done top-down or does the lower level management submit budgets for their areas that later are consolidated in one big budget?

17. Is the forecasting based on prehistoric averages-last year data?

18. Is your program affected by any significant trends? If so, which seasonality effects?

19. Is your organization efficient at utilizing the budget as an evaluation tool? Does it timely compare—i.e., midyear results year-to-date with overall budget, etc.?—Does it step in if a budget variance is inevitable?

CASE 1: SADDLEBACK MEMORIAL HOSPITAL

The hospital has within its framework several subprograms, of which The Jonathan Jacques children's cancer program is one. As per our questionnaire, Maggie Thomas, the administrative manager, gave the following overall information:

1. The budget is made annually.

2. The budget is made by the hospital board of directors with the assistance of the administrative manager.

3. The program is fully nonprofit as all income arises from fund-raising activities and endowment interest income from the Jonathan Jacques family. Fifty percent of the program is subsidized by the hospital.

4. The budgeting method is incremental; only increases above last year's basis are considered.

5. The hospital projects based on the year before a 6% salary increase and a 6% growth rate. However, due to the poor economic conditions, the program has lately had to take up to 16% decreases in overhead/administration cost to survive and it foresees another upcoming 5–10% cut in the following year. Currently 20% of the budget is for overhead/administrative and approximately 70% goes to the actual mission. Approximately 35% of the mission funds are used for research and development and the rest is used for providing professional help/support groups/counseling/psycho-social assistance to the patients/families with pediatric cancer.

6. A subject program is not funded by the government so the primary regulations to follow are the ones set by the Memorial Hospital. (It is important to note that the Memorial Hospital itself has a foundation office. Fund-raising activities have to be approved by the subject unit, as the foundation office itself has its own way of raising money to the hospital as a whole. The overall program and the subprograms are not allowed to overlap. The foundation office will restrict the institutions solicited for income for it not to interfere with its business.)

7. The Jonathan Jacques program is a subprogram to The Saddleback Memorial Hospital.

8. A line item budget is made, counting every administrative item such as salary for staff members, supplies, and services.

9. The only documentation required is the in-house one supplied in the hospital. All billing is done directly to the hospital and it then makes monthly statements that are sent to the program's administrative manager for her to compare with the original budget.

10. A subject program is a year ahead of itself as the money raised for the budget year 1995 is raised in 1994 by a fund-raising activity. The picture is set in that the manager knows how much income is budgeted for the next year.

11. The budget is fixed for the reasons mentioned in (10).

12. The budgeting is done top-down by the hospital board based on the suggestions made by the administrative manager.

13. The forecasting is based on last year's data with percentage increases for the following year.

14. The program is affected by economic trends. As indicated above, due to the shortage of philanthropical money, the program has had to face severe reductions.

15. The hospital accounting department accumulates the bills and management makes monthly reports to tell the program leaders where they are. There is an analysis of money spent by program. Auditors attempt to intervene immediately if the administration is off track and spends too much money. The fiscal year of a subject program is July 1 through June 30.

CASE 2: THE LEUKEMIA SOCIETY OF LOS ANGELES

The Leukemia Society of America, Inc. is a national voluntary health agency dedicated solely to seeking the cause and eventual cure of leukemia and allied diseases. The society, which was established in 1949, supports five major programs: research, patient aid, public and professional education, and community service. The society has chapter offices located across the United States and all local and national programs are supported by contributions from individuals, commerce and industry, unions and foundations, bequests and memorials, and voluntary help.

Based on a questionnaire, Samuel E. Thomas, a senior administrator, provided us with the following overall feedback:

1. The budget is made both annually and every 5 years. However, the local LA office only shows the annual figures whereas the 5-year budget is a consolidated budget for the overall organization.

2. The president and the treasurer are responsible for the budget as well as Samuel Thomas on a local basis.

3. The program is fully nonprofit with donations from individuals and revenue from special events. The organization does not get large government grants because there are too many strings attached.

4. There is no operating income.

5. Zero-base budgeting is used.

6. The responsible parties make a budget assessment based on the expected amount of fund raising.

7. There are certain filing requirements. The LA office has to file its year-end statements with IRS (Form 990), with the state of California (charitable division), with the city of LA and the County of LA (social services). Additionally, the organization submits its figures to different agencies such as the watch dog agencies.

8. There are no restrictions on the funds raised currently.

9. The LA office pursues the original program goals but is a subchapter of the overall organization.

10. Due to guidelines usually the programs do not clash. Approximately 25% of the programs are utilized for overhead/administration and the rest for the mission itself. Of the mission funds, 50% of the funds are used for research and development and 50% are used for patient help. There is a medical/scientific advisory committee that is always revising the desired split for the overall program.

11. The documentation requirement to the funders looks a bit more "fancy" with nice graphs.

12. The money is raised for the same year, so the budget is established based on expectations for the upcoming fund raising events.

13. A line item budget is used as well as function budgets for external use.

14. The budget is fixed.

15. The budgeting is done both top-down and with participation by local offices for their local figures.

16. The forecasting is done based on last year's data.

17. The program is affected primarily by the overall economic trend.

18. The organization reviews monthly at executive meetings the income/expense picture. Additionally, the figures are reviewed every 6 months by the financial committee as well as annually on a consolidated basis. The organization attempts to monitor overall performance and tries to fine-tune its costs. In bad situations for a local office (such as 20 years ago when St. Louis had an unexpected outbreak of leukemia that strained local resources), the other national offices will assist financially. However, each office works independently with a clearly stated objective and financial goal.

Figures 6 and 7 show the 5-year master budget (1994–1998), based on the following assumptions:

1. 4% growth increase from 1993

2. 5% growth increase from 1994

3. 6% growth increase from 1995

4. 7% anticipated increase from 1996

5. 8% anticipated increase from 1997

FIGURE 6

LEUKEMIA SOCIETY OF AMERICA, INC
GREATER LOS ANGELES CHAPTER

STATEMENT OF SUPPORT, REVENUE AND EXPENSES
AND CHANGES IN FUND BALANCE

YEAR ENDS JUNE

	ACTUAL 1992 TOTAL FUNDS	ACTUAL 1993 TOTAL FUNDS	PERCENT CHANGE	1994 TOTAL FUNDS	PROJECTED 1995 TOTAL FUNDS	1996 TOTAL FUNDS	1997 TOTAL FUNDS	1998 TOTAL FUNDS
PUBLIC SUPPORT & REVENUE								
PUBLIC SUPPORT								
RECEIVED DIRECTLY								
RESIDENTIAL CAMPAIGNS	$181,587	$289,022	59 16%	$300,583	$315,612	$334,549	$357,967	$386,605
COMMERCE & INDUSTRY	$47,882	$40,604	-15 20%	$42,228	$44,340	$47,000	$50,290	$54,313
SPECIAL GIFTS	$13,153	$13,799	4 91%	$14,351	$15,069	$15,973	$17,091	$18,458
MEMORIALS & DONORS	$40,063	$45,715	14 11%	$47,544	$49,921	$52,916	$56,620	$61,150
COINBOARDS	$36,259	$31,072	-14 31%	$32,315	$33,931	$35,966	$38,484	$41,563
LEGACIES & BEQUESTS	$4,596	$188,187	3994 58%	$195,714	$205,500	$217,830	$233,078	$251,725
SPECIAL EVENTS	$195,567	$170,235	-12 95%	$177,044	$185,897	$197,050	$210,844	$227,711
RADIOTHON	$125,480	$199,180	58 73%	$207,147	$217,505	$230,555	$246,694	$226,429
FOUNDATIONS	$89,650	$27,700	-69 10%	$28,808	$30,248	$32,063	$34,308	$37,052
TOTAL RECEIVED DIRECTLY	$734,237	$1,005,514	36 94%	$1,045,735	$1,098,021	$1,163,903	$1,245,376	$1,345,006
RECEIVED INDIRECTLY								
COMBINED HEALTH APPEAL	$1,059	$7,125	572 80%	$7,410	$7,781	$8,247	$8,825	$9,531
FEDERAL EMPLOYEES	$22,312	$24,822	11 25%	$25,815	$27,106	$28,732	$30,743	$33,203
CLUBS/ORGANIZATIONS	$22,349	$22,833	2 17%	$23,746	$24,934	$23,430	$28,280	$30,542
CONFEDERATED FUNDS	$175,794	$138,311	-21 32%	$143,843	$151,036	$160,098	$171,305	$185,009
UNITED/COMMUNITY FUNDS	$11,455	$8,132	-29 01%	$8,457	$8,880	$9,413	$10,072	$10,878
TOTAL RECEIVED INDIRECT	$232,969	$201,233	-13 63%	$209,272	$219,736	$232,920	$249,224	$269,162
TOTAL PUBLIC SUPPORT	$967,206	$1,206,737	24 77%	$1,255,006	$1,317,757	$1,396,822	$1,494,600	$1,614,168
REVENUE INTEREST	$4,327	$3,929	-9 20%	$4,086	$4,290	$4,548	$4,866	$5,256
LOSS ON DISPOSAL OF ASSETS	$0	($4,624)		$0	$0	$0	$0	$0
TOTAL PUBLIC SUPPORT/REV	$971,533	$1,206,042	24 14%	$1,259,093	$1,322,047	$1,401,370	$1,499,466	$1,619,423

FIGURE 6, continued

EXPENSES:								
PROGRAM SERVICES:								
PATIENT SERVICE	$116,996	$137,481	17.51%	$142,980	$150,129	$159,137	$170,277	$183,899
PUBLIC HEALTH EDUCATION	$123,074	$140,444	14.11%	$146,062	$153,365	$162,567	$173,946	$187,862
PROFESSIONAL EDUC.	$56,321	$48,303	-14.24%	$50,235	$52,747	$55,912	$59,826	$64,612
COMMUNITY SERVICE	$97,874	$137,269	40.25%	$142,760	$149,898	$158,892	$170,014	$183,615
TOTAL PROGRAM SERVICES	$394,265	$463,497	17.56%	$482,037	$506,139	$536,507	$574,063	$619,988
SUPPORTING SERVICE:								
MANAGEMENT & GENERAL	$65,346	$66,875	2.34%	$69,558	$73,028	$77,409	$82,828	$89,454
FUND RAISING	$104,541	$163,807	56.69%	$170,359	$178,877	$189,610	$202,883	$219,113
TOTAL SUPPORTING SERVICES	$169,887	$230,682	35.79%	$239,909	$251,905	$267,019	$285,710	$308,567
ADMITTANCES TO HEAD-QUARTERS	$446,325	$512,081	14.37%	$532,564	$559,192	$592,744	$634,236	$684,975
TOTAL EXPENSES	$1,010,477	$1,206,260	19.38%	$1,254,510	$1,317,236	$1,396,270	$1,494,009	$1,613,530
EFFICIENCY OF SUPPORT AND REVENUE OVER EXPENSES	($38,944)	($218)	-99.44%	$4,582	$4,811	$5,100	$5,457	$5,894
OTHER CHANGES IN FUND BALANCES:								
MNTS CAPITAL LEASE	$0	$0	0.00%	$0	$0	$0	$0	$0
EQUIPMENT ACQUISITION	$0	$0	0.00%	$0	$0	$0	$0	$0
REIMBURSEMENT FROM HEADQRTS:								
PATIENT SERVICE	$16,146	$10,913	-32.41%	$11,350	$11,917	$12,632	$13,516	$14,598
CHAPTER SYMPOSIA	$371	$0	-100.00%	$0	$0	$0	$0	$0
TOT. INCREASE (DECREASE) FOR THE YEAR	($22,427)	$10,695	-147.69%	$15,932	$16,728	$17,732	$18,973	$20,491
FUND BALANCES:								
BEGINNING OF YEAR	$12,597	($9,830)	-178.03%	$865	$16,797	$33,525	$51,257	$70,230
END OF YEAR	($9,830)	$865	-108.80%	$16,797	$33,525	$51,257	$70,230	$90,722

FIGURE 7

LEUKEMIA SOCIETY OF AMERICA, INC
GREATER LOS ANGELES CHAPTER

BALANCE SHEET

| | ACTUAL | | PROJECTED | | | | |
	1992 TOTAL FUNDS	1993 TOTAL FUNDS	1994 TOTAL FUNDS	1995 TOTAL FUNDS	1996 TOTAL FUNDS	1997 TOTAL FUNDS	1998 TOTAL FUNDS
ASSETS							
Cash	$75	$1,837	$1,910	$2,006	$2,126	$2,275	$2,457
Due from National Headquarters	$3,281	$3,464	$3,603	$3,783	$4,010	$4,290	$4,634
Deposits	$3,262	$3,262	$3,392	$3,562	$3,776	$4,040	$4,363
Prepaid expenses	$802	$2,848	$2,962	$3,110	$3,297	$3,527	$3,810
Equipment at cost Less accumulated depreciation	$24,268	$23,678	$24,625	$25,856	$27,408	$29,326	$31,672
TOTAL ASSETS	$31,688	$35,089	$36,493	$38,317	$40,616	$43,459	$46,936
LIABILITIES AND FUND BALANCES							
Accounts payable	$23,748	$9,388	$9,764	$10,252	$10,867	$11,627	$12,558
Obligations under capital Lease	$5,013	$10,087	$10,490	$11,015	$11,676	$12,493	$13,493
Accrued expenses:							
Payroll	$8,896	$5,918	$6,155	$6,462	$6,850	$7,330	$7,916
Payroll taxes	$105	$280	$291	$306	$324	$347	$375
Due to National Headquarters-other	$3,756	$8,551	$8,893	$9,338	$9,898	$10,591	$11,438
TOTAL LIABILITIES	$41,518	$34,224	$35,593	$37,373	$39,615	$42,388	$45,779
Fund balances (deficit)	($9,830)	$865	$16,797	$33,525	$51,527	$70,230	$90,722
TOTAL LIABILITIES AND FUND BALANCES	$31,688	$35,089	$18,796	$3,848	($11,642)	($27,842)	($44,943)

Note: Usually assets and liabilities must be equal. However, the Leukemia Society—with continued growth—can end up with positive balances for additional spending on the program or investment in equipment. We have let the financial balances at the bottom show the amount by which the program assets exceed the liabilities, i.e., the amount in surplus.

Notes for Chapter 10

1. This chapter was coauthored by Patricia Guardado and Louise Nowel, our graduate assistants at California State University, Long Beach.

2. This case was provided by David Saad, our graduate assistant, who during the summer of 1992 interviewed the Chief Administrative Officer, Nancy Kindelan, of the Los Angeles Chapter of the American Red Cross.

3. Vinter, Robert. *Budgeting for Not-For-Profit Organizations* (The Free Press, 1984).

4. The information in this section is provided by John Van Haaster, Budget Analyst for a managed health maintenance organization.

5. This survey was provided by our graduate assistant, Mette B. Karapetian.

Chapter 11

Budgeting for Colleges, Universities, and Private Schools

Many colleges, universities and private schools find themselves in the throes of managing under conditions of financial restraint, which present problems related to both institutional management and external affairs. At the same time, these organizations face the task of developing resource planning and budgeting systems that produce the programmatic information necessary for defining institutional priorities to guide budget allocation and program reduction decision-making. The budget and planning system is expected to provide the information system and data base to permit comprehensive and equitable program evaluation.

A school budget is a multifaceted planning document that links educational policy to financial decisions. It contains the institution's goals, priorities and the strategies for meeting them, such as whether or not accelerated programs are offered to gifted students, whether bilingual education classes for students and language specialist credential training for teachers will be offered, if after-school sports activities are offered, and the ratio of students to teachers.

BUDGETING FOR COLLEGES AND UNIVERSITIES

The budgeting process for colleges and universities is highly dependent on the size of the institution. A very small school can develop a budget with simple forms and the administration of its budget can be done through simple budget status reports.

The first step in the budgeting process is to estimate the income from all sources for the upcoming year. Once the income items have been established, expenditures for each of the various programs are estimated. If expected expenditures are greater than income, then some difficult decisions must be made by the administrative staff. The first option is to either increase estimated income or to decrease expected expenditures. Another option is to look for ways to increase income during the year or decrease expenditures during the year. This involves risks because if the additional income is not forthcoming or the expenditures are not decreased, the university could be in serious financial trouble.

Most universities prepare their budgets on fiscal years either from September 1 through August 31, or July 1 through June 30. One year is the traditional time frame for budgeting; however, many schools are now planning and budgeting several years into the future, especially when campus expansions or facility improvements are scheduled in upcoming years.

FUND GROUPS

The fund groups for colleges and universities include:

Current funds—resources available to conduct primary educational objectives of the institution. It may be restricted or unrestricted. University unrestricted current funds, derived from tuition, student fees, and endowment revenue, can be transferred to various operating activities, unless otherwise indicated by the governing board. On the other hand, the use of restricted current funds is specified by the donors or other outside agencies. These funds are typically obtained from contracts, gifts, grants, appropriations, and endowments.

Annuity and life income funds—these are restricted funds which provide for repayment to the donor of part of the fund income.

Loan funds—repayment of principal and interest are returned to the fund and made available for further loans to staff and students.

Plant funds—these funds include plant assets and related debt, and assets to be used for future acquisition.

Endowment funds—principal cannot be used but income earned may or may not be.

Agency funds—the resources are managed by the institiution as an agent on behalf of others. These funds are restricted. Examples are when the university serves as an agent for faculty organization or student government.

ADDING UP REVENUE BUDGET ITEMS

When a university or college is preparing a budget of expected cash inflows, some of the largest categories of revenues are enrollments, tuition and fees, endowments, financial aid and special fees. Each of these is discussed below:

Enrollments

An accurate and reliable estimation of the number of students attending the university is vital in preparing the budget. This number will be the principal guide for many other areas of the budget when other income and expenditure estimates are made. Management uses past experience and new student enrollment as ways of compiling this budget item. Universities having relatively stable enrollments find it easier to estimate income. Those schools with growing or declining enrollments have a riskier position and must evaluate carefully. It is also important to have a firm estimate of the yearly attrition rate of students and the time of year they are most likely to leave the university. In order to maintain stable enrollment numbers, it is often helpful to establish freshmen and other student grade quotas.

Tuition and Fees

The number of students attending the university multiplied by the tuition rate will produce the gross tuition for the school. From this number, the amounts for attrition and uncollectible accounts must be deducted to yield the net tuition income. Many schools charge students a different rate for the individual school they study in at the university. For example, there will be separate rates used for the School of Engineering, the School of Social Sciences, and the School of Business. Managers must also take into account the number of part-time and evening students who will be paying a different rate.

Endowments

The university usually estimates endowments based on historical patterns. However, careful consideration must be made of the current economic conditions and the manager's personal experience in developing this estimate. It is also important to remember that many endowments are made with conditions and restrictions, such as scholarships for minority students, fellowships, or athletic awards. These restricted funds cannot be used to offset general university expenditures.

Financial Aid

It is fairly easy to estimate the amount of assistance the university will receive from federal grants, funds for fellowships, and other sources. However, it is vital that these funds be monitored and analyzed for changing attitudes in the federal, state, and local governments to ensure that the funds will continue to be received at current levels. As mentioned above in the endowment section, a manager will have more trouble making a judicious evaluation if that person lacks experience.

Special Fees

Similar to the restrictions on endowments, many of the collected fees are targeted for specific purposes and cannot be used to pay off the general expenditures of the university. Some examples of such fees include those for health services, residence hall programs, parking, and laboratories. These amounts can be predicted from enrollment numbers while taking attrition and refunds into consideration. Additionally, any amounts the university will receive for late fees and examination fees must be taken into consideration. The most expedient estimate of this income category is derived from historical trends.

Other sources of income, while minor compared to the above categories, still must be included when total revenues are budgeted. These classifications for colleges and universities include rental income from the use of facilities, short-term investments, income from bookstores and other auxiliary services, and revenues from athletic events.

DETERMINING EXPENDITURE BUDGET ITEMS

When preparing a budget of expected cash outflows, many managers begin with the continuing commitments of the university or college. These types of expenditures include salaries, benefits, and all other operating expenses. Added to these amounts are the new items for the coming year.

These would include negotiated salary increases and automatic experience step increases, increases in employment budgets, new programs, new staff, expected maintenance and renovations, and others. The total of all of these expenditures gives an estimated total of obligations to be incurred by the university. This total is compared to the estimated total for revenues, and it is often at this point that the painful process of cutting the budget begins in order to balance revenues with expenditures. One other consideration to remember is that, by law, some colleges and universities must maintain sufficient reserves in their fund balance to meet contingencies. Accordingly, expenditures must be decreased enough to ensure the revenues will cover upcoming costs during the year *and* still allow the college to maintain the required reserves.

DEVELOPING THE UNIVERSITY BUDGET

The procedure for developing and compiling the university's budget is extensive yet systematic. There are several stages in the approval process leading to the final university-wide budget. Typically, the process starts with the department head and moves to the dean, then to the vice president, and finally to the president. At each level, the required checks and approvals are necessary. Although the governing board (i.e., the trustees) is the final authority of approval for the budget, the majority of the checks and approvals for the budget are done with the university administrators.

Many of the larger colleges and universities have established "budget centers" to bring together and control expenditures for departments, buildings, projects, programs, etc. The number of budget centers depends on the requirements of the individual organization. Having too many budget centers could result in a waste of effort and resources. Examples of budget centers are the Athletic Department, the University Bookstore, the Housing and Residence Life, and the Accounting Department. Establishing a criterion for each budget center to follow helps to maintain a consistency across the university and allows for easy compilation of the university-wide budget. For example, all budget centers would be instructed to use line 10000 for certificated salaries, line 20000 for classified salaries, line 30000 for employee benefit costs, line 40000 for supplies, etc. Not every budget center will use every line classification of the budget; they should use only those lines that are relevant to their operations.

All of the budget centers are under the supervision of one of the vice presidents or the president him or herself. These people are responsible for the budgets under them and establish and communicate the control procedures for their budgets. Each budget center prepares a budget for its area which is forwarded to the dean, who compiles all of the budgets and forwards them to the vice president. This administrator reviews and questions the division budget and then forwards it to the president, who then compiles the university-wide budget.

Before passing the budget on to the president and board of trustees, it is vital that all expenses match income and all figures are verified as being in the correct line. In presenting the final draft of the budget to the trustees, the budget manager, usually the vice president for finance, will prepare exhibits that show a condensed and concise version of the budget. Even though it is abbreviated, all of the significant information must be available for the trustees to make an informed decision. The supporting information for budget items should be available during the presentation when the trustees will ask some tough questions. They must have full and complete information on the budget because the fiscal responsibility of the university rests with them. If all of the information is in order and questions are answered to its satisfaction, the board will approve the budget for the next fiscal year.

After the budget has been approved, copies of each department's budget are forwarded to the appropriate dean or department head. The budget manager retains the master copy of all budgets and is in charge of administering it over the course of the next year. This is also the time that planning for the next budget year begins. When the department heads receive their area's budget, they are asked to submit to the budget manager a detailed plan of expenditures to match the budgeted expenditures. This will be used as a control over the course of the academic year. As a final check, department heads are usually asked to submit a monthly or semesterly status report of expenditures and revenues received to date.

A university must also prepare a budget for the college library.

CASE-STUDY—UNIVERSITY LIBRARY BUDGET

Library Y is a medium size college library. It serves 16,000 full-time and part-time undergraduate and graduate students. Its primary mission is to support the college curriculum with resources including acquiring the materials to support college instruction, providing access to the resources and offering reference and instructional services that facilitate use of the collection. The research needs of faculty are only partially fulfilled by on-site collections, but the library does actively borrow needed materials.

The library has several separate service points that include reference, reserve, circulation, periodicals, etc. Each service point requires staffing.

The university administration allocates funds among the various units or divisions. Monies allocated for specific purposes must be used for such including security, day care, services for disabled students, and library support.

The Library Director prepares the budget with input from library department heads and academic administrators.

The library budget includes funding for Other Than Personal Services also known as OTPS and part time personnel needs also known as temporary services.

INCOME SOURCES

Matching Funds

Cash and in-kind gifts to the library are matched with cash grants. There is a maximum figure each year and such money must be used to buy library materials. The amount is identified mid-way into the fiscal year.

Collection Development

Money is granted to the library to help maintain research level collections in a few areas. The Library is committed to sharing the collections outside the institution when it accepts the funds. Spending is limited to buy materials in specific subject areas identified in the original request.

Department Accounts

Small amounts of money may be available to the Library through individual accounts. Such accounts might include money collected for lost books and commissions from vendors such as a copy service. There are specific conditions under which the money may be spent.

Endowment Accounts

The interest generated by the library's endowment accounts is available for the purchase of library materials. Such accounts are usually established as memorials and are restricted to specific types of materials.

EXPENSES

Library Materials

The greatest expense in the library is the amount spent on library materials. Included here is the purchase of monographs (some of which are required on standing order), periodicals, online databases, microfilms, and non-print materials such as slides, compact discs, pictures, videos, etc. The annual cost of periodical subscriptions, online databases and materials on standing order are usually accurately projected. Early in the fiscal year the library is able to identify the amount that needs to be allocated in order to meet these commitments. If the total budget can not be balanced and there is a predicted shortfall, the library administration may opt for cancellation of subscriptions and standing orders in order to bring down the costs.

The money allocated for library materials is usually divided using established guidelines or a collection development formula. Many criteria are used by libraries to establish such guidelines and the division may vary from year to year. Nevertheless, constant examination of such formulas results in balanced collections that meet the needs of patrons.

Personnel

Salaries and fringe benefits for full-time employees in the library are not computed in the library budget but rather the overall college budget. However, money for part time employees must be allocated from the lump sum given to the library. These funds cover payment for part time librarians, clericals and student assistants. Early in the fiscal year, the Library Director identifies the amount needed for such part time personnel services and encumbers that amount.

Equipment

Equipment and equipment upgrades are required every fiscal year. Particularly as library automation accelerates the need for more equipment grows. Equipment needs include PC work stations, terminals, printers, book trucks, audio and video equipment, microfilm readers, etc. Allocations vary each year and are dictated by the total budget figure.

Supplies

Expenses here are for materials such as tattletape, binding and mending supplies, processing supplies and specific items that are library specific and not available through central supply.

Contracts and Maintenance

Items covered in this area include service contracts, bibliographic utility (OCLC), online public catalog upkeep and repair costs.

Bindery

Bindery costs are required to pay an outside binder for monographic and periodical binding.

Memberships

Amount needed for American Library Association (ALA) membership and regional consortiums.

Travel and Staff Development

Includes funds for professional conferences and staff development workshops.

Special Project

The scope of such projects varies yearly but may include funding for special initiatives such as database cleanup, inventories, local area networks, and retrospective projects.

A typical budget request for this library follows:

TYPICAL BUDGET REQUEST

Library resources	
Print and non-print materials and databases	$ 700,000
Resources on standing order	110,000
Periodicals	685,000
Personnel—Part time	230,000
Equipment	75,000
Supplies	40,000
Contracts and maintenance (includes OCLC)	125,000
Bindery	20,000
Memberships	2,500
Travel and staff development	3,000
Total Request	$1,990,500

BUDGETING FOR PRIVATE SCHOOLS

Private schools are operated by nonprofit organizations, and many of them are associated with churches, temples, or other religious groups. Their budgeting needs for planning and controlling operations are often the same as the larger, public organizations. Likewise, private schools, regardless of size, must compete with the public schools for funding from national and local organizations, and for qualified teachers and support staff. Since the purpose of a school is to teach, it might appear that the budget would be a most routine matter. But there are many policy decisions that have to made. For example:

❐ Should the music program be expanded?

❐ Should more emphasis be placed on computer learning?

❐ Should the school increase salaries in the coming year and try to upgrade the staff?

❐ Should the athletic field be resodded this year?

❐ Should the fund-raiser be hired?

❐ Should tuition be raised?

These and many more questions face the board. The decision as to what are the goals and their relative priority has to be a board-level function. Ultimately, the board is responsible for policy and the budget represents "policy."

EXAMPLE: A SMALL CHURCH SCHOOL

An example of a small church school will be used to illustrate the differences in budgeting for a small nonprofit organization vs. a large nonprofit institute as illustrated in the two sections discussed above. This school is located in Southern California and has a total enrollment of 280 students. In contrast, a typical public elementary school in the same community has an average enrollment of over 800 students. As expected, the revenue and expenditure budgets to be prepared are significantly smaller and the whole budget process is less cumbersome for the private school.

Some budgets for the larger public schools have four plans that are treated separately: revenue, expenditure, educational, and priority. Even though it will not treat each of these individually, the private school still must consider all of these categories.

The larger public schools can also enjoy the benefits of economies of scale that are not possible in the small private school. Public administrators, however, must answer to all of the taxpayers in their community, whether or not they have children who attend the school, because public schools are funded with state tax revenues. One example of a program that is offered by the public school to the general community is a remedial speech program based on the child's need and not on whether the child is enrolled in the public school.

In contrast, private school administrators are accountable only to the parents of the children currently enrolled and the contributors to the school. The private school offers no special programs to the general community; they are funded privately and have their own goals and objectives. They are not accountable to the general community like the public schools that receive state tax revenues.

Before preparing a budget, the historical records are reviewed comparing budget to actual data. Pro forma financial statements are then prepared manually, not using a spreadsheet program, on the basis of the group's objectives. Measures are identified that will be used to evaluate progress during the year towards goals and objectives. At the private school used in our example, the budget is two pages long and is developed using percentages of increases and/or decreases on the prior year's budget. The budget is then approved by the parish head pastor. No revisions are made and no public hearings are held.

In contrast, a public school's budget is presented to the board and the general public by the superintendent. Comments and discussion would be invited and several revisions are usually made before the final, lengthy budget document is adopted for the next fiscal year.

For the small private school, the primary sources of revenue are the monthly tuition payments and the fees charged for each family. The rate schedule differs depending on whether the family is a member of the parish, a non-member, or is non-Catholic. The tuition payments also depend on whether one or more children per family are enrolled. Only an incremental tuition is charged for each additional child.

Other revenue sources include the general fee used to buy textbooks and supplies, the parish subsidy, and funds collected from fund-raising activities, such as candy sales, jog-a-thon, and bingo.

The largest category of expenditure is the salaries and related payroll taxes and benefit costs. Other large expenditures are those related to the purchase of textbooks and the costs of utilities. Salary schedules are set by the archdiocese, while textbook costs are set by the publisher. Utility budgets are based on previous period costs and repairs are based on previous bids for similar maintenance jobs. Figure 1 is a spreadsheet comparing budgeted data with actuals for school years 1990/1991 and 1991/1992 and budgets for school years 1992/1993 and 1993/1994. (The actuals for the year 1992/1993 were not available at this writing.) This data has also been plotted on Figures 2 and 3 for comparative purposes and illustration of the trend in revenues and expenses.

FIGURE 1

BUDGET DATA:
REVENUES EXPENSES IN DOLLARS

ACCOUNT TITLES	BUDGET 90/91	ACTUAL 90/91	ACTUAL OVER (UNDER) BUD DOLLARS	ACTUAL OVER (UNDER) BUD %	BUDGET 91/92	ACTUAL 91/92	ACTUAL OVER (UNDER) BUD DOLLARS	ACTUAL OVER (UNDER) BUD %	BUDGET 92/93	BUDGET 92/93	INC (DEC) IN BUDGET DOLLARS	INC (DEC) IN BUDGET %
REVENUES												
Scholarship Endowment	1,500.00	0.00	(1,500.00)	-100.00%	1,000.00	600.00	(400.00)	-40.00%	500.00	1,000.00	500.00	100.00%
Tuition	312,300.00	306,723.40	(5,576.60)	-1.79%	331,350.00	355,414.14	24,064.14	7.26%	423,680.00	427,850.00	4,170.00	0.98%
Annual Fee	40,350.00	40,857.20	507.20	1.26%	41,250.00	42,261.00	1,011.00	2.45%	41,772.00	45,250.00	3,478.00	8.33%
Registration Fee	2,640.00	0.00	(2,640.00)	-100.00%	2,700.00	4,562.01	1,862.01	68.96%	0.00	2,700.00	2,700.00	100.00%
In Lieu of Service					0.00	1,000.00	1,000.00	100.00%				
PTO Activities	50,000.00	50,000.00	0.00	0.00%	50,000.00	50,000.00	0.00	0.00%	50,000.00	50,000.00	0.00	0.00%
Donations (Restricted)		0.00			0.00	30,000.00	30,000.00	100.00%				
Food Service	0.00	9,883.17	9,883.17	100.00%	0.00	9,138.40	9,138.40	100.00%	0.00	0.00		
Day Care	15,000.00	23,634.00	8,634.00	57.56%	20,000.00	32,453.05	12,453.05	62.27%	0.00	20,000.00	20,000.00	100.00%
Exchange						11,369.72	11,369.72	100.00%	0.00	0.00		
Archdiocesan Subsidy	0.00	1,500.00	1,500.00	100.00%								
Parish Subsidy	45,000.00	42,350.00	(2,650.00)	-5.89%	45,000.00	32,150.00	(12,850.00)	-28.56%	22,500.00	22,500.00	0.00	0.00%
Bingo (Parish Operated)	15,000.00	17,650.00	2,650.00	17.67%	15,000.00	11,850.00	(3,150.00)	-21.00%	15,000.00	15,000.00	0.00	0.00%
TOTAL REVENUES	481,790.00	492,597.77	10,807.77	2.24%	506,300.00	580,798.32	74,498.32	14.71%	553,452.00	584,300.00	30,848.00	5.57%
EXPENSES												
Religious Salaries	79,380.00	64,741.21	(14,638.79)	-18.44%	91,080.00	90,113.50	(966.50)	-1.06%	81,300.00	82,215.00	915.00	1.13%
Lay Salaries	253,025.00	258,489.45	5,464.45	2.16%	254,980.00	259,742.24	4,762.24	1.87%	287,450.00	300,985.00	13,535.00	4.71%
Health Insurance	18,438.00	28,028.04	9,590.04	52.01%	34,683.00	28,694.69	(5,988.31)	-17.27%	52,046.00	56,948.00	4,902.00	9.42%
Retirement	5,956.00	16,350.67	10,392.67	174.43%	16,867.00	23,478.02	6,611.02	39.19%	20,016.00	18,912.00	(1,104.00)	-5.52%
FICA-Employer	17,010.90	16,183.45	(827.45)	-4.86%	17,271.00	17,275.19	4.19	0.02%	21,990.00	23,025.00	1,035.00	4.71%
Workmen's Compensation	3,900.00	2,957.00	(943.00)	-24.18%	3,045.00	3,273.00	228.00	7.49%	3,150.00	5,500.00	2,350.00	74.60%
Office Expenses	4,000.00	1,922.35	(2,077.65)	-51.94%	3,500.00	4,138.24	638.24	18.24%	3,200.00	4,000.00	800.00	25.00%
Property Taxes	3,000.00	3,059.68	59.68	1.99%	3,500.00	2,549.28	(450.72)	-15.02%	3,100.00	3,500.00	400.00	12.90%
Telephone	3,388.00	1,924.85	(1,463.15)	-43.19%	2,500.00	2,590.27	90.27	3.61%	2,300.00	2,500.00	200.00	8.70%
Utilities	15,357.95	12,315.58	(3,042.37)	-19.81%	12,800.00	13,502.72	702.72	5.49%	11,000.00	12,000.00	1,000.00	9.09%
Insurance-Stdnt. Accdnt.	1,500.00	1,441.00	(59.00)	-3.93%	1,500.00	1,441.00	(59.00)	-3.93%	1,700.00	2,000.00	300.00	17.65%
Classroom Supplies	8,000.00	4,638.53	(3,361.47)	-42.02%	6,000.00	6,038.03	38.03	0.63%	5,000.00	6,000.00	1,000.00	20.00%
Office Supplies	3,000.00	2,090.93	(909.07)	-30.30%	3,000.00	4,256.65	1,256.65	41.89%	3,000.00	3,000.00	0.00	0.00%
Bldg. & Ground Supplies	8,832.15	9,417.34	585.19	6.63%	6,000.00	9,235.74	3,235.74	53.93%	6,000.00	6,000.00	0.00	0.00%
Textbooks	20,000.00	21,130.73	1,130.73	5.65%	18,000.00	20,747.02	2,747.02	15.26%	21,700.00	24,000.00	2,300.00	10.60%
Computer Sftwe. & Supplies	3,000.00	757.23	(2,242.77)	-74.76%	2,000.00	9,784.28	7,784.28	389.21%	1,000.00	1,000.00	0.00	0.00%
Auto Expense	1,000.00	609.22	(390.78)	-39.08%	1,000.00	0.00	(1,000.00)	-100.00%	2,000.00	2,000.00	0.00	0.00%
Staff Development	2,000.00	1,730.00	(270.00)	-13.50%	2,000.00	1,458.00	(542.00)	-27.10%	3,000.00	3,000.00	0.00	0.00%
P.E./Athletic Program	4,000.00	2,918.51	(1,081.49)	-27.04%	3,000.00	4,246.63	1,246.63	41.55%	3,500.00	5,000.00	1,500.00	42.86%
Land/Bldg. Repr & Maint.	4,500.00	2,847.93	(1,652.07)	-36.71%	3,500.00	21,979.26	18,479.26	527.98%	1,000.00	1,000.00	0.00	0.00%
Library Books/Periodicals	1,000.00	493.96	(506.04)	-50.60%	1,000.00	1,045.58	45.58	4.56%	3,000.00	3,000.00	0.00	0.00%
Equipt. Repr. & Maint.	3,000.00	2,296.97	(703.03)	-23.43%	3,000.00	6,504.42	3,504.42	116.81%	4,000.00	4,000.00	0.00	0.00%
Office/Classroom Equipt.	2,500.00	0.00	(2,500.00)	-100.00%	2,500.00	7,299.73	4,799.73	191.99%	5,000.00	5,000.00	0.00	0.00%
Other Capital Expenditures	6,000.00	18,455.61	12,455.61	207.59%	6,000.00	18,537.82	12,537.82	208.96%	4,000.00	4,000.00	0.00	0.00%
Convent Repr. & Maint.	4,000.00	3,150.00	(850.00)	-21.25%	4,000.00	1,642.85	(2,357.15)	-58.93%	5,000.00	5,000.00	0.00	0.00%
Food Program		9,035.21	9,035.21	100.00%		9,538.21	9,538.21	100.00%	0.00	2,000.00	2,000.00	100.00%
Day Care	5,000.00	2,832.40	(2,167.60)	-43.35%	3,074.00	2,367.11	(706.89)	-23.00%	1,000.00	715.00	(285.00)	-28.50%
Student Activities	1,000.00	491.75	(508.25)	-50.83%	1,000.00	407.89	(592.11)	-59.21%	2,000.00	2,000.00	0.00	0.00%
Exchange						11,369.72	11,369.72	100.00%				
Convent Utilities					0.00							
TOTAL EXPENSES	481,790.00	490,309.60	8,519.60	1.77%	506,300.00	583,257.09	76,957.09	15.20%	553,452.00	584,300.00	30,848.00	5.57%
DIFFERENCES	0.00	2,288.17	2,288.17		0.00	(2,458.77)	(2,458.77)		0.00	0.00	0.00	

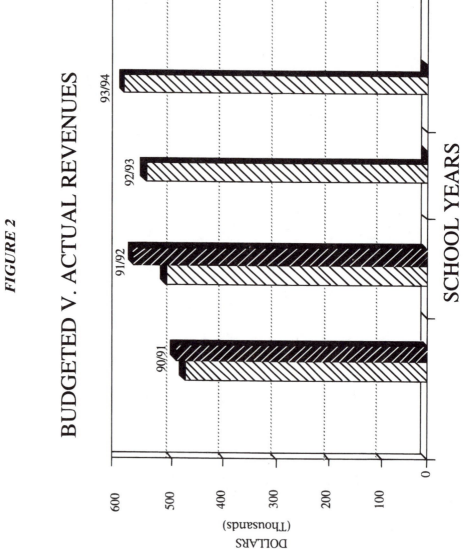

FIGURE 2

BUDGETED V. ACTUAL REVENUES

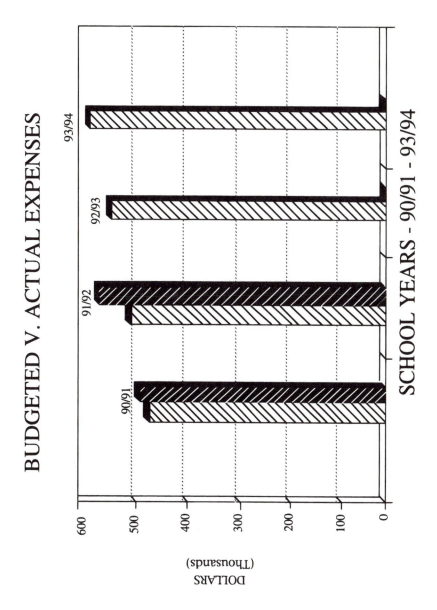

FIGURE 3

BUDGETED V. ACTUAL EXPENSES

Chapter 12

Budgeting for Churches[*][+]

The management of church financial activities and operations is a serious responsibility. Most churches have ambitious programmatic objectives but operate with limited financial resources. Therefore, modern budgeting techniques are absolutely essential for church financial management.

Church budgets have both revenue and expenses sections, but there has been a tendency to place more emphasis on the outgo portion. A thorough analysis of income is seldom completed. Not enough time has been spent on analyzing and researching the revenue trends and changes therein.

Generally, there are three objectives for the church budget:

❑ To act as a guide for the governing board to follow so that they can raise funds and pay expenses in keeping with the desires of the congregation;

*This chapter was written by Stephen W. Hartman, Ph.D., a budgeting consultant and Professor at the School of Management of the New York Institute of Technology.

+Special mention is given to Jeff Runyan, Misi S. Tagaloa, and Roger Yee for their research on church budgets.

❏ To be a tool that can be used to measure progress and to guide operations during the year. A comparison of actual income to anticipated income at designated intervals of the year can be made to determine whether or not contributions are being made at the anticipated rate. If they are not, it may be necessary to revise the budget based on the new information that is presented;

❏ To encourage contributions to the church in the area of tithing or stewardship.

Most churches carry over their budget from the previous year with only a few changes. The general format for budget preparation is outlined below and some of the questions that should be answered when formulating the budget are given:

1. Estimate the revenues for the church.

   a. Collect data from the previous two to four years and analyze the collection trends.

   b. Look at local economic conditions: What is the cost of living in the area?

   c. Look at member demographics and social conditions: Is the population changing? Are younger members being attracted to the church? What would be the effect of the death or retirement of current members?

   d. Have there been any changes to the religious education programs that would affect the contributions received from the congregation?

2. Estimate the expenses for the congregation's needs.

   a. Have a person from each department submit an estimate indicating the cost necessary for program needs for the coming year.

   b. Have the treasurer supply comparative data about actual expenses for the past few years.

   c. Analyze the information, then prioritize programs and allocate resources.

   d. If necessary, delete some items from the budget to stay within estimated income.

3. Submit the budget to the governing board.

4. Present the proposed budget to the congregation and allow time for members to respond with questions or proposed recommendations for modifications.

During the year, the actual expenditures should be compared with the relevant portion of the budget. This is almost always done on a quarterly basis. Potential trouble areas should be brought to the attention of the governing board and responsible department heads so that corrective action can be taken early.

CONDUCTING CHURCH BUSINESS WITH A PROGRAM PLANNING AND BUDGETING SYSTEM

Although the budget process proceeds as described above, many times there is no communication between the different departments and the finance committee. Where there is this lack of communication, funds may be over-budgeted in departments where they are not really needed and underbudgeted in departments where increases in financial support are necessary for the programs to function effectively. The solution to this problem is to take a systems approach to conducting business in the church by using a Program Planning and Budgeting System (PPBS).

There are many subsystems in a church that should be included in the PPBS; some of them are the governing board, the council on ministries, the education department, the Sunday School department, the finance committee, the building and grounds committee, the missions committee, etc. The objective of PPBS is to provide a structure and process for the church as a whole and for each of its departments. It will help to identify the church's mission or purpose and to connect the departmental plans to the budget-building process. To accomplish this objective, the PPBS focuses on intergroup communication and decision-making.

Some of the input needed for PPBS to operate in a church are as follows:

❐ A mission statement that is acknowledged and accepted by the congregation. This will give guidance and establish program priorities.

❐ A set of plans and budgets prepared by each department to accomplish the program's specific purpose and to support the congregation's priorities.

❒ An indication from the congregation on the total budget figure it will approve.

❒ Some guidelines and timetables to assist departmental planning groups.

The outputs from a church PPBS are as follows:

❒ A clear understanding of the organization's mission—what it hopes to accomplish within its environment.

❒ A clear understanding for each program administrator on the objective of the program and how it relates to the work of all other departments in the church.

❒ A clear definition of departmental goals and objectives.

❒ Understandable budgets for each goal, department, and for the entire church.

❒ A communication and reporting network that allows the congregation to approve the budget considering specific department plans and objectives.

PPBS is designed to allow a broader participation for members in deciding the mission and the programs of the church and the departments through the allocation of resources during the budgeting process. PPBS concentrates on gathering, organizing, and distributing useful information throughout the entire organizational system, so that individual members and departments may use it to set goals for the growth of the church and its members. With the center of the planning and budgeting as close as possible to the congregation, the utilization of PPBS will propel the church towards a decentralized structure. Some of the end results are as follows:

❒ The mission, departments, programs, and budget are decided by the congregation or from information taken directly from them.

❒ The departmental plans and budgets are prepared by each respective department.

❒ The administrative committees coordinate the plans and budgets, communicate with the congregation, and seek to provide the necessary resources to ensure the success of each program. The PPBS system as used in the church environment is illustrated in Diagram 1:[1]

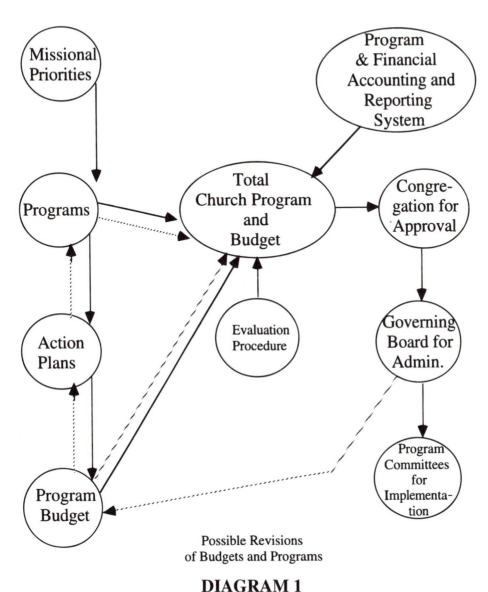

Possible Revisions
of Budgets and Programs

DIAGRAM 1

*Adapted from Lindgren & Shawchuck, *Management for Your Church* (Nashville, TN: Abingdon Publishing Co., 1977).

SAN GABRIEL VALLEY ALLIANCE CHURCH[2]

The San Gabriel Valley Alliance Church (SGVAC) is a predominately Chinese congregation located in Temple City, California. It has a membership of about 200 people attending on holidays and about 150 weekly attendees. The governing board of SGVAC which determines the direction of the church, consists of 14 members, including 3 pastors. A treasurer and financial secretary take care of all accounting functions for the church, although it is the financial secretary who is responsible for making up the budget for the church.

The budget for SGVAC is prepared by examining the previous year's budget, and new allotments to departments and programs are increased based on certain percentages or decreased where budget cuts were designated. Exhibits 1 and 2 illustrate the 1991 actual budget and the 1992 proposed budget. The amounts in revenue and expense categories were either increased or decreased from 1991 to 1992. Although the 1992 budget projected a loss of $3,742, it was accepted by the congregation. The reasoning was that a "rabbit would be pulled from the hat" sometime during the year to cover the projected deficit. This thinking is based on a faith that God will deliver the church into a more positive financial picture. The exhibits show the budget for the year 1992 with actual numbers for the first quarter. Already, there is a deficit of $935.50, well on the way to the projected $3,742.

The budgeting process consists of having the financial secretary prepare the budget and then present it to the governing board at the annual business meeting, where the budget is approved regardless of the net income expected. There is no feedback mechanism in which the congregation is allowed to give input on where it feels more funds need to be directed and where cost cuts should be made. Since no PPBS procedure is being used, the individual departments have no communication with the finance department in determining the budgeted amount to that department for the year. It does need to be pointed out that due to the relatively small size of the church, some department heads hold seats on the governing board and from that standpoint, some input can be given during the budgeting process. However, even with representation on the governing board, most departments do not present any information that is necessary in order for a PPBS system to be implemented.

EXHIBIT 1
SGV Alliance Church
Income and Expense from January to March, 1992

		1992 Budget	1991 Actual
Revenue:			
Rent:		$0.00	$7,620.00
Operating:			
	General	$85,000.00	$82,172.98
	Sunday	$14,000.00	$11,829.64
	Children	$180.00	$159.35
	Thanksgiving	$19,000.00	$18,667.00
	Sunday	$500.00	$262.87
Lunch		$0.00	$90.00
Others:			
	V.B.S.	$1,100.00	$1,020.00
	Revival	$0.00	$0.00
	Summer	$0.00	$0.00
	Xmas &	$1,400.00	$1,323.25
	Speaker's Fee	$0.00	$0.00
	Library	$0.00	$0.00
	Computer	$0.00	$0.00
	Flower	$550.00	$625.00
	New Church	$0.00	$0.00
	Interest	$1,160.00	$1,157.41
	Misc.	$2,230.00	$1,858.00
Transfer:			
	Mission	$25,000.00	$19,630.30
	Building	$4,500.00	$3,705.00
	Benevolent	$4,770.00	$4,443.10
	Gift/Fund	$0.00	$0.00
Total		$159,390.00	$154,563.90
Expenses:			
	Rent:	$12,600.00	$12,000.00
	Pastors:		
	Salary + Allow.	$91,600.00	$81,200.00
	Pension	$0.00	$0.00
	Health	$2,300.00	$3,105.58
	Life Insurance	$1,032.00	$1,392.00
	Speaker's	$1,600.00	$1,520.00
	Sunday	$2,100.00	$1,963.29

EXHIBIT 1, continued

	Lunch	$400.00	$296.00
	Other		
	Summer	$850.00	$0.00
	Easter	$100.00	$40.75
	V.B.S.	$1,500.00	$1,312.32
	Conference	$2,000.00	$2,067.76
	Revival	$100.00	$0.00
	Xmas	$600.00	$577.29
	Un-Halloween	$150.00	$0.00
	Computer	$150.00	$0.00
	Misc.	$500.00	$438.54
	Others:		
	Property Tax	$0.00	$861.84
	Utilities	$3,100.00	$3,509.52
	Cleaning	$2,600.00	$1,680.00
	Flower	$350.00	$321.69
	Liability	$2,100.00	$4,087.98
	Office/Printing	$2,800.00	$1,298.04
	C&MA	$3,800.00	$3,438.00
	Advertising	$900.00	$708.00
	Improvement	$2,300.00	$2,703.66
	Repairs/Maint	$1,000.00	$0.00
	Recreation &	$400.00	$0.00
	Gift & P/R	$1,000.00	$1,266.72
	Hitchcock	$100.00	$0.00
	Library	$500.00	$1,256.69
	Recruitment	$0.00	$455.47
	Internship	$0.00	$0.00
	Copy Machine	$1,000.00	$1,570.88
	Bank Charges	$0.00	$0.00
	Misc.	$1,500.00	$1,232.87
	Transfer:		
	Mission	$14,200.00	$15,296.77
	Building	$4,500.00	$4,788.60
	Benevolent	$3,400.00	$3,724.15
	Gift/Fund	$0.00	$0.00
	Total	$163,132.00	$154,114.41
	Net	($3,742.00)	$449.49

EXHIBIT 2
SGV Alliance Church
Income and Expense from January to March, 1992

		1992 Budget	3 Months Actual	3 Months Budget
Revenue:				
Rent		$0.00	$0.00	$0.00
Operating				
	General	$85,000.00	$22,895.00	$21,250.00
	Sunday Worship	$14,000.00	$2,692.98	$3,500.00
	Children Worship	$180.00	$27.87	$45.00
	Thanks giving	$19,000.00	$6,810.00	$4,750.00
	Sunday School	$500.00	$78.41	$125.00
Lunch Program:		$0.00	$0.00	$0.00
Others:				
	V.B.S.	$1,100.00	$0.00	$275.00
	Revival Meeting	$0.00	$182.00	$0.00
	Hymn Books	$0.00	$239.00	$0.00
	Summer Retreat	$0.00	$0.00	$0.00
	Xmas & Thanks giving	$1,400.00	$0.00	$350.00
	Speaker's fee	$0.00	$0.00	$0.00
	Library	$0.00	$0.00	$0.00

EXHIBIT 2, continued

	Computer	$0.00	$0.00	$0.00
	Flower	$550.00	$305.00	$137.50
	New Church	$0.00	$0.00	$0.00
	Interest	$1,160.00	$158.70	$290.00
	Misc.	$2,230.00	$32.50	$557.50
Transfer:				
	Mission	$25,000.00	$4,495.00	$6,250.00
	Building	$4,500.00	$3,780.15	$1,125.00
	Benevolent	$4,770.00	$2,866.94	$1,192.50
	Gift Fund	$0.00	$0.00	$0.00
Total Revenue:		$159,390.00	$44,563.55	$39,847.50
Expenses:				
	Rent:	$12,600.00	$3,150.00	$3,150.00
	Pastors:			
	Salary + Allowance	$91,600.00	$22,340.00	$22,900.00
	Pension	$0.00	$0.00	$0.00
	Health Insurance	$2,300.00	$477.48	$575.00
	Life Insurance	$1,032.00	$258.00	$258.00
	Speaker's Fee	$1,600.00	$0.00	$400.00
	Sunday School Material:	$2,100.00	$987.96	$525.00
	Lunch Program	$400.00	$0.00	$100.00
	Other Programs:			
	Simmer Retreat	$850.00	$0.00	$212.50
	Easter Program	$100.00	$0.00	$25.00

EXHIBIT 2, continued

	V.B.S.	$1,500.00	$0.00	$375.00
	Conference	$2,000.00	$165.00	$500.00
	Revival Meeting	$100.00	$908.32	$25.00
	Xmas	$600.00	$601.53	$150.00
	UN-Halloween	$150.00	$0.00	$37.50
	Computer	$150.00	$0.00	$37.50
	Misc.	$500.00	$0.00	$125.00
Others:				
	Property Tax	$0.00	$0.00	$0.00
	Utilities	$3,100.00	$1,105.30	$775.00
	Cleaning	$2,600.00	$717.00	$650.00
	Flowers	$350.00	$200.00	$87.50
	Liability Insurance	$2,100.00	$524.58	$525.00
	Office/Printing	$2,800.00	$729.21	$700.00
	C&MA Contribution	$3,800.00	$962.00	$950.00
	Advertising	$900.00	$487.00	$225.00
	Improvement	$2,300.00	$0.00	$575.00
	Repairs/ Maintenance	$1,000.00	$42.50	$250.00
	Recreation & Festivals	$400.00	$202.37	$100.00
	Gifts & P/R	$1,000.00	$0.00	$250.00
	Hitchcock Fund	$100.00	$0.00	$25.00
	Library	$500.00	$44.81	$125.00
	Recruitment (Speakers)	$0.00	$0.00	$0.00
	Internship Expenses	$0.00	$0.00	$0.00
	Copy Machine	$1,000.00	$603.85	$250.00
	Bank Charges	$0.00	$72.96	$0.00
	Misc.	$1,500.00	$350.68	$375.00
Transfer:				

EXHIBIT 2, continued

	Mission	$14,200.00	$4,055.02	$3,550.00
	Building	$4,500.00	$900.00	$1,125.00
	Benevolent	$3,400.00	$3,005.40	$850.00
	Gift/Fund	$0.00	$0.00	$0.00
Total Expenses:		$163,132.00	$42,890.97	$40,783.00
Net Income		($3,742.00)	$1,672.58	($935.50)

Since SGVAC is currently in a growth stage, it is recommended that the church implement some sort of PPBS and move away from the budgeting process currently used. A larger congregation would be more interested in having some say in how their contributions are distributed, and it would also give different departments some autonomy in determining what goals they want to achieve and how much they need to achieve those goals. Currently, the departments work with a budget amount well below what is necessary for them to reach their goals. Moreover, PPBS would more easily accommodate a large congregation because the operation is more organized and congregational input is facilitated. PPBS would serve the needs of a larger congregation more effectively than the current system.

USING MICROCOMPUTER BUDGETING APPLICATIONS AT SGVAC

The church could use many microcomputer budgeting and other applications, including word processing documents, maintaining a congregational attendance database, preparing desktop publications for advertising and promotional events during the year, and spreadsheets for facilitating the budget process.

SGVAC currently has one PC clone in its office facility. The computer is primarily configured for word processing office pastoral staff documents. There also are a few bible reference programs facilitating scriptural references. A spreadsheet program is not used in preparing the budget at SGVAC. Each line item is budgeted after an examination of the previous year's budget, and the previous allotment to that item is then increased or decreased by a percentage amount.

If SGVAC's budget would be put on a spreadsheet program such as Lotus 1-2-3, it would enable a "what if" analysis to be performed. Different line items could be increased or decreased by a given amount and the effect on the rest of the budget could be readily seen. Not only would the impact on the bottom line be immediately seen when changes were made in the revenue or expense categories, but cuts or increases in percentages for whole groups on the budget can be changed and the impact on the remaining items can quickly be determined. This analysis can help departments within the church see how increases or cuts for funding for their departments affect the financial status of other departments in the budget.

One church-focused software program is Automated Accounting System's *General Ledger* (G/L), *Contribution* (A/R), and *Membership Information* (M/I). This software was written with a church organization identified as the primary user. Recently it was used by a church much larger than SGVAC that was searching for software to aid in running church business as well as supporting the technical expertise and data entry capabilities of its congregation. The entire system fits well into the plan of the church without complex modifications. It allows the user to input budget allowances for the accounting year on the chart of account file. By using this file, the user can determine if the degree of detail required in the comparison to the budget is provided in the accounts established by the system. Also, the user can input data for a full year, specific month, or numbers of months. The user manual provides a clear description for creating control files. Upon creation of the control parameters, the system is operational.

The *Automated Accounting Systems* software provides standard formats for a profit-and-loss statement and for a balance sheet. The balance sheet can be presented in the usual end-of-period format or displayed in a comparative format where the status at the end of two periods can be compared. The receivables software—the Contribution System—can be interfaced with the general ledger system or run standalone, and journal entries can be prepared automatically.

The user can create a membership file containing profile data on each member or family-giving unit of the church. As revenues are received, they are credited to each member's account, and, where a pledge has been recorded, the outstanding balance is available in both screen display and printout.

The membership module offers a database facility and basic report-writing function. The database can accommodate ten individual data elements and ten individual dates related to each member of the congregation.[3]

CHOOSING THE RIGHT BUDGETARY METHOD

There are various methods of developing church-related budgets. In the profit sector, most budgets are developed by top management and imposed on the organization. This budgetary method is thus termed an imposed budget. The imposed budget is prevalent in large organized religions with their headquarters located in Europe. These budgets are usually developed with little or no consultation with the members of the congregation and are simply mandated.

An imposed budget can cause the development of congregational resentments. For example, in the Reorganized Church of Jesus Christ of Latter Day Saints, a group of lay preachers broke away from the mother church and formed its own organized church. The major difference the lay preachers had was with the imposed budgetary process that they felt did not adequately represent their interests.

Imposed budgets also have serious implications for organizational morale. It can lead to perceptions of inequalities and lack of representatives as well as opening the door for charges of favoritism. Nonetheless, an imposed budget is a much more manageable budget from an organizational point of view in that it is much more easily developed than other formats which emphasize closer coordination with the congregation.

CONSULTATIVE BUDGETS

A format that may be more amenable to some churches is the consultative budget. In the consultative budget top management has in-depth consultations with lower management and some key line personnel. Committees are often developed and utilized in the consultative budgetary format. This format can be very time consuming, but it does overcome some of the more objectionable elements of the imposed format, while offering some strong advantages.

One of the biggest advantages of the consultative budget is that it allows the sharing of many points of view. The consultative format creates a cooperative environment that can draw the congregation closer together.

CONSULTATIVE BUDGETING AT THE SAMOAN CHURCH COUNCIL

The Samoan Church Council in California consists of five different autonomous churches: two in Long Beach, one in Los Angeles, one in Wilmington, and one in Huntington Beach. They use the consultative budgetary method exclusively. All members who attend the budgetary meetings vote on all issues. Additionally, all issues are subject to the approval of all five congregations. The Church Council meets four times a year. At the beginning of each assembly meeting, the attendees are divided into three groups:

❒ Women's association

❒ Deacons and Deaconesses (mostly men with a handful of women)

❒ Lay personnel (preachers, assistant pastors and retired ministers)

Each group formulates and brings to the entire assembly any matter it wishes to address and/or recommend, ranging from budgets to missionary work. The entire assembly then debates and votes on all issues. Meetings can last three to four hours. At the conclusion of the meeting, everyone gathers at the fellowship hall for tea. There is a strong sense of accomplishment as well as an air of euphoria, since everyone participated in the decision-making process.

PARTICIPATORY BUDGETS

In the participatory budget, personnel at the lowest level of the organization take part in the budgetary process. As one of the most contemporary budgetary methods, it is closely identified as a strong motivator. Nonetheless, the participatory budget method has many disadvantages.

Similar to the consultative budgetary method, the participatory method is extremely time consuming. Additionally, certain choices must be made. Who should participate in this process and to what degree? Should there be no distinction between management and operating personnel participation?

However, the participatory method does work well in a small church setting where everyone has enough time to fully utilize the process and develop a budget. Participants become extremely motivated and the end product is a quality budget.

The selection of the appropriate budgeting method for a church requires developing a match between the culture of the organization and the needs of the parishioners. The consultative or participatory budgeting method requires a fair degree of sophistication on the part of the participants with value awareness of the overall needs of the organization. They also require a willingness to consider one's own values in view of competing demands.

Whereas the imposed budget is far more easily accepted in a traditional organizational environment, the consultative and participatory methods may be a good fit with a more sophisticated and educated congregation. Thus, the appropriate choice requires a careful analysis of the level of education and expectancies of a church's congregation. As the concept of organizational democracy becomes more widespread, consultative and participatory budgets increasingly become more essential as ways of involving and motivating interested parishioners.

SPECIAL BUDGETING PROBLEMS OF THE CATHOLIC CHURCH

Many church organizations have a centralized management system that does not permit a consultative or participatory budgetary system. The Catholic church is organized into archdioceses and dioceses, each headed by an Archbishop or Bishop respectively. All of the parishes within a diocese are under the financial control of the Bishop. However, under church canon law each diocese and parish has a finance council/committee. The Bishop can specify instructions regarding financial management procedures including accounting procedures and financial reports to insure financial accountability.[4] The reality is that many conventional religious organizations traditionally have an imposed budgetary system as a consequence of a centralized management system. A consultative or participatory budgeting system would not be appropriate for these traditional churches without modifications.

Nonetheless, whether one is using an imposed, consultative, or participatory budgeting system, the rational distribution of limited programmatic resources mandates a value system or ranking mechanism that prioritizes these resources within the goals, objectives and value of the religious organization. The most advantageous method for achieving consistent outcomes is the development of a financial management manual.

In 1983 the National Conference of Catholic Bishops (NCCB) and the United States Catholic Conference (USCC) issued an updated "Accounting Principles and Reporting Practices for Churches and Church-Related Organizations" financial management manual. This manual provides "guidance for Catholic Church organizations in classifying and recording financial activities relating to their mission and establishing norms for reporting these activities externally to actual or potential user groups."[5]

The reality is, however, the average individual parish either does not have access to this financial manual or does not find it to be useful. Therefore, individual diocesan parishes find they do not have substantial budgetary guidance or even guidelines to pursue. Not surprisingly, individual parish budgetary practices have little standardization.

In recent years, Catholic parishes have experienced steadily increasing programmatic costs in delivering services for their parishioners. While many have pursued collaborative ventures with other parishes, the lack of budgetary standards often results in a breakdown in financial accountability, placing a severe strain on already thin resources.

In 1985, one midwestern Archbishop spearheaded a committee to examine parish financial management practices. This resulted in the development of a Parish Financial Management Manual for all parishes. It provides guidance to parish administrators having budgetary and financial responsibilities. It addresses practices and procedures for parish accounting, budgeting, financial reporting and periodic financial review, and is meant to serve a key role in establishing consistent parish financial accountability throughout the archdiocese.[6]

Another problem for the Catholic church is internal control. This is particularly manifest in offertory collection accountability. The areas of concern include actual collection practices, accounting and recording functions, and depositing of bank proceeds. Other aspects of financial accountability include "affiliated" but financially independent church-related organizations such as athletic associations and parish societies. Fund-raising activities, investment management, and payroll are also matters of great importance for financial accountability.

The development of a useful and consistent financial management manual is essential for the Catholic church and other church-related organizations.

HOW CHURCHES CAN CONTROL COSTS

In an environment of increasingly scarce resources, churches must be concerned with cost containment. However, the nonsecular mission of a church increases the sensitivity to budgetary reduction efforts. The whole question of defining "wasteful" spending is particularly difficult. Many church-related activities do not, after all, have a clearly measurable financial objective. For example, the historic church-related practice of establishing missionaries in far corners of the world is extremely expensive and has no tangible financial benefit. Yet, it is often considered a vital element to a church's overall objective.

Nonetheless, prudent budgetary management empowers a church's long-run survival and success. A church's cost containment objectives allow it to continue its essential elements of service, ministry and outreach while reducing waste and increasing quality and performance. Several steps must be considered in any church-related budgetary cost containment effort.

STEP 1: Surveying potential cost containment areas

An accountant or church-affiliated financial officer such as a treasurer or deacon would assist in identifying areas where cost reductions could be accomplished while still achieving the church's overall objectives. Comparisons with previous budgets may help to identify areas where expenditures have been growing most rapidly. Comparisons with other churches may also be instrumental in helping reveal above-average expenses.

When expenditure categories are revealed as probable targets of cost containment efforts, research must be conducted to determine what the acceptable expenditure level would be and what effect that will have on the delivery of services. Most church-related cost items are considered fixed. However, there are variable costs relating to fluctuating attendance, festivals, or other events.

STEP 2: Establishing a cost containment program

A cost containment program must be developed and coordinated very carefully between the administrative pastor, deacon and board members as it could have a serious negative effect on individual programs and the attainment of a church's overall goals.

The best approach is to establish open board meetings where the overall containment targets can be established subject to input from interested parishioners. This would be followed by subsequent meetings where progress can be reported toward determining the cost containment targets. This will develop and nurture the concept of open financial accountability leading to the ultimate goal of acceptance and support by the parishioners.

STEP 3: Preparing and verifying the actual cost containment programs

This involves an analysis of costs from several different perspectives. One method is to compare actual costs in an observation period with those of the previous period. Another is to compare actual costs with the target costs of the observation period in the report year; finally, an analysis of the cost containment factors to determine if reductions in one area are offset by cost increases elsewhere.

STEP 4: Determining the implementation plans of the cost containment program

Since most churches are small, this is done by a relatively few people who have financial management responsibility. The only exception to this is if a central diocesan authority is involved.

STEP 5: Addressing the church's human resource management responsibility

It is extremely important that the management of the church interfaces with its personnel to insure productivity and loyalty. As a general rule, most church employees earn a smaller salary than in other organizations, and tangible results are often difficult to determine. Therefore, it is essential to motivate the employees by stressing the greater good they are accomplishing and how essential they are to achieving the church's overall goals. Increased productivity translates into lower unit cost and higher quality.

It is also important for the church to continually recruit and attract volunteers. Volunteers tend to be highly motivated and can be an extremely important source of increased productivity and reduced costs. They can help achieve cost containment targets that might otherwise not be possible.

STEP 6: Establishing a cost-of-goods reduction program

Churches normally purchase finished products, usually not for resale. The basic concept of price comparison is important, but equal consideration has to be given to reliability, quality, and availability. It may make more sense for a church to develop a strong relationship with one supplier than to continually change suppliers. The advantage of the former is that the supplier understands the church's needs while the latter may produce short-term cost reductions but have increased problems of reliability and quality, not to mention availability.

Another method of achieving a reduction in the cost of goods is product or service substitution as long as there are no quality tradeoffs. For example, substitutions can be explored in the staff automobiles and lodging expenses.

Since churches normally produce ample amounts of printed materials, it may be worth considering acquiring a sophisticated desktop publishing system to reduce the dependence on outside printers. This will often require the services of a full time employee or volunteer. The key consideration here is whether the volume and quality produced will offset the cost of the system. In many cases it will.

Achieving acceptable cost-of-goods reductions is the goal, rather than simply achieving cost-of-goods reductions. This requires a knowledgeable consumer as well as a concerted effort to develop a strong positive relationship with suppliers.

STEP 7: Reducing warehouse rental costs by reducing inventory

This may only apply to a selected number of churches. However, many churches may find themselves storing an accumulating amount of materials for a bookstore or a future fair in areas that could be used for current activities that may, in fact, be revenue producing. Selling off and reducing the inventory may not only raise money, but will also open up valuable space.

STEP 8: Evaluating the use of current materials

This involves a utilization survey of materials and equipment the church currently has. Are all of the children's play accessories, including video games, getting adequate use? Is there other specialized equipment not being properly used? How about the utilization of building space? Is the meeting room used adequately? Are there other room areas that are dedicated to some purpose that have, in fact, little use?

A basic utilization survey will help the church determine where needs are not being served and where resources are not needed. An open and sharing approach by management holding budgetary meetings with all interested parties can be extremely useful in achieving positive outcomes. This may require a rethinking of the budget and help to achieve cost containment targets.

STEP 9: Reducing manufacturing costs

While churches are not in the manufacturing business, they do have operational costs that are essential to their survival. Principal among these are utility costs. This includes electricity, heat, water, and telephone. Of these utility costs, electricity and heat are preeminently most important. An energy audit conducted by the local utility company may help to reveal areas where significant cost savings can be achieved. Recycling of materials may also be significant in achieving savings.

Substituting volunteer labor for paid labor may also be a feasible method of containing labor costs. This has already been referred to, but it is particularly pertinent in this area.

STEP 10: Reducing fixed asset costs

For a church, the principal fixed asset is its land and buildings. Depending on the financial condition of the church, many churches own their own property. However, where leases or rental contracts are involved, serious attention should be given to the terms and conditions of the lease or rental contracts. It may be that if more favorable terms cannot be negotiated, the church should consider another location or an outright purchase if this is within its financial ability.

In the event a church has excess land or space, the church may consider either selling or leasing it. However, in the case of a lease, the church would have tax implications. Where churches have excess land, the land may be utilized for holding special fund-raising events. An outright sale must be weighed against the property's future value.

STEP 11: Reducing development costs

If you consider fund-raising to be a development activity, then one has to consider a reduction in the cost of raising those funds. For example, professional fund-raisers charge a fee for their services. The question is whether the amount of money they raise is a realistic offset to their cost. Perhaps, the church management, including the pastor, can become fairly proficient at the whole concept of fund-raising and reduce the reliance upon professional fund-raisers. Fund-raising activities have to be considered based upon their net return.

STEP 12: Reducing administrative costs

Here improvements in work office procedures are emphasized in order to increase productivity. Automating as much as possible of the administrative work routine is important. Word processing, databases, spreadsheets, and fax machines are invaluable for instilling order and productivity in day-to-day administrative activities.

Normal supervision of mailing and telephone costs also play an important role in administrative cost containment.

STEP 13: Reducing distribution costs

Many churches have extensive mailing lists that are utilized for a wide variety of purposes. The use of a commercial mailing service may be helpful in obtaining lower mailing costs by utilizing bulk zone mailing and other methods. Additionally, combining appropriate mailing at specific times may have more impact while costing less.

STEP 14: Reducing publicity costs

While individual churches can and do engage in promotional campaigns, normally their campaigns are local in nature. While cable TV campaigns can at times be appropriate, typical church promotion campaigns focus on the print media. The question any church has to answer in a cost containment program is the age-old question of how to get the best response using limited resources. As was suggested earlier, developing one's own in-house desktop publishing capabilities may assist in reducing costs for the production of flyers and other promotional literature as well as encouraging creativity and in-house expertise.

Demographically targeted campaigns may be more cost effective for certain purposes than the more costly wide distributions. Screening existing mailing lists for those who have moved or have not responded can contain costs without affecting the total impact of the promotional campaign.

Asking the parishioners to start a word-of-mouth campaign can be extremely cost effective at little or no cost. Word-of-mouth advertising is, of course, the best advertising.

An innovative idea is the use of a computer bulletin board open to the community where a dialogue can be maintained between the church and its members on current events and problems as well as providing specific information. This can be done easily and may eliminate the need for some mailings or other promotional activities.

STEP 15: Developing a cost containment report

A cost containment report can be issued on an interim or annual basis. It should make a comparison about previous year spending levels and current targets as well as actual spending totals. A cost containment report should be positive in tone noting progress in meeting cost containment targets as well as discussing management innovations in achieving church goals.

NOTES TO CHAPTER 12

1. Adapted from a text by Alvin J. Lindgren and Normal Shawchuck, Management for Your Church, Nashville, TN: Abingdon Publishing Co. 1977.

2. This section is taken from an unpublished manuscript written by Roger Yee, "An Examination of the Budgeting Process for Nonprofit Religious Organizations (Churches)," California State University at Long Beach, 1992.

3. Alfred M. King, "Computers & Accounting, Hardware/Software Reviews," *Management Accounting* (March, 1988), pp. 18–20.

4. Robert L. Armacost and Wayne A. Scheider, "Financial Management in Church Operations," *CPA Journal* (April, 1989), p. 37.

5. Ibid., p. 37.

6. Ibid., p. 38.

Chapter 13

Budgeting for Credit Unions, Fraternities, and Clubs*

This chapter addresses budgeting issues surrounding other nonprofit organizations, such as credit unions, fraternities, and clubs. It also looks at their unique features.

BUDGETING FOR CREDIT UNIONS

When credit unions started in this country over 100 years ago, many people recognized the benefits they would provide for their members. Credit unions were formed by groups of professionals, trade associates, or common interest groups to allow nonprofit financial support and stability for group members.

The financial support these credit unions offered their members were basically savings and lending. Members would deposit their money into the credit union so the organization could loan it out to other members. Each member derived a benefit from this; the member who saved money in the credit union got a reasonable rate of return on his/her money, secure in the

---

*This chapter was coauthored by Adrian Fitzsimons, Ph.D., CPA, CFA, and CMA. Dr. Fitzsimons is a Professor of Accounting and Finance at St. John's University and a consultant to Deloitte, Touche, and Company, CPAs.

knowledge that the money was being invested in the other members of the union, while the member who borrowed got a loan at a reasonable interest rate and always knew the credit union was there in time of need.

The early credit unions were run usually by a few of the members out of a member's house or place of business. Most members of the same credit union were good friends. Some credit unions had basic procedures for their lending and savings practices, but that was about all. There was really no need for any formalized budgeting or accounting practices because of the small size of the organization.

ACCOUNTING AND FINANCIAL REPORTING

As credit unions grew rapidly in the early part of the 1900s, there was a growing need to standardize the industry, especially pertaining to the areas of government policy and regulations. The government established the National Credit Union Administration (NCUA) to administer and standardize all credit union policies. The NCUA then began implementing certain basic accounting procedures that all credit unions were required to follow.

One of the first accounting practices forced upon the credit unions was the use of general ledger cards for the tracking of monetary transactions. This created a permanent record of all organizational transactions for audit purposes by the NCUA.

During the mid 1900s, credit unions grew in size and number. They were able to receive tax benefits that other financial institutions were not able to receive because of their nonprofit status. Although the credit union industry was entering the mature stage, budgeting still did not play an important role during this time because the accounting systems in use were modified cash-basis accounting systems. This means expenses were recognized when they were paid out and not at the time of accrual. There were a few exceptions to the cash-basis of accounting, including:

- ❏ liabilities which were not promptly paid when due

- ❏ deferred income or expenses applicable to future periods

- ❏ depreciation on fixed assets

- ❏ estimated losses to be sustained on loans outstanding and other risk assets

Having their expenses recognized and accounted for only when the funds were actually paid out allowed credit unions to use simple bookkeeping procedures. At that time, the modified cash-basis accounting systems were highly recommended by the NCUA.

Because the cash-basis accounting systems did not give credit unions an accurate picture of their financial position at any one time, they started looking into an accrual-based accounting system. The principal bookkeeping records of the accrual-based system for credit unions consisted of the Journal, Cash Record, and the General Ledger.

With the accrual-based system, credit unions had to start deciding what and when to recognize and record as an expense. If expenses were unknown, the credit union employees who were in charge of the accounting systems had to estimate them. This is when the need for budgeting was first recognized as an important aspect of the accounting process of the credit unions.

Along with the new accrual-based accounting systems used in credit unions, budgets started being formed around the revenue and expenses of credit unions. Planning managers were noticing the same yearly expenses from year to year and started to budget these expenses accordingly. Member growth in the unions was also being studied and the revenue received was being budgeted along with the yearly expenses. These accounting and budgeting systems worked very well for credit unions during the 1950s, 1960s and 1970s, but as times changed, so did the role of the credit unions in the financial industry.

In the late 1970s and early 1980s, the credit unions made a big impact on the financial industry. They were no longer looked upon as small community groups or associations where you could get a small loan or save some extra money for a rainy day. They were growing financial institutions that offered members more and more financial services. The NCUA noticed this change in the organizations and realized they needed to redefine and modify the accounting practices. Subsequently, the NCUA set forth a purpose and scope for credit unions to use in planning their accounting systems.

MANAGERIAL ACCOUNTING AND BUDGETING

The first and most important purpose of a credit union's accounting system is to provide comprehensive and dependable financial information so that credit union management can make effective and intelligent decisions on matters that affect the operation of the organization. Profit or cost centers may be identified. Profit centers include collection and investment. Cost centers include loan processing, data processing, and marketing.

Second, all financial information received from the accounting records must be stated in financial statement form to present fairly the financial position of the credit union at a given date. The statements that are required are the *Statement of Financial Condition* and the *Statement of Activities*. Also, all accounting records must be in accordance with the NCUA accounting guidelines and must meet all government regulations set forth under the National Credit Union Act.

While the NCUA was redefining the accounting systems used by credit unions, the credit union members were redefining what services they needed from their organization. Members asked for a variety of financial services and products like some of the other major financial institutions; services such as checking accounts, retirement accounts, holiday saver accounts, various types of vehicle loans, and even VISA and MasterCard accounts. With these new services and products, credit unions needed to develop budgeting systems that would accommodate them as well as conform to the new NCUA accounting guidelines.

The NCUA gave credit union executives the flexibility to determine the types of checking and savings accounts they offered to their members. The planners had to consider the needs of the members as well as the credit union's economic and operational capabilities before putting these services and products in place. Some of the major operational considerations were the amount of existing shares that would roll over into the new type of account, the amount of new share capital that might be generated, the cost of printing the certificates and new forms, and the increase in office staff needed to operate these programs. Suddenly, the credit unions needed to focus their budgeting efforts on long-term as well as short-term operating cash flow budgets.

DEVELOPING CREDIT UNION BUDGETS

Credit union executives began to design cash flow budgets using historical data and seasonal fluctuations based on projected usage of these new products and services. Managers needed separate budgets for staffing increases, overhead increases, and variable expenses that were based on the volume of these new services and products. These budgets were not just yearly saving and lending activity budgets, but became monthly operational budgets that covered almost every activity that was performed by the credit union.

Within a short time, every level of management started to become part of the budgeting process. There were short-term budgets being created by front-line managers in regard to staffing levels to serve the members. There were other short-term and mid-term budgets being created by middle-level management on projected membership growth, product growth in shares and certificates, and personnel growth. Top-level management began developing long-term budgets for the expansion of the credit union facilities, adding new branch offices, and maintaining reserve requirements while increasing the membership base. The new focus for credit unions was to develop a budgeting system that would help allocate resources and plan for the future. The accrual-based accounting system was still being used in most credit unions, but was not so supportive as it needed to be with the new budgeting systems. To remedy this situation, most credit unions adopted a budgeting/accounting process known as *managerial accounting*.

The primary purpose of managerial accounting was to provide management with data that was necessary for planning and controlling credit union operations. Management needed to balance the needs and desires of savers against the needs and desires of borrowers within a regulatory framework. To satisfy these often conflicting demands, management instituted a comprehensive budgetary process, established written policies and measured performance against established goals and objectives.

How the Budgetary Process Works for Credit Unions

The budgetary process begins with the *planning process*. During planning, the operating budget, financial controls, and the evaluation measures are developed. The planning process is critical for credit unions because of the need to avoid the consequences of competition like cost price squeezes. The environment, both internal and external, must be evaluated, goals must be set and contingency plans made in case objectives are not being met.

The next step is *budget preparation*. Once the planning process establishes certain goals and objectives, the budget preparation process will develop program and project plans to accomplish the goals. The programs and projects should identify tasks and target dates for achieving the desired goals. Once the plans are completed, the annual budget should be prepared with actual dollar amounts allocated to various operational categories.

The third step, after planning and budget formulation, is *financial control*. Procedures are established to collect, categorize, and report data on daily operations. During this part of the evaluation, profit centers or cost centers might be identified within the credit union. Some examples of cost centers are the data processing department, loan processing operations, and the marketing department. Some examples of profit centers in credit unions are the collection department and the investment department. Once the financial control process is completed, the whole budgetary process must be evaluated.

The *evaluation*, the final step, should be a thorough review to determine the progress being made towards goals and objectives. If results are not as expected, contingency plans should be implemented. Moreover, management must determine whether its goals and objectives are still desirable given the changes in the credit unions's economic, political, or operational environments.

WHAT DOES THE FUTURE HOLD?

The managerial accounting and budgeting system has worked well for credit unions until now. However, if the credit union's environment starts to change, then changes must also occur in the budgeting process. The environment did change for the credit unions with the default of hundreds of savings and loans and thrift financial organizations. Even some credit unions failed. This alerted planners and executives to begin looking at their costs very closely and to adjust their budgeting allocation procedures accordingly.

Many credit unions performed detailed evaluations of their overall financial position during this time of crisis. Credit unions became very concerned about their bottom line and counted on their accounting systems to develop accurate figures to be used during the budgeting process. Since managerial and accrual-based accounting systems really didn't give credit unions the cost evaluations they needed during this industry crisis, credit unions modified their accounting systems to focus more on a cost-based accounting system.

Under the cost-base accounting system, credit unions could identify their cost centers and budget for them, and compute individual costs associated for each center, something they could not do under the managerial system. This allowed credit unions to get a more complete and accurate picture of their financial position and to use more accurate estimates on future processing costs for their services. With this new emphasis on cost accounting, credit unions were able to allocate their resources more effectively.

The NCUA saw this change in credit unions and started to evaluate their own rules and regulations that pertained to the accounting systems in credit unions. They knew that credit unions would not be able to comply with all of their accounting regulations and still meet their demands in the financial industry. Slowly, the NCUA started to modify its accounting requirements for credit unions. The major change that NCUA allowed was the ability of the credit unions to adopt and follow Generally Accepted Accounting Principles (GAAP). By allowing credit unions to follow GAAP, more and more credit unions were able to adjust their accounting and budgeting systems to compete more competitively with banks and savings and loans in the industry.

Even though credit unions are considered nonprofit and excluded from federal and state taxes, they are still subject to mismanagement, poor budgeting and planning, and poor economic conditions. Generally, credit unions do not have the resources the major banks and other institutions have and, for them to stay competitive, they must continue to efficiently manage their resources and plan for the future.

The future for credit unions will be determined by efficient operations. With increasing competition, the cost of funds for credit unions will rise along with the thinning of their profit margins on many of their services and products. Since most credit union costs were covered by these shrinking profit margins, other budgeting alternatives had to be evaluated. Now credit unions are looking at new ways to adjust their current accounting and budgeting systems to meet the demands of the future. They are moving towards a "business plan" and away from a short-term budgeting process. A business plan has the same cycles as a budget, but each cycle is more thoroughly analyzed. Business plans are long-term oriented with an emphasis on cost control.

Another type of program that credit unions are starting to use is the *Functional Cost Analysis Program*. This program develops credit union income and cost data along functional lines and provides comparisons of this data among various credit unions and banks. Since the cost accounting systems that the credit unions use are not an exact science, it has been hard for credit unions to compare costs among themselves and banks with much accuracy. This is especially true in cases where different methods of accounting are being used among the organizations.

The Functional Cost Analysis Program uses adjustment techniques to help standardize the comparison process. Credit unions feel that if they can obtain reasonable approximations of functional costs, year-to-year cost comparisons within the credit union and cost comparisons among other credit unions can be greatly enhanced.

With the continuing changes in the financial industry there will be ongoing consolidations of many of the financial institutions and their regulatory agencies. In the near future, a standard accounting and budgeting system will no doubt be implemented throughout the financial industry.

Are goals and objectives still practical given changes in the economic, operational, and political environment? If the environment changes, changes in the budget process must be made.

BUDGETING FOR FRATERNITIES

In the post-World War II era, college fraternities flourished at an accelerating rate. They offered the camaraderie that many veterans were used to and provided immediate social contacts and affordable housing (colleges were short on housing space). In addition, fraternities helped to provide a job network for graduating members.

Budgeting was very easy since the income stream was large and continuous. Many fraternities built new houses and started organizations on new campuses during this period.

Then came the 1960s when student unrest and the associated effects on college campuses cast a disparaging shadow on the fraternities' reputation. Fraternities were now unpopular and their membership began to decrease. Only the fraternities that budgeted reserves were able to continue their operations. Many local chapters lost their houses because they could not pay mortgages, while others spent half their budget on "Animal House"-style parties to desperately attract members, only to go broke getting the prospective members and other students intoxicated.

The 1970s was a period of slow growth and most of the poorly run chapters were no longer in business. College fraternities were now focusing on new issues to justify their existence with college administrators. Food drives, awareness seminars, blood donations, and other philanthropies benefitted from the volunteer labor in the fraternities. The Internal Revenue Service was also taking away the nonprofit status of many party-oriented fraternities and taxing income. This was also the time when the national headquarters of each fraternity started to impose guidelines for financial reporting and the setting of yearly budgets.

In the 1980s, fraternities experienced continued growth and expansion. The liability issues of alcohol, rape, and hazing put considerable pressure on fraternities to clean up their act. Insurance premiums became so high that many chapters had to suspend operations.

The 1990s have seen the national fraternities cooperating with one another on several issues. Cooperative insurance pools, co-op food buying, and new policies and procedures were created. With all the new programs created, the National Interfraternity Conference realized one disturbing trend; the majority of chapters were not budgeting reserves for the replacement of existing facilities. In fact, they found that the majority of rebuilt houses have been completed with insurance money from fires.

If fraternities are to survive in the long run, proper budgeting must be taught to all fraternity officers. Most current chapter houses were purchased after World War I or World War II and they are now reaching an age where they are no longer cost-efficient to repair. Instead, they must be entirely rebuilt. City codes won't allow most fraternities to refurbish without meeting current standards. The location of the chapter house is vital to its success, especially since there are seldom vacant lots around a college campus. This leaves no choice but to rebuild completely new facilities on the existing property. In addition to budgeting for everyday operations, the planning for the replacement of existing facilities is the major budgeting task that most fraternities face in the 1990s.

ESTABLISHING CORPORATION STATUS

College fraternities are considered nonprofit corporations by the Internal Revenue Service. The chapter houses are considered 501 C-7 corporations and are required to file Form 990 every year. They also pay tax on income earned and not contributed over 15%. Local chapters, however, must place a disclaimer on bills and receipts that says: "not tax deductible." They are also limited to raising money from members only and cannot have members make $50,000 from cookie sales. Furthermore, they cannot receive more than 35% of their income from non-members (i.e., renters, summer boarders). This is one of the reasons why most local fraternities operate as two separate corporations.

The undergraduate chapter is a corporation that is responsible for collecting dues, recruiting members, socializing, and catering to the daily needs of a college student. Officers of this corporation are elected yearly and members stay one to four years. This turnover accounts for a variety of instability problems and the lack of any long-range planning.

The housing corporation solves the above problems by having alumni members act as officers who seek to keep the fraternal experience going. The housing corporation is responsible for mortgages, property titles, insurance, physical upkeep, and other long-range plans. The corporation acts separately and has the undergraduate chapter sign a lease every year. This creates a "landlord-tenant" relationship that is generally successful in keeping away creditors and expensive litigation.

The dual corporation role also keeps the Internal Revenue Service from implementing the 35% non-member income rule. The housing corporation exists solely to provide housing for college students in general, but preferably members of its fraternity. The housing corporation cannot violate this rule because it is not a social nonprofit corporation. The 35% rule only applies to the undergraduate chapter.

The national fraternity is considered a 501 C-3 corporation by the Internal Revenue Service. This allows the fraternity to accept tax-deductible contributions from anyone. Most alumni donate their money to the national headquarters, which can then disperse the money for educational purposes to deserving local chapters. This money can be used for scholarships, libraries, computer rooms, lighting, and anything else that can be reasonably used toward academic pursuits. The guidelines for this are very stringent since the national fraternity would not want to lose its tax-deductible status.

The national fraternity can also earn tax-free money from income property while the local chapters cannot. Some local chapters have ended up with income property and have donated it to their national headquarters. In return, they receive an educational stipend.

BUDGETING FOR THE FRATERNITY

Establishing Income Levels

The undergraduate chapter establishes a budget for the coming year during the summer. The chapter officers develop the budget with help from alumni advisors, school officials, faculty, or an accountant. Many budget preparers simply increase or decrease the previous year's budget according to the Consumer Price Index (CPI). The danger in this kind of practice is that the budget may not reflect the current environmental conditions. For example, a surplus of brand new student housing may become available that is less expensive than the previous year. The college may be subsidizing its housing while the fraternity simply follows the standard CPI increase. The result is that only a few members move into the fraternity house in the fall semester, and the miscalculated budget causes the chapter's bankruptcy. The fraternity must therefore compare its basic charges with other fraternities, Guaranteed Student Loan (GSL) studies, and rent formulas.

Other fraternities that are successful at the same campus are the best ones with which to compare operations. The campus Inter-Fraternity Council can often be of help since some collect budgets of campus fraternities, but politics often means that access to these budgets is denied. Asking the officers of other fraternities what they charge is an alternative, and both sides can learn from each other. This type of exchange is best done at housing corporation meetings. Also, different fraternities at some campuses may employ the same accountant and, while the accountant obviously cannot disclose his/her clients' budgets, an astute officer can ask for the high and low charges for each cost category.

Each school that offers financial aid must have a housing-cost study from the GSL department. This study is a federal requirement and shows housing costs for the campus and its surrounding areas. It also has food costs, meal plans, parking fields, and averages of other necessities that college students require.

Rent formulas can help establish per-room or per-person pricing for the fraternity. Since most chapters sign a one-year lease with the housing corporation, the per-person price is the responsibility of the undergraduate chapter. The housing corporation can also use these formulas to determine what income is fair or adequate when the yearly lease is signed.

Regulating Cash Flow with a Payment Plan

The payment plan that the fraternity chooses must consider budgetary concerns, or else a cash flow problem may occur. Not only must the plan be realistic, it must also be clearly stated to all the members before school begins. Money collected in the spring has to help sustain the chapter house during the summer break, when income is very low. Both corporations must work together to make sure the expenses are paid in a timely fashion. The housing corporation has large, but few, transactions, such as mortgage, insurance, and property tax payments. The chapter has smaller, but more numerous expenditures, such as food, utilities, and social events. The collection of payments is vital to the success of the budget. If cash flow forecasts are not met, then items in the budget are revised to compensate.

Controlling Operating Expenses

It is typical for fraternities to go over budget figures when expenses are not kept under control. The best budget possible will not keep expenses in line if each officer does not receive a breakdown of the costs he is expected to control. The budget must be broken down and distributed to those in charge of each section.

Fixed expenses for the undergraduate chapter are not so great as the variable expenses. Flexible budgeting using percentages or ratios is helpful. Most expenses will vary according to how many members the fraternity has. When the budget is developed, an accurate count of how many members will return for the fall semester is hard to ascertain. A separate column should be left blank in the budget so the exact membership total can reflect true variable expenses. The members still pay the same rate, but the social and other variable expenses will differ.

Fixed expenses, however, are the majority of a housing corporation's budget. The mortgage payment, property taxes, insurance, and others are all relatively fixed. The only variable expenses for the housing corporation are the maintenance costs, which vary according to the number of members living in the building. The housing corporation is wise to make this a variable figure in its budget and have the undergraduate chapter pay an additional maintenance charge above its monthly rent. If this is neglected, the structure will show its age to a point where it will no longer attract members or it will be condemned by local agencies.

The social budget is a large percentage of the variable expenses for the chapter. To keep this expense from getting out of control, it must be submitted from the prior year showing any areas of cost overruns and explanations. This will allow a proper social budget to be developed that won't miss important events.

Many fraternities employ a full or part-time cook. Not only does this involve payroll and tax withholdings, but it also requires working with the cook to develop a realistic food budget. The cook's salary is fixed, but most of the food expenses are variable relating to the number of members who opt for the meal plan. The majority of cooks will not follow a budget unless they are involved in planning. A monthly breakdown of food purchases should be submitted by the cook to the treasurer as a control measure.

Putting Aside a Reserve for Bad Debts

A very important category that is usually underestimated with most nonprofit organizations is the reserve for bad debts. Using historical data provides a good base and accurately entering this total will keep other parts of the budget from going over budget. Underestimating this reserve will inflate the revenue available and cause many expense categories to exceed cost estimates at the end-of-the-year income statement.

LOOKING BEYOND BREAKING EVEN

Once the revenue and expenses are accounted for, an effective non-profit budget will go beyond merely trying to break even. This is not to say nonprofit accounting methods should mirror for-profit businesses, but non-profits should think in terms of budgeting for surpluses or reserves. The most successful fraternities use regular yearly surpluses to accumulate for use in designated funds (i.e., repairs, education, building replacement). The Internal Revenue Service does not tax extra income retained in this manner. These retained funds do not have to remain idle; they can be used in loans to other nonprofit organizations and the interest earned is not taxable.

SETTING LONG-RANGE BUDGETING PLANS

Once proper short-term budgeting has been successful, one must turn to the long run. Establishing and maintaining reserves is the budgeting duty of the housing corporation, because its function is to provide stability and perpetuity. A plan detailing the purchase or replacement of the building at a future date is necessary for determining the reserve amount needed. Future value predictions must be part of this calculation since the reserve money will earn interest and buildings will increase in price. Once this long-range plan is explained to the membership, the yearly amounts needed can become part of the yearly budgets. Reserves must also be planned for that cover unexpected emergencies and repairs.

FINANCING FRATERNITY OPERATIONS

As a general rule, fraternities need to stay under 80% debt in financing their operations. Mortgages generally do not go above this figure, but secondary financing can often make total debt go above the 80% mark. If the debt is too high, a mortgage buydown can quickly alleviate this problem.

The primary financing for fraternities has been bank loans for the purchase or remodeling of a chapter house. These loans are long-term, usually 15 to 30 years, and a majority are obtained with a co-signer. This is becoming very hard to do in most states, however, since home prices are high and fraternities are considered risky. One option some fraternities have started using is to apply for a business loan instead of a home loan. This is another good reason for the fraternity to implement accurate budgeting and cost controls.

A financing method that was popular prior to 1950 was to sell corporate bonds to members or their parents to purchase a building. This method has seen some renewed interest since home loans are more difficult to obtain.

Fund-raising has always been a way of fraternity life. Since the national headquarters are now stronger than ever, they have been the main fundraisers. This, together with a revised tax status, has left the local chapters with few donations. Hiring a professional fund-raising company can bring in extra revenues and allows the housing and chapter corporations to focus their attention on other areas.

Bequests are another way in which the fraternity can finance operations. Since the principal can't be touched, they can establish a perpetuity upon a person's death that can become a source of yearly income.

Budgeting for a fraternity is a behind-the-scenes process, as it is for most nonprofit organizations. Members are quick to blame someone else when complaints about finances arise. The increasing costs of college tuition will no longer allow students to spend freely on fraternities as they did in the past. The fraternities have to demonstrate what they can offer to students, and a must for effective planning and operations is the implementation of a conscientious and comprehensive budgeting process.

CASE STUDY: PACIFIC SOCCER LEAGUE—STRIKERS[1]

HISTORY AND BACKGROUND

The Pacific Soccer League, Premier Division Strikers, is registered as a nonprofit organization. The Pacific Soccer League (PSL) is recognized as the strongest league in Southern California with 50 teams and 4 divisions. The Strikers have been a semi-professional soccer club since 1978 with players ranging in age from 19 to 35. Some of the players have played professionally before joining the team and others have experience playing on college teams. Currently, the Strikers have a wide variety of soccer backgrounds with college experience from Rochester Tech, Cincinnati, Cerritos, Fullerton, and Cornell University and professional experience from Argentina, Brazil, and Los Angeles. The team was originally funded by a wealthy soccer enthusiast. However, after frustrations with rising costs to compete in the Pacific Soccer League and a losing season, the Strikers lost their sole source of financing in 1991. It was at this time the budget came under discussion and review so team playing could continue.

The team has no employees, just volunteers who offer to coach, doctor, manage, and try to organize the financial records for the team. At this point, a budget was developed by first choosing a fiscal year.

The Strikers season begins in October and ends in April. For this reason the fiscal year was chosen to start in September and end in August of the next year. With the first game scheduled in October, September brings several fees due, including PSL registration, California State Soccer Association registration, and Premier Division Prize Fund. The remainder of the fees are incurred throughout the year and are largely based on the number of games played and tournaments entered. With April ending the season, this leaves at least four months to organize and close the books for that year. Therefore, the 1993 budget reflects costs incurred from September 1, 1993 through August 31, 1994. The 1994 budget reflects costs for September 1, 1994 through August 31, 1995.

THE BUDGET

The simple and straightforward nature of the Strikers' financial system led to the choice of using the cash-basis accounting system. The financial transactions were recorded only when cash changed hands. Because all fees were written from one central checking account and all deposits were made from the same account, this involved no more than just accurate check balancing.

The most important step in the budget process was to accurately figure out how much income the team would take in and how much would be spent throughout the year. The budget was grouped into two main sections: income and expenses (costs). Within these two sections were further subdivisions into specific income and expense categories. Each of these categories was placed on its own line with a dollar value attached to it in a *Lotus 1-2-3* spreadsheet program. (See Figure 1.)

Figure 2 presents graphical display of expense categories.

The largest of the cost categories is the field fees followed by the referee fees. Field fees include costs to reserve the field, maintain, line with chalk for games, and light the field for night games. Referee fees include money paid to the three referees to work the game.

Budgeting is directly related to the overall planning process of the organization. In order to plan for the future, a clear sense of what the available resources are and what the team goals are must be used strategically. For this part of the budgeting process, the team manager, captain, and coach were involved in both the budgeting and general planning process. Because these team members must set long-range goals for the team, decide on team priorities, and ultimately assume fiscal accountability, it is important that they be involved in the budgeting process both in the forecasting stages and later when the budget is monitored and compared to actual results. The setting up of a contingency/reserve account was facilitated through the budgeting process. Roughly 5 percent of the team's total income was budgeted for this purpose. It helped serve as a form of self-insurance in case some unexpected expense comes up during the year, such as fines, injuries not covered by insurance, equipment emergency repairs, and miscellaneous costs not accounted for in the initial budget process. If at the end of the fiscal year there is money left over after all contingencies have been taken care of, the reserve simply becomes just that, and the unallocated money can be put into some kind of savings account, market fund, or stock as determined by the team vote. Each year funds should be put aside until such time as the team has from 25 to 50 percent of an entire year's budget in reserve, mainly because no one can guarantee the success of a fund drive or the number of sponsors who will give money to the team year after year. Eight steps were taken to complete a successful budgeting cycle, each of which is discussed below.

FIGURE 1

PACIFIC SOCCER LEAGUE STIKERS BUDGETS

	1991	1992	1993
(1) Income			
Sponsors			
Arrowhead	$250.00	$600.00	$300.00
Soup Plantation	$150.00	$100.00	$ 0.00
Lamp Post Pizza	$100.00	$400.00	$250.00
Toyota	$500.00	$700.00	$500.00
Westdoor & Frame	$2,000.00	$1,000.00	$1,500.00
Players ($50/player)	$800.00	$1,000.00	$1,000.00
John Medel	$500.00	$400.00	$200.00
Brett Wood	$500.00	$200.00	$350.00
Bill Gerring	$500.00	$400.00	$400.00
Nigel Barrett	$500.00	$550.00	$450.00
JUSA League	$800.00	$2,700.00	$2,700.00
Total Income	$6,600.00	$8,050.00	$7,650.00
(2) Expenses			
Players:	16	20	20
Games Played	20	30	25
PSL League Fee	$250.00	$280.00	$308.00
CA Registration	$300.00	$300.00	$330.00
PSL Prize Fund	$160.00	$160.00	$176.00
League Referee Fees	$1,000.00	$1,500.00	$1,650.00
($50/game)			
Liability Insurance	$ 30.00	$ 30.00	$ 33.00
PSL Dinner	$125.00	$125.00	$137.50
Tournament Fees:			
Tournament Referee	$480.00	$320.00	$352.00
($40/game)			
Budweiser Open Cup	$ 60.00	$ 60.00	$ 66.00

FIGURE 1, continued

Las Vegas	$200.00	$200.00	$220.00
State Cup	$ 50.00	$ 50.00	$ 55.00
National Open Cup	$ 50.00	$ 80.00	$ 88.00
National Amateur	$ 60.00	$ 40.00	$ 44.00
Oregon Tournament	$ 0.00	$ 80.00	$ 88.00
Supplies:			
Newletters	$100.00	$110.50	$121.55
Stamps	$ 29.00	$ 32.05	$ 35.25
Paper/envelopes	$ 50.00	$107.45	$118.20
Field ($58/game)	$250.00	$475.00	$522.50
Field Maintenance	$200.00	$157.50	$173.25
Chalk	$100.00	$205.00	$225.50
Lights ($100/game)	$1,000.00	$1,330.00	$1,463.00
Reserve	$330.00	$372.50	$382.50
(5% of total income)			
Total Costs	**$4,824.00**	**$6,015.00**	**$6,589.24**
Year balance	$1,776.00	$2,035.01	$1,060.76

FIGURE 2

STRIKER EXPENSES

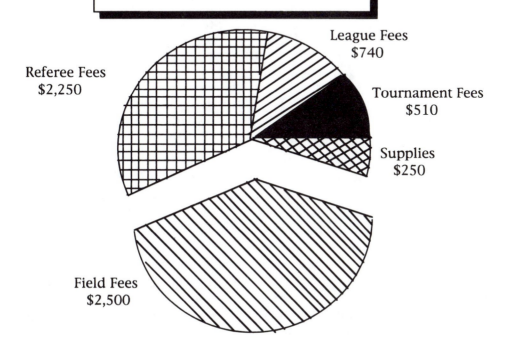

League Fees
$740

Referee Fees
$2,250

Tournament Fees
$510

Supplies
$250

Field Fees
$2,500

Making a "Wish" List

The first step was a review of what the team manager, captain, and coach wanted to accomplish during the year. At the beginning of the budget cycle, the team representatives sat down to consider a number of questions about the upcoming soccer season:

1. What tournaments does the team wish to enter this year?

2. Should the players pay for team travel expenses?

3. What additional activities might be undertaken if costs are not an issue?

4. Are there special one-time expenditures that might be considered for things such as equipment, the improvement of physical facilities, or special consultants in marketing the team?

Each year the team enters the league cup (this is mandatory), the Budweiser Open Cup, the Las Vegas Open, the State Cup, the National Open Cup, the National Amateur Cup, and the Oregon Cup. Each cup has an entry fee to help pay for tournament expenses; usually half of the collected entry fees go to the first-, second-, and third-place teams. The payoff for entering the tournaments is that those tournaments with weaker teams and large prize money are a good investment for the team, provided they win. The tournaments that have stronger teams should be limited because the chances of winning the prize money are not so great as the challenge to win. Tournaments that the Strikers wish they could enter include the Santa Barbara Cup and the San Francisco Open.

The Strikers have paid for their own travel expenses to and from games and tournaments ever since the founding of the team. Other teams with larger budgets pay for all their players' travel expenses, thus attracting some of the more talented players to their team and away from the Strikers. To stay competitive in the PSL, travel expenses should be paid for.

Travel to Europe to compete against European semi-professional leagues has long been a dream of many of the players. Although the cost would be exorbitant, it is a goal worth aiming for provided that careful planning and budgeting takes place. This would definitely be a long-term planning goal for the team.

The Strikers have played in the same uniforms for the past two years. Last year shorts and socks were donated to the team from a soccer store, but cleats, chin guards, sweats and soccer bags are still financed by each individual player. If cost were no object, the team would like to supply each player with complete new uniforms, sweats, soccer bag, and shin guards. In addition, the team also needs new soccer balls, nets for the goals, and flags for the field. The ultimate wish would be a team van for travelling to and away from games.

Costing Out the "Wish" List

The next step in the budgeting process was to cost out the "wish" list. Obviously, this is done after the basic costs are covered first so the Strikers can keep playing in the PSL. The basic costs were budgeted using an incremental method that relied on the previous year's is actual expenses and income. Each item was carefully evaluated to insure this was indeed an accurate budgeted figure.

The new "wish list" items required estimates to be made. This was done using a zero-base budgeting method with costs being estimated on the high side, adding an additional 10 percent to each figure to protect the team from under budgeting for those activities that had never been done before. See Figure 3 for "wish" list cost estimates.

Estimating Income

The third step was to estimate income from each business sponsor and/or fund-raising activity. Again, the previous year's actuals were helpful. However, because most of the money was funded from one person who did not wish to fund the team this year, a new approach had to be taken. The most dependable income was the required player fee paid by each team member before he/she could actually play. As the number of players increases, so does the amount of money the team collects. Other additional income is largely dependent on the individual contributions from the coach, manager, and two devout Striker fans.

The largest and most underdeveloped area of income is outside sponsorships. In 1991, the Strikers had Arrowhead Water, Soup Plantation, Lamp Post Pizza, Toyota Industrial Equipment (T.I.E.), and Westdoor & Frame as sponsors. In the first half of the 1992 season, the Strikers lost the sponsorship of the Soup Plantation due to lack of reciprocal sales. At the same time, however, Westdoor & Frame increased its contribution as did Arrowhead and Lamp Post Pizza. It is more cautious to understate all income estimates by at least 10 percent. Another undeveloped area is prize

FIGURE 3

WISH LIST EXPENSES	'93 COSTS
CUP REGISTRATION FEES:	
SANTA BARBARA CUP	$ 120.00
SAN FRANCISCO OPEN	$ 200.00
TRAVEL EXPENSES (CUP GAMES ONLY)	
PLANE	
LAS VEGAS	$ 1,800.00
SAN FRANCISCO	$ 2,000.00
OREGON	$ 4,000.00
BUS	
LAS VEGAS	$ 1,000.00
SANTA BARBARA	$ 600.00
TRAVEL TO EUROPE	
REGISTRATION FEE	$ 500.00
PLANE	$ 22,000.00
HOTEL	$ 5,600.00
INTER-COUNTRY TRAVEL	$ 1,000.00
EMERGENCY RESERVE	$ 1,000.00
TOTAL EUROPE	**$ 30,100.00**
NEW UNIFORMS	
SHIRTS	$ 640.00
SHORTS	$ 300.00
SOCKS	$ 160.00
SHIN GUARDS	$ 200.00
CLEATS	$ 1,500.00
SWEATS	$ 1,500.00
SOCCER BAGS	$ 400.00

FIGURE 3, continued

SOCCER BALLS	$ 300.00
NETS	$ 200.00
FLAGS	$ 80.00
TOTAL NEW UNIFORMS	**$ 5,280.00**
VAN	$ 20,000.00
PRO COACH/RECRUITER	$ 18,000.00
PRO MARKETING CONSULTANT	$ 8,000.00

money for winning tournaments. This is an untapped resource if the Strikers opt to enter less popular tournaments with teams that are not so talented as they are, thus being a good bet that the Strikers would win the prize money. This could help generate some much needed income. (See Figure 4 for graphical representations of 1991, 1992 and 1993 income budgets.)

FIGURE 4
PSL Strikes Yearly Income

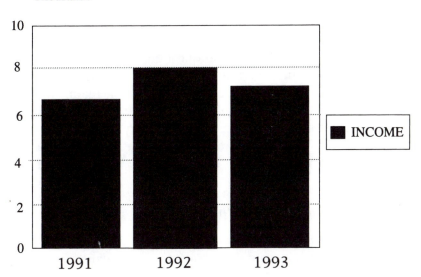

Assigning Priorities

During step four of the budgeting process, priorities were assigned to each of the "wish" list activities and the regular costs for the team. It was at this point that the real negotiating took place after the basics were budgeted. The following list resulted after negotiations:

❏ League/player registration fees

❏ Referee fees

❏ Field use and maintenance

❏ Tournament fees

❏ New uniforms

❏ New equipment

❏ Travel expenses

❏ Extended travel games/tournaments

❏ Professional coach/recruiter

❏ Professional marketing team

❏ Team van

The priority-setting must relate not only to dollars and cents, but to a fundamental assessment of the team's reason for being. For this purpose, each priority was held up to the question, "Does this help the team get where it should be in a year, in two years, in five years?" This forced every member to evaluate what he/she expected from the team. Was this a just-for-fun team or was the ultimate goal to branch out and be recognized as one of the top semi-professional teams in the country? These were difficult questions, but in asking them the team representatives fulfilled a fundamental role in deciding what course is best for the team and is most clearly in the league's interest.

Adjusting and Balancing the Budget

The fifth step was to adjust and balance the budget. It was clear that some activities had to be given up if the budget was to balance. Too many expenses and not enough income! All of the projects should be considered and examined even though only some will be undertaken immediately. The review of a potential activity one year is very valuable in planning goals and activities for the next year. Once activities have been put in some semblance of order, a little negotiation is still possible as the budget is adjusted and brought into balance. Some examples of areas that could be adjusted include the number of players (more players increases income) and the number of tournaments (less tournaments mean less cost in registration fees, field costs, and referee fees).

The 1991 year balance was added to the 1992 year balance and the result was $3,811.01, which was available for spending on the "wish list" items. This amount represented monies available after the normal yearly costs had been paid. Looking at the priorities list, the team began to choose which alternatives would be met with the available budget. After comparing costs, the following items from the "wish list" were chosen to purchase at the end of the 1992 fiscal year:

1. Registration fees for Santa Barbara and San Francisco

2. New uniforms of shirts, shorts, sweats, and new balls.

3. Travel expenses

After subtracting the purchase amounts of items 1 and 2, the amount left was $751.01, and this was put into a travel expenses fund to be built upon so that eventually the team could afford to pay for one game's travel expenses. It was also agreed that those items the team could not afford this year would be retained on a separate list to be reviewed in next year's wish list.

Discussing and Approving the Proposed Budget

The sixth step in the budget process was for the full team to discuss and approve the proposed budget for the next fiscal year. This was more than a mere formality because, by voting, the team exercises its fiduciary responsibility in setting financial limits and boundaries. It also forces the team to implicitly agree to meet the projected revenues through a commitment to fund-raising.

Cash-flow projections are most commonly prepared on a monthly basis for the upcoming fiscal year. In this analysis, the team's income and expenses are projected for each month. This protects the team from a potential cash shortage problem and can provide it with enough warning to be proactive in revising problem areas. See Figure 5 for the 1993 monthly cash budget.

FIGURE 5

1993 PACIFIC SOCCER LEAGUE STRIKERS MONTHLY CASH BUDGET

	SEPT	OCT	NOV	DEC	JAN	FEB	MAR	APR	MAY	JUNE	JULY	AUG	TOTAL
Tournament Games Played (Nov. - April)													
Games Played	4	4	4	0	0	1	4	3	2	0	0	0	22
Players	18	25	25	25	25	25	25	25	25	25	25	25	
PSL League Fee	$280.00	$0.00	$0.00	$0.00	$0.00	$0.00	$0.00	$0.00	$0.00	$0.00	$0.00	$0.00	$280.00
CA Registration	$300.00	$0.00	$0.00	$0.00	$0.00	$0.00	$0.00	$0.00	$0.00	$0.00	$0.00	$0.00	$300.00
PSL Prize Fund	$160.00	$0.00	$0.00	$0.00	$0.00	$0.00	$0.00	$0.00	$0.00	$0.00	$0.00	$0.00	$160.00
League Referee Fees ($50/game)	$200.00	$200.00	$250.00	$150.00	$150.00	$150.00	$0.00	$0.00	$0.00	$0.00	$0.00	$0.00	$1,160.00
Liability Insurance	$30.00	$0.00	$0.00	$0.00	$0.00	$0.00	$0.00	$0.00	$0.00	$0.00	$0.00	$0.00	$30.00
PSL Dinner	$0.00	$0.00	$0.00	$0.00	$0.00	$0.00	$0.00	$125.00	$0.00	$0.00	$0.00	$0.00	$125.00
Tournament Fees:													
Tournament Referee Fees ($40/game))	$40.00	$0.00	$0.00	$0.00	$0.00	$40.00	$40.00	$120.00	$80.00	$0.00	$0.00	$0.00	$320.00
Budweiser Open Cup	$0.00	$0.00	$60.00	$0.00	$0.00	$0.00	$0.00	$0.00	$0.00	$0.00	$0.00	$0.00	$60.00
Las Vegas	$0.00	$0.00	$200.00	$0.00	$0.00	$0.00	$0.00	$0.00	$0.00	$0.00	$0.00	$0.00	$200.00
State Cup	$0.00	$0.00	$0.00	$0.00	$50.00	$0.00	$0.00	$0.00	$0.00	$0.00	$0.00	$0.00	$50.00
National Open Cup	$0.00	$0.00	$0.00	$0.00	$80.00	$0.00	$0.00	$0.00	$0.00	$0.00	$80.00	$0.00	$80.00
National Amateur Cup	$0.00	$0.00	$0.00	$0.00	$40.00	$0.00	$0.00	$0.00	$0.00	$0.00	$0.00	$0.00	$40.00
Oregon Tournament	$0.00	$0.00	$0.00	$0.00	$0.00	$0.00	$0.00	$0.00	$80.00	$0.00	$0.00	$0.00	$80.00
Total Tournament Entry Fees	$0.00	$0.00	$0.00	$0.00	$0.00	$0.00	$0.00	$0.00	$0.00	$0.00	$0.00	$0.00	$510.00
Supplies:													
Newsletters	$50.00	$0.00	$0.00	$0.00	$60.50	$0.00	$0.00	$0.00	$0.00	$0.00	$0.00	$0.00	$110.50
Stamps	$14.50	$0.00	$0.00	$0.00	$17.55	$0.00	$0.00	$0.00	$0.00	$0.00	$0.00	$0.00	$32.05
Paper/envelopes	$50.00	$0.00	$0.00	$0.00	$57.45	$0.00	$0.00	$0.00	$0.00	$0.00	$0.00	$0.00	$107.45
Field ($25/game)	$62.50	$50.00	$62.50	$37.50	$37.50	$50.00	$62.50	$62.50	$50.00	$0.00	$0.00	$0.00	$475.00
Field Maintenance	$17.50	$17.50	$17.50	$17.50	$17.50	$17.50	$17.50	$17.50	$17.50	$0.00	$0.00	$0.00	$157.50
Chalk	$25.00	$25.00	$25.00	$25.00	$25.00	$25.00	$25.00	$25.00	$15.00	$0.00	$0.00	$0.00	$205.00
Lights ($70/game)	$175.00	$140.00	$175.00	$105.00	$105.00	$140.00	$175.00	$175.00	$140.00	$0.00	$0.00	$0.00	$1,330.00
Total Field Fees													$2,167.50
Reserve (5% of total income)	$90.00	$35.00	$60.00	$20.00	$50.00	$15.00	$25.00	$30.00	$30.00	$17.50	$0.00	$0.00	$372.50
Total Costs	$1,494.50	$467.50	$850.00	$345.50	$690.50	$437.50	$545.00	$655.00	$432.50	$17.50	$80.00	$0.00	$6,015.00
Income:													
Sponsor:													
Arrowhead	$0.00	$0.00	$300.00	$0.00	$0.00	$0.00	$100.00	$100.00	$100.00	$0.00	$0.00	$0.00	$600.00
Soup Plantation	$100.00	$0.00	$0.00	$0.00	$0.00	$0.00	$0.00	$0.00	$0.00	$0.00	$0.00	$0.00	$100.00
Lamp Post Pizza	$0.00	$0.00	$0.00	$0.00	$100.00	$0.00	$100.00	$100.00	$100.00	$0.00	$0.00	$0.00	$400.00
Toyota	$0.00	$0.00	$500.00	$0.00	$0.00	$0.00	$0.00	$0.00	$0.00	$200.00	$0.00	$0.00	$700.00
Westcoer & Frame	$500.00	$0.00	$0.00	$0.00	$500.00	$0.00	$0.00	$0.00	$0.00	$0.00	$0.00	$0.00	$1,000.00
Players ($50/player)	$900.00	$100.00	$0.00	$0.00	$100.00	$0.00	$0.00	$0.00	$0.00	$0.00	$0.00	$0.00	$1,000.00
John Model	$100.00	$100.00	$0.00	$100.00	$0.00	$100.00	$0.00	$0.00	$0.00	$0.00	$0.00	$0.00	$400.00
Brett Wood	$100.00	$100.00	$0.00	$0.00	$0.00	$0.00	$0.00	$0.00	$0.00	$0.00	$0.00	$0.00	$200.00
Bill Gerring	$0.00	$200.00	$0.00	$0.00	$0.00	$0.00	$0.00	$0.00	$0.00	$200.00	$0.00	$0.00	$400.00
Nigel Barrett	$0.00	$300.00	$100.00	$0.00	$0.00	$0.00	$0.00	$0.00	$0.00	$150.00	$0.00	$0.00	$550.00
JUSA League	$300.00	$300.00	$300.00	$300.00	$300.00	$300.00	$300.00	$300.00	$300.00	$0.00	$0.00	$0.00	$2,700.00
Total Income	$1,800.00	$700.00	$1,200.00	$400.00	$1,000.00	$300.00	$500.00	$600.00	$600.00	$350.00	$0.00	$0.00	$8,050.00
Accrued Balance	$1,800.00	$1,005.50	$1,738.00	$1,288.00	$1,943.00	$1,552.51	$1,615.01	$1,670.01	$1,615.01	$1,532.51	$1,515.01	$1,435.01	$18,709.54
Month Balance	$305.50	$538.00	$888.00	$943.00	$1,252.51	$1,115.01	$1,070.01	$1,015.01	$1,182.51	$1,515.01	$1,435.01	$1,435.01	$12,694.54

Monitoring and Revising the Budget

The last step in the budgeting process for the Strikers was to monitor and revise the budget as new information and new conditions took place during the year. One common mistake is to assume the budgeting process has come to an end once the team approves the budget. This flexible approach to updating the budget is extremely valuable in keeping the budget current with rising or changing costs. Any changes that are made during the year should be reviewed so that errors can be avoided when a new budget is prepared during the next budget cycle.

MAINTAINING FINANCIAL HEALTH

As the financial budgets indicate, the PSL Strikers are maintaining moderate financial health. However, if real future growth for the team is expected, then income needs to increase significantly. Some recommendations the Strikers should consider in an effort to obtain some of the items on their "wish list" and maintain financial health include:

1. Have a field donated by an organization to cut field fees, which are the most expensive cost category. The Strikers can offer to maintain the field themselves in return for having no field fees.

2. Recommend to the PSL that only day games, not night games, should be played. This would cut light fees for the field.

3. Offer camps for young soccer players a few hours before the Strikers' scheduled games. Charge $5 a player or $20 a team and help develop basic soccer skills in these younger players. Field fees would not have to be paid for the camp because they already would be paid under the game expenses.

4. Actively and aggressively seek out more sponsors. With the 1994 World Cup held in the United States, this could be the ideal time to find sponsors and ride the wave of popularity that soccer experiences as a result of the World Cup.

Before this budget planning took place, the Strikers had been hit with expenses that were forgotten, because they had never been written down and team members would either pool their own money quickly or request the fans to do so. Now, with an updated budget and monthly cash-flow projection, costs can be expected and organized so that planning for future growth can take place.

NOTE TO CHAPTER 13

1. Adapted from Jamie Wood, *Budgeting for Nonprofit Organizations: Strikers*, an unpublished graduate thesis, California State University at Long Beach, 1992.

ADDITIONAL READINGS

AICPA SOP 78-10 *Accounting Principles and Reporting Practices for Certain Nonprofit Organizations*, paragraph 12.

AICPA, Inc. *Audits of Providers of Health Care Services*, 2nd Edition (New York, 1991).

American Hospital Association—1976 Chart of Accounts for Hospitals, p. 6.

Anderson, H. J. "CFOs: Cost-Shift Pressures Will Spur Health Care Policy Reform," *Hospitals*, August 1991, pp. 38–43.

Anthony, R. and D. Young. *Management Control in Nonprofit Organizations*, 3rd Edition (Richard D. Irwin, 1988).

Armacost, R. and W. Schneider. "Financial Management In Church Operations," *CPA Journal*, Vol. 59, Number 4, April 1989, pp. 36–41.

Bailey, Larry P. *Miller Comprehensive GAAP Guide* (Harcourt Brace Jovanovich, 1987).

Bedell, Kenneth. *Using Personal Computers in the Church* (Judson Press, 1983).

Bolster, C. J. and R. Binion. "Linkages Between Cost Management and Productivity," *Topics in Health Care Management*, Summer 1987, pp. 67–75.

Burda, D. "DRGs: Five Years of PPS Have Fostered Division and Fierce Competition," *Modern Healthcare*, November 4, 1988, p. 26.

Butler, R. J. and D. C. Wilson. *Managing Voluntary and Nonprofit Organizations* (Routledge, 1990).

Caplan, Edwin H. *Management Accounting & Behavioral Science* (Addison-Wesley, 1971).

Cleaverly, W. *Essentials of Health Care Finance* (Aspen Publications, 1992).

Cleaverly, W. "ROI: Its Role in Voluntary Hospital Control," *Hospital Health Services Administration*, Spring 1990, pp. 71–82.

Cook, Donald. "Strategic Plan Creates a Blueprint for Budgeting," *Healthcare Financial Management*, Vol. 44, May 1990, pp. 21–27.

Cook, J. "How Good Are Our Nonprofit Hospitals?" *Forbes*, April 30, 1990, p. 104.

Dabbs, Gordon. "Nonprofit Businesses in the 1990s: Models for Success," *Business Horizons*, Sept. 1991, Vol. 34, p. 68.

Douglas, Patricia. *Governmental & Non-Profit Accounting, Theory and Practice* (Harcourt Brace Jovanovich, 1991).

Drucker, P. F. *Managing the Non -Profit Organization* (Harper Collins, 1990).

Forbes, "Consultant in a Bind," November 13, 1989, pp. 285–286.

Freeman, Robert L., Craig Shoulders, and Edward Lynn, *Governmental and Nonprofit Accounting: Theory and Practice* (Prentice Hall, 1983).

Gies, D. L., J. S. Ott, and J. M. Shafritz, *The Nonprofit Organization* (Brooks/Cole, 1990).

Goldschmidt, Y. and A. Gafni, "A Managerial Approach to Allocating Indirect Fixed Costs in Health Care Organizations," *Health Care Management Review*, Spring 1990, pp. 43–51.

Governmental Accounting and Financial Reporting Principles, authoritative pronouncement NCGA-1, pp. 13, 14, 78, and 94–97.

Griffith, John R. *The Well Managed Community Hospital* (AUPHA, 1992).

Gross, Malvern J. Jr., and Stephen F. Jablonsky. *Principles of Accounting and Financial Reporting for Nonprofit Organizations* (John Wiley & Sons, 1979).

Hax, Arnoldo C. and Nicolas S. Majluf. *The Strategy Concept and Process: A Pragmatic Approach* (Prentice Hall, 1991).

Helmi, M. A. and M. N. Tanju, "Activity-Based Costing May Reduce Costs, Aid Planning," *Healthcare Financial Management*, November 1991, p. 95.

Henke, Emerson O. *Introduction to Nonprofit Organization Accounting*, 2nd edition (Kent Publishing Company, 1985).

Herkimer, A. G. Jr., *Understanding Hospital Financial Management*, (Aspen Publication, 1988).

Hunter, J. E., F. L. Schmidt and T. Daniel Coggin. "Problems and Pitfalls in Using Capital Budgeting and Financial Accounting Techniques in Assessing the Utility of Personnel Programs," *Journal of Applied Psychology*, August 1988, pp. 522–528.

Johnson, E. A. and R. L. Johnson. *Hospitals Under Fire* (Aspen Publication, 1986).

Jones, Charles O. *An Introduction to the Study of Public Policy*, 3rd edition (Brooks/Cole, 1984).

Jones, L. R. *University Budgeting for Critical Mass and Competition* (Praeger Publishers, 1985).

Kenkel, P. J. "DRG Study Shows Disparity Among Hospitals," *Modern Healthcare*, January 28, 1991, p. 18.

Kennedy, L. W. *Quality Management in the Nonprofit World* (Jossey-Bass, 1991).

Kirk, R. *Identifying Costs and Pricing Nursing Services*, Aspen Publication, Rockville, Maryland, 1987.

Kuchler, Joseph. "Tax-Exempt Yardstick: Defining the Measurements," *Healthcare Financial Management*, February 1992, Vol. 46, pp. 20–32.

Lane, Frederick S. *Current Issues in Public Administration*, 3rd edition (St. Martin's Press, 1986).

Lindgren, Alvin J. and Norman Shawchuck. *Management for Your Church* (Abingdon Publishing Co., 1977).

Lineman, Harold F. *Business Handbook for Churches* (Warner Press, 1964).

Lynch, Thomas. *Public Budgeting in America* (Prentice Hall, 1990).

Mastromo, Frank. "Automating Church Accounting," *Management Accounting*, Vol. 69, Issue 9, March 1988, pp. 18–20.

Nemes, J. "Not-for-Profit Margins Fall Again," *Modern Healthcare*, November 24, 1989, p.4.

PC-Computing, "Budget Express Fine-Tunes 1-2-3," August 1989, p. 83.

PC Week, "Lotus 1-2-3 Add-In Proffers Corporate Budgeting Help," April 26, 1988, p. 89.

Potter, Margaret. "Taxation of Nonprofit Hospitals: A Cost Impact Model," *Hospital & Health Services Administration*, Spring 1992, Vol. 37, pp. 89–102.

Richardson, Ivan L. and Sidney Baldwin. *Public Administration: Government in Action* (Charles E. Merrill, 1976).

Roper, M. L. "Cost Accounting Slow to Influence Hospital Pricing," *Hospitals*, December 5, 1988, p. 18.

Seymour, Danelle. "On a PC and a Prayer," *Personal Computing*, Vol. 12, Issue 10, October 1988, pp. 178–180.

Shim, Jae K. and Joel Siegel. *Complete Budgeting Workbook and Guide* (Prentice Hall, 1994).

Shim, Jae K. and Joel Siegel. *Budgeting for Nonfinancial Managers* (Prentice-Hall, 1995).

Siegel, J. and Jae K. Shim. *Accounting Handbook* (Barrons, 1990).

Smith, L. et al. "An Internal Audit of a Church," *Internal Auditing*, Vol. 5, Number 1, Summer 1989, pp. 34–42.

Starling, Grover. *The Politics and Economics of Public Policy: An Introductory Analysis with Cases* (The Dorsey Press, 1979).

Tracey, O. M. et al. "Hospital Cost Accounting: Who's Doing What and Why," *Health Care Management Review*, Fall 1990, pp. 73–78.

Vinter, Robert D., and Rhea K. Kish. *Budgeting for Not-For-Profit Organizations* (Collier Macmillan Publishers, 1984).

Wolf, T. *Managing a Nonprofit Organization* (Prentice Hall, 1990).

Williams, Grant. "1991: A 'Modest' Rise in Charitable Giving," *The Chronicle of Philanthropy*, June 30, 1992, Vol. IV, No. 18, pp. 15–20.

Young, D. W. *Financial Control in Health Care* (Dow-Jones-Irwin, 1984).

Part *IV*

Financial Analysis For the Nonprofit Organization

A Case Study in Financial Statement Analysis and the New Reporting Standards of the FASB—Part I

THE SOURCES OF FINANCIAL REPORTING STANDARDS

This chapter and the following two chapters present a case study in financial analysis for a not-for-profit organization. Financial analysis is carried out to meet the needs of both internal users and external users. The difference between financial analysis for internal versus external use is dependent on the fact that internal users normally have access to highly disaggregated financial data in contrast to the highly aggregated data available to external users.

The organizing principle for the presentation of financial data to meet the needs of managers is that of usefulness. Data presented for the use of external users is subject to significant limitations as compared to that available to internal users. Data provided external users is also guided by financial reporting standards.

Financial reporting standards are currently largely crafted by the Financial Accounting Standards Board (FASB). The American Institute of Certified Public Accountants (AICPA) has also played a significant role in providing financial reporting standards. The AICPA produced a series of publications that set out auditing guidance for NPOs. These audit manuals also included financial reporting standards for a diverse population of not-for-profit organizations: *Audits of Colleges and Universities* (1973), *Audits of Voluntary Health and Welfare Organizations* (1974), and *Audits of*

Providers of Health Care Services (1990).[1] In addition, the AICPA produced a separate publication in the nonprofit area that was concerned exclusively with financial reporting standards. The AICPA issued *Statement of Position 78-10*, "Accounting Principles and Reporting Practices for Certain Nonprofit Organizations." This "Statement of Position" (SOP) was issued by the AICPA to cover those not-for profit entities that were not subject to the audit guides. During this period of financial reporting standards included in AICPA audit guides, the real authority for financial reporting standards was with the FASB. However, the FASB has been rather slow to issue modifications and replacements for the standards in the AICPA audit guides. Recently, the FASB seems to be finally diminishing the financial reporting role of the AICPA. The FASB issued a financial reporting standard on depreciation in 1987.[2] In 1993, the FASB issued two new reporting standards for not-for-profit entities. One of these reporting standards applies to the financial statements of nonprofit entities, *Statement of Financial Accounting Standards No. 117*, "Financial Statements of Not-for-Profit Organizations."[3]

UNDERSTANDING THE RESOURCES AND ACTIVITIES OF A NONPROFIT ORGANIZATION THROUGH ITS ACCOUNTS AND ACCOUNTING SYSTEM

The basic source of financial data both for internal and external use is the accounting systems of the nonprofit entity. A basic model will be constructed using the accounting system to provide the necessary data for both internal and external financial analysis.

The accounting system analyzes and organizes the financial data generated by the activities of the not-for-profit organization as it engages in a series of transactions with other entities. The data is accumulated in terms of a series of accounts. The accounts are the analytic categories used to organize the data so that we can understand the impact of the transactions on the organization.

The basic accounts used by the accounting systems will tell us what sorts of data will be collected for financial analysis. Below, we show a simplified set of illustrative accounts for a typical not-for-profit organization.

First, we look at a series of illustrative asset accounts in Exhibit 1.

EXHIBIT 1 IIllustrative Asset Accounts and What They Account For

The Accounts | Account for

UNRESTRICTED CURRENT ASSETS

1. Cash—Unrestricted

Cash held for everyday operations, amounts in excess of operating requirements are invested in very low-risk and very short-term debt instruments recorded in separate accounts and reported as cash equivalents.

2. Accounts Receivable

Amounts owed for fees charged for services.

3. Allowance for Uncollectible Accounts Receivable

Lowers the value of accounts receivable by an estimate for uncollectible accounts.

4. Pledges Receivable—Unrestricted— Contributions

Unconditional promises to contribute resources to support day-to-day activities of the NPO.

5. Allowance for Uncollectible Pledges Receivable

Lowers the value of pledges receivable by an estimate for uncollectible pledges.

6. Investment Income Receivable

Interest and dividends earned on investments but not yet paid.

7. Inventories of Supplies

Stocks of unused supplies.

8. Prepaid Expenses

Payments in advance for services to be received.

UNRESTRICTED NONCURRENT ASSETS

9. Property, Plant and Equipment

Land, buildings and equipment used in the everyday operations of the NPO.

10. Accumulated Depreciation—Property, Plant and Equipment	Depreciation accumulated for depreciable assets past and current periods.

TEMPORARILY RESTRICTED ASSETS

11. Cash—Temporarily Restricted Grants	Cash received from grants and segregated to satisfy grant requirements and restrictions.
12. Cash—Temporarily Restricted Contributions	Cash received from restricted contributions and segregated to satisfy requirements specified by the restricted contributions.
13. Pledges Receivable—Temporarily Restricted for Operating Activities	Unconditional promises to contribute resources to support specific day-to-day activities of the NPO or to be available for use in future time periods.
14. Allowance for Uncollectible Pledges Receivable	Lowers the value of pledges receivable by an estimate for uncollectible pledges.
15. Governmental Grants Receivable —Temporarily Restricted for Operating Purposes	Cash owed and to be received from grants that have been awarded for specific operating purposes.
16. Pledges Receivable—Temporarily Restricted for Capital Purposes	Unconditional promises to contribute resources to finance the acquisition of fixed assets such as plant, property, equipment.
17. Allowance for Uncollectible Pledges Receivable	Lowers the value of pledges receivable by an estimate for uncollectible pledges.

18. Investments—Temporarily Restricted for Capital Purposes	Investment in income earning securities of cash temporarily restricted for the acquisition of fixed assets.

PERMANENTLY RESTRICTED ASSETS

19. Cash—Permanently Restricted —Contributions	Cash received from contributions to a permanent endowment.
20. Investments—Permanently Restricted Endowment	Investment in income earning securities of cash contributed to a permanent endowment.

The different types of asset accounts have been grouped into several categories of assets. For purposes of financial analysis, we need to understand both the types of assets used by the not-for-profit organization and the categories into which these assets are grouped.

The basic categories used to group the assets are *unrestricted, temporarily restricted*, and *permanently restricted*. These categories are required for external reporting purposes by *Statement of Financial Accounting Standards (SFAS) No. 117*.

Unrestricted Assets

First, we have the *unrestricted* assets. These are assets that are available for the day-to-day operating activities of the not-for-profit organization as spelled out in its bylaws. The *unrestricted* assets are further separated into *current* and *noncurrent unrestricted* assets. The *current unrestricted* assets are those that are *expected* to be transformed into a cash form over the course of the normal operating cycle or over a year, whichever comes later. The transformation into cash form is generally through the use of the asset in the operating activities of the not-for-profit organization. *Noncurrent unrestricted* assets are not *expected* to be transformed to cash form or, if ultimately transformed to cash form, it is *expected to be beyond* a year or the normal operating cycle, whichever is later.

The distinction between *current* and *noncurrent* is based on expectations and is therefore a subjective judgment. The judgment is by the management of the not-for-profit organization. The purpose of the distinction between *current* and *noncurrent* is to provide information on liquidity. In a retail business, the normal operating cycle is composed of obtaining merchandise and selling it. Merchandise is obtained on credit. Cash is paid to the vendors. Merchandise may be sold for cash or credit. If for credit, then cash is received from customers to pay off their accounts. The normal operating cycle using cash transactions begins with the payment for the acquisition of merchandise and ends with the receipt of cash from customers.

The cash cycle is a liquidity cycle. Some businesses have short operating cycles; others may have long operating cycles. If the operating cycle is less than a year, then the yearly cycle is used to separate current from noncurrent assets and liabilities. If the normal operating cycle is significantly beyond a year, then it is used to separate current from noncurrent items.

Each nonprofit organization needs to identify its normal operating cycle, if it has one. Otherwise, the annual cycle would be used to separate current from noncurrent assets and liabilities.

Restricted Assets

Second, we have *restricted* assets. *Restricted* assets are those assets that are available to be used for particular purposes as specified through contractual or legal requirements that cannot be altered unilaterally by the not-for-profit organization. These assets may be *temporarily* or *permanently* *restricted*. If *temporarily restricted*, the assets become *unrestricted* when a particular condition or circumstance is fulfilled as specified by contractual or legal requirements. *Permanently restricted* assets will not become *unrestricted*, since there are no conditions or circumstances that will permit such a change in character. *Permanently restricted* assets are normally in the form of investments that will generate income that normally is specified as fully or partially *unrestricted or may be specified as temporarily restricted*, and ultimately will become available for the normally operating activities of the not-for profit organization.

In Exhibit 2, we look at *illustrative* liability accounts.

EXHIBIT 2 Illustrative Liabillity Accounts and What They Account For

The Accounts   Account for

UNRESTRICTED CURRENT LIABILITIES
21. Accounts Payable   Amounts owed vendors for
                                             supplies, merchandise, and

	equipment acquired, and for professional and other services received.
22. Prepaid Services	Fees paid in advance for services to be rendered in the future by a NPO.
23. Notes Payable	Short-term amounts on notes owed to the bank on a line of credit.
24. Interest Payable	Amounts of interest owed on short-term or long-term debt at the end of the fiscal period. The interest is to be paid in a future fiscal period.
25. Long-term Debt—Current Installment	Amount of long-term debt that will mature and is expected to be paid in the next fiscal year.

UNRESTRICTED NONCURRENT LIABILITIES

26. Long-term Debt—Noncurrent	Amount of long-term debt that matures beyond the next fiscal year.

TEMPORARILY RESTRICTED LIABILITIES

27. Accounts Payable	Amounts owed vendors for supplies, merchandise, and equipment acquired, and for professional and other services received to be paid out of restricted resources.

The liability accounts are grouped in similar categories to the asset accounts. The distinction between current and noncurrent unrestricted liabilities parallels the distinction between *current* and *noncurrent unrestricted* assets. The restricted liabilities are *temporarily restricted*.

The asset and liability accounts are followed by the *illustrative* net asset accounts in Exhibit 3.

EXHIBIT 3 Illustrative Net Asset Accounts and What They Account For

The Accounts	Account for
UNRESTRICTED NET ASSETS	
28. Unrestricted Net Assets	The *difference* between the total assets less the total liabilities less the total restricted net assets. Represents the unrestricted equity of the NPO.
TEMPORARILY RESTRICTED NET ASSETS	
29. Contributions for Operating Purposes	Contributions temporarily restricted to be used for specified operating purposes that do not become unrestricted until resources are expended for the purposes of the gift.
30. Grants for Operating Purposes	Grants temporarily restricted to be used for specified operating purposes that do not become unrestricted until resources are expended for the purposes of the grant.
31. Contributions for Capital Purposes	Contributions temporarily restricted to be used for specified capital purposes that do not become unrestricted until resources are expended for the purposes of the gift (i.e., the acquisition of fixed assets).

32. Investment Income for Capital Purposes   Investment income earned and temporarily restricted to be used for capital purposes (i.e., the acquisition of fixed assets).

PERMANENTLY RESTRICTED NET ASSETS

33. Permanently Restricted Net Assets   Represents the equity in the permanently restricted assets.

The net asset accounts represent the equity of the NPO. The equity is the difference between the total assets and the total liabilities of the NPO. The net assets or equity of the NPO is divided into the three categories of unrestricted, temporarily restricted, and permanently restricted. In a sense we have a rather loose approximation to the traditional fund accounting used by those NPOs that receive significant amounts of restricted resources to finance their activities.

In Exhibit 4, we turn to the first of *illustrative* operating accounts, the revenue accounts. The "revenue" accounts cover both nonexchange transactions from support and exchange transactions. In *SFAS No. 116*, the FASB defines "revenue" so that it includes both support or nonexchange transactions and exchange transactions. Note that some types of nonprofit accounting have reserved the term "support" for nonexchange transactions and "revenue" for exchange transactions. *SFAS No. 116* does not reserve the term "support" for nonexchange transactions. We will follow the usage in *SFAS No. 116*; however, it probably would have made the discussion simpler to reserve the term "revenue" for exchange transactions. Support is reserved for nonexchange transactions.

EXHIBIT 4 *Illustrative Support Revenue Accounts and What They Account For*

The Accounts   Account for

SUPPORT ACCOUNTS

34. Unrestricted Contributions for   Increase in unrestricted equity
    Operating Activities   resulting from unrestricted gifts for operating purposes.

35. Allocations from Federated Fund-Raising NPOs

Allocations are grant-like funds received from fund-raising organizations such as the United Way.

36. Provision for Federated Fund-Raising Expenses

Reported as a reduction in the amount of allocated fund-raising received by the organization; it is the share of the costs of federated fund-raising agreed to be borne by the recipient NPO.

37. Net Assets Released from Restrictions —Contributions for Operating Activities

Increase in unrestricted equity for temporarily restricted contributions for which resources were expended releasing restrictions.

38. Net Assets Released from Restrictions —Grants for Operating Activities

Same as #35 above, except temporarily restricted grants were involved.

39. Net Assets Released from Restrictions —Contributions for Capital Purposes

Same as #35 above, except gifts were for the acquisition of fixed assets.

40. Provision for Uncollectible Pledges

An estimated reduction of the amount of asset pledges receivable also reported as a reduction of the corresponding amount of contributions included in the NPOs equity; may also be treated as an expense by some NPOs (see account #69 below).

REVENUE ACCOUNTS

41. Revenues from Fees for Services

Increase in unrestricted equity resulting from fees earned in exchange for rendering services.

42. Investment Income

Increase in unrestricted equity resulting from interest and dividends earned on investments.

43. Gain on Sales of Fixed Assets

Increase in unrestricted equity resulting from gains on the disposal of fixed assets.

The support accounts accumulate information on nonexchange transactions that arise from gifts or grants to the NPO that do not involve quid pro quo exchanges. The gift or grant from the donor or granting agency is made without any expectation or requirement that the NPO provide services in exchange. The revenue transactions also cover exchange transactions. The "revenues from fees for services" accounts for exchange transactions between the NPO and the recipient of its services. The NPO expects to receive a payment from the recipient in exchange for those services it provides.

The support transactions arise out of both unrestricted and restricted gifts and restricted grants. Separate accounts are provided for each type of support transaction so that information is accumulated for each type.

Both the revenue from nonexchange support transactions and the revenue from exchange type transactions increase the equity or net assets of the NPO. In Exhibit 5, we turn to illustrative accounts that record transactions that decrease the equity of the NPO.

EXHIBIT 5 *Illustrative Expense Accounts and What They Account For*

The Accounts   Account for

EXPENSE ACCOUNTS BY OBJECT OF EXPENSE

44. Salaries

Cost of employees' gross salaries and wages for services *rendered* whether or not paid.

45. Employee benefits

Cost of employees' benefits in addition to gross salaries for health, vacation, pension, sick leave, etc.

46. Payroll taxes	Cost of employer payroll taxes on employees' gross salaries.
47. Allocations to Beneficiary Agencies	Cost of supporting beneficiary agencies when this is a mission or specific program of the NPO.
48. Professional fees	Cost of services of independent professionals such as doctors, lawyers, accountants.
49. Contractual services	Cost of services of independent contractors for administrative, cleaning, or other services.
50. Facilities rents	Cost of rental of facilities to provide program services and support activities such as management & general activities.
51. Insurance	Cost of insurance against various risks from losses due to fire hazards, to car hazards, to liability hazards, etc.
52. Utilities	Cost of gas, electric, and water services received.
53. Telephone	Cost of telephone services received.
54. Heating	Cost of heating where this is significant.
55. Equipment rentals	Cost of rentals of office, automotive, or other equipment required for NPO activities.
56. Maintenance and repairs	Cost of maintenance and repairs of facilities and equipment, etc.

57. Projects materials	Cost of materials used for projects for program and support activities.
58. Supplies	Cost of supplies used for program activities, management & general and fund-raising activities.
59. Printing and publications	Cost of printing services and publications produced or acquired.
60. Postage and shipping	Cost of mailing and shipping services incurred.
61. Conferences and meetings	Cost of conferences, conventions and other meetings authorized for employees of the NPO.
62. Travel	Cost of authorized travel to carry out the activities of the NPO.
63. Assistance to clients	Cost of various types of aid in the form of money assistance or goods-in-kind assistance to families and individuals under programs designed to provide assistance.
64. Grants to National Association	Cost of grants and awards to the national association of which the NPO is a member to support mutually beneficial projects.
65. Membership Dues	Cost of memberships in national or other associations formed to meet particular needs of the NPO.

| 66. Miscellaneous | Cost of very minor items for which separate accounts are not set up. |

The accounts in Exhibit 5 record costs generated by program activities and support activities of the NPO. The support activities involve management and general activities; basically, the administrative costs of managing the NPO. Support activities also involve fund-raising activities to provide the NPO the financial support that it requires to fulfill its mission.

The expenses shown in Exhibit 5 are by *object*, not by *program*. The objects of expense are for the most part common to all types of NPOs with quite varied programs and mission. All NPOs incur personnel costs in terms of salaries and wages, employee benefits, and payroll taxes. All NPOs incur such expenses as supplies, utilities, telephone, postage, etc. Other expense items may be common to most, but not all NPOs. Certain expense items are quite specific to particular types of NPOs, incurred as a result of the particular mission or programs of that type of NPO. Some NPOs have the mission of fund-raising for other NPOs. Thus, for these NPOs, we would find as an expense item, Allocations to Beneficiary Agencies.

In Exhibit 6 we show particular additional *illustrative* expenses that can arise from the overall activities of an NPO.

EXHIBIT 6   *Illustrative Expense Accounts and What They Account For*

The Accounts   Account for

EXPENSE ACCOUNTS BY OBJECT OF EXPENSE

| 67. Depreciation Expense | An estimated expense that is the result of allocating the historical cost of depreciable plant and equipment over its forecasted useful service life to the NPO. |
| 68. Provision for Uncollectible Accounts | An estimated or forecasted expense for the amount of accounts receivable that is not expected to be collected or recovered. |

69. Provision for Uncollectible Pledges	An estimated reduction of the amount of the asset pledges receivable, also reported as an expense. See account #40 above, for an alternative approach that is a reduction of the corresponding amount of contributions included in the NPOs equity. Some NPOs use the alternative approach rather the expense approach.
70. Interest Expense on Short-Term Debt	Cost incurred of short-term borrowing interest is recorded up-to-the-date of the financial statements, whether or not paid fully.
71. Interest Expense on Long-Term Debt	Cost incurred of long-term borrowing, interest is recorded up-to-the-date of the financial statements, whether or not paid fully.

Exhibit 6 includes such items as Provision for Uncollectible Accounts and Provision for Uncollectible Pledges. The Provision for Uncollectible Accounts has been treated as an expense and as a reduction of the associated revenue item in the not-for-profit area. However, there has been a movement to treat the Provision for Uncollectible Accounts consistently as an expense item. The item Provision for Uncollectible Pledges has generally been treated as a reduction of the associated amount of contributions arising from pledges. The current financial reporting standards as promulgated by the FASB seems silent on this matter. It is likely that this estimated amount for uncollectible pledges is more likely to be treated as a reduction of the associated contributions arising from the pledges than as an expense item. This is what we shall assume in our illustrated financial statements.

Depreciation expense is an allocation of the historical cost of the related fixed asset, whether it be plant or equipment, over the forecasted beneficial life of the asset to the NPO. In a sense, depreciation expense is an estimate for each period of the cost of the services being provided to the NPO by the fixed assets. The depreciation method is systematic but rather arbitrary relative to the actual services rendered by particular fixed assets so that this amount is difficult to interpret. It is not really a measure of the true aging or productivity of the fixed assets nor is it a good guide to planned spending to replace such assets.

Interest expense, whether short-term or long-term, is recorded as it is incurred whether or not it has been paid.

FINANCIAL ANALYSIS AND ILLUSTRATIVE TRANSACTIONS OF THE MODEL NPO

Now that we have reviewed the typical accounting categories that one would expect to find for a not-for-profit organization, let us turn to an illustrative model of the NPO we intend to subject to financial statement analysis.

We are going to assume this NPO has engaged in a series of transactions that arise from its activities. Basically, it is responsible for three major programs that provide services that its contributors support. These programs will be called simply Program A, Program B, and Program C. In addition to its program-driven activities, the NPO incurs "management and general" costs and "fund-raising" costs.

UNRESTRICTED ASSETS

CURRENT ASSETS

UNRESTRICTED CASH

The first set of transactions are the ones that impact the Cash account of our NPO. Note that strictly speaking when we speak of the Cash account we are describing both Cash and Cash Equivalents. A separate account will be shown for Cash Equivalents in order to simplify the control over cash and distinguish clearly between cash and cash equivalents. Cash Equivalents are temporary investments of excess cash in very low-risk and very short maturity debt instruments.

The following *illustrative* transactions and calculations were run through a standard spreadsheet using certain predetermined relationships so that *totals and balances may reflect rounding differences.*

The impact on the *illustrative* unrestricted Cash account can be shown in the following analysis of that account:

ANALYSIS OF THE UNRESTRICTED CASH ACCOUNT*

Transactions	Increase	(Decrease)	Balance
Balance, 7/1/19X1			$ 200,000
Collections—Fees—Entry #4	$ 3,000,000		3,200,000
Contributions—Entry #5	9,282,706		12,482,706
Investment income—Entry #6	300,032		12,782,738
Prepaid expense—Program-A— Entry #8		$(18,378)	12,764,360
Disposal of Fixed Assets— Entry #20	50,000		12,814,360
Transferred Temporarily Restricted Cash from Grants for Operating Purposes— Entry #25	499,956		13,314,315
Transferred Temporarily Restricted Cash for Capital Purposes—Entry #27	614,524		13,928,839
Interest Income—Short-Term —Entry #30	24,276		13,953,115
Interest Expense—Short-Term —Entry #31		(13,607)	13,939,508
Cash for Operating Purposes —Time Restrictions Released —Entry #32	316,870		14,256,379
Paid Accounts Payable —Entry #33		(12,942,448)	1,313,931
Adjust Cash Equivalents —Entry #37		(1,113,931)	$ 200,000
	$14,088,364	($14,088,364)	

*Totals and balances may reflect rounding differences.

The Cash account has an opening balance in it of $200,000. All of the illustrative entries are made once a year. In reality cash is flowing into and out of the Cash account all during our hypothetical year, 19X2. Ultimately, we will break down the annual entries into monthly flows to provide a somewhat closer approximation to actual transactions.

Eight *illustrative* transactions are shown as increasing the Cash account. The transactions are numbered so that we can follow their impact on the NPO through the accounting system.

TRANSACTIONS THAT INCREASE CASH

4. Fees for services collected from the beneficiaries of such services for the year 19X2 amounted to $3,000,000. Note that the collections include both services rendered during the current year and also for services rendered the prior year but owed and unpaid at the end of that year.

5. Contributions collected in cash for the year 19X2 amounted to $9,282, 706. Note that contributions collected are both for contributions relevant to 19X2 and unpaid contributions pledged and owed for prior years.

6. Unrestricted investment income received in cash form from endowment investment for the year 19X2 amounted to $300,032.

20. Cash collected from the sale of the disposal of used fixed assets for the year 19X2 amounted to $50,000.

25. Temporarily Restricted Cash for Operating Purposes from grants was transferred to the Unrestricted Cash account when restrictions were satisfied by the expenses from operating activities as specified in the grants for Program A in the amount of $499,956.

27. Temporarily Restricted Cash for Capital Purposes was transferred to the Unrestricted Cash account when restrictions were satisfied by the acquisition of $614,524 of fixed assets.

30. Interest earned and collected on very short-term low-risk debt securities for the year 19X2 amounted to $24,276.

32. Cash in the amount of $316,870 is transferred from Cash Temporarily Restricted for Operating Purposes when time restrictions are satisfied.

Four *illustrative* transactions are shown that decrease the cash account.

TRANSACTIONS THAT DECREASE CASH

8. Advance payment on services to be received by Program A in the amount of $18,378.

31. Paid interest expense on short-term debt for 19X2 in the amount of $13,607.

33. Paid accounts payable for 19X2 that amounted to $12,942,448. Payments covered both current year expenses and other items purchased as well as prior year amounts owed on accounts payable.

37. A summary entry that shows the net effect of transferring amounts of cash in excess of $200,000 to a cash equivalents account as a result of investing in very low-risk and very short-term debt instruments. The amount transferred is $1,113,931.

The increases to the Cash account outweigh the decreases by $1,113,931. The amounts above $200,000 are transferred to a cash equivalents account. The accounting system is designed to record increases and decreases in the accounts through accounting entries that must balance out.

While the cash account had an opening balance of $200,000, in fact, there was an additional $33,422 of cash that had been invested in "cash equivalents." Excess amounts over $200,000 are automatically invested in "cash equivalents" to earn interest until needed for operating purposes.

UNRESTRICTED CASH EQUIVALENTS

Below is an analysis of the *illustrative* Cash Equivalents account.

ANALYSIS OF THE UNRESTRICTED CASH EQUIVALENTS ACCOUNT

Transactions	Increase	(Decrease)	Balance
Balance, 7/1/19X			$33,422
Adjust cash equivalents Entry #37	$1,113,931		$1,147,353

As noted earlier, cash equivalents represent investment in very low-risk and very short-term debt instruments issued by highly credit-worthy borrowers. Also noted was that cash equivalents would be recorded in a separate account for control purposes. Interest earned on investment in cash equivalents is recorded as earned.

The transactions that affected the Cash Equivalents account through the year are represented by transfers into and out of the account. The transactions that affected the Cash Equivalents account had one source.

37. The basic source is the transfer of excess amounts of cash from the unrestricted cash account, discussed above. The excess amount transferred was $1,113,931.

Accounts Receivable

In order to better understand our entries, we need to follow them to accounts other than the Cash account. We shall be able to do so as we work our way through the accounts that interact directly with the cash account.

First, we look at the Accounts Receivable account. The Accounts Receivable can be analyzed in a manner similar to that for the Cash account.

ANALYSIS OF ACCOUNTS RECEIVABLE

Transactions	Increase	(Decrease)	Balance
Balance, 7/1/19X1			$ 485,879
Fees for services —Entry #3	$2,894,231		3,380,110
Collections—19X2 —Entry #4		($2,889,643)	490,467
Identified uncollectible Accounts—Entry #38		(30,000)	$ 460,467
	2,894,231	(2,919,643)	
Decrease in Accounts Receivable	25,412		
	$2,919,643	($2,919,643)	

There are three basic summary *illustrative* transactions that affected accounts receivable. These are:

3. Fees charged to beneficiaries for services rendered for the current year, 19X2, amount to $2,894,831.

4. Fees for services collected in cash for the year 19X2 amounted to $2,889,643. Note that the fees collected are both for fees for services relevant to 19X2 and unpaid accounts receivable owed to the NPO for prior years. See above, for the associated transactions as they affect the cash account.

38. Identified actual specified accounts receivable that are judged to be uncollectible. Such accounts are removed from the *active* Accounts Receivable account.

Again, we show the illustrative transactions that affected the Accounts Receivable on an annual basis. The decreases outweighed the increase by $25,412 so that the opening balance of $485,879 was reduced to $460,467 at the end of the year. There is a reduction in the Accounts Receivable of $30,000 for those beneficiaries from whom fees proved to be uncollectible. That reduction more than accounts for the overall reduction in the Accounts Receivable of $25,412.

We would need more information in order to understand the circumstances that resulted in certain of the accounts receivable being uncollectible. We would also need to know more about the nature of our Accounts Receivable to understand whether or not the $30,000 of uncollectible accounts is to be expected or is considered excessive.

Note that entry #4 that records cash collections and thus decreases Accounts Receivable is clearly associated with entry #4 in the Cash account which records the complementary increase in cash. However, the two amounts do not match, which must mean that some other accounts were also affected by entry #4.

The account directly associated with Accounts Receivable is the *Allowance for Uncollectible Accounts Receivable*. Below is an illustrative analysis of this account.

ANALYSIS OF ALLOWANCE FOR UNCOLLECTIBLE ACCOUNTS RECEIVABLE

Transactions	Decrease	(Increase)	Balance
Balance, 7/1/19X1			($40,000)

Identified Uncollectible Accounts Receivable Entry #38	$30,000		(10,000)
Estimated Uncollectible Accounts Receivable —Entry #39		($35,000)	($45,000)
	30,000	(35,000)	
Increase in the Allowance for Uncollectible Accounts Receivable	5,000	_____	
	$35,000	($35,000)	

The columns for increases and decreases are reversed as compared to what was shown earlier for the Cash and Accounts Receivable accounts. This reversal is the result of the fact that the Allowance for Uncollectible Accounts Receivable is considered a *contra-asset* account. That is, it is an account that is associated with a particular asset account but it behaves in a contra or contrary fashion to the asset account. It is also considered an asset valuation account. The account is used to revalue the asset account with which it is associated for external reporting purposes.

The purpose of the Allowance for Uncollectible Accounts Receivable is to revalue the Accounts Receivable account for external financial reporting purposes. The Allowance account basically is an estimated or forecasted figure. It reduces the Accounts Receivable so that the reduced amount of Receivables is the amount that management judges to be ultimately collectible from the current balance in the account.

Entry #38 is shown reducing the Accounts Receivable for those Receivables identified as uncollectible which also reduces the Allowance account. Entry #39 which records the current estimate for uncollectible receivables is recorded only in the Allowance account and not in the Receivables account. Entry #39 records the expense in the allowance account, and as we shall see, there will be a matching expense account we will discuss later. In any case, the estimated uncollectibles cannot be recorded in the Receivables account itself since actual uncollectible Receivables have not been identified as yet. Entry #38 is the entry that identifies uncollectibles that are associated with last year's estimated uncollectibles.

PLEDGES RECEIVABLE

We turn to another receivables account, the Pledges Receivable account.

The account Pledges Receivable records *unconditional* promises of unrestricted gifts of money and other resources to fund the socially beneficial services provided by our model NPO. These unconditional and unrestricted gifts are also available to fund the supporting activities such as management and general activities and fund-raising activities that make it possible to provide the socially beneficial program activities of the NPO.

The FASB has set the reporting standard for reporting unconditional promises of gifts, be they *unrestricted* or *restricted*. The account we are currently looking at records unconditional and unrestricted promises to donate money and other resources. The FASB reporting standard covering contributions and promises to contribute is found in *SFAS No. 116*.

Paraphrasing *SFAS No. 116*, a

Conditional promise to give is a promise that is *expected* to be fulfilled on the occurrence of a future and uncertain event.[4]

The complementary concept

Unconditional promise is a promise that is *expected* to be fulfilled simply with the passage of time or upon the demand of the recipient of the promised gift.[5]

The promised contributions recorded in this Pledges Receivable are also described as *unrestricted*. Again we turn to *SFAS No. 116* for descriptions of these concepts.

Again, paraphrasing *SFAS No. 116*,

Unrestricted support arises from contributions that are not subject to any restrictions by the donors.[6]

The complementary concept

Restricted support arises from contributions that increase either *temporarily* restricted net assets or *permanently* restricted net assets.[7]

Unfortunately, we have to define the terms *"temporarily* restricted" and *"permanently* restricted" within the concept of *restricted support.* Fortunately, we have already discussed both temporarily restricted and permanently restricted net assets.

In Exhibit 3, "Illustrative Net Asset Accounts," there is an example of an item that increases

> *Temporarily restricted* net assets arises from temporarily restricted contributions given to be used for specified operating purposes which do not become *unrestricted* until resources are expended for the purposes of the gift.

Earlier the concept of *"permanently restricted"* assets was discussed, so that we can recall that

> For permanently restricted assets there are no conditions or circumstances that will permit them to become unrestricted. Rather such assets are normally in the form of investments that will generate income that will become fully or partially *unrestricted* or *temporarily restricted* and ultimately available for the operating activities of the not-for-profit organization.

Next, we have an analysis of the *illustrative* transactions that affected the Pledges Receivable account.

ANALYSIS OF PLEDGES RECEIVABLE

Transactions	Increase	(Decrease)	Balance
Balance 7/1/19X1			
Reclassify Pledges —Entry #1	$2,134,624		$2,134,624
Pledges—19X2 —Entry #2	9,911,407		12,046,031
Collections—Entry #5		($9,282,706)	2,763,325
Identified Uncollectible Pledges Receivable Entry #40		(315,000)	2,448,325

Reclassify Pledges
—Entry #48 $ 2,448,325   0
                    $12,046,031   ($12,046,031)

There are five transactions that affect Pledges Receivable:

1. To reclassify pledges receivable for $2,134,624 to its normal account for control purposes, Pledges Receivable, Unrestricted, from its reporting account, Pledges Receivable, Temporarily Restricted. This entry is made at the beginning of the year, July 1, 19X1.

2. To record unconditional and unrestricted promised gifts for 19X2 that amounted to $9,911,407.

5. To record cash collections that amounted to $9,282,706 from promised gifts of the current year, 19X2, and from Pledges Receivable at the beginning of the year.

40. To remove from active status those specifically identified accounts receivable that have been judged to be uncollectible as the result of a strenuous effort to collect them. The amount totalled $315,000.

48. To reclassify pledges receivable from its normal account for control purposes Pledges Receivable, Unrestricted, to its year-end reporting account, Pledges Receivable, Temporarily Restricted for Reporting Purposes. This entry is made at the end of the year, June 30, 19X2.

First, note that the Pledges Receivable, Unrestricted account is not reported as such on the NPOs financial statements. Rather, Pledges Receivable are reported as Pledges Receivable, Temporarily Restricted. This is in accordance with the requirements of *SFAS No. 116*.

For management and accounting control, the normal account used to account for pledges is Pledges Receivable, Unrestricted. Unconditional and unrestricted pledges are recorded in this account. Once a year, for external reporting purposes, the amount in the Pledges Receivable, Unrestricted, is reclassified to the account Pledges Receivable, Temporarily Restricted, for external financial reporting purposes.

According to *SFAS No. 116*

Receipts of unconditional promises to give with payment due in future periods shall be reported as restricted support unless explicit donor stipulations or circumstances surrounding the receipt of a promise make clear that the donor intended it to be used to support activities of the current period. For example receipt of promises to give cash in future years generally increase temporarily restricted net assets.[8]

Promises to give exceeded collections on gifts by $628,701. However, the increase in Pledges Receivable is far less than this. Pledges Receivable increased according to our analysis above, but only by $313,701. That increase is short of the $628,701 by $315,000. The third entry into the Pledges Receivable account is a reduction to that account of exactly $315,000 described as "Identified Uncollectible Pledges Receivable." As in the case of Accounts Receivable, we have significant amounts of receivables that are uncollectible. Again, we do not have information on the circumstances that underlie the uncollectibility nor do we have information on whether the amount is within expected limits.

Since we have just discussed the issue of uncollectible receivables, let us look next at the Allowance for Uncollectible Pledges.

The Allowance for Uncollectible Pledges Receivable is a *contra-asset* account in the same fashion as the Allowance for Uncollectible Accounts Receivable. It is a *contra-asset* account to the related asset account, Pledges Receivable. This account also functions as a valuation asset account. It is a valuation asset account for the related asset account, Pledges Receivable. Its purpose is to reduce the *reported* value of the related asset account Pledges Receivable to an amount judged by the management of the NPO to be the collectible value of Pledges Receivable at June 30, 19X2.

An analysis of the *illustrative* transactions that affect this account shows the following:

ANALYSIS OF ALLOWANCE FOR UNCOLLECTIBLE PLEDGES RECEIVABLE

Transactions	Decrease	(Increase)	Balance
Balance, 7/1/19X1			
Reclassify Allowance —Entry #1		($300,00)	($300,000)
Identified Uncollectible Pledges Receivable Entry #40	$315,000		15,000

Estimated Uncollectible
Pledges Receivable
—Entry #41   _____   ($350,000)   ($335,000)
                              315,000   (650,000)

Reclassify Allowance
—Entry-#48   335,000   _____
                              $650,000   ($650,000)

The first transaction that affects the Allowance for Uncollectible pledges account is transaction #1. This entry reclassifies the Allowance for Uncollectible Pledges Receivable for $300,00 to its normal account for control purposes, Allowance for Uncollectible Pledges Receivable, Unrestricted, from its reporting account, Allowance for Uncollectible Pledges Receivable, Temporarily Restricted for Reporting Purposes. This entry is made at the beginning of the year, July 1, 19X1.

In entry #40, the Allowance account is reduced for those pledges receivable that have been identified as uncollectible in the amount of $315,000. This is the amount shown earlier by which the Pledges Receivable account is reduced. A new estimate for uncollectible pledges is recorded in the Allowance account at $350,000 in Entry #41. This is a forecasted amount whose estimate rests on the judgment of the management of the NPO.

Entry #48 reclassifies the allowance for uncollectible pledges receivable for $350,000 from its normal account for control purposes, Allowance for Uncollectible Pledges Receivable, Unrestricted, to its year-end reporting account, Allowance for Uncollectible Pledges Receivable, Temporarily Restricted for Reporting Purposes. This entry is made at the end of the year, June 30, 19X2.

INVESTMENT INCOME RECEIVABLE

The next unrestricted current asset to be examined is Investment Income Receivable. This account records unrestricted investment income earned on the endowment which is accounted for in a permanently restricted Investment Account.

An analysis of the *illustrative* Investment Income Receivable account is as follows:

ANALYSIS OF INVESTMENT INCOME RECEIVABLE

Transactions	Increase	(Decrease)	Balance
Balance 7/1/19X1			$20,947
Investment Income— Collected—Entry #6		($20,947)	0
Investment Income to Be Received (i.e., Accrued) —Entry #47	$32,918		$32,918
	32,918	(20,947)	
Increase in Investment Income Receivable	_____	(11,971)	
	$32,918	($32,918)	

Two transactions and two entries affect the Investment Income Receivable account. The first transaction recognizes the collection of interest and dividends earned in the prior year, but owed and unpaid at the end of that year. Collections of the unpaid amounts are made and recorded this year. The second transaction and entry recognizes that interest has been earned and dividends for the current year declared but that these have not yet been paid.

INVENTORIES OF SUPPLIES

We now turn to the inventories of supplies maintained for facilitating the operating activities of our NPO. The inventories of supplies are used in the activities of each program and in management and general and fundraising activities.

The management of the NPO is concerned with accurate costs for its program and support activities. As such, separate inventory accounts are maintained for each of the programs as well as for the support activities.

An analysis of the Inventory of Supplies account is shown for each of the programs and for the Management and General supporting activity. The entries into the accounting records are indicated as journal entries (JE).

ANALYSIS OF INVENTORIES OF SUPPLIES

Transactions	A	B	C	M&G	FR	Total
Balance, 7/1/X1	$156,684	$137,733	$80,393	$25,406	$8,400	$408,616

Purchases, 19X2- JE#7	171,548	90,086	29,339	16,700	307,673
Consumption, 19X2-JE #35	(42,268)	(184,170)	(95,397)	(19,331)	(14,475)	(355,641)
Balance, 6/30/X2.	$114,416	$125,111	$75,082	$35,414	$10,625	$360,648

There are two basic transactions and thus two basic entries that affect this account. These are:

7. Purchases of supplies for the activities of the NPO and accounted for through inventories of supplies accounts—Program B—$171,548, Program C—$90,086, Management & General—$29,339, and Fund-Raising—$16,700.

35. Consumption of supplies for the activities of the NPO and accounted for through inventories of supplies accounts—Program A—$42,268, Program B—$184,170, Program C—$95,397, and Management & General—$19,331, and Fund-Raising—$14,475.

Supplies of all types are accounted for through the inventories. Office supplies—from paper clips to stationery to folders, etc.—are accounted for through the Inventory of Supplies. The types of supplies needed for particular programs are determined by the nature of the activities and services that are associated with each program. However, note that generally Inventory of Supplies would be accounted for through the periodic method in order to minimize paperwork. Once a year, a physical inventory would be taken to help provide accurate costing for the programs and activities of the NPO. During the year, control over purchase of supplies would be maintained through a budgeting system.

PREPAID EXPENSES

Prepaid expenses are the result of advance payments to vendors for services to be received. Prepaid expenses might better be called prepaid services. The advance payments generally occur as a result of the common practice in place for a particular type of service. For example, it is the practice to prepay for certain types of insurance services. For example, fire insurance and automotive insurance are examples of insurance services that are prepaid in advance of the receipt of the services. Thus, a typical prepaid expense would be prepaid insurance.

An analysis of the Prepaid Expenses is shown, as it was for the Inventories of Supplies, on a program-by-program basis and for Management & General (M&G) activities.

ANALYSIS OF PREPAID EXPENSES

Transactions	A	B	C	M&G	Total
Balance, 7/1/19X1	$ 26,313	$103,124	$48,217	$36,803	$214,457
Purchases, 19X2-JE #8	18,378				18,378
Consumption, 19X2-JE #36	(9,189)	(33,926)	(16,063)	(12,835)	(72,013)
Balance, 6/30/19X2	$ 35,502	$ 69,198	$32,154	$23,968	$160,822

The *illustrative* transactions for Prepaid Expenses are:

8. Advance payments of certain expenses of the NPO that are accounted for through prepaid expense accounts for Program A—$18,378.

36. Incurring of expenses that have been prepaid and are accounted for through prepaid expense accounts for—Program A $ 9,189, Program B—$ 33,926, Program C—$16,063, and Management & General—$12,835.

A look at the *illustrative* transactions suggests that perhaps one would like a bit more information about the nature of these prepaid expenses and how these services are managed to obtain target levels of services at minimum costs. Why were there advance payments for services for one program and not for the others?

NONCURRENT ASSETS: PROPERTY, PLANT AND EQUIPMENT

The Property, Plant and Equipment of a NPO are long-lived assets and are therefore classified as noncurrent assets. Fund-Raising for these assets is often treated as a separate and distinct activity from fund-raising for the normal operating programs and the support activities of the NPO. The Property, Plant and Equipment assets are also considered part of the fixed tangible assets of the entity. Accounting for such assets can be quite complex and involved. We shall provide for our accounting illustration a relatively simple example.

Property, Plant and Equipment is carried in the accounts at the original market value paid to acquire the equipment. When such assets are received as gifts, an approximation to market value known as fair value at the date of the gift is used to record a value for such items on the books.

The financial numbers on the books for Property, Plant and Equipment do not provide us with information on the productivity of these assets.

The two basic *illustrative* transactions that affect the Property, Plant and Equipment account are as follow:

20. Disposal of either excess or obsolete Property, Plant and Equipment through sale or abandonment which had an original cost of $257,450. The original cost maintained on the books does not represent the current market value of such assets.

26. Acquisition of Property, Plant and Equipment to meet the need of the program and support activities of the NPO in the amount of $614,524.

Below, we show an analysis of the Property, Plant, and Equipment account and its *illustrative* transactions.

ANALYSIS OF PROPERTY, PLANT AND EQUIPMENT

Transactions	Increase	(Decrease)	Balance
Balance 7/1/19X1			$5,951,227
Disposals—Entry #20		($257,450)	$5,693,777
Acquisitions—Entry #26	$614,524		6,308,301
Increase in Property, Plant, and Equipment		(357,074)	
	$614,524	($614,524)	

Just as Accounts Receivable and Pledges Receivable had associated *contra asset* or *valuation asset* accounts, Property, Plant and Equipment also has such an account. It is Accumulated Depreciation for Property, Plant and Equipment. The Accumulated Depreciation account is a *valuation asset* account for Property, Plant and Equipment. The purpose of the account is to reduce the value of Property, Plant and Equipment for the cumulative amount of depreciation expense that has been recorded for these assets over their useful lives to the entity.

The transactions that affect the Accumulated Depreciation account are as follows:

20. Reduction of Accumulated Depreciation on property, plant and equipment that has been disposed of as recorded by Entry #20 in the Appendix.

42. The current year's estimate of depreciation expense on the property plant, and equipment in use during the year in the amount of $937,589.

An analysis of this account would be as follows:

ANALYSIS OF ACCUMULATED DEPRECIATION—PROPERTY, PLANT AND EQUIPMENT*

Transactions	Decrease	(Increase)	Balance
Balance 7/1/19X1			($2,549,506)
Disposals—Entry #20	$232,544		(2,316,962)
Provision for Depreciation—Entry #42	_____	($937,589)	($3,254,551)
	232,544	(937,589)	
Increase in Accumulated Depreciation—Property Plant, and Equipment	705,045	_____	
	$937,589	($937,589)	

* Rounding difference.

A second analysis shows the distribution of Property, Plant and Equipment (PPE) to each program and functional support activity. The analysis also shows Accumulated Depreciation (AD) for Property, Plant and Equipment distributed by program and support activity. Note, in the calculations for the distributions of across program and activities, the amounts in the second analysis may show some rounding differences from the amounts in our earlier analyses of these accounts.

ANALYSIS OF PROPERTY, PLANT AND EQUIPMENT AND TRANSACTIONS BY PROGRAM AND SUPPORT ACTIVITY*

	Programs				
	A	B	C	M&G	19X2
PPE, 7/1/X1	$612,976	$3,535,029	$1,588,978	$214,244	$5,951,227
Acquisitions	63,296	365,027	164,078	22,123	614,524
	676,272	3,900,056	1,753,056	236,367	6,565,751

Disposals	(26,517)	(152,925)	(68,739)	(9,268)	(257,450)
PPE, 6/30/X2	649,755	3,747,131	1,684,317	227,099	6,308,301
AD, 7/1/X1	262,599	1,514,406	680,718	91,783	2,549,506
Disposals	(23,952)	(138,131)	(62,089)	(8,372)	(232,544)
	238,647	1,376,275	618,629	83,411	2,316,962
Depreciation	96,572	556,928	250,336	33,753	937,589
AD, 6/30/X2	335,219	1,933,203	868,965	117,164	3,254,551
PPE, net	$314,536	$1,813,928	$ 815,351	$109,935	$3,053,750

* Totals may reflect rounding differences.

LIABILITIES

UNRESTRICTED CURRENT LIABILITIES

ACCOUNTS PAYABLE

The Property, Plant and Equipment represents the last of the unrestricted assets. At this point we turn to the liability side so that unrestricted assets and liabilities can be considered together. What is happening in the accounting system is much easier to understand by examining the unrestricted assets and liabilities before considering the restricted assets.

The first liability account that we look at is Accounts Payable.

ANALYSIS OF ACCOUNTS PAYABLE

Transactions	Decrease	(Increase)	Balance
Balance, 7/1/19X1			($1,298,095)
Purchase of Inventory —Entry #7		($307,673)	(1,605,768)
Expenses—Other than Personnel—Entry #21		(2,915,365)	(4,521,133)
Expenses—Wages & Salaries—Entry #22		(7,264,561)	(11,785,694)
Expenses—Employee Benefits—Entry #23		(1,398,109)	(13,183,803)
Expenses—Employer Payroll Taxes —Entry #24		(556,581)	(13,740,384)

Acquisition of Capital Assets —Entry #26		(614,524)	(14,354,908)
Paid Accounts Payable —Entry #33	12,942,448	_____	($1,412,460)
	12,942,448	(13,056,813)	
Increase in Accounts Payable	114,365	_____	
	$13,056,813	($13,056,813)	

The major *illustrative* transactions that increase Accounts Payable are:

1. Purchases of inventories of supplies.

2. Expenses of program activities.

3. Expenses of supporting activities such as Management & General and Fund-Raising transactions.

4. Acquisition of fixed assets such as equipment.

The major *illustrative* transaction that decreases Accounts Payable is the payment of vendor bills. The payment of vendors' bills is from the Unrestricted Cash account in the amount of $12,942,448.

PREPAID SERVICES

The NPO receives advance payments of Fees for Services prior to rendering those services. The NPO thus owes Prepaid Services to its beneficiaries. The Prepaid Services account is basically shown with year-end entries to show its balance at the end of the year for reporting purposes. For control purposes it would be used during the year, but we have simplified the entries for our discussion.

There are two *illustrative* transactions that affect this account. These are:

4. Advance payments from beneficiaries for future services that have been included in the cash-collected entry along with other types of cash collections.

45. At year end, this entry records the amount of advance payments for which future services were not yet rendered at June 30, 19X2. This is the amount of prepaid services owed in future years.

The analysis of the Prepaid Services account is as follows:

ANALYSIS OF PREPAID SERVICES

Transactions	Decrease	(Increase)	Balance
Balance, 7/1/19X1			($97,264)
Prepaid Services —6/30/19X2—Entry #4		($110,357)	(207,621)
Prepaid Services —7/1/19X1—Entry #45	$ 97,264	_____	(110,357)
	97,264	(110,357)	
Increase in Prepaid Services	13,093	_____	
	$110,357	($110,357)	

Note that Prepaid Services is a liability account that will not be settled in terms of money but in terms of services to be rendered in the future. The account could also be called Advance Payments from Beneficiaries or Advance Payments from Clients. In the business arena this account would be called Advance Payments from Customers or Deferred Revenue. It could also be called Prepaid Revenue or simply the nondescript Deferred Credit.

LONG-TERM DEBT—CURRENT INSTALLMENT

The Long-Term Debt—Current Installment account is used primarily for external reporting. It is usually not even an account on the books. Rather, it is treated as a reporting requirement to maintain the distinction between *current* and *noncurrent* liabilities. We show it as an account to simplify the discussion and not get bogged down in such niceties as workpapers. The transactions that affect this account are as follows:

28. Payment of the prior year's current installment of principal.

46. Recording the current year's current installment of principal.

The analysis of this account is shown next.

ANALYSIS OF LONG-TERM DEBT—CURRENT INSTALLMENT

Transactions	Decrease	(Increase)	Balance
Balance, 7/1/19X1			($304,498)

Debt service on principal —Entry #28	$304,498		0
Current installment —Entry #46	_____	($333,062)	($333,062)
	304,498	(333,062)	
Decrease in current installment	28,564	_____	
	$333,062	($333,062)	

The amounts for the prior and current year installments are the result of the fact that the long-term debt is a mortgage note payable whose principal and interest are repaid simultaneously on a monthly basis throughout the year.

UNRESTRICTED NONCURRENT LIABILITIES

LONG-TERM DEBT

We move from the current liabilities to the noncurrent liabilities. In this case, the noncurrent liability is a single 9.0 percent, 10-year mortgage note payable to the bank. The discussion of the Long-Term Debt-Current Installment account provides us with a partial analysis of the long-term debt, but only a partial analysis.

The basic *illustrative* summarized annual transaction that affects long-term debt is simply:

46. Recording the current year's current installment of principal.

This simplified *illustrative* annual transaction is the result of the use of the Long-Term Debt—Current Installment account. The analysis of this simplified illustration is as follows:

ANALYSIS OF SIMPLIFIED ILLUSTRATIVE LONG-TERM DEBT

Transactions	Decrease	(Increase)	Balance
Balance, 7/1/19X1			(2,529,926)
Current installment —Entry #46	333,062		(2,196,864)

An analysis of a Less Simplified Illustrative Long-Term Debt account is shown below. The balance in the Long-Term Debt account includes the current installment at 7/1/19X1 that was paid during 19X2.

ANALYSIS OF ILLUSTRATIVE LONG-TERM DEBT SERVICE —PRINCIPAL AND INTEREST*

Transactions		Decrease	(Increase)	Balance
Balance, 7/1 (includes current installment at 7/1)				($2,834,424)
Payment No.	Monthly Payment	Interest	Principal	
37	$45,603	$21,258	$24,345	(2,810,079)
38	45,603	21,076	24,528	(2,785,552)
39	45,603	20,892	24,712	(2,760,840)
40	45,603	20,706	24,897	(2,735,943)
41	45,603	20,520	25,084	(2,710,859)
42	45,603	20,331	25,272	(2,685,588)
43	45,603	20,142	25,461	(2,660,126)
44	45,603	19,951	25,652	(2,634,474)
45	45,603	19,759	25,845	(2,608,629)
46	45,603	19,565	26,039	(2,582,591)
47	45,603	19,369	26,234	(2,556,357)
48	45,603	19,173	26,431	($2,529,926)
	$547,239	$242,742	$305,500	

*Totals may reflect rounding differences.

Of course, the actual account would show amounts to the last penny. Normally it would not show the amount of the debt service payment including interest.

For external financial reporting, a look into the future is required for disclosing long-term debt repayment obligations.

At June 30, 19X2, the payment schedule for this note is as follows:

19X3	$333,062
19X4	364,306

19X5	398,480
19X6	435,861
19X7	476,747
19X8	<u>521,470</u>
	<u>$2,529,926</u>

Unrestricted Net Assets (Unrestricted Equity)

The classic fundamental accounting equation of

Assets = Liabilities + Owner's Equity

has its parallel in

Assets = Liabilities + NPO Equity

or restated as

NPO Equity = Assets – Liabilities

Thus far, the discussion and analysis have concentrated on the *unrestricted* assets and liabilities. The fundamental accounting equation should hold as follows:

Unrestricted NPO Equity = *Unrestricted* Assets – *Unrestricted* Liabilities

An analysis of the *Unrestricted* Net Assets (or Equity) account is as follows:

ANALYSIS OF UNRESTRICTED NET ASSETS (EQUITY)

Transactions	Decrease	(Increase)	Balance
Balance, 7/1/19X1			($1,495,258)

The unrestricted net assets are shown at the beginning balance at 7/1/19X1 of $1,495,258. At the end of the fiscal year when the books are closed, the Unrestricted Net Assets will increase by $822,956. This will represent the difference between revenues from all sources and the total of all program and supporting services activities of the NPO. The balance in the Unrestricted Net Assets account also equals the difference between the Totals of the Unrestricted Assets and Liabilities both at the beginning of the fiscal year, 7/1/19X1, and at the end of the fiscal year, 6/30/19X2. Of course, this equality also holds all during the fiscal year. We shall deal subsequently with the revenue and expense perspective. We turn next to the equality of assets and the sum of liabilities and equity.

THE FUNDAMENTAL ACCOUNTING EQUATION AND THE UNRESTRICTED NET ASSETS

In Exhibit 7, we show an accounting trial balance of the balances in the *unrestricted* asset, liability, and net asset accounts as of July 1, 19X1 and June 30, 19X2. The trial balance shows that the Unrestricted Net Assets account is in fact the balancing account both on July 1, 19X1 and June 30, 19X2. There is nothing surprising about this fact, since the accounting system is so structured that this must be the outcome.

EXHIBIT 7 Unrestricted Resources—General Fund—Trial Balance

TRIAL BALANCE

Unrestricted Assets, Liabilities & Net Assets	19X2		19X1	
	Dr	Cr	Dr	Cr
Cash	$200,000		$200,000	
Cash Equivalents	1,147,353		33,422	
Accounts Receivable	460,467		485,879	
Allowance for Uncollectible Accounts		$45,000		$40,000
Pledges Receivable	0		0	
Allowance for Uncollectible Pledges		0		0
Investment Income Receivable	32,918		20,947	
Inventory of Supplies —Program A	114,416		156,684	
Inventory of Supplies —Program B	125,111		137,733	

Inventory of Supplies —Program C	75,082		80,393	
Inventory of Supplies Management & General	35,414		25,406	
Inventory of Supplies Fund-Raising	10,625		8,400	
Prepaid Expenses —Program A	35,502		26,313	
Prepaid Expenses —Program B	69,198		103,124	
Prepaid Expenses —Program C	32,154		48,217	
Prepaid Expenses Management & General	23,968		36,803	
Property, Plant and Equipment	6,308,301		5,951,227	
Accumulated Depreciation —Property, Plant and Equipment		3,254,550		2,549,506
Accounts Payable		1,412,460		1,298,095
Prepaid Services		110,357		97,264
Long-Term Debt —Current Installment		333,062		304,498
Long-Term Debt		2,196,864		2,529,926
Unrestricted Net Assets, July 1, 19X1		495,258		495,258
	8,670,509	7,847,552	$7,314,548	$7,314,548
Increase in Unrestricted Net Assets		822,956		
Totals	$8,670,509	$8,670,509		

Dr= Debt; Cr=Credit

*Totals may reflect rounding differences.

Both on July 1 and June 30, the Unrestricted Net Assets account is shown with the July 1 balance in it. This only means that the end-of-the-period accounting procedures have not been completed that will add the increase in the unrestricted net assets in the amount of $701,102 to the opening balance of $495,258 in the account.

The trial balance in Exhibit 7 demonstrates that the fundamental accounting equation is satisfied in the case of the unrestricted assets, liabilities, and equity. The analysis in Exhibit 8 shows that the fundamental accounting equation has been satisfied.

EXHIBIT 8 Unrestricted Net Assets and the Fundamental Accounting Equation*

	Unrestricted Net Assets	=	Unrestricted Assets	–	Unrestricted Liabilities
Total Debits and Credits	$ 0	=	$8,670,509	–	$8,670,509
Allowance for Uncollectible Accounts	0		(45,000)	–	(45,000)
Accumulated Depreciation Property, Plant and Equipment	0	=	(3,254,550)	–	(3,254,550)
	0	=	5,370,959	–	5,370,959
Unrestricted Net Assets Balances, July 1, 19X1	495,258	=		–	(495,258)
	495,258	=	5,370,959	–	4,875,701
Increase in Unrestricted Net Assets, 19X2	822,956	=	822,956	–	
Totals	$1,318,214	=	$6,193,915	–	$4,875,701

*Totals may reflect rounding differences.

THE REVENUE/EXPENSE PERSPECTIVE

THE REVENUE SIDE

A second and vitally important perspective must now be explored, the revenue/expense perspective. Revenues are analyzed and accumulated by type and source. The two major types of revenue are those that arise from

1. Nonexchange transactions

2. Exchange transactions

The major sources of nonexchange revenues would be

1. Direct contributions of monetary and other resources from individuals

2. Indirect allocations of monetary resources from fund-raising organizations

3. Grants from private and governmental organizations that do not require quid pro quo services

The major sources of revenues arising from exchange transactions would include, among others:

1. Fees for services rendered

2. Investment income

3. Rental income

4. Realized gains from the disposal of operating assets

5. Realized gains from trading in financial assets

6. Unrealized gains from the holding of financial assets

ILLUSTRATIVE REVENUE TRANSACTIONS

The following *illustrative* revenue transactions affected the NPO:

1. An entry recorded at the beginning of the fiscal year that reclassifies the prior year's ending balance in unconditional and unrestricted pledges receivable to unrestricted contributions in accordance with the requirements of *SFAS No. 116*. These requirements will be discussed in greater detail when temporarily restricted assets are discussed. See also Entry #48 below that is the fiscal year-end entry to reclassify the ending balance of unconditional and unrestricted pledges receivable.

2. Unrestricted contributions arising from unconditional and unrestricted pledges solicited during the annual campaign to fund the programs and supporting activities of the NPO.

3. Fees for services charged to beneficiaries of the services program by the activities of Program B.

6. Unrestricted investment income earned and received on the investments of the endowment of the NPO created to fund the programs and support activities of the NPO.

20. Realized gains from the disposal of fixed assets.

25. Increase in net assets from grants—released from restrictions for operating activities.

27. Increase in net assets from contributions—released from restrictions for the acquisition of fixed assets, i.e., for capital purposes.

28. Increase in net assets from contributions—released from restrictions for debt service, i.e., for the repayment of interest and principal of long-term debt used for the acquisition of fixed assets, again for capital purposes.

30. Unrestricted interest income earned and received on cash equivalents.

32. Increase in net assets from contributions released from time dependent restrictions for operating activities.

41. Estimated amount of uncollectible pledges receivable to be treated as a reduction of the associated unrestricted contributions.

45. Fees for services earned but not yet paid.

47. Unrestricted investment income earned but not yet paid on endowment investments.

48. An entry that reclassifies revenue from unconditional and unrestricted pledges of gifts of resources to net assets temporarily restricted due to timing differences in accordance with the requirements of *SFAS No. 116*. These requirements will be discussed in greater detail when temporarily restricted assets are discussed.

The *illustrative* revenue transactions for the NPO can be summarized in the following analysis:

*ANALYSIS OF REVENUE ACCOUNTS FROM EXCHANGE AND NONEXCHANGE TRANSACTIONS**

	Unrestricted Contributions	Released from Restrict-tions—Grants and Contributions	Fees for Services	Investment Income	Gain from Dis-posal of Fixed Assets
Entry #2	$9,911,407				
Entry #3			$2,894,231		
Entry #6				$279,086	
Entry #20					$25,094
Entry #25		$ 499,956			
Entry #27		614,524			
Entry #28		547,239			
Entry #30				24,276	
Entry #32		316,870			
Entry #45			97,264		
Entry #47				32,918	
Balances	9,911,407	$1,978,589	$2,991,495	$336,280	$25,094
Entry #41	(350,000)				
	9,561,407				
Entry #1	1,834,624				
Entry #48	(2,113,325)				
	$9,282,706				

*Some totals may differ from account balances due to rounding differences.

The Expense Side—Illustrative Transactions

Expenses are analyzed and accumulated by the accounting system in terms of programs and support activities and also in terms of object of expense.

There are six *illustrative* categories of transactions that affect the expense accounts of a program or supporting activity of the NPO. These are:

1. Entry #21 AP—Other than personnel services expenses through accounts payable

2. Entry #22 PR—Wages and salaries expense

3. Entry #23 EB—Employees benefits expense

4. Entry #24 PT—Employer's payroll taxes expense

5. Entry #35 CI—Consumption of inventory from the inventory of supplies

6. Entry #36 CP—Consumption of prepaid expenses from the prepaid expenses

First, we look at expense transactions of Programs A, B, C, Management & General, and Fund-Raising in terms of the six *illustrative* categories.

ANALYSIS OF EXPENSES OF PROGRAM A, B, & C, MANAGEMENT & GENERAL, AND FUND-RAISING*

Transactions	A	B	C	M&G	FR
JE 21 AP	$ 488,287	$1,549,696	$ 680,303	$ 98,090	$ 98,989
JE 22 PR	1,095,186	3,877,349	1,766,935	335,223	189,868
JE 23 EB	210,775	746,219	340,057	64,516	36,541
JE 24 PT	83,909	297,067	135,375	25,683	14,547
JE 35 CI	42,268	184,170	95,397	19,331	14,475
JE 36 CP	9,189	33,926	16,063	12,834	
Balances	$1,929,614	$6,688,427	$3,034,131	$555,667	$354,420

*Totals reflect rounding differences from account balances

THE EXPENSE SIDE—ANALYSIS BY OBJECT OF EXPENSE

The expenses of program and support activities can also be analyzed in terms of objects of expense. Exhibit 9 contains the expense analysis by object of expense.

EXHIBIT 9   Expenses—by Object Classification—Programs A, B, C, Management & General, and Fund-Raising*

Expense Object Classifications	Program A	Program B	Program C	Management & General	Fund-Raising
Salaries	$1,095,186	$3,877,349	$1,766,935	$336,223	$189,869
Employee benefits	210,775	746,219	340,057	64,516	36,541
Payroll Taxes	83,909	297,067	135,375	25,683	14,547
	1,389,869	4,920,635	2,242,368	425,422	240,957
Professional fees	41,721	242,334	0	32,258	0
Contractual services	20,861	166,726	55,328	0	0
Facilities rents	58,807	164,787	0	15,846	0
Insurance	9,189	33,927	16,063	12,770	0
Utilities	18,377	92,087	37,480	7,480	0
Telephone	25,728	53,314	31,591	10,259	35,442
Heating	45,943	145,401	69,607	12,877	0
Equipment rentals	55,499	213,258	26,772	0	0
Maintenance and repairs	20,215	103,719	14,278	7,480	0
Projects materials	37,765	0	187,402	0	0
Supplies	42,268	184,170	95,397	19,418	22,784
Printing and publication	5,513	29,080	49,974	3,702	37,973
Postage and shipping	23,890	140,554	38,462	2,710	17,265
Conferences and meetings	35,744	87,240	66,037	3,526	0
Travel	13,783	82,394	99,948	1,603	0
Assistance to clients	80,860	0	0	0	0
Miscellaneous	3,579	28,801	3,425	526	
	1,929,613	6,688,427	3,034,131	555,667	354,421
Depreciation	96,572	556,928	250,336	33,753	
Provision of Uncollectible Accounts		35,000			
Interest on Short-Term Debt				13,606	

Interest on Long-Term
  Debt   242,741

| Totals | $2,026,185 | $7,280,355 | $3,284,467 | $845,767 | $354,421 |

*Totals may reflect rounding differences.

ADDITIONAL EXPENSES

Additional expenses incurred by the NPO to be presented are:

1. Depreciation Expenses

2. Provision for Uncollectible Accounts

3. Interest on Short-Term Debt

4. Interest on Long-Term Debt

In fact, all of these expenses were presented as part of the analysis of particular asset and liability accounts. These expenses are also shown in Exhibit 8.

The accounting system maintains separate expense accounts for each of these expenses. Here is a summary analysis of these expenses.

ANALYSIS OF ADDITIONAL EXPENSES

	Depreciation Expense	Provision for Uncollectibles Accounts	Interest Expense Long-Term Debt	Interest Expense Short-Term Debt
Entry #28			$242,741	
Entry #31				$13,607
Entry #39		$35,000		
Entry #4	$937,589			

Depreciation expense has been allocated to the three programs and to Management & General in Exhibit 9. That allocation was shown earlier in the analysis of the Accumulated Depreciation—Property, Plant and Equipment account. Many times, allocations of depreciation expense can be quite arbitrary. Whether these allocations are arbitrary or not would require additional information to that shown directly in the accounting system.

The Provision of Uncollectibles Accounts expense is assigned to Program B since that is the program that extends credit to its beneficiaries that results in Accounts Receivable. The two types of interest expense have been assigned to the Management & General category since financing via credit is an overall decision of the NPO and not the responsibility of the individual programs.

The analysis of Interest on Long-term Debt was provided earlier in the analysis of the Long-Term Debt account.

The Interest on Short-Term Debt will be discussed when cash flows are analyzed.

THE FUNDAMENTAL ACCOUNTING EQUATION AND THE RESTRICTED NET ASSETS

We have demonstrated for our illustrative accounting model of the NPO that the fundamental accounting equation is satisfied for the unrestricted assets, liabilities, and net assets.

The same fundamental accounting equation holds for the restricted assets, liabilities, and net assets. There are three categories of restricted resources:

1. Temporarily restricted resources available for operating purposes

2. Temporarily restricted resources available for capital purposes such as acquisition of fixed assets and debt service on debt used to acquire fixed assets

3. Permanently restricted resources held as endowment

RESTRICTED ASSETS

CASH FROM GRANTS—TEMPORARILY RESTRICTED FOR OPERATING ACTIVITIES

We turn from the unrestricted assets, liabilities and equity accounts to the restricted accounts. The first group of accounts we illustrate are the temporarily restricted assets.

Cash received from temporarily restricted government grants that have been awarded to support particular programs of the NPO is accounted for through the Cash and Cash Equivalents—Temporarily Restricted account. Cash and cash equivalents are shown in a single account to simplify the exposition. Cash equivalents are interest bearing so that the Interest Receivables—Temporarily Restricted account is analyzed at the same time as the cash and cash equivalents account.

The analysis of these accounts is below:

ANALYSIS OF CASH—TEMPORARILY RESTRICTED—FROM GRANTS FOR OPERATING ACTIVITIES

Transactions	Increase	(Decrease)	Balance
Balance, 7/1/19X1			$ 0
Received from Grants —Entry #10	$499,956		499,956
Cash Transferred— Restrictions released —Entry #25		(499,956)	$ 0

CASH FROM CONTRIBUTIONS—TEMPORARILY RESTRICTED FOR OPERATING ACTIVITIES

A second temporarily restricted cash account results from contributions subject to timing restrictions. With the appropriate passage of time, the timing restrictions are satisfied and cash is transferred from the temporarily restricted account to the unrestricted cash account.

ANALYSIS OF CASH—TEMPORARILY RESTRICTED—FROM CONTRIBUTIONS FOR OPERATING ACTIVITIES

Transactions	Increase	(Decrease)	Balance
Balance, 7/1/19X1			$ 0
Received from Contributions—Entry #5	$316,870		$316,870
Cash Transferred— Restrictions released —Entry #32		($316,870)	$ 0

GRANTS RECEIVABLE—TEMPORARILY RESTRICTED FOR OPERATING ACTIVITIES

The Grants Receivable account carries the initial amounts of the grants awarded as of 7/1/19X1. This amount represents cash owed from such grants at the beginning of the fiscal year, thus it is treated as a Grants Receivable. The amount of grants awarded for 19X2 in entry #9 increases Grants Receivable. Entry #10, which was shown earlier in the temporarily restricted Cash and Cash Equivalent account as an increase, is shown as reducing the amounts of Grants Receivable owed.

ANALYSIS OF GOVERNMENT GRANTS RECEIVABLE—TEMPORARILY RESTRICTED—FOR OPERATING ACTIVITIES

Transactions	Increase	(Decrease)	Balance
Balance, 7/1/19X1			$ 55,022
Grants awarded —Entry #9	$524,905		579,927
Grants—19X2 —Entry #10	_____	($499,956)	$ 79,971
	524,905	(499,956)	
Increase in grants awarded	_____	(24,949)	
	$524,905	($524,905)	

Normally receivables are subject to an estimate for uncollectibles for external reporting purposes. The estimate for uncollectibles is accounted for through a separate Allowance for Uncollectibles account. In the case of the government grants, management has judged that an estimate for uncollectibles is not necessary given the credit worthiness of the granting agency.

PLEDGES RECEIVABLE—TEMPORARILY RESTRICTED FOR OPERATING PROCEDURES

Temporarily restricted resources are obtained through contributions as well as through grants. Pledges receivable arising from temporarily restricted contributions are analyzed along with the associated Allowance for Uncollectibles.

The *illustrative* transactions affecting the Receivables and Allowance accounts are as follows:

2. Pledges of contributions subject to time restrictions.

5. Cash collections of pledges.

43. Reducing pledges receivable for inactive pledges that management has determined to be uncollectible after an exhaustive effort to collect the pledges. This entry also affects the Allowance for Uncollectible Pledges.

44. The estimate of the amount of uncollectible pledges that are expected to occur from those accounts presently active but not yet specifically identified as uncollectible.

ANALYSIS OF PLEDGES RECEIVABLE—TEMPORARILY RESTRICTED—FOR OPERATING ACTIVITIES

Transactions	Increase	(Decrease)	Balance
Balance, 7/1/19X1			$316,870
Pledges—19X2			
—Entry #2	$281,497		598,367
Collections			
—Entry #5		($316,870)	281,497
Identified uncollectible			
pledges—Entry #43		(25,000)	$256,497
	281,497	(341,870)	
Decrease in temporarily			
restricted pledges	60,373		
	$341,870	($341,870)	

ANALYSIS OF ALLOWANCE FOR UNCOLLECTIBLE PLEDGES—TEMPORARILY RESTRICTED FOR OPERATING ACTIVITIES

Transactions	Decrease	(Increase)	Balance
Balance, 7/1/19X1			($30,000)
Identified uncollectible			
pledges—Entry #43	$25,000		(5,000)

Provision for uncollectible Pledges —Entry #44	_____	($25,000)	($30,000)
	$25,000	($25,000)	

PLEDGES RECEIVABLE—TEMPORARILY RESTRICTED FOR REPORTING PURPOSES

The Pledges Receivable—Unrestricted account is reclassified at year-end for reporting purposes to a Pledges Receivable—Temporarily Restricted for Reporting Purposes account. This means that on the financial statements the Unrestricted Pledges receivable will be shown as Temporarily Restricted Pledges Receivable.

The purpose of treating unconditional and unrestricted pledges receivable as restricted on the financial statements is to meet the requirements of *SFAS No. 116.*

The same reclassification is done for the related Allowance account. The two entries, #1 and #48, that affect these two accounts have already been discussed earlier as part of the analysis of the Pledges Receivable, Unrestricted account and its related Allowance account.

ANALYSIS OF PLEDGES RECEIVABLE—TEMPORARILY RESTRICTED—FOR REPORTING PURPOSES

Transactions	Increase	(Decrease)	Balance
Balance, 7/1			$2,134,624
Reclassify Pledges —Entry #1		($2,134,624)	0
Reclassify Pledges —Entry #48	$2,448,325		$2,448,325

ANALYSIS OF ALLOWANCE FOR UNCOLLECTIBLE PLEDGES—TEMPORARILY RESTRICTED FOR REPORTING PURPOSES

Transactions	Decrease	(Increase)	Balance
Balance, 7/1			($300,000)
Reclassify Allowance —Entry #1	$300,000		0

Reclassify Allowance
    —Entry #48   ($335,000)   ($335,000)

NET ASSETS—TEMPORARILY RESTRICTED REVENUE RECOGNITION AND TEMPORARILY RESTRICTED NET ASSETS

Grants, contributions, and other gifts that are subject to temporary restrictions are not to be recognized at the time of the gift. Revenue recognition is deferred until the temporary restriction is satisfied. The Temporarily Restricted Assets represent "deferred revenues." In business accounting deferred revenue is treated as a liability. Deferred revenue usually arises as a result of advance payments from customers. The advance payment is made with the expectation that future performance in terms of goods, services or other assets are expected in exchange for the payment. Gifts or grants that do not involve expectation of a future exchange would not be treated as deferred revenue and a liability. Rather, the deferred recognition of revenue at the time of the gift is treated as an increment to the equity of the NPO. The temporarily restricted gifts or grants are accounted for as additions to the assets and as additions to the temporarily restricted equity of the NPO. In the terminology of *SFAS No. 116*, the temporarily restricted equity is called Temporarily Restricted Net Assets.

We shall be reviewing a number of examples of Temporarily Restricted Net Assets.

NET ASSETS—FROM GRANTS

We have reviewed all of the asset accounts that are temporarily restricted for operating purposes. These accounts are balanced by a series of Net Assets—Temporarily Restricted accounts, just as the unrestricted assets and liabilities accounts were balanced by the Unrestricted Net Assets account. It was unnecessary to establish any liability accounts related to the temporarily restricted asset accounts.

There are two transactions and entries that affect the Net Asset—Temporarily Restricted—from Grants.

9. Grants awarded to the NPO specifically restricted to support the operating activities of Program A.

37. An adjusting entry that recognizes the amount of revenues arising under the grants in the current period because grant restrictions were satisfied as a result of actual expenditures incurred under purposes of the grants.

ANALYSIS OF NET ASSETS (EQUITY)—TEMPORARILY RESTRICTED—FROM GRANTS*

Transactions	Decrease	(Increase)	Balance
Balance, 7/1/19X1			($55,022)
Temporary Restrictions —19X2—Entry #9		($524,905)	(524,905)
Restrictions released —19X2—Entry #25	499,956	_____	($79,972)
	$499,956	(524,905)	
Increase in Temporarily Restricted Pledges	24,949	_____	
	$524,905	($524,905)	

*Totals may reflect rounding differences.

NET ASSETS—FROM CONTRIBUTIONS

Contributions that are subject to timing restrictions are treated as temporarily restricted. Pledges Receivable from such contributions have been discussed earlier. We now turn to balancing Net Assets—Temporarily Restricted—from Contribution account.

There are three transactions and entries that affect the Net Asset—Temporarily Restricted—from Contributions.

2. To record the Pledges for 19X2 subject to timing restrictions.

37. An adjusting entry that recognizes the amount of revenues arising under the pledges subject to timing restrictions in the current period because timing restrictions were satisfied.

44. An adjusting entry that reduces the Net Assets account for the estimated amount of uncollectible pledges.

ANALYSIS OF NET ASSETS (EQUITY)—TEMPORARILY RESTRICTED—FROM CONTRIBUTIONS

Transactions	Decrease	(Increase)	Balance
Balance, 7/1/19X1			($286,870)
Temporary Restrictions —19X2—Entry #2		($281,497)	(568,367)
Restrictions released —19X2—Entry #32	$316,870		(251,497)
Provisions for Uncollectible Pledges —Entry #44	25,000	_____	($226,497)
		341,870	($281,497)
		_____	(60,373)
	$341,870	($341,870)	

NET ASSETS—TEMPORARILY RESTRICTED FOR REPORTING PURPOSES

The third Temporarily Restricted Equity account is the Net Assets—Temporarily Restricted for Reporting Purposes. The equity account balances the associated temporarily restricted assets account.

ANALYSIS OF NET ASSETS (EQUITY)—TEMPORARILY RESTRICTED—FOR REPORTING PURPOSES

Transactions	Decrease	(Increase)	Balance
Balance, 7/1/19X1			($1,834,624)
Adjustment for Reporting Purposes-Entry #1	$1,834,624		0
Adjustment for Reporting purposes—Entry #48		($2,113,325)	($2,113,325)
Increase in Receivables Restricted for Reporting	278,701		
	$ 2,113,325		

THE FUNDAMENTAL ACCOUNTING EQUATION AND TEMPORARILY RESTRICTED NET ASSETS FOR OPERATING PURPOSES

Temporarily restricted assets for operating purposes are balanced by temporarily restricted equity for operating purposes. The fundamental accounting equation is satisfied as follows:

GRTROP + (PRTROP – AUPR) + (PRTRRP – AUPR) = NAGRTROP + NAPRTROP + NAPRTRRP

$79,971 + (256,497 – 30,000) + (2,448,325 – 335,000) = 79,971 + 226,497 + 2,113,325

Definition of Symbols

GRTROP = Grant Receivable—Temporarily Restricted—Operating Purposes

PRTROP = Pledges Receivable—Temporarily Restricted—Operating Purposes

AUPRTROP = Allowance for Uncollectible Pledges Receivable—Temporarily Restricted—Operating Purposes

PRTRRP = Pledges Receivable—Temporarily Restricted—Reporting Purposes

AUPRTRRP = Allowance for Uncollectible Pledges Receivable—Temporarily Restricted—Reporting Purposes

NAGRTROP = Net Assets—Grants Receivable—Temporarily Restricted—Operating Purposes

NAPRTROP = Net Assets—Pledges Receivable—Temporarily Restricted—Operating Purposes

NAPRTRRP = Net Assets—Pledges Receivable—Temporarily Restricted—Reporting Purposes

A trial balance of the assets and equities temporarily restricted for operating purposes is set out in Exhibit 10. This trial balance is set out in the traditional accounting format of debits (dr) and credits (cr). It shows the equality demonstrated by the fundamental accounting equation. The trial balance also provides a summary overview of the assets and equities that are temporarily restricted for operating purposes. Note that the assets and equities temporarily restricted for reporting purposes for external financial reporting are temporarily restricted for operating purposes for internal reporting purposes.

EXHIBIT 10 Temporarily Expendable Restricted Operating Resources—Restricted Purposes Fund—Trial Balance*

	TRIAL BALANCE			
	19X2		19X1	
Restricted Assets, Liabilities & Net Assets	Dr	Cr	Dr	Cr
Cash—Temporarily Restricted—Grants	$0			
Governmental Grants Receivable —Temporarily Restricted for Operating Purposes	79,972		$55,022	
Pledges Receivable—Temporarily Restricted for for Operating Purposes	256,497		351,870	
Allowance for Uncollectible Pledges—Temporarily Restricted for Operating Purposes		$30,000		$30,000
Pledges Receivable—Temporarily Restricted for Reporting Purposes	2,448,325		2,134,624	
Allowance for Uncollectible Pledges Temporarily Restricted for Reporting Purposes		335,000		300,000
Net Assets—Temporarily Restricted Contributions for Operating Purposes		226,497		286,870
Net Assets—Temporarily Restricted Grants for Operating Purposes		79,972		55,020

Net Assets—Temporarily Restricted
 Pledges Receivable for Reporting
 Purposes   _____ 2,113,325 _____ 1,834,624

                               $2,784,793 $2,784,793 $2,506,517 $2,506,517

*Totals may reflect rounding differences.

RESTRICTED ASSETS FOR CAPITAL PURPOSES

Earlier, temporarily restricted contributions, initially, in the form of pledges were for operating purposes. Those pledges were obtained during the annual fund-raising campaign. The NPO has also been engaging in a capital campaign. The capital campaign has led to pledges of gifts that are temporarily restricted for capital purposes. Capital purposes involve first and foremost the acquisition of property, plant and equipment (tangible fixed assets) to be used in the operating activities of the NPO. The acquisition of capital assets such as property, plant and equipment may be paid for directly through normal short-term credit followed by payment or financed through long-term borrowing. The financial resources raised through the capital campaign are to finance the acquisition of plant assets either by direct payment for those assets as they are acquired or by the repayment of long-term debt as it matures that was borrowed to finance the acquisition of such assets.

First, we look at the cash account that is used for cash collected from pledges temporarily restricted for capital purposes.

CASH FROM CONTRIBUTIONS—TEMPORARILY RESTRICTED FOR CAPITAL PURPOSES

A temporarily restricted cash account is maintained to account for contributions collected from temporarily restricted pledges for the acquisition of tangible fixed assets. These temporarily restricted contributions are also available to service both short-term and long-term debt incurred in the acquisition of fixed assets.

There are five transactions that affect this account.

12. Records the cash collected from pledges to finance the acquisition of fixed assets and debt service to finance such acquisitions.

26. Transferred cash to the Unrestricted Cash account since restrictions were satisfied as a result of the acquisition of fixed assets eligible to be funded through contributions for capital purposes.

27. Transferred cash to a temporarily restricted cash account for the servicing of long-term debt.

29. A summary entry that transferred excess cash to a short-term investments account for income-earning purposes.

34. To record investment income earned on investments of excess cash.

ANALYSIS OF CASH—TEMPORARILY RESTRICTED—FROM CONTRIBUTIONS—FOR CAPITAL PURPOSES

Transactions	Increase	(Decrease)	Balance
Balance, 7/1/19X1			$ 0
Contributions Collected —Entry #12	$2,000,000		$2,000,000
Cash Transferred—Debt Service—Entry #19		($ 547,239)	1,452,761
Cash Transferred —Restrictions Released —Entry #27		(614,524)	838,237
Invested Excess Cash —Entry #29		(838,237)	0
Interest Income —Short-Term —Entry #34	15,886	_____	$ 15,886
	2,015,886	(2,000,000)	
	_____	(15,886)	
	$2,015,886	($2,015,886)	

CASH FROM CONTRIBUTIONS—TEMPORARILY RESTRICTED FOR DEBT SERVICE

A separate cash account is maintained for debt service. Two transactions affect this account. The first transaction transfers cash into this account from the cash from the contributions restricted to capital purposes. The second transaction pays debt service on long-term debt. An analysis of such debt service was provided when the Long-Term Debt account was analyzed. The amount shown as paid, $547,239, is the annual amount. The earlier analysis is on a monthly basis.

ANALYSIS OF CASH—TEMPORARILY RESTRICTED—FOR DEBT SERVICE

Transactions	Increase	(Decrease)	Balance
Balance, 7/1/19X1			$ 0
Cash Transferred—Debt Service—Entry #19	$547,239		$547,239
Paid Debt Service —Entry #28		($547,239)	$ 0

PLEDGES RECEIVABLE—TEMPORARILY RESTRICTED FOR CAPITAL PURPOSES

The next two accounts to be analyzed are the Temporarily Restricted Pledges Receivable account and the related Allowance account.

The Receivables account is affected by three *illustrative transactions*.

11. Pledges of contributions subject to temporary restrictions that limit the contributions to capital purposes.

12. Cash collections of pledges.

43. Reducing pledges receivable for inactive pledges that management has determined to be uncollectible after an exhaustive effort to collect the pledges. This entry also affects the Allowance for Uncollectible Pledges.

The Allowances account is affected by two *illustrative* transactions.

43. Described above.

44. The estimate of the amount of uncollectible pledges that are expected to occur from those accounts presently active but not yet specifically identified as uncollectible.

ANALYSIS OF PLEDGES RECEIVABLE—TEMPORARILY RESTRICTED—FOR CAPITAL PURPOSES

Transactions	Increase	(Decrease)	Balance
Balance, 7/1/19X1			$ 138,000
Pledges—19X2 —Entry #11	$2,104,000		2,242,000
Collected Pledges —Entry #12		($2,000,000)	242,000

Identified Uncollectible Pledges—Entry #43	_____	(20,000)	$222,000
	2,104,000	(2,020,000)	
Increase in Pledges Receivable	_____	84,000	
	$2,104,000	($2,104,000)	

ANALYSIS OF ALLOWANCE FOR UNCOLLECTIBLE PLEDGES —TEMPORARILY RESTRICTED FOR CAPITAL PURPOSES

Transactions	Decrease	(Increase)	Balance
Balance, 7/1/19X1			($10,000)
Identified Uncollectible Pledges—Entry #43	$20,000		10,000
Provision for Uncollectible Pledges—Entry #44		($20,000)	($10,000)

INVESTMENTS—TEMPORARILY RESTRICTED FOR CAPITAL PURPOSES

The excess amount of Cash Temporarily Restricted for Capital Services is invested in short-term debt instruments that do not qualify as cash equivalents and therefore must be accounted for and reported separately from Cash and Cash Equivalents. The analysis shows only one summary transaction as affecting this account. In fact, throughout the year there were a number of transfers into and out of the account as the amounts of excess cash varied from month to month.

ANALYSIS OF INVESTMENTS—TEMPORARILY RESTRICTED —FOR CAPITAL PURPOSES—SIMPLIFIED PRESENTATION

Transactions	Increase	(Decrease)	Balance
Balance, 7/1/19X1			$ 0
Invested Excess Cash —Entry #29	$838,237		$838,237

NET ASSETS—TEMPORARILY RESTRICTED FOR CAPITAL PURPOSES

There are five *illustrative* summary transactions that affect the Net Assets—Temporarily Restricted from Contributions for Capital Purposes.

11. Records $2,104,000 in pledges receivable during 19X2 that were temporarily restricted for capital purposes as both assets and increases in the Net Assets—Temporarily Restricted for Capital Purposes.

26. The acquisition of equipment and other tangible fixed assets for operating purposes in the amount of $614,524 means that restrictions were satisfied and, thus, this amount of net assets should be treated as having had restrictions released.

28. The "payment" of debt service on matured long-term debt that was used to finance the acquisition of property, plant and equipment also acts to satisfy restrictions and results in a decrease of restricted net assets.

34. Interest income of $15,886 on temporarily restricted investments is itself treated as temporarily restricted and to be used only for the acquisition of capital assets.

44. The estimate of $20,000 for uncollectible pledges is treated as a reduction of the Temporarily Restricted Net Assets.

ANALYSIS OF NET ASSETS (EQUITY)—TEMPORARILY RESTRICTED—FOR CAPITAL PURPOSES

Transactions	Decrease	(Increase)	Balance
Balance, 7/1/19X1			($ 128,000)
Temporary Restrictions —19X2—Entry #11		($2,104,000)	(2,232,000)
Restrictions Released —19X2—Entry #27	$614,524		(1,617,476)
Restrictions Released —19X2—Entry #28	547,239		(1,070,237)
Interest Income —Temporarily Restricted—Entry #34		(15,886)	(1,086,123)
Provision for Uncollectible Pledges —Entry #44	20,000		($1,066,123)
	1,181,763	(2,119,886)	

Increase in Temporarily
Restricted Net Assets   938,123   _____
                        $2,119,886   ($2,119,886)

THE FUNDAMENTAL ACCOUNTING EQUATION AND TEMPORARILY RESTRICTED NET ASSETS FOR CAPITAL PURPOSES

Temporarily restricted assets for capital purposes are balanced by temporarily restricted equity for capital purposes. The fundamental accounting equation is satisfied as follows:

$$CTRCP + (PRTRCP - AUPR) + ITRCP = NATRCP$$

$$\$15,886 + (222,000 - 10,000) + 838,237 = \$1,066,123$$

Definitions of Symbols

CTRCP = Cash—Temporarily Restricted—Capital Purposes

PRTRCP = Pledges Receivable—Temporarily Restricted—
            Capital Purposes

AUPRTROP = Allowance for Uncollectible Pledges Receivable
              —Temporarily Restricted—Capital Purposes

ITRCP = Investment—Temporarily Restricted—Capital
          Purposes

NATRCP = Net Assets—Temporarily Restricted—Capital
           Purposes

A trial balance of the assets and equities temporarily restricted for capital purposes is set out in Exhibit 11. This trial balance is also set out in the traditional accounting format of debits (dr) and credits (cr). It also shows the equality demonstrated by the fundamental accounting equation. The trial balance also provides a summary overview of the assets and equities that are temporarily restricted for capital purposes.

EXHIBIT 11 *Temporarily Restricted Expendable Plant Resources— Expendable Plant Fund—Trial Balance**

	TRIAL BALANCE			
	19X2		19X1	
Restricted Assets, Liabilities & Net Assets	Dr	Cr	Dr	Cr
Cash—Temporarily Restricted —for Capital Purposes	$ 15,886			
Cash—Temporarily Restricted for Debt Service	0			
Pledges Receivable—Temporarily Restricted for Capital Purposes	222,000		$138,000	
Allowance for Uncollectible Pledges Temporarily Restricted for Capital Purposes		$ 10,000		$ 10,000
Investment—Temporarily Restricted for Capital Purposes	838,237			
Net Assets—Temporarily Restricted Contributions for Capital Purposes		1,066,123		128,000
	$1,076,123	$1,076,123	$138,000	$138,000

*Totals may reflect rounding differences.

ENDOWMENT—PERMANENTLY RESTRICTED RESOURCES

An NPO has two periodic fund-raising campaigns; the annual operating campaign and the recurring but less frequent capital campaign. There is a third fund-raising activity; the activity on the behalf of endowment. This is a continuous fund-raising activity. Endowment can generate a separate income stream.

CASH—PERMANENTLY RESTRICTED ENDOWMENT

A separate cash account is maintained to receive contributions permanently restricted for endowment as well as investment income from endowment investments.

There are four *illustrative* transactions that affect the Cash— Permanently Restricted for Endowment.

14. Contributions of $288,795 collected from pledges permanently restricted for endowment.

15. Investment of the $288,795 of collections on pledges.

16. Cash of $18,196 received on investment income to be added to the permanent endowment to maintain its purchasing power value.

17. Investment of the cash from investment income.

ANALYSIS OF CASH—PERMANENTLY RESTRICTED—FROM CONTRIBUTIONS FOR ENDOWMENT PURPOSES

Transactions	Increase	(Decrease)	Balance
Balance, 7/1/19X1			
Contributions Collected —Entry #14	$288,795		$288,795
Investment—Entry #15		(288,795)	0
Investment Income —Entry #16	18,196		18,196
Investment—Entry #17		(18,196)	0

Note that contributions will also include bequests from estates that are given for endowment purposes. If the amounts of the bequests are material, they should be accounted for and reported separately for information and control purposes.

The Board of Trustees took action to include a certain amount of investment income in the endowment in order to maintain its value after adjustment for the effect on purchasing power of inflation.

INVESTMENT INCOME RECEIVABLE—PERMANENTLY RESTRICTED ENDOWMENT

Investment income was earned at the end of the prior fiscal year on permanent endowment investment but not paid. *Illustrative* transaction #16 which was reflected earlier in the Cash-Permanently Restricted for Endowment account, records the effect on the Investment Income Receivable of the receipt of cash. Illustrative transaction #18 records the investment of the cash.

ANALYSIS OF INVESTMENT INCOME RECEIVABLE—PERMANENTLY RESTRICTED FOR ENDOWMENT PURPOSES

Transactions	Increase	(Decrease)	Balance
Balance, 7/1/19X1			$1,168
Investment—Entry #16		($1,168)	0
Investment Income —Entry #18	$1,916		$1,916

As noted earlier, the Board of Trustees took action to maintain its value of the endowment in purchasing power terms by including a certain amount of investment income in endowment investments.

PLEDGES RECEIVABLE—PERMANENTLY RESTRICTED ENDOWMENT

Pledges of contributions to the permanent endowment are accounted for through their own account for planning and control purposes.

Three *illustrative* transactions affect this Pledges Receivables account as has been the case for the prior Pledges Receivables accounts.

13. Pledges of contributions subject to permanent restrictions that limit the contributions to endowment.

14. Cash collections of pledges.

43. Reducing pledges receivable for inactive pledges that management has determined to be uncollectible after an exhaustive effort to collect the pledges. This entry also affects the Allowance for Uncollectible Pledges.

The Allowances account is affected by two *illustrative* transactions.

43. Described above.

44. The estimate of the amount of uncollectible pledges that are expected to occur from those accounts presently active but not yet specifically identified as uncollectible.

*ANALYSIS OF PLEDGES RECEIVABLE—PERMANENTLY RESTRICTED—FOR ENDOWMENT PURPOSES**

Transactions	Increase	(Decrease)	Balance
Balance, 7/1/19X1			$29,215

Endowment Contributions —Entry #13	$316,423		345,639
Contributions Collected —Entry #14		($288,795)	56,844
Identified uncollectible Pledges—Entry #43	_____	(2,000)	$54,844
	$316,423	(290,795)	
Increase in Pledges Receivable	_____	(25,628)	
	$316,423	($316,423)	

*Totals may reflect rounding differences.

ANALYSIS OF ALLOWANCE FOR UNCOLLECTIBLE PLEDGES —PERMANENTLY RESTRICTED FOR ENDOWMENT PURPOSES

Transactions	Decrease	(Increase)	Balance
Balance, 7/1/19X1			($2,500)
Identified Uncollectible Pledges—Entry #43	$2,000		(500)
Provision for Uncollectibles —Entry #44	_____	($4,500)	($5,000)
	2,000	(4,500)	
Increase in Allowance	2,500	_____	
Increase in Allowance	$4,500	($4,500)	

INVESTMENT—PERMANENTLY RESTRICTED ENDOWMENT

The endowment investments account increased as a result of permanently restricted cash from pledged contributions to endowment, entry #15. Investments also increased because of the Board of Trustees' action to maintain the purchasing power value of the endowment by adding permanently restricted cash from investment income to the endowment, entry #17. Finally, the unrealized and realized gains from endowment investments are recognized and recorded by entry #49 which is a requirement of *SFAS No. 117.*

ANALYSIS OF INVESTMENTS—PERMANENTLY RESTRICTED FOR ENDOWMENT PURPOSES

Transactions	Increase	(Decrease)	Balance
Balance, 7/1/19X1			$4,412,006
Investment—Entry #15	$288,795		4,700,801
Investment—Entry #17	18,196		4,718,997
Unrealized and Realized Gains—Entry #49	125,000		$4,843,997
Increase in Investments	$431,991		

NET ASSETS—PERMANENTLY RESTRICTED FOR ENDOWMENT

The endowment equity account provided a matching increase that resulted from permanently restricted pledges to contribution to endowment, entry #13. Investments also increased because of the Board of Trustees' action to maintain the purchasing power value of the endowment by adding investment income to the endowment, entry #17. An additional amount was added to the endowment equity from investment income earned but to be received, transaction #18.

Unrealized and realized gains added to permanent endowment will also increase the permanent endowment equity as recorded in entry #49.

There was also a decrease to the permanent endowment equity by virtue of the estimate for uncollectible permanently restricted pledges, entry #44.

ANALYSIS OF NET ASSETS (EQUITY)—PERMANENTLY RESTRICTED—FOR ENDOWMENT PURPOSES

Transactions	Decrease	(Increase)	Balance
Balance, 7/1/19X1			($4,439,890)
Endowment Contributions —Entry #13		($316,423)	(4,756,313)
Investment Income —Entry #16		(17,028)	(4,773,341)
Investment Income Receivable—Entry #18		(1,916)	(4,775,257)
Provision for Uncollectible Pledges —Entry #44	$4,500		(4,770,757)

Unrealized and Realized			
Gains—Entry #49	_____	(125,000)	($4,895,757)
	4,500	(460,367)	
Increase in Permanently			
Restricted Net Assets	455,867	_____	
	$460,367	($460,367)	

THE FUNDAMENTAL ACCOUNTING EQUATION AND PERMANENTLY RESTRICTED NET ASSETS FOR ENDOWMENT PURPOSES

Permanently restricted assets for endowment purposes are balanced by permanently restricted equity for endowment purposes. The fundamental accounting equation is satisfied as follows:

$$IIRPREP + (PRPREP - AUPR) + IPREP = NAPREP$$

$$\$1,916 + (54,844 - 5,000) + 4,718,997 = \$4,770,757$$

Definitions of Symbols

IIRPREP = Investment Income Receivable—Permanently Restricted—Endowment Purposes

PRPREP = Pledges Receivable—Permanently Restricted—Endowment Purposes

AUPRPREP = Allowance for Uncollectible Pledges Receivable—Permanently Restricted—Endowment Purposes

IPREP = Investment—Permanently Restricted—Endowment Purposes

NAPREP = Net Assets—Permanently Restricted—Endowment Purposes

A trial balance of the assets and equities permanently restricted for endowment purposes is set out in Exhibit 12. This trial balance is again set out in the traditional accounting format of debits (dr) and credits (cr). It also shows the equality demonstrated by the fundamental accounting equation.

The trial balance also provides a summary overview of the assets and equities that are temporarily restricted for capital purposes.

***EXHIBIT 12** Permanently Restricted Endowment Resources—*
Endowment Fund—Trial Balance*

	TRIAL BALANCE			
	19X2			19X1
Restricted Assets, Liabilities & Net Assets	Dr	Cr	Dr	Cr
Cash—Permanently Restricted Endowment	$ 0		$ 0	
Investment Income Receivable—Permanently Restricted Endowment	1,916		1,168	
Pledges Receivable— Permanently Restricted Endowment	54,844		29,215	
Allowance for Uncollectible Pledges —Permanently Restricted		5,000		$ 2,500
Investment—Permanently Restricted Endowment	4,843,997		4,412,006	
Net Assets—Permanently Restricted for Endowment		4,895,757		4,439,890
	$4,900,757	$4,900,757	$4,442,390	$4,442,390

*Totals may reflect rounding differences.

APPENDIX TO PART I

To provide you with a fuller picture of the accounting system, the Appendix to the chapter has the full set of journal entries that would have been used to record the transactions.

NOTES FOR CHAPTER 14

1. *Audits of Providers of Health Care Services* replaced the *Hospital Audit Guide* (1972).

2. *Statement of Financial Reporting Standards No. 93*, "Recognition of Depreciation by Not-for-Profit Organizations," (Norwalk, CT: FASB, August 1987). The effective date of the standard was deferred by *Statement of Financial Reporting Standards No. 99*, "Deferral of Effective Date of Recognition of Depreciation by Not-for-Profit Organizations," (Norwalk, CT: FASB, August 1988).

3. This pronouncement was issued in June 1993 to take effect for fiscal years beginning after December 15, 1994 for not-for-profit organizations with total assets greater than or equal to $5 million and annual expenses greater than or equal to $1 million. Not-for-profits with less than $5 million and annual expenses less than $1 million are subject to this pronouncement for fiscal years beginning after December 15, 1995. At the same time that the FASB issued *Statement No. 117*, it also issued *Statement of Financial Reporting Standards (SFAS) No. 116*, "Accounting for Contributions Received and Contributions Made," (Norwalk, CT: FASB, June 1993).

4. *SFAS No. 116*, p. 67.

5. *Ibid.*, p. 69

6. *Ibid.*

7. *Ibid.*, p. 68.

8. *Ibid.*, p. 4.

APPENDIX—NPO—JOURNAL ENTRIES—19X2

	Dr	Cr
Entry #1		
Net Assets—Temporarily Restricted		
for Reporting Purposes	1,834,624	
Pledges Receivable	2,134,624	
Allowance for Uncollectible Pledges		
—Temporarily Restricted		
for Reporting Purposes	300,000	
Pledges Receivable—Temporarily		
Restricted for Reporting Purposes		2,134,624
Allowance for Uncollectible Pledges.		300,000
Revenues from Contributions		1,834,624

To reclassify Pledges Receivable and the associated Allowance amounts from accounts set up for reporting purposes to normal accounts for internal processing and control.

Entry #2

Pledges Receivable	9,911,407	
Pledges Receivable—Temporarily Restricted	281,497	
Revenue from Contributions		9,911,407
Net Assets—Temporarily Restricted from Contributions for Operating Purposes		281,497

To record pledges of unconditional and unrestricted contributions for 19X2 in the amount of $9,911,407 and temporarily restricted pledges due to timing restrictions for periods beyond June 30, 19X2 in the amount of $281,497.

Entry #3

Accounts Receivable	2,894,231	
Revenue from Fees for Services		2,894,231

Fees charged for services rendered by Program B during 19X2.

Entry #4

Cash—Unrestricted	3,000,000	
Accounts Receivable		2,889,643
Prepaid Services		110,357

Cash collected on Accounts Receivable and prepaid services

Accounts Receivable	2,889,643
Prepaid Services	110,357
	3,000,000

Entry #5

Cash—Unrestricted	9,282,706	
Cash—Restricted	316,870	
Pledges Receivable		9,282,706
Pledges Receivable—Temporarily Restricted for Operating Purposes		316,870

Cash collected on unconditional and unrestricted pledges and on temporarily restricted pledges.

Unrestricted	9,282,706		
Temporarily Restricted	316,870		
	9,599,576		

Entry #6

Cash—Unrestricted		300,032	
Investment Income Receivable			20,947
Investment Income			279,086

Cash collected on unconditional and unrestricted
investment income on endowment investments due from
the prior year and earned during the current year.

Receivable, July 1, 19X1	20,947
Earned during 19X2	279,086
	300,032

Entry #7

Inventories of Supplies—Program B		171,548	
Inventories of Supplies—Program C		90,086	
Inventories of Supplies—Management & General		29,339	
Inventories of Supplies—Fund-Raising		16,700	
Accounts Payable			307,673

Purchases of supplies for the following
functions:

Program B	171,548
Program C	90,086
Management & General	29,339
Fund-Raising	16,700
	307,673

Entry #8

Prepaid Expense—Program A		18,378	
Cash—Unrestricted			18,378

Advance payments of expenses for
Program A

Entry #9

Government Grants Receivable—Temporarily Restricted for Operating Purposes		524,905	
Net Assets from Temporarily Restricted from Grants for Operating Purposes			524,905

Government grants awarded during 19X2 that are
temporarily restricted for specific operating
purposes of Program A.

Entry #10

Cash—temporarily Restricted—Grants	499,956	
Government Grants Receivable—Temporarily		
Restricted for Operating Purposes		499,956

Cash received under temporarily restricted
government grants.

Entry #11

Pledges Receivable—Temporarily		
Restricted for Capital Purposes	2,104,000	
Net Assets Temporarily Restricted—		
for Capital Purposes		2,104,000

Unconditional but temporarily restricted pledges
to contribute to a major capital campaign
undertaken by NPO.

Entry #12

Cash—Temporarily		
Restricted-Capital Contributions	2,000,000	
Pledges Receivable—Temporarily		
Restricted for Capital Purposes		2,000,000

Cash received from pledged contributions to the
major capital campaign.

Entry #13

Pledges Receivable—Permanently Restricted		
for Endowment	316,423	
Net Assets—Permanently Restricted for		
Endowment		316,423

Unconditional pledged contributions to the
permanently restricted endowment

Entry #14

Cash—Permanently Restricted for Endowment	288,795	
Pledges Receivable—Permanently Restricted		
for Endowment		288,795

Cash received from pledged contributions to the
permanently restricted endowment.

Entry #15

Investment—Permanently		
Restricted Endowment	288,795	
Cash—Permanently Restricted Endowment		288,795

Investment of cash received from the pledged
contributions to the permanently restricted
endowment.

Entry #16

Cash—Permanently Restricted Endowment	18,196	
Investment Income Receivable—		
Permanently Restricted for Endowment		1,168
Net Assets Permanently Restricted for		
Endowment		17,028

Cash received from pledged restricted investment
income on current contribution to the permanently
restricted endowment.

Entry #17

Investment—Permanently		
Restricted Endowment	18,196	
Cash—Permanently Restricted Endowment		18,196

Investment of cash received on investment income
from current contributions to the permanently
restricted endowment.

Entry #18

Investment Income Receivable—		
Permanently Restricted Endowment	1,916	
Net Assets Permanently Restricted for		
Endowment		1,916

Records investment on interest earned and dividends
declared but not paid to be treated as permanently
restricted on current contributions received on pledges
to endowment by formal action of the Board of Trustees.

Entry #19

Cash Temporarily Restricted for Debt Service	547,239	
Cash—Temporarily Restricted—		
Contributions for Capital Purposes		547,239

Transfer of cash temporarily restricted for the
acquisition of fixed assets and debt service on fixed
assets to cash temporarily restricted for debt service
in accordance with bond indenture requirements.

Entry #20

Cash—Unrestricted	50,000	
Accumulated Depreciation—		
Property, Plant and Equipment	232,544	
Property, Plant and Equipment		257,450
Gain on Sales of Fixed Assets		25,094

To record disposal of fixed assets, cash received
on disposal and gain realized from disposal.
The following programs and activities were affected:

	Fixed Assets	Accumulated Depreciation
Program A	$ 26,517	$ 23,952
Program B	152,925	138,131
Program C	68,739	62,089
Management & General	9,268	8,372
	$257,450	$232,544

Entry #21

Expenses—Program A	488,287	
Expenses—Program B	1,549,696	
Expenses—Program C	680,303	
Expenses—Management & General	98,090	
Expenses—Fund-Raising	98,989	
Accounts Payable		2,915,365

Expenses for other than personnel service
for 19X2 for program activities and for
supporting activities.

Entry #22

Expenses—Program A	1,095,186	
Expenses—Program B	3,877,349	
Expenses—Program C	1,766,935	
Expenses—Management & General	335,223	
Expenses—Fund-Raising	189,868	
Accounts Payable		7,264,561

Salaries and Wages Expenses for 19X2 for
program activities and for supporting
activities.

Entry #23

Expenses—Program A	210,775	
Expenses—Program B	746,219	
Expenses—Program C	340,057	
Expenses—Management & General	64,516	
Expenses—Fund-Raising	36,541	
Accounts Payable		1,398,108

Employees' fringe benefits expenses for
19X2 for program activities and for
supporting activities.

Entry #24

Expenses—Program A	83,909	
Expenses—Program B	297,067	
Expenses—Program C	135,375	
Expenses—Management & General	25,683	
Expenses—Fund-Raising	14,547	

Accounts Payable		556,581

Employers' payroll tax expenses for 19X2 for
program activities and for supporting activities.

Entry #25

Net Assets Temporarily Restricted from Grants		
for Operating Purposes	499,956	
Cash—Unrestricted	499,956	
Cash—Restricted from Grants		499,956
Net Assets Released from Temporary Restrictions		
from Grants for Operating Purposes		499,956

To record the effect on the unrestricted cash
equivalents account as a result of transfers of
temporary cash when restrictions have been satisfied.

Entry #26

Property, Plant and Equipment	614,524	
Accounts Payable		614,524

To record acquisition of fixed assets for use in the
    following activities:

Program A	$ 63,296
Program B	365,027
Program C	164,078
Management & General	22,123
	$614,524

Entry #27

Cash—Unrestricted	614,524	
Net Assets—Temporarily Restricted		
for Capital Purposes	614,524	
Net Assets Released from Temporary		
Restrictions for Capital Purposes		614,524
Cash—Restricted for Capital Purposes		614,524

To record cash and net assets restricted for capital
purposes released by the acquisition of plant assets.

Entry #28

Net Assets—Temporarily Restricted		
for Capital Purposes	547,239	
Interest Expense on		
Long-term Debt	242,741	
Long-term Debt—		
Current Installment	304,498	
Cash—Temporarily Restricted for Debt Service		547,239
Net Assets Released from Temporary		
Restrictions for Capital Purposes		547,239

Paid the prior year's current installment of 6/30/19X1 and interest for 19X2 on long-term debt, a mortgage note payable.

Entry #29

Investments—Temporarily Restricted for Capital Purposes	838,237	
Cash—Temporarily Restricted— Contributions for Capital Purposes		838,237

To transfer excess cash resources for investments temporarily restricted for capital acquisition and for debt service on capital acquisitions.

Entry #30

Cash—Unrestricted	24,276	
Investment Income—Unrestricted		24,276

To record short-term interest expense on temporary investment of unrestricted excess cash in cash equivalents. Cash equivalents are very low-risk and very short-term, 90 days or less to maturity on debt instruments.

Entry #31

Interest Expense on Short-Term Debt	13,607	
Cash—Unrestricted		13,607

Interest expense on short-term borrowing through a bank line of credit.

Entry #32

Net Assets Temporarily Restricted for Operating Purposes	316,870	
Cash—Unrestricted	316,870	
Cash—Restricted from Pledges		316,870
Net Assets Released from Temporary Restrictions for Operating Purposes		316,870

To record the effect on the unrestricted cash equivalents account as a result of the transfer of temporarily restricted cash when timing restrictions have been satisfied.

Entry #33

Accounts Payable	12,942,448	
Cash—Unrestricted		12,942,448

Paid accounts payable for 19X2.

Entry #34

Cash-Temporarily Restricted Contributions

—for Capital Purposes	15,886	
Net Assets—Temporarily Restricted		
for Capital Purposes		15,886

Interest income on cash temporarily restricted
for operating and for capital purposes.

Entry #35

Expenses-Program A	42,268	
Expenses-Program B	184,170	
Expenses-Program C	95,397	
Expenses-Management & General	19,331	
Fund-Raising	14,475	
Inventories of Supplies—Program A		42,268
Inventories of Supplies—Program B		184,170
Inventories of Supplies—Program C		95,397
Inventories of Supplies—Management & General		19,331
Inventories of Supplies—Fund-Raising		14,475

Inventory of supplies used during 19X2.

Entry #36

Expenses-Program A	9,189	
Expenses-Program B	33,926	
Expenses-Program C	16,063	
Expenses-Management & General	12,835	
Prepaid Expenses—Program A		9,189
Prepaid Expenses—Program B		33,926
Prepaid Expenses—Program C		16,063
Prepaid Expenses—Management & General		12,835

Services arising from prepaid expenses used
during 19X2.

Entry #37

Cash Equivalents—Unrestricted	1,113,931	
Cash—Unrestricted		1,113,931

To record net effect on the unrestricted cash
equivalents account as a result of continuous
investment of excess cash in cash equivalents.

Entry #38

Allowance for Uncollectible Accounts	30,000	
Accounts Receivable		30,000

Specific accounts receivable identified as
uncollectible that were removed as active
accounts from accounts receivable.

Entry #39

Provision for Uncollectibles Accounts Receivable	35,000	

Allowance for Uncollectible Accounts		35,000

Estimated forecasted amount of uncollectible
accounts receivable expected from current
receivables owed.

Entry #40

Allowance for Uncollectible Pledges	315,000	
Pledges Receivable		315,000

Specific pledges receivable identified as
uncollectible were removed as active pledges
from pledges receivable.

Entry #41

Unrestricted Contributions	350,000	
Allowance for Uncollectible Pledges		350,000

Estimated forecasted amount of uncollectible
pledges receivable expected from current receivables
owed. The Provision for Uncollectible Pledges is
treated either as an expense or as a reduction of the
related revenue from contributions.

Entry #42

Depreciation Expense	937,589	
Accumulated Depreciation—		
Property, Plant and Equipment		937,589

Depreciation expense for the following activities:

Program A	96,572
Program B	556,928
Program C	250,336
Management & General	33,753
	937,589

Entry #43

Allowance for Uncollectible Pledges—Temporarily		
Restricted for Operating Purposes	25,000	
Allowance for Uncollectible Pledges—		
Temporarily Restricted for Capital Purposes	20,000	
Allowance for Uncollectible Pledges—		
Permanently Restricted for Endowment	2,000	
Pledges Receivable—Temporarily Restricted		
for Operating Activities		25,000
Pledges Receivable—Temporarily Restricted		
for Capital Purposes		20,000
Pledges Receivable—Permanently Restricted		
Endowment		2,000

Specific pledges receivable identified as uncollectible

were removed as active pledges from pledges receivable.

Entry #44

Net Assets—Temporarily Restricted—		
Contributions for Operating Purposes	25,000	
Net Assets—Temporarily Restricted		
for Capital Purposes	20,000	
Net Assets—Permanently Restricted		
for Endowment	4,500	
Allowance for Uncollectible Pledges—		
Temporarily Restricted for Operating		
Purposes		25,000
Allowance for Uncollectible Pledges—		
Temporarily Restricted for Capital Purposes		20,000
Allowance for Uncollectible Pledges—		
Permanently Restricted for Endowment		4,500

Estimated forecasted amount of uncollectible pledges receivable expected from current receivables owed.

Entry #45

Prepaid services	97,264	
Revenues from fees for services		97,264

To recognize advance payments as revenues because prepaid services have been rendered.

Entry #46

Long-term Debt—Noncurrent	333,062	
Long-term Debt—Current Installment		333,062

To reclassify the current installment of long-term.

Entry #47

Investment Income Receivable	32,918	
Investment Income—Unrestricted		32,918

To record investment income from interest income earned and dividends declared but not yet paid.

Entry #48

Unrestricted Contributions for Operating Purposes	2,113,325	
Pledges Receivable—Temporarily Restricted for		
Reporting Purposes	2,448,325	
Allowance for Uncollectible Pledges	335,000	
Pledges Receivable—Unrestricted		2,448,325
Allowance for Uncollectible Pledges for		
Reporting Purposes		335,000
Net Assets-Temporarily Restricted for		

Reporting Purposes		2,113,325
Entry #49		
Long-Term Investments	125,000	
Net Assets—Permanently Restricted		125,000
	76,804,346	76,804,346

Chapter 15

A Case Study in Financial Statement Analysis and the New Reporting Standards of the FASB—Part II

THE ANNUAL FINANCIAL STATEMENTS AND THE NEW FASB REPORTING STANDARDS

The next stage in preparing a foundation for financial statement analysis is to understand financial statements prepared according to the new standards for not-for-profit entities set out in *SFAS No. 117*.

We have taken a detailed journey through the accounting records of our *illustrative* NPO. That journey provided us with a look at a series of transactions and entries that summarized the activities for the fiscal year. These are the *illustrative* transactions that will be the foundation for our *illustrative* financial statements.

GUIDING PRINCIPLE FROM *SFAS No. 117*

One of the important guiding principles from *SFAS No. 117* is that

This Statement discusses how to report assets, liabilities, net assets, revenues, expenses, gains, and losses in financial statements; however, it does not specify when to recognize or how to measure those elements. The degree of aggregation and order of presentation of items of assets and liabilities in statements of financial position or items of revenues and expenses in statements of activities of not-for-profit organizations, although not specified by this Statement, generally should be similar to those required or permitted for business enterprises.[1]

BASIC FINANCIAL STATEMENTS

The basic financial statements to be presented by a not-for-profit entity according to *SFAS No. 117* are:

1. The Statement of Financial Position (also known as a Balance Sheet)

2. A Statement of Activities

3. Statement of Cash Flows

Voluntary Health and Welfare Organizations have traditionally presented a fourth basic statement:

4. The Statement of Functional Expenses

SFAS No. 117 does not require such a statement, but provides the alternative of presenting functional expense information in a note disclosure.

SFAS No. 117 also provides for certain alternative statements. For example, in place of the Statement of Activities, the NPO could present:

2.a. A Statement of Unrestricted Revenues, Expenses, and Other Changes in Unrestricted Net Assets, and

2.b. A Statement of Changes in Net Assets.

SFAS No. 117 illustrates a Statement of Cash Flows in terms of the two formats used in its pronouncement on cash flows, *SFAS No. 95.*[2] Therefore the Statement of Cash Flows can be presented using either the

3.a. direct method of presenting cash flows, or

3.b. indirect method of presenting cash flows.

FUND ACCOUNTING

SFAS No. 117 does not require the use of fund accounting for external financial reporting. The authors of *SFAS No. 117* state that the financial statements are intended to be those of the NPO entity as a whole and not of the individual funds of the entity. With respect to the Statement of Financial Position, for example, *SFAS No. 117* provides that

A statement of financial position shall focus on the organization as a whole and shall report the amounts of its total assets, liabilities and net assets.[3]

With respect to a Statement of Activities, *SFAS No. 117* states that

A statement of activities provided by a not-for-profit organization shall focus on the organization as a whole and shall report the amount of the change in net assets for the period. It shall use descriptive terms such as *change in net assets* or *change in equity*.[4]

In discussing the Statement of Activities, *SFAS No. 117* has a specific note on fund accounting that states

This Statement does not use the terms *fund balance* or *changes in fund balance* because in current practice those terms are commonly used to refer to individual groups of assets and related liabilities rather than to the entity's net assets or changes in net assets taken as a whole. Reporting by fund groups is not a necessary part of external financial reporting; however this statement does not preclude providing disaggregated information by fund groups.[5]

Because of the FASB's requirements that the financial statements focus on the entity as a whole, we do not illustrate the traditional fund accounting format in the Statement of Financial Position as such. However, we provide an approximation to the fund accounting presentation by illustrating an alternative *columnar format* for the Statement of Financial Position. The columnar format emphasizes the *unrestricted*, *temporarily restricted* and *permanently restricted* distinctions required by *SFAS No. 117*. It does not focus on funds. The use of a "total column" is required because the focus must be ultimately on the entity as a whole.

We do not directly address the issue of the internal use of fund accounting for planning and control. Clearly, where fund accounting is considered essential for internal planning and control, it should be used. External financial reporting standards such as those found in *SFAS No. 117* are not intended to provide guidance to managers for internal planning and control.

CURRENT/NONCURRENT CLASSIFICATION

SFAS No. 117 also does not require the incorporation of the current/noncurrent distinction in classifying the assets and liabilities. We have incorporated that distinction into the *illustrative* Statement of Financial Position to make it more useful for financial statement analysis.

COMPARATIVE FORMAT

Comparative financial information is quite useful in understanding and analyzing financial statements. *SFAS No. 117* illustrates a comparative format for the Statement of Financial Position and indicates that

> Comparative statements of financial position are provided to facilitate understanding of the statement of cash flows.[6]

The other financial statements are not illustrated using a comparative format. There is no explicit discussion in the body of the pronouncement itself concerning the comparative format. Nevertheless, since *SFAS No. 117* states that financial reporting by business entities is the best guide, the comparative format should be used where possible.

ILLUSTRATIVE FINANCIAL STATEMENTS

The following financial statements will be presented and discussed:

1.a. Statement of Financial Position

2.a. Statement of Unrestricted Revenues, Expenses, and Other Changes in Unrestricted Net Assets, and the complementary

2.b. Statement of Changes in Net Assets

2.c. Statement of Activities (in place of (2a) and (2b) above)

3.a. Statement of Cash Flows (Direct Method)

Alternative formats to be presented and discussed:

1.b. Statement of Financial Position (Columnar Format)

2.d. Statement of Changes in Net Assets (Columnar Format)

2.e. Statement of Activities (Columnar Format)

3.b. Statement of Cash Flows (Indirect Method)

NOTES TO FINANCIAL STATEMENTS

We will also discuss what might be expected to appear in the critical Notes to the Financial Statements. The Notes to the Financial Statements are considered an essential and integral part of the basic financial statements. The basic financial statements and the notes are the basic disclosure instruments required of an NPO to meet the reporting standards of the FASB as set out in *SFAS No. 117.*

THE STATEMENT OF FINANCIAL POSITION

The first of the basic financial statements that will be reviewed is an *illustrative* Statement of Financial Position. Exhibit 1 presents an *illustrative* Statement of Financial Position for the NPO following the reporting standards in *SFAS No. 117* and using the *illustrative* transactions of the previous chapter.

EXHIBIT 1

NPO Organization
Statement of Financial Position
June 30, 19X2 and 19X1*

	19X2	19X1
Assets:		
Unrestricted assets:		
Current assets:		
Cash & cash equivalents	$1,347,353	$ 233,422
Accounts receivable, net (Note B)	415,467	445,879
Investment income receivable	32,918	20,947
Inventories (Note C)	360,648	408,616
Prepaid expenses (Note D)	160,822	214,457
Total unrestricted current assets	2,317,207	1,323,321
Property, plant, and equipment (Note E)	3,053,750	3,401,721

Total unrestricted assets	$ 5,370,957	$ 4,725,042
Restricted assets:		
Temporarily restricted assets:		
Cash & cash equivalents	$ 15,886	
Pledges receivable (Notes F, G)	2,551,822	$ 2,249,494
Grants receivable	79,972	55,022
Short-term investments (Note I)	838,237	
Permanently restricted assets:		
Investment income receivable	1,916	1,168
Pledges receivable (Note H)	49,844	26,715
Long-term investments (Note I)	4,843,997	4,412,006
Total restricted assets	$ 8,381,673	$ 6,744,406
Total assets	$13,752,630	$11,469,448
Liabilities and net assets:		
Liabilities:		
Accounts payable & accrued expenses	$ 412,460	$ 298,095
Long-term debt—current installment	333,062	304,498
Prepaid services	110,357	97,264
Total current liabilities	855,879	699,857
Long-term debt (Note J)	2,196,864	2,529,926
Total liabilities	$ 3,052,743	$ 3,229,783
Net assets:		
Unrestricted	$ 2,318,214	$ 1,495,258
Temporarily restricted (Note K)	3,485,916	2,304,517
Permanently restricted	4,895,757	4,439,890
Total net assets	10,699,887	8,239,665
Total liabilities and net assets	$13,752,630	$11,469,448

*The accompanying notes are an integral part of this statement.

On the face of the Statement of Financial Position there is an important reminder that the financial statements must include a set of Notes to the

Financial Statements that are an integral part of the statements. The other financial statements will contain the same reminder.

SFAS No. 117 introduced a new and important distinction into financial reporting by NPOs: that between *temporarily restricted* and *permanently restricted* assets. The *illustrative* Statement of Financial Position shown in Exhibit 1 incorporates this distinction throughout.

The *illustrative* Statement of Financial Position that is presented in this chapter incorporates the distinction between *temporarily and permanently restricted* more completely than the *illustrative* Statement of Financial Position in *SFAS No. 117*. Both the asset and equities sides of the *illustrative* Statement of Financial Position presented in this chapter incorporate the *temporarily* versus *permanently restricted* distinction. *SFAS No. 117* incorporates the distinction primarily in the equities section of the Statement of Financial Position. The reason we incorporate the distinction more completely is to show both managers of NPOs and users of financial statements of NPOs how to meet the requirements of *SFAS No. 117* and at the same time serve the needs of those wishing to understand and analyze the financial statements of the NPO in a more complete fashion.

The trial balances of the previous chapter are used by the NPOs' accountants as the link between the accounting records and the financial statements. As such, those trial balances need to be transformed into what are called Working Trial Balances to provide a sufficient documentary bridge between the accounting records and the financial statements.

The *illustrative* transactions were sufficiently simplified for a typical NPO so that the trial balance of the prior chapter can be used without overly complex calculations to tie directly into the figures shown in the financial statements. The Notes to the Financial Statements also should provide sufficient additional information to help understand how the financial statements were compiled from the accounting records.

THE STATEMENT OF FINANCIAL POSITION AND NOTES TO FINANCIAL STATEMENTS

CASH AND CASH EQUIVALENTS

The first of the unrestricted assets is cash and cash equivalents, which is simply the sum of two accounts that appear in the trial balance in Exhibit 7 of Chapter 14, Unrestricted Cash at $200,000 and Unrestricted Cash Equivalents at $1,147,353 for the amount that appears in the Statement of Financial Condition at $1,347,353. The trial balance is an internal document so that this information would not be available to external users of the financial statements. Generally, the breakdown between cash and cash equivalents would not be provided in the Notes to the Financial Statements. At most, the Notes would provide a description of "cash equivalents" that would appear in the first of the Notes. The first note to the financial statement is the note on the "Summary of Significant Accounting Policies." This note is shown in Exhibit 2.

EXHIBIT 2 *Notes to Financial Statements*

NOTE A—SUMMARY OF SIGNIFICANT ACCOUNTING POLICIES

Fund Accounting

Fund accounting is used for internal planning and control purposes. Unrestricted assets are accounted for internally through the use of an Operating Fund. Temporarily restricted assets to be used for day-to-day operating activities are accounted for through the Operating Fund.

Cash Equivalents

Cash equivalents are temporary investments of cash in excess of operating needs in short-term (90 days or less to maturity), very low-risk debt instruments issued by highly credit-worthy entities

Receivables

Accounts Receivable and Pledges Receivable are shown net of an allowance for uncollectible pledges that reflect the annual provision for bad debts.

Grants Receivable from Governments are not reduced for an estimated allowance for uncollectibles because the risk is judged to be minimal and such an estimate not measurable.

Pledges

Receipts of unconditional promises to contribute money in future periods are reported as restricted support, unless the donor or the circumstances attending the pledge explicitly intend to support current period activities.

Restricted Gifts

Receipts of gifts of cash or other assets are reported as restricted support if the donor limits the use of the assets.

Donor limits that may be satisfied through use of the assets for the limited purpose specified or through the passage of time are reported in the Statement of Activities or (the Statement of Changes in Net Assets if that is presented as one of the basic financial statements) as temporarily restricted net assets released from restrictions.

Inventories of Supplies

Inventories of supplies are valued at cost.

Property, Plant and Equipment

Property, Plant and Equipment are accounted for internally through the Operating Fund. Resources restricted for plant acquisition are accounted for internally through the use of a Plant Fund.

Depreciation is calculated using the straight-line method and estimated useful lives.

Endowment

Gifts that are contributed as principal or corpus as an endowment trust arrangement to be invested and maintained in perpetuity and only income is to be used for general or limited purposes are accounted for internally through the use of Endowment Funds.

Investments

Investments are carried at market or appraised value, and realized and unrealized gains and losses are reflected in the statement of activities.

Temporarily Restricted Net Assets

The temporarily restricted net assets account for amounts that have been deferred for recognition to future periods.

ACCOUNTS RECEIVABLE

The second unrestricted asset is Accounts Receivable. Generally, there is a required disclosure of the amount of the Allowance for Uncollectible

Accounts at the end of each fiscal year presented either directly in the Statement of Financial Position or in the Notes.

We have provided an *illustrative* Note B which is shown in Exhibit 3. This *illustrative* note provides information not only on the Allowance for Uncollectible Accounts, but also the amount of accounts receivable specifically identified as uncollectible. This information is usually not available in the Notes to the Financial Statements *nor is it a required disclosure* even though it could be a useful disclosure to external users of financial statements.

There is a reference to Note B that is part of the Accounts Receivable disclosure shown directly in the Statement of Financial Condition.

EXHIBIT 3 Note B—Accounts Receivable**

Accounts receivable are shown net of an allowance for uncollectible accounts that reflect the annual provision for bad debts.

		19X2	19X1
Accounts receivable, before reduction for identified uncollectibles, June 30		$490,467	$515,879
Less: Accounts receivable determined to be uncollectible		30,000	30,000
Accounts receivable, June 30, 19X2		460,467	485,879
Allowance for uncollectible accounts, July 1, 19X1	$40,000		40,000
Less: Accounts receivable determined to be uncollectible	(30,000)		
Subtotal	10,000		
Add: Estimated annual provision for bad debts	35,000		
Allowance for uncollectible accounts, June 30, 19X2		45,000	
Accounts receivable, net, June 30		$415,467	$445,879

**This note is not a required disclosure, as long as information is provided directly in the Statement of Financial Position on the amount of the Allowance for Uncollectibles at the end of each fiscal year presented. The note is useful to external users of financial statements.

INVESTMENT INCOME RECEIVABLE

Investment income arising from long-term endowment investment is unrestricted and available for operating purposes. Under the accrual basis of accounting such interest income that has been earned but not paid and dividend declared but also not paid should be accrued and shown as a receivable.

INVENTORY OF SUPPLIES AND PREPAID EXPENSES

The next two items, inventories of supplies and prepaid expenses, have separate disclosures in the Notes to the Financial Statements. Note C for inventory of supplies and Note D for prepaid expenses are shown in Exhibits 4 and 5, respectively. Notes C and D are purely illustrative and are not required disclosures.

EXHIBIT 4 NOTE C—INVENTORIES[**]

Inventories are composed of supplies used in the various program and in the functional support activities.

	19X2	19X1
Program A	$114,416	$156,684
Program B	125,111	137,733
Program C	75,082	80,393
Management & General	35,414	25,406
Fund-Raising	10,625	8,400
Total	$360,648	$408,616

[**]This note is not a required disclosure but is useful to external users of financial statements. Information on inventories of supplies by program would be maintained only if required for planning and control by managers of those programs.

EXHIBIT 5 Note D—Prepaid Expenses[**]

Prepaid expenses cover services paid for and expected to be received in future periods after June 1, 19X2.

	19X2	19X1
Program A	$ 35,502	$ 26,313
Program B	69,198	103,124
Program C	32,154	48,217
Management & General	23,968	36,803
Total Prepaid Expenses	$160,822	$214,457

**This note is not a required disclosure but is useful to external users of financial statements. Information on prepaid expenses by program would be maintained only if required for planning and control by managers of those programs.

The disclosures in Notes C and D provide information on inventory of supplies and prepaid expenses by program and functional activity. Detailed inventory records by program activity would only be maintained where it was necessary for management to maintain such records for planning and control. Generally, the same limitation would apply to disclosing prepaid expenses by program where this is feasible. But it is not a required disclosure and such information would be prepared for internal use only if the managers of the programs found it useful for planning and control purposes.

PROPERTY, PLANT AND EQUIPMENT

In Exhibit 6, there is Note E, the *illustrative* note disclosure for Property, Plant and Equipment. *SFAS No. 117* does not provide an illustrative note disclosure for Property, Plant and Equipment. Such a note disclosure is standard in external reporting for business entities. While the note is a standard disclosure, the form of the note is not standard and varies quite a bit.

The fact that business disclosure requirements would apply is indicated by our earlier discussion of the "Guiding Principle" in *SFAS No. 117* when it states that the principles of external financial reporting for business entities generally apply to not-for-profit organizations.

Disclosure for Property, Plant and Equipment does not require a breakdown by subdivision of an entity such as by program activity. *SFAS No. 117* does take note of the usefulness of information on major programs when it discusses "Information about an Organization's Service Efforts."[7] However, there is no requirement about program information related to the Statement of Financial Position.

While business external financial reporting rules apply in general, there are specialized reporting requirements with respect to Property, Plant and Equipment for certain not-for-profit organizations. *SFAS No. 93*, "Recognition of Depreciation by Not-for-Profit Organizations," does not require that values be estimated and assigned to "inexhaustible collections," owned by museums, art galleries, botanical gardens, other not-for-profit organizations.[8] Nevertheless, even though assets are not actually recorded in the financial accounting records, there are records, kept of these items for planning and control purposes. Even though there are no dollar values assigned to these assets, they should be listed on the Statement of Financial Condition among the assets without any dollar value. In addition, there should be a reference next to the asset that refers to a note in the Notes to the Financial Statements that describes the collection.

EXHIBIT 6 Note E—Property, Plant and Equipment**

Property, plant and equipment is utilized in each program and functional support activity.

	A	B	C	M & G	19X2
PPE, 7/1/X1	$612,976	$3,535,029	$1,588,978	$214,244	$5,951,227
Acquisitions	63,296	365,027	164,078	22,123	614,524
	676,272	3,900,056	1,753,055	236,367	6,565,751
Disposals	(26,517)	(152,925)	(68,739)	(9,268)	(257,450)
PPE, 6/30/X2	$649,755	$3,747,131	$1,684,316	$227,099	$6,308,301
AD, 7/1/19X1	$262,599	$1,514,406	$ 680,718	$ 91,782	$2,549,506
Disposals	(23,952)	(138,131)	(62,089)	(8,372)	(232,544)
	238,647	1,376,275	618,629	83,411	2,316,961
Depreciation	96,572	556,928	250,336	33,753	937,589
AD, 6/30/X2	335,219	1,933,203	868,965	117,164	3,254,551
FA, net	$314,536	$1,813,928	$ 815,351	$109,935	$3,053,750

**SFAS No. 117 requires disclosures similar to those for business entities. Business entities generally have a required disclosure for Property, Plant and Equipment. The form of this disclosure varies. Information by subdivisions such as program activities for a not-for-profit entity would not be required. Note that there are special limited reporting requirements for certain not-for-profit entities for certain special types of plant assets such as "inexhaustible collections" of museums and art galleries as well as for certain "individual works of art" and "historical treasures."

Totals may reflect rounding differences.

TEMPORARILY RESTRICTED CASH AND CASH EQUIVALENTS

We turn from the unrestricted assets to the restricted assets. First, we look at the *temporarily restricted* assets. The first of these assets involve cash and cash equivalents. Temporarily restricted cash and cash equivalents are held for acquisition of capital assets. They are not available for day-to-day operating activities.

TEMPORARILY RESTRICTED PLEDGES RECEIVABLE

The next of the temporarily restricted assets is Pledges Receivable. There are three types of Pledges Receivable reported as *temporarily restricted*.

Exhibit 7 presents Note F. Note F deals with two types of *temporarily restricted* Pledges Receivable. As discussed for Note B with respect to Accounts Receivable, Note F is not a required note disclosure as long as the amount of the Allowance for Uncollectible Pledges at the end of each *fiscal year* presented is disclosed either in the Notes to the Financial Statements or directly on the Statement of Financial Position.

EXHIBIT 7 *Note F—Temporarily Restricted Pledges Receivable***

A. Temporarily Restricted Pledges for Operating Purposes

There are two types of restricted pledges receivable shown below. First are those pledges receivable that are subject to time restrictions and the result of contributions for operating purposes. Second are those pledges receivable that are restricted by purpose and the result of contributions to fund capital asset acquisitions. Provisions for uncollectible pledges are shown for both categories of pledges receivable. Presented first are those pledges to fund operating activities after June 30, 19X2.

		19X2	19X1
Pledges receivable, June 30		$281,497	$351,870
Less: Pledges receivable determined to be uncollectible		25,000	35,000
Account receivable, June 30		256,497	316,870
Allowance for uncollectible pledges, July 1, 19X1	$30,000		30,000
Less: Pledges receivable determined to be uncollectible	(25,000)		
Subtotal	5,000		
Add: Estimated annual provision for uncollectibles	25,000		
Allowance for uncollectible pledges, June 30		30,000	
Pledges receivable, net, June 30		$226,497	$286,870

B. Temporarily Restricted Pledges for Capital Purposes

The following temporarily restricted pledges receivable are for financing capital asset acquisitions.

		19X2	19X1
Pledges receivable, June 30		$242,000	$148,000
Less: Pledges receivable determined to be uncollectible		20,000	10,000
Account receivable, June 30		222,000	138,000
Allowance for uncollectible pledges, July 1, 19X1	$10,000		10,000
Less: Pledges receivable determined to be uncollectible	(20,000)		
Subtotal	(10,000)		
Add: Estimated annual provision for uncollectibles	20,000		
Allowance for uncollectible pledges, June 30, 19X2		10,000	
Pledges receivable, net, June 30		$212,000	$128,000
Pledges Receivable for Operating and for Capital Purposes, net June 30		$438,497	$414,870

**This note is not a required disclosure, as long as information is provided directly in the Statement of Financial Position on the amount of the Allowance for Uncollectibles at the end of each fiscal year presented. The note is useful to external users of financial statements.

PLEDGES RECEIVABLE—TEMPORARILY RESTRICTED FOR REPORTING PURPOSES

As discussed earlier, unconditional and unrestricted promises to make future gifts are to be treated as Temporarily Restricted Pledges Receivable for external financial reporting purposes. Note G is presented in Exhibit 8 to provide an *illustrated* disclosure for Pledges Receivable—Temporarily Restricted for Reporting Purposes.

As is the case for other receivables, Note G is not a required disclosure as long as the amount of the Allowance for Uncollectible Pledges at the end of each fiscal year presented is disclosed directly on the face of the Statement of Financial Condition.

EXHIBIT 8 Note G—Pledges Receivable Temporarily Restricted for Reporting Purposes[**]

Unconditional and Unrestricted Pledges Receivable—Reported as Temporarily Restricted

As specified in Note A, pledges of unconditional and unrestricted contributions are promises to make a future gift and are to be treated as temporarily restricted until cash is received.

		19X2	19X1
Pledges receivable, June 30		$2,763,325	$2,434,624
Less: Pledges receivable determined to be uncollectible		315,000	300,000
Pledges receivable, June 30		2,448,325	2,134,624
Allowance for uncollectible pledges, July 1, 19X1	$300,000		300,000
Less: Pledges receivable determined to be uncollectible	(315,000)		
Subtotal	(15,000)		
Add: Estimated annual provision for uncollectibles	350,000		
Allowance for uncollectible pledges, June 30		335,000	
Pledges receivable, net, June 30		$2,113,325	$1,834,624

[**]This note is not a required disclosure, as long as information is provided directly in the Statement of Financial Position on the amount of the Allowance for Uncollectibles at the end of each fiscal year presented. The note is useful to external users of financial statements.

PERMANENTLY RESTRICTED PLEDGES RECEIVABLE

We have not as yet dealt with temporarily restricted investments, but these will be discussed later. At this point, we look at permanently restricted Pledges Receivable. These are pledges to contribute to the NPO's endowment, which is a permanently restricted asset. The *illustrative* note disclosure with respect to this asset, Note H, is shown in Exhibit 9. Unlike the other *illustrative* notes with respect to receivables, this is a standard type of disclosure. Note H discloses the amount of the Allowance for Uncollectibles at the end of each of the fiscal years presented in the financial statements. This disclosure does not have to be in a note but can be alternatively on the face of the Statement of Financial Position.

EXHIBIT 9 Note H—Permanently Restricted Pledges Receivable**

	19X2	19X1
Pledges Receivable, June 30	$59,844	$36,715
Less: Allowance for Uncollectible		
Permanently Restricted Pledges Receivable	10,000	10,000
Pledges Receivable, net, June 30	$49,844	$26,715

**This note is not a required disclosure, as long as information is provided directly in the Statement of Financial Position on the amount of the Allowance for Uncollectibles at the end of each fiscal year presented. The note is useful to external users of financial statements.

SHORT-TERM AND LONG-TERM RESTRICTED INVESTMENTS

The last two types of major assets to be discussed are short-term and long-term restricted investments. Short-term restricted investments arise from contributions temporarily restricted for financing the acquisition of property plant and equipment or repaying debt incurred in the acquisition of such assets. Unspent monies to be used for such capital purposes are invested short-term to earn income while waiting to be expended. Long-term investments arise from contributions to the permanent endowment of the NPO.

In Exhibit 10, Note I is set out to provide the required note disclosure for both short-term and long-term investments. The note provides details on the contributions invested, investment income earned, unrealized and realized gains on long-term investments, and the amount allocated to operating activities and for other purposes.

SFAS No. 117 requires the recognition of both unrealized and realized gains on long-terms investments. This means that long-term investments are not subject to the historical cost principle, but their valuation is now subject to market forces to be recognized each period in the financial statements.

EXHIBIT 10—Note I—Investments

Investments are maintained in two investment pools or portfolios. Endowment investments are maintained in pool A and all other short-term investments in a separate portfolio.

With respect to endowment, the Board of Trustees determined that it was necessary to add a portion of investment income to endowment in order to maintain its value after adjustment for the effect of inflation on purchasing power.

	Pool A	Other
Investments, July 1, 19X1	$4,412,006	$0
Contributions for permanent endowment	288,795	
Contributions for capital asset acquisition added to short-term investments		838,237
	$ 288,795	$838,237
Interest and dividends received	318,228	15,886
Realized and unrealized gains	125,000	
Total return on investment	$443,228	$15,886
Amounts appropriated for operations	300,032	
Amount held as cash for expenditure		15,886
	$300,032	$15,886
Net amount added to permanent endowment	431,991	
Net amount added to short-term investments		838,237
Investments, June 30, 19X2	$4,843,997	$838,237

LONG-TERM DEBT

A significant note disclosure is required with respect to long-term debt. That note disclosure is in Exhibit 11 as Note J. The note discloses that the long-term debt is in the form of a 10-year, 9% mortgage note payable. The note also discloses the debt service payment schedule over a 5-year period on a year-by-year basis. After five years this long-term note will be fully paid.

EXHIBIT 11—Note J—Long-Term Debt

Long-term debt is composed of a single 9.0 percent, 10-year mortgage note payable to the bank. At June 30, 19X2, the payment schedule for this note is as follows:

19X3	$ 333,062
19X4	364,306
19X5	398,480
19X6	435,861
19X7	476,747
19X8	521,470
	$2,529,926

TEMPORARILY RESTRICTED NET ASSETS

The temporarily restricted net assets (or equity) balance the temporarily restricted assets. The assets being balanced are (1) grants receivable, (2) cash and cash equivalents, pledges receivable, and short-term investments, all temporarily restricted for capital purposes, (3) and unconditional and unrestricted pledges receivable. Revenues will be recognized when temporarily restricted assets are freed from their restrictions either through the passage of time or by being used for the purposes specified by the restrictions.

Exhibit 12 sets out Note K, which is a required disclosure with respect to temporarily restricted net assets. Exhibit 13 sets out an alternative disclosure as Note K.

EXHIBIT 12—Note K—Temporarily Restricted Net Assets

The temporarily restricted net assets account for amounts that have been deferred for recognition to future periods. The first such deferrals involve temporarily restricted items that are specified for Program A and items that have been deferred for use in periods after June 30, 19X2. In each case the contributions are destined to fund operating activities. The second item involves deferred recognition of contributions to fund the acquisition of capital assets and debt service on long-term debt issued to finance the acquisition of capital assets. The third item represents unconditional and unrestricted pledges that are expected to be collected.

Temporarily restricted net assets are available for the following purposes or periods:

	19X2	19X1	Increase (Decrease)
Program A activities	$ 79,972	$ 55,022	$ 24,950
For capital purposes	1,066,123	128,000	938,123
Timing restrictions for periods after June 30, 19X2	226,497	286,870	(60,373)
Restricted for reporting purposes	2,113,325	1,834,624	278,701
	$3,485,917	$2,304,516	$1,181,401

EXHIBIT 13—Note K—Temporarily Restricted Net Assets [Alternative disclosure]

The temporarily restricted net assets account for amounts that have been deferred for recognition to future periods. The first such deferrals involve temporarily restricted items that are specified for Program A and items that have been deferred for use in periods after June 30, 19X2. In each case the contributions are destined to fund operating activities. The second item involves deferred recognition of contributions to fund the acquisition of capital assets and debt service on long-term debt issued to finance the acquisition of capital assets. The third item represents unconditional and unrestricted pledges that are expected to be collected.

Temporarily restricted net assets are available for the following purposes or periods:

	19X2	19X1	Future Revenues for Operations	Future Additions to Capital Assets
Temporarily restricted :				
Program A grants	$ 79,972	$ 55,022	$ 24,950	
Contributions for Operating Activities	226,497	286,870	(60,373)	
Contributions for Operating Activities	2,113,325	1,834,624	278,701	
Contributions for acquisition of capital assets	1,050,237	128,000		$922,237
Investment Income for acquisition of capital assets	15,886			15,886
	$3,485,916	$2,304,517	$243,277	$938,122

STATEMENT OF FINANCIAL POSITION—COLUMNAR FORMAT

Exhibit 14 presents an alternative and more traditional format for the Statement of Financial Position. The columnar format has been a traditional format for external financial reporting for not-for-profit entities that utilize fund accounting. The Statement of Financial Position in Exhibit 14 does not focus on fund accounting per se. The use of the "total" column, generally *not* used in the fund accounting format, indicates that the reporting focus continues to be the entity as a whole.

The columnar approach does offer the advantage of providing a more complete reporting according to the current/noncurrent disctinction that is useful in financial statement analysis. Recall, however, that *SFAS No. 117* does not require the classification of assets and liabilities into the current and noncurrent categories.

EXHIBIT 14

NPO Organization
Statement of Financial Position
June 30, 19X2*

	Unrestricted	Temporarily Restricted	Permanently Restricted	Total
Assets:				
Cash & cash equivalents	$1,347,353	$ 15,886		$ 1,363,238
Accounts receivable, net (Note B)	415,467			415,467
Investment income receivable	32,918			32,918
Inventories (Note C)	360,648			360,648
Prepaid expenses (Note D)	160,822			160,822
Pledges receivable (Notes F, G)		2,551,822		2,551,822
Grants receivable		79,972		79,972
Short-term investments (Note I)		838,237		838,237
Total current assets	$2,317,207	$3,485,916		$ 5,803,123
Investment income receivable			$ 1,916	$ 1,916
Pledges receivable (Notes H)			49,844	49,844
Property, plant, and equipment (Note E)	3,053,750			3,053,750
Long-term investments (Note I)			4,843,997	4,843,997
Total noncurrent assets	$3,053,750	$ 0	$ 4,895,757	$ 7,949,507
Total assets	$5,370,957	$3,485,916	$ 4,895,757	$13,752,630
Liabilities and net assets:				
Liabilities:				
Accounts payable & accrued expenses	$ 412,460			$ 412,460
Long-term debt—current installment	333,062			333,062
Prepaid services	110,357			110,357
Total current liabilities	$ 855,879			$ 855,879
Long-term debt (Note J)	2,196,864			2,196,864
Total liabilities	$ 3,052,743			$ 3,052,743

Net assets:

Unrestricted	$2,318,214			$ 2,318,214
Temporarily restricted (Note K)		$3,485,916		3,485,916
Permanently restricted			4,895,757	4,895,757
Total net assets	$2,318,214	$3,485,916	$4,895,757	$10,699,887
Total liabilities and net assets	$5,370,957	$3,485,916	$4,895,757	$13,752,630

*The accompanying notes are an integral part of this statement.

Totals may reflect rounding differences.

STATEMENT OF UNRESTRICTED REVENUES, EXPENSES, AND OTHER CHANGES IN UNRESTRICTED NET ASSETS

The basic operating statement for the NPO is the Statement of Unrestricted Revenues, Expenses, and Other Changes in Unrestricted Net Assets. This statement reports support, revenues, expenses, gains and losses. An *illustrative* statement is shown in Exhibit 15.

The statement has three major sections. The first section reports "support, revenues and other gains." *SFAS No. 117* describes this section simply as "revenue and other gains." Revenue has been defined in *SFAS No. 117* to include support.

The reporting of unconditional and unrestricted contributions is on the cash basis since pledges receivable are treated as temporarily restricted and not included in the amount shown for pledges. Note L in Exhibit 16 discloses the manner of recognizing unconditional and unrestricted contributions. It can be seen that such contributions are basically reported on a cash basis.

The second section of the statement reports temporarily restricted contributions and grants that have been recognized as revenue when restrictions have been satisfied. Note M in Exhibit 17 is a required disclosure for temporarily restricted contributions and grants that were recorded originally as temporarily restricted net assets and are now recognized as revenues when restrictions have been satisfied. The satisfaction of restrictions may be through the incurring of appropriate expenses for particular program activities or the acquisition of equipment for particular programs or for supporting services. The satisfaction of restrictions may be simply through the passage of time. The payment of debt service on long-term debt used to finance the acquisition of capital assets may also satisfy a restriction, if donors have specified that their restricted gifts can be used for this purpose.

The third section reports program expenses and supporting services expenses. Depreciation expense is reported separately as is interest expense and the provision for uncollectible accounts receivable. Interest expense on long-term debt is reported separately from interest expense on short-term borrowing. The *illustrative* statement in *SFAS No. 117* does not separately report depreciation expense, interest expense, and provision for uncollectibles.

Voluntary Health and Welfare Organizations also provide a separate statement on objects of expense. *SFAS No. 117* provides that object of expense information may be disclosed in the Notes to the Financial Statements. Such a note disclosure, Note N, is set out in Exhibit 18.

EXHIBIT 15

NPO Organization
Statement of Unrestricted Revenues, Expenses, and
Other Changes in Unrestricted Net Assets
Year Ended June 30, 19X2*

Unrestricted support, revenues and other gains:

Contributions (Note L)	$ 9,282,706
Fees for services	2,991,495
Income on long-term investments	312,004
Income on short-term investments	24,276
Net gain on disposal of fixed assets	25,094
Total unrestricted support, revenues, and gains	$12,635,574

Net assets released from restrictions

Satisfaction of program restrictions	499,456
Satisfaction of equipment acquisition restrictions	1,161,753
Expiration of time restrictions	316,870
Net assets released from restrictions	$ 1,978,589
Total unrestricted support, revenues, and other gains	$14,614,163

Expenses:

Program A	1,929,613
Program B	6,688,427
Program C	3,034,131
Management & General	555,677
Fund-Raising	354,421
Depreciation	937,589
Interest expense on line of credit	13,607
Provision for uncollectible accounts	35,000
Total expenses before interest on long-term debt	$13,548,466
Excess (deficiency) of support and revenue over expenses before interest on long-term debt	1,065,697
Interest expense on long-term debt	242,741
Increase in unrestricted net assets	$ 822,956

*The accompanying notes are an integral part of this statement.

Totals and carryforward amounts may reflect rounding differences.

EXHIBIT 16 Note L—Contributions: The Annual Campaign—Pledges and Collections**

Unconditional and unrestricted promises to contribute to the annual campaign—19X2	$9,911,407
Plus: unconditional and unrestricted promises to contribute to the annual campaign-19X1—uncollected at 7/1/19X1, net of allowance	1,834,624
Total collectible pledges	11,746,031
Less: unconditional and unrestricted promises to contribute to the annual campaign-19X1—uncollected at 6/30/19X2	2,463,325
Cash collected from pledges and reported	

as revenue from contributions $\underline{\$9,282,706}$

**This note is not a required disclosure, as long as information is provided directly in the Statement of Financial Position on the amount of the Allowance for Uncollectibles at the end of each fiscal year presented. The note is useful to external users of financial statements.

EXHIBIT 17 Note M—Net Assets Released from Restrictions

Temporarily restricted contributions and grants that were recorded as temporarily restricted net assets have been released from their restrictions by the passage of time or by the incurring of appropriate expenses.

Purpose restriction accomplished

Program A expenses incurred $ 499,956

Equipment acquired and placed in service
  for the following program and
  supporting activities:

Program A	$63,296	
Program B	365,027	
Program C	164,078	
Management & General	22,123	614,524

Debt service on long-term debt used
  to finance the acquisition of equipment   547,239

Time restrictions satisfied $\underline{316,870}$

Total restrictions released and revenue
  recognized $\underline{\$1,978,589}$

EXHIBIT 18 Note N—Expenses—by Object Classification—Programs A, B & C, Management & General, and Fund-Raising*

Expense by Object Classifications	Program A	Program B	Program C	Management & General	Fund Raising
Salaries	$1,095,186	$3,877,349	$1,766,935	$336,223	$189,869
Employee benefits	210,775	746,219	340,057	64,516	36,541
Payroll Taxes	$\underline{83,909}$	$\underline{297,067}$	$\underline{135,375}$	$\underline{25,683}$	$\underline{14,547}$
	$1,389,869	$4,920,635	$2,242,368	$425,422	$240,957

Professional fees	41,721	242,334	0	32,258	0
Contractual services	20,861	166,726	55,328	0	0
Facilities rents	58,807	164,787	0	15,846	0
Insurance	9,189	33,927	16,063	12,770	0
Utilities	18,377	92,087	37,480	7,480	0
Telephone	25,728	53,314	31,591	10,259	35,442
Heating	45,943	145,401	69,607	12,877	0
Equipment rentals	55,499	213,258	26,772	0	0
Maintenance and repairs	20,215	103,719	14,278	7,480	0
Projects materials	37,765	0	187,402	0	0
Supplies	42,268	184,170	95,397	19,418	22,784
Printing and publication	5,513	29,080	49,974	3,702	37,973
Postage and shipping	23,890	140,554	38,462	2,710	17,265
Conferences and meetings	35,744	87,240	66,037	3,526	0
Travel	13,783	82,394	99,948	1,603	0
Assistance to clients	80,860	0	0	0	0
Miscellaneous	3,579	28,801	3,425	526	0
	1,929,613	6,688,427	3,034,131	555,667	354,421
Depreciation	96,572	556,928	250,336	33,753	
Provision of Uncollectible Accounts		35,000			
Interest on Short-Term Debt				13,606	
Interest on Long-Term Debt				242,741	
Totals	$2,026,185	$7,280,355	$3,284,467	$845,767	$354,421

[*]Voluntary Health and Welfare Organizations present a fourth basic financial statement, The Statement of Functional Expenses. This note provides that disclosure.

Totals may reflect rounding differences.

STATEMENT OF CHANGES IN NET ASSETS

The Statement of Changes in Net Assets complements and completes the reporting of changes in equity for the NPO as a result of operating and non-operating transactions. It is shown in Exhibit 19.

This statement has four sections. The first section provides summary information from the Statement of Unrestricted Revenues, Expenses, and Other Changes in Net Assets. The focus is not on detailed disclosures concerning revenues, expenses, and gains and losses but summarizes the totals of these changes in unrestricted net assets. Net assets released from restrictions are disclosed separately from other revenue items.

The second section discloses information on items that result in changes in temporarily restricted net assets. Temporarily restricted contributions, grants, and investment income are examples of items that increase temporarily restricted net assets. Satisfaction of restrictions decreases temporarily restricted net assets and simultaneously increases unrestricted net assets.

The third section provides disclosures on items that increase or decrease permanently restricted net assets. The NPO basically has a permanent endowment. The endowment is held primarily in the form of long-term investments. Generally, investment income on such investments is unrestricted. However, the Board of Trustees that is required to maintain the purchasing power of the endowment may allocate some investment income to the endowment to meet this requirement.

The last section summarizes the impact of changes in permanently restricted net assets on the balance of such net assets at fiscal year end.

EXHIBIT 19

NPO Organization
Statement of Changes in Net Assets
Year Ended June 30, 19X2*

Unrestricted net assets:

Total unrestricted support, revenues and other gains	$12,635,574
Net assets released from restrictions	1,978,589
Total expenses before provision for uncollectibles	(13,548,466)
Interest on long-term debt	(242,741)
Increase in unrestricted net assets	$ 822,956

Temporarily restricted net assets:

Contributions restricted for operating purposes	$ 535,198
Grants restricted for operating purposes	524,905

Contributions restricted for capital purposes	2,084,000
Investment income for capital purposes	15,886
Net assets released from restrictions	(1,978,589)
	$ 1,181,399
Permanently restricted net assets:	
Contributions	$ 311,923
Investment income on current contributions to endowment	18,944
Net unrealized and realized gains on long-term investments (Note I)	125,000
	$ 455,867
Increase in net assets	$ 2,460,222
Net assets, 7/1/19X1	8,239,665
Net assets, 6/30/19X2	$10,699,887

*The accompanying notes are an integral part of this statement.

Totals may reflect rounding differences.

STATEMENT OF CHANGES IN NET ASSETS—COLUMNAR FORMAT

An alternative format for the Statement of Changes in Net Assets is illustrated in *SFAS No. 117*. The alternative format is shown in Exhibit 20.

The three basic categories of changes in (a) unrestricted, (b) temporarily restricted, and (c) permanently restricted are organized in columnar format. This is similar to the columnar format illustrated for the Statement of Financial Position.

EXHIBIT 20

NPO Organization
Statement of Changes in Net Assets
Year Ended June 30, 19X2

	Unrestricted	Temporarily Restricted	Permanently Restricted	Total
Support, revenues and gains:				
Total unrestricted support, revenues and other gains	$12,635,574			$12,635,574

Total restricted support, revenues and other gains	$3,144,102		311,923	3,456,026
Income from long-term investments			18,944	18,944
Income on short-term investments		15,886		15,886
Net realized and unrealized gains on long-term investments			125,000	125,000
Net assets released from restrictions	1,978,589	(1,978,589)	————	0
Total support, revenue and other gains	$ 14,614,163	$1,181,399	$ 455,867	$16,251,429
Temporarily restricted net assets:				
Total expenses before interest on long-term debt	$(13,548,466)			$(13,548,466)
Interest on long-term debt	(242,741)			(242,741)
Total expenses	$(13,791,207)			$(13,791,207)
Change in net assets	$ 822,956	$1,181,399	$ 455,867	$ 2,460,222
Net assets, 7/1/19X1	1,495,258	2,304,517	4,439,890	8,239,665
Net assets, 6/30/19X2	$ 2,318,214	$3,485,916	$4,895,757	$10,699,887

*The accompanying notes are an integral part of this statement.

Totals may reflect rounding differences.

STATEMENT OF ACTIVITIES

The Statement of Activities can be presented in place of two statements: (a) the Statement of Unrestricted Revenues, Expenses, and Other Changes in Net Assets and (b) the Statement of Changes in Net Assets. The Statement of Activities presents the details present in the two prior statements in one overall statement. The Statement of Activities is also illustrated in two formats. The two formats for the *illustrative* Statement of Activities are shown in Exhibits 21 and 22.

EXHIBIT 21

NPO Organization
Statement of Activities
*Year Ended June 30, 19X2**

Changes in unrestricted net assets:

Revenues and gains:

Contributions (Note L)	$ 9,282,706
Fees for services	2,991,495
Income from long-term investments	312,004
Income from short-term investments	24,276
Net gain on disposal of fixed assets	25,094
Total unrestricted support, revenues, and gains	$12,635,574

Net assets released from restrictions:

Satisfaction of program restrictions	$ 499,456
Satisfaction of equipment acquisition restrictions	1,161,753
Expiration of time restrictions	316,870
Net assets released from restrictions	$ 1,978,589
Total unrestricted support, revenues, and other gains	$14,614,163

Expenses:

Program A	1,929,613
Program B	6,688,427
Program C	3,034,131
Management & General	555,677
Fund-Raising	354,421
Depreciation	937,589
Interest expense on line of credit	13,607
Provision for uncollectible accounts	35,000
Total expenses before interest on long-term debt	$13,548,466

Excess (deficit) of support and revenue over expenses before interest on long-term debt	$ 1,065,697
Interest expense on long-term debt	242,741
Increase in unrestricted net assets	$ 822,956
Changes in temporarily restricted net assets:	
Contributions restricted for operating purposes	$ 535,198
Grants restricted for operating purposes	524,905
Contributions restricted for capital purposes	2,084,000
Investment income for capital purposes	15,886
Net assets released from restrictions	(1,978,589)
Increase in temporarily restricted net assets	$ 1,181,399
Changes in permanently restricted net assets:	
Contributions	$ 311,923
Investment income on current contributions to endowment	18,944
Net unrealized and realized gains on long-term investments (Note I)	$ 125,000
Increase in permanently restricted net assets	455,867
Increase in net assets	$ 2,460,222
Net assets, 7/1/19X1	8,239,665
Net assets, 6/30/19X2	$10,699,887

*The accompanying notes are an integral part of this statement.

Totals may reflect rounding differences.

EXHIBIT 22

NPO Organization
Statement of Activities
Year Ended June 30, 19X2*

	Unrestricted	Temporarily Restricted	Permanently Restricted	Total
Support, revenues and other gains:				
Contributions (Note L)	$9,282,706	$2,619,198	$311,923	$12,218,326

Grants for operating purposes		524,905	524,905
Fees for services	2,991,495		2,991,495
Income from long-term investments	312,003	18,944	326,447
Income from short-term investments	24,276	15,886	40,162
Gain on sales of fixed assets	25,094		25,094
Net realized and unrealized gains on long-term investments		125,000	125,000
Total support, revenues, and gains	$12,635,574	$3,159,988	$455,8671	$ 6,251,429

Net assets released from restrictions:

Satisfaction of program restrictions	$ 499,956	$(499,956)	0
Satisfaction of equipment acquisition restrictions	1,161,763	(1,161,763)	0
Expiration of time restrictions	316,870	(316,870)	0
Net assets released from restrictions	1,978,589	(1,978,589)	0
Total support, revenues, and other gains	$14,614,163	$ 1,181,399	$ 455,867	$16,251,429

Expenses:

Program A	$ 1,929,613	$ 1,929,613
Program B	6,688,427	6,688,427
Program C	3,034,131	3,034,131
Management & General	555,677	555,677
Fund-Raising	354,421	354,421
Depreciation	937,589	937,589
Interest expense on line of credit	13,607	13,607
Provision for uncollectible accounts	35,000	35,000
Total expenses before interest on long-term debt	$13,548,466	$13,548,466

Change in net assets before:				
Interest on long-term debt	$1,065,697	$1,181,399	$ 455,867	$ 2,702,963
Interest expense on long-term debt	242,741			242,741
Change in net assets	$ 822,956	$1,181,399	$ 455,867	$ 2,460,222
Net assets, 7/1/19X1	1,495,258	2,304,517	4,439,890	8,239,665
Net assets, 6/30/19X2	$2,318,214	$3,485,916	$4,895,757	$10,699,887

*The accompanying notes are an integral part of this statement.

Totals may reflect rounding differences.

CASH FLOWS FROM ANNUAL TO MONTHLY DATA

In Chapter 14, we took a detailed journey through the accounting records of our *illustrative* NPO. That journey provided us with a look at a series of transactions and entries that summarized the activities for the fiscal year. In this chapter, the data in the accounting records are presented in the form of financial statements with accompanying note disclosures. The last of the basic financial statements to be presented is the Statement of Cash Flows. Before we present such a statement, let's look more closely at cash flows.

From the accounting records, only summarized annual data has been presented. For cash flows information, we shall present illustrative monthly cash flow data.

CASH INFLOWS/OUTFLOWS FROM OPERATING ACTIVITIES

First, the cash inflow side will be examined. Monthly cash inflow information is presented in Exhibit 23. The cash inflows are those that are used to finance the day-to-day operating activities of the NPO. Cash inflows are shown for (a) contributions for operating activities, (b) grants for the program activities of Program A, (c) fees for services rendered from the program activities of Program B, and (d) unrestricted investment income from endowment investments.

In Exhibit 24, the cash inflows from contributions, grants, fees, and investment income are totaled on a monthly basis. Other inflows are added from (a) sales of equipment, (b) interest income, and (c) transfers from resources contributed for capital acquisitions that have been released from temporary restrictions.

With monthly data you can discern that cash inflows from contributions show a seasonal pattern. This may be the result of the annual fund-raising campaign. You would need more information on the process of fund-raising to better understand the seasonal pattern.

Cash outflows are the result of program and supporting services expenses, acquisition of inventories of supplies and prepayment of certain types of expenses. Monthly data on cash outflows for operating activities is shown in Exhibit 25. These outflows also include interest expense incurred and paid as a result of short-term borrowing due to the seasonal pattern of inflows relative to outflows.

Exhibit 26 provides an overview of all cash outflows for operating purposes. This exhibit adds monthly cash flow data on (a) purchase of new equipment, (b) sale of old equipment, and (c) net impact of short-term interest income versus short-term interest expense. The data on cash outflows for operating activities is on a monthly basis for the entire year, 19X2. It shows precisely when during the fiscal year short-term borrowing was required and when cash surpluses built up. Whether that pattern is one that was planned for is not available from the nature of our case study.

Exhibit 27 shows monthly cash flow data for nonoperating items. The major nonoperating item on the inflow side are cash inflows from contributions from the capital fund-raising campaign. The outflows are for (a) acquisition of equipment and (b) debt service on long-term debt.

EXHIBIT 23 Contributions, Grants, Fees, Investment Income for Operating Activities—Monthly Cash Collections

	Contributions	Grants	Fees for Services	Investment Income on Endowment
July	$ 480,404	$ 20,009	$ 249,000	$ 33,000
August	576,265	35,013	237,000	20,999
September	479,546	125,016	255,000	21,039
October	623,534	20,007	258,000	33,000
November	1,488,071	49,981	261,000	20,999
December	2,591,934	7,497	249,000	20,999

January	1,248,014	92,501	243,000	33,000
February	335,612	44,984	249,000	20,999
March	624,102	22,487	252,000	20,999
April	671,724	2,489	255,000	33,000
May	192,164	59,996	243,000	20,999
June	288,206	19,975	249,000	20,999
Totals collected	$9,599,576	$499,955	$3,000,000	$300,032

EXHIBIT 24 Summary of Cash Inflows Related to Operating Activities —by Month and Source

	Contributions, Grants, Fees Investment Income	Sale of Equipment	Interest Income	Transfers of Cash for Capital Acquisition	Totals	Cumulative Balance
July	$ 782,413	$ 0	$ 0		$ 782,413	$ 782,413
August	869,277	0	2		869,280	1,651,693
September	880,601	0	0		880,601	2,532,294
October	934,541	0	0	$153,631	1,088,172	3,620,466
November	1,820,051	10,000	0		1,830,051	5,450,517
December	2,869,430	0	646		2,870,076	8,320,592
January	1,616,515	0	4,993	307,262	1,928,770	10,249,362
February	650,595	15,000	5,327		670,922	10,920,284
March	919,587	0	3,631		923,218	11,843,502
April	962,213	0	4,097		966,310	12,809,812
May	516,160	25,000	3,110		544,270	13,354,082
June	578,180	0	2,471	153,631	734,282	$14,088,363
	$13,399,564	$50,000	$24,276	$614,524	$14,088,363	

EXHIBIT 25 Summary of Cash Outflows Related to Operating Activities by Month

	Prepaid Exp., Inventory of Supplies & Expenses	Short-term Interest	Total	Cumulative
July	$ 908,034	$ 0	$ 908,034	$ 908,034

August	682,102	931	683,033	1,591,067
September	1,024,743	0	1,024,743	2,615,810
October	1,425,419	505	1,425,924	4,041,734
November	1,297,744	5,979	1,303,723	5,345,458
December	1,970,750	6,191	1,976,941	7,322,399
January	496,661	0	496,661	7,819,060
February	532,830	0	532,830	8,351,891
March	1,602,943	0	1,602,943	9,954,834
April	781,037	0	781,037	10,735,870
May	939,755	0	939,755	11,675,625
June	837,915	0	837,915	$12,513,540
	$12,499,933	$13,607	$12,513,540	

EXHIBIT 26 Summary of Net Cash Inflows (Outflows) Related to Operating and Investing Activities

	Cash Inflows & Outflows from Operations	Purchase & Sale of Equipment	Short-term Interest Income less Expense	Transfer Cash for Capital Acquisition	Totals	Cumulative Balance
July	$(125,621)		$ 0		$(125,621)	$(125,621)
August	187,176		(929)		186,247	60,626
September	(144,142)		0		(144,142)	(83,516)
October	(490,878)	$(153,631)	(505)	$153,631	(491,383)	(574,899)
November	522,306	10,000	(5,979)		526,327	(48,572)
December	898,680		(5,546)		893,135	844,563
January	1,119,853	(307,262)	4,993	307,262	1,124,847	1,969,409
February	117,765	15,000	5,327		138,092	2,107,501
March	(683,356)		3,631		(679,725)	1,427,776
April	181,176		4,097		185,273	1,613,049
May	(423,595)	25,000	3,110		(395,485)	1,217,564
June	(259,735)		2,471	153,631	(103,633)	1,113,930
	$ 899,630	$(410,893)	$10,669	$614,524	$1,113,930	

EXHIBIT 27 Cash Inflows (Outflows) Related to Investing and Financing

	Cash Inflow	Cash Outflows				
	Contribution Restricted for Capital Purposes	Cash for Purchase of Fixed Assets	Payment of Long-term Debt Interest	Princi-pal	Net Cash Monthly Inflows	Interest Income
July	$ 72,000		$ 21,258	$ 24,345	$ 26,397	
August	66,000		21,076	24,528	20,397	
September	126,000		20,892	24,712	80,397	
October	280,000	$153,631	20,706	24,897	80,766	$ 318
November	380,000		20,520	25,084	334,397	520
December	500,000		20,331	25,272	454,397	1,357
January	152,000	307,262	20,142	25,461	(200,865)	2,494
February	96,000		19,951	25,652	52,397	1,995
March	86,000		19,759	25,845	40,397	2,127
April	96,000		19,565	26,039	50,397	2,233
May	88,000		19,369	26,234	42,397	2,365
June	58,000	153,631	19,173	26,431	(141,234)	2,476
Cash inflows & outflows	$2,000,000	$614,524	$242,741	$304,498	$838,237	$15,886

*Cash from sales of fixed assets is part of the unrestricted cash of the NPO.

Totals may reflect rounding differences.

Exhibit 28 presents cash flow from endowment contributions.

EXHIBIT 28 Cash Flow from Contributions for Endowment—Pledged and Collected, Investment Income from Endowment, and Investment in Endowment on a Monthly Basis

	Contributions to Endowment	Investment Income from Endowment	Invested in Endowment
July	$56,986	$2,001	$58,987
August	72,013	1,274	73,287

September	10,499	1,276	11,775
October	4,501	2,001	6,502
November	6,012	1,274	7,286
December	7,493	1,274	8,767
January	14,987	2,001	16,988
February	5,993	1,274	7,266
March	19,509	1,274	20,782
April	21,004	2,001	23,005
May	40,510	1,274	41,783
June	29,289	1,274	30,562
Totals	$288,795	$18,196	$306,991

THE STATEMENT OF CASH FLOWS—DIRECT METHOD

The presentation of cash flows data both on annual and monthly bases has set the stage for the presentation of the last of the major financial statements, the Statement of Cash Flows (SCF).

The SCF comes in two forms. The first presented is the "direct method." The second method, the "indirect method," will be presented later. The SCF is presented in Exhibit 29 using the direct method.

EXHIBIT 29

NPO Organization
Statement of Cash Flows
Year Ended June 30, 19X2*

Cash flow from operating activities:

Cash received from fees for services rendered	$3,000,000
Cash received from contributors for operating activities	7,448,082
Cash collected on pledges receivables, 7/1/19X1	1,834,624
Cash collected on pledges receivables, 7/1/19X1	316,870
Cash received from grants for operating activities	444,933
Cash received from grants receivable, 7/1/19X1	55,022

Cash from interest and dividends on endowment investments	300,032
Cash received from short-term interest income	24,276
Cash released from temporary restrictions for equipment acquisition	153,631
Cash paid for employee services—salaries and benefits	(9,219,251)
Cash paid to vendors for operating expenses	(3,262,304)
Cash used for prepaid expenses	(18,378)
Cash paid on interest on long-term debt	(242,741)
Cash paid on interest on short-term debt	(13,607)
Net cash provided by operating activities	$ 821,190

Cash flow from investing activities:

Purchase of equipment	$(614,524)
Proceeds from sale of equipment	50,000
Purchase of investments—restricted for capital purposes	(838,237)
Purchase of investments—restricted for endowments	(306,991)
Net cash used in investing activities	$(1,709,752)

Cash flow from financing activities:

Proceeds from contributions restricted for:

Investment in plant	$ 2,000,000
Investment in endowment	288,795
	$ 2,288,795

Other financing activities:

Interest and dividends restricted to endowment	18,196
Interest and dividends restricted to investment in plant	15,886
Principal payments on long-term debt	(304,498)
	$(270,417)
Net cash provided by financing activities	$ 2,018,378
Net increase in cash and cash equivalents	$ 1,129,816
Cash and cash equivalents, July 1, 19X1	$ 233,422
Cash and cash equivalents, June 30, 19X2	$ 1,363,238

Supplemental Data for Noncash Investing and Financing Activities:

Increase in value of endowment investment from
  unrealized gains $125,000
Decrease in long-term debt from current installment   333,062

*The accompanying notes are an integral part of this statement.
Totals may reflect rounding differences.

The statement is organized in five major sections. Cash flows are reported in terms of (a) operating activities, (b) investing activities, (c) financing activities, (d) a summary showing the impact of all sources of cash flows on the ending balance of cash and cash equivalents, and (e) pertinent non-cash flow information that should be reported.

First, we have cash flows from operating activities. In this section, the cash inflows are shown first. The fees for services rendered of $3,000,000 can be traced back to the cash flow data presented in Exhibit 23. The next two items represent cash flows from unconditional and unrestricted contributions for operating activities from prior-year pledges for $1,834,624 and from current-year pledges for $7,448,082. These two sources total to $9,282,706. The third item of cash flows from contributions is subject to timing restrictions for $316,870. This third item added to the first two items gives us a total of cash flows from contributions for operating activities of $9,599,576. That amount ties directly into the cash flows from contributions amount in Exhibit 23.

The next two items of cash inflows add up to the amount of grants shown in Exhibit 23. Cash received from the current year's grants is shown at $444,933 and cash from grants receivable at the beginning of the year is shown at $55,022, which together equal $499,955, the amount in Exhibit 23.

The seventh item in Exhibit 29, investment income from endowment investments at $300,032, also is in Exhibit 23. The eighth cash inflow item in the operating activities section, interest income at $24,276, is in the monthly cash flows set out in Exhibit 24. The last cash inflow item is $153,631, which represents cash inflow released from temporary restrictions by the acquisition of equipment. This item appears earlier in Exhibit 26.

The first three items of cash outflows in Exhibit 29 result from operating activities: (a) cash paid for employee services at $9,219,251, (b) cash paid to vendors for operating expenses at $3,262,304, and (c) prepaid expenses at $18,378 together total to $12,499,933. This is the amount of cash outflow shown in Exhibit 25 expended on prepaid expenses, inventory of supplies and program and supporting activities expenses. The fourth item of cash outflow of payment of interest on long-term debt of $242,741 appears earlier in Exhibit 27. The last item of cash outflow, interest on short-term debt of $13,607, appears earlier in Exhibit 25.

In the second section of the SCF we have cash flows from investing activities. The four items in this section appear earlier in Exhibits 24, 26, 27, and 28.

Information on financing activities is presented in the third section of the SCF. The five items in this section appear earlier in Exhibits 27 and 28.

The overall impact on the beginning cash balance is shown by adding the impact of the changes in cash flows to it. The Statement of Financial Position shows Unrestricted Cash and Cash Equivalents of $1,347,353 and temporarily restricted Cash and Cash Equivalents of $15,885 which together total $1,363,238. This ending balance in Cash and Cash Equivalents agrees with the amount shown in the SCF.

The final section contains some information on noncash flows that affect investing and financing activities. In our *illustrative* example, we have only two noncash items to report. One involves an investing item which is the increase in the value of the endowment investments through the recognition of unrealized gains that result from increases in the market value of such investments. The second item involves financing that results from the decrease in the long-term debt due to the maturity of the current installment due in the next fiscal year.

THE STATEMENT OF CASH FLOWS—INDIRECT METHOD

Exhibit 30 sets out the second version of the SCF using the indirect method. The basic difference between the direct and indirect methods is that the indirect method does not show explicitly cash flows from operations. The indirect method was provided as an alternative for those entities whose accounting records could not provide the needed cash flows data easily. The direct method is the preferred format for the SCF, but the indirect method is an acceptable alternative.

EXHIBIT 30

NPO Organization
Statement of Cash Flows
Year Ended June 30, 19X2*

Operating activities:

Changes in net assets	$2,460,222
Adjustments to reconcile changes in net assets to net cash flows from operating activities:	
Depreciation & amortization	937,589
Gain on sale of fixed assets	(25,094)
Decrease in accounts receivable	30,412
Increase in investment income receivable	(11,971)
Decrease in inventories	47,968
Decrease in prepaid expenses	53,635
Increase in accounts payable	114,365
Increase in prepaid services to be delivered	13,093
Increase in temporarily restricted pledges receivable	(302,328)
Increase in temporarily restricted grants receivable	(24,950)
Increase in permanently restricted investment receivable	(748)
Increase in permanently restricted pledges income receivable	(23,128)
Unrealized gain on long-term investments	(125,000)
Contributions restricted for capital purposes	(2,000,000)
Contributions restricted for endowment	(288,795)
Investment income restricted for capital purposes	(15,886)
Investment income restricted for endowment	(18,196)
Net cash provided by operating activities	$ 821,190

Cash flow from investing activities:

Purchase of equipment	$(614,524)
Proceeds from sale of equipment	50,000
Purchase of investments—restricted to fixed asset acquisitions	(838,237)
Purchase of investments—restricted for endowments	(306,991)
Net cash used in investing activities	$(1,709,752)
Financing activities:	
Proceeds from contributions restricted for:	
Investment in plant	$ 2,000,000
Investment in endowment	288,795
	$ 2,288,795
Other financing activities:	
Interest and dividends restricted to endowment	$ 18,196
Interest and dividends restricted to investment in plant	15,886
Principal payments on long-term debt	(304,498)
	(270,417)
Net cash provided by financing activities	2,018,378
Net increase in cash and cash equivalents	1,129,816
Cash and cash equivalents, July 1, 19X1	233,422
Cash and cash equivalents, June 30, 19X2	$1,363,238

Supplemental Data for Noncash Investing and Financing Activities:

Increase in value of endowment investment from unrealized gains	$ 125,000
Decrease in long-term debt from current installment	333,062

*The accompanying notes are an integral part of this statement.

Totals may reflect rounding differences.

The SCF using the indirect method has the same structure overall as under the direct method. It has cash flows from: (a) operating activities, (b) investing activities, and (c) financing activities. It also has a summary showing the impact on the beginning balance of the change in cash flows as well as information on noncash investing and financing activities.

The indirect method begins with the amount shown for the Change in Net Assets from the Statement of Changes in Net Assets or from the Statement of Activities. In Exhibit 21, we have the Statement of Activities that shows the Change in Net Assets to be $2,460,222. This amount is carried over into the SCF in Exhibit 30. The Changes in Net Assets' figure contains the effects of a number of noncash items. As a result, there are a number of items that transform the amount for Changes in Net Assets into Cash Flows from Operating Activities. Some items can be taken directly from other exhibits but other items are not shown in other exhibits and must be calculated separately.

The first noncash adjustment is depreciation shown at $937,589. It can usually be found in the Notes to the Financial Statements. It may or may not be shown directly in the Statement of Unrestricted Revenues, Expenses and Other Changes in Net Assets (SURE) or in the Statement of Activities (SA). This noncash item was added to arrive at the Changes in Net Assets figure so that now it is subtracted to arrive at a Cash Flows from Operating Activities amount.

The second, noncash item, Gain on Sale of Fixed Assets at $25,094, is subtracted and can be found in Exhibits 15 and 21. The third item a decrease in Accounts Receivable for $30,412, is not found directly in another exhibit. Instead, it must be calculated from the two balances given for Accounts Receivable in the Statement of Financial Position (SFP) in Exhibit 1. In Exhibit 1 we find the Balance for Accounts Receivable at June 30, 19X2 to be $415,467 while the balance at June 30, 19X1 is $445,879. There has been a decrease of $30,412. A decrease in Accounts Receivable means that cash in the amount of $30,412 has been collected that is not reflected in SURE or in SA. Therefore, the $30,412 has not been reflected in the figure shown for Changes in Net Assets in SA. This amount has to be added to Changes in Net Assets to arrive at Cash Flows from Operating Activities.

The same calculation and analysis must be done for a number of other increases or decreases in certain of the assets and liabilities using the information given in Exhibit 1. Investment Income Receivable increased by

$11,971 and must be subtracted from Changes in Net Assets to arrive at Cash Flows from Operating Activities. Inventories decreased by $47,968 and must be added. Prepaid Expenses decreased by $53,635 and must also be added.

The above changes are in the current unrestricted assets. There are also changes in current unrestricted liabilities that must be considered. Accounts Payable increased by $114,365. An increase in Accounts Payable means that less cash was used to pay vendors than is reflected in the amount shown for Changes in Net Assets. The increase in Accounts Payable must be added to Changes in Net Assets to arrive at the amount for Cash Flows from Operating Activities. The second liability that affects operating activities, Prepaid Services, increased by $13, 093. The amount has to be added to the Changes in Net Assets to arrive at Cash Flows from Operating Activities.

We turn next to the temporarily and permanently restricted assets. The temporarily restricted pledges increased by $302,328 using the amounts shown in Exhibit 1. Temporarily restricted Grants Receivable shows an increase of $24,950 in Exhibit 30 that can be confirmed from the figures shown in Exhibit 1. The same applies to the increase of $748 for permanently restricted investment income receivable. All of these increases must be subtracted.

The unrealized gains on long-term investments of $125,000 is a noncash item that also must be subtracted. This item is shown explicitly in Exhibit 21.

The last group of adjustments is somewhat different from the earlier groups. The adjustments can all be found directly in Exhibit 30. The $2,000,000 of Contributions restricted for capital purposes is subtracted in the Cash Flows from Operating section and added to the Cash Flows from Financing Activities section. The same applies to the $288,795 of contributions restricted for endowment. The last two adjustment items of investment income, in this first section, are subtracted in this section and added in the Cash from Financing Activities section.

The other sections of the SCF using the indirect method are the same as for the SCF using the direct method.

NEXT FINANCIAL STATEMENT ANALYSIS

This completes the review and discussion of the basic financial statements for a not-for-profit organization. In the next chapter we turn to the analysis of the financial statements.

NOTES TO CHAPTER 15

1. *SFAS No. 117*, paragraph 8, p. 3.

2. *SFAS No. 95*, "Statement of Cash Flows" (Norwalk, CT: FASB, 1987).

3. *SFAS No. 117*, paragraph 10, p. 4.

4. *Ibid.*, paragraph 18, pp. 6–7.

5. *Ibid.*, footnote 5, p. 7.

6. *Ibid.*, paragraph 156, p. 55.

7. *Ibid.*, footnote 6, p. 9.

8. *SFAS No. 93*, "Recognition of Depreciation by Not-for-Profit Organizations" (Norwalk, CT: FASB, August 1987).

Chapter 16

A Case Study in Financial Statement Analysis and the New Reporting Standards of the FASB—Part III

In Parts I and II, the accounting system and the financial statements of the illustrative NPO were covered. This chapter centers its discussion on financial statement analysis. It covers the ways in which a not-for-profit organization's financial position, results of operations, and cash flows may be evaluated. The analysis includes an examination of financial stress.

In the business area, analysis of financial statements is directed at measuring risk and return. Investors must ultimately judge risk and return in selecting investments. In the not-for-profit area, the basic objective of financial statement analysis is the judgment of risk. Profitability is not the key objective of a not-for-profit entity. The value of services to society rendered by not-for-profit organizations must be evaluated by methods separate from analysis of financial statements. Of course, when not-for-profit organizations are involved in investing activities, risk and return are of prime concern in evaluating the performance of their investments.

RESPONSIBILITY OF TRUSTEES AND MANAGERS AND THE FIDUCIARY NATURE OF NPO ACTIVITIES

Providers of gifts, contributions and grants that do not involve exchange transactions stand in a critically different position from customers who obtain products and services in exchange for payment of monies. Trustees, officers and managers of NPOs have a continual fiduciary obligation to those who provide support in the form of gifts, contributions and grants without a *quid pro quo* exchange of goods, services or other resources. In an important sense NPOs have a greater fiduciary responsibility to the providers of support than even to creditors or investors. That fiduciary responsibility places a higher level of reporting responsibility on NPOs than envisaged by the FASB in *SFAS No. 117*. We have followed SFAS No. 117 closely but, at the same time, have tried to take account of the needs of the external user as well as the special fiduciary responsibility of NPOs.

The *illustrative* examples cannot fully provide for the reporting requirements of the individual circumstances of each NPO. Therefore, the trustees, officers and managers of an NPO must bring to bear their own judgment to meet their fiduciary responsibilities in reporting to external users.

ANALYSIS OF THE STATEMENT OF FINANCIAL POSITION

There is a standard series of measures used in the analysis of the Statement of Financial Position. These measures will be described and their usefulness and limitations for a nonprofit entity discussed. The ultimate objective of all of these measures will be to provide information on risk.

COMMON SIZE ANALYSIS AND ANALYSIS OF CHANGES

An examination of the composition of the assets, liabilities and equities can provide a useful starting point for an analysis of the Statement of Financial Position. The Statement of Financial Position for the NPO was presented in Exhibit 1 of Chapter 15. Exhibit 1 of this chapter presents an analysis of the composition of the assets, liabilities and equities presented in Exhibit 1 of the previous chapter. The composition of the assets, liabilities, and equities is calculated as percentages of the total assets. This is known as *"common size"* analysis of the Statement of Financial Position.

Additional analysis of the Statement of Financial Position is provided in Exhibit 2. In this exhibit, an analysis of the changes in assets, liabilities, and equities is shown along with the composition of these changes.

EXHIBIT 1

NPO Organization
Common Size Analysis
of the Statement of Financial Position
June 30, 19X2 and 19X1*

	19X2	19X1
Assets:		
Unrestricted assets:		
Current assets:		
Cash & cash equivalents	9.80%	2.04%
Accounts receivable, net (Note B)	3.02%	3.89%
Investment income receivable	0.24%	0.18%
Inventories (Note C)	2.62%	3.56%
Prepaid expenses (Note D)	1.17%	1.87%
Total unrestricted current assets	16.85%	11.54%
Property, plant, and equipment (Note E)	22.20%	29.66%
Total unrestricted assets	39.05%	41.20%
Restricted assets:		
Temporarily restricted assets:		
Cash & cash equivalents	0.12%	0.00%
Pledges receivable for operating purposes (Notes F & G)	17.02%	18.50%
Pledges receivable for capital acquisition (Note F)	1.54%	1.11%
Grants receivable	0.58%	0.48%
Short-term investments (Note I)	6.10%	0.00%
Permanently restricted assets:		
Investment income receivable	0.01%	0.01%
Pledges receivable (Note H)	0.36%	0.23%
Long-term investments (Note I)	35.22%	38.47%
Total restricted assets	60.95%	58.80%

Total assets:	100.00%	100.00%

Liabilities and net assets:

Liabilities:

Accounts payable & accrued expenses	3.00%	2.60%
Long-term debt—current installment	2.42%	2.65%
Prepaid services	0.80%	0.85%
Total current liabilities	6.22%	6.10%
Long-term debt (Note J)	15.97%	22.06%
Total liabilities	22.20%	28.16%

Net assets:

Unrestricted	16.86%	13.04%
Temporarily restricted (Note K)	25.35%	20.09%
Permanently restricted	35.60%	38.71%
Total net assets	77.80%	71.84%
Total liabilities and net assets	100.00%	100.00%

*Totals may reflect rounding differences.

EXHIBIT 2

NPO Organization
Analysis of Changes in the Financial Position
Year Ended June 30, 19X2

	Amount of Change	Percent of Total Assets	Percentage Increase (Decrease)
Assets:			
Unrestricted assets:			
Current assets:			
Cash & cash equivalents	$1,113,931	48.79%	477.22%
Accounts receivable, net (Note B)	(30,412)	–1.33%	–6.82%
Investment income receivable	11,971	0.52%	57.15%
Inventories (Note C)	(47,968)	–2.10%	–11.74%
Prepaid expenses (Note D)	(53,635)	–2.35%	–25.01%
Total unrestricted current assets	$ 993,887	43.53%	75.11%

Property, plant, and equipment (Note E)	(347,971)	–15.24%	–10.23%
Total unrestricted assets	$ 645,916	28.29%	13.67%
Restricted assets:			
Temporarily restricted assets:			
Cash & cash equivalents	$ 15,886	0.70%	Undefined
Pledges receivable for operating purposes (Notes F & G)	218,327	9.56%	10.29%
Pledges receivable for capital purposes (Note F)	84,000	3.68%	65.63%
Grants receivable	24,950	1.09%	45.34%
Short-term investments (Note I)	838,237	36.71%	Undefined
Permanently restricted assets:			
Investment income receivable	748	0.03%	64.00%
Pledges receivable (Note H)	23,128	1.01%	86.57%
Long-term investments (Note I)	431,991	18.92%	9.79%
Total restricted assets	$1,637,267	71.71%	24.28%
Total assets	$2,283,182	100.00%	19.91%
Liabilities and net assets:			
Liabilities:			
Accounts payable & accrued expenses	$ 114,365	5.01%	38.37%
Long-term debt—current installment	28,564	1.25%	9.38%
Prepaid services	13,092	0.57%	13.46%
Total current liabilities	$ 156,022	6.83%	22.29%
Long-term debt (Note J)	(333,062)	–14.59%	–13.16%
Total liabilities	$(177,041)	–7.75%	–5.48%
Net assets:			
Unrestricted	$ 822,956	36.04%	55.04%
Temporarily restricted (Note K)	1,181,399	51.74%	51.26%
Permanently restricted	455,867	19.97%	10.27%
Total net assets	$2,460,223	107.75%	29.86%
Total liabilities and net assets	$2,283,182	100.00%	19.91%

CASH AND CASH EQUIVALENTS

Total assets were $13,752,630 at June 30, 19X2 and $11,469,448 at June 30, 19X1 from the *illustrative* data in Exhibit 1 of Chapter 15. Exhibit 1 of this chapter shows that cash rose significantly as a proportion of the total assets, from 2.04% at the prior year-end, June 30, 19X1, to 9.8% at the current year-end, June 30, 19X2. This major change in the relative importance of cash and cash equivalents as an asset between 19X1 and 19X2 is readily apparent from the common size analysis in Exhibit 1 of this chapter. Why did management choose to permit cash to rise so significantly? It is a question that cannot be answered directly from the information provided by the financial statements. An external analyst would have to seek information directly from the management of the NPO to understand its decision to permit cash and cash equivalents to rise so abruptly.

While cash and cash equivalents represent 9.8% of total assets, the rise in cash and cash equivalents is even greater as a proportion of the overall rise in total assets between June 30, 19X1 and June 30, 19X2. The *illustrative* Analysis of the *Changes* in Financial Position in Exhibit 2 reveals that total assets rose by $2,283,182, a rise of 19.91% using June 30, 19X1 as the base to calculate the percentage change between the two year-ends. The increase in the total assets is a *net* increase, since it is the result of combining both increases and decreases in assets. The rise in cash and cash equivalents is shown in Exhibit 2 to be $1,113,931 which is the greatest rise of any of the assets in absolute dollars. This rise represents 48.79% of the *net* increase in the total assets, i.e., the rise in cash and cash equivalents is almost 50% of the *net* rise in all of the assets. Again, the question would arise for the financial analyst as to the justification for the concentrated and dominant rise in the cash position of the NPO.

TEMPORARILY RESTRICTED SHORT-TERM INVESTMENTS

Temporarily restricted short-term investments held for capital purposes such as the acquisition of plant assets shows the second highest rise as a proportion of the total assets in Exhibit 1. This investment rose from 0.0% of the total assets at June 30, 19X1, to 6.1% at June 30, 19X2. In Exhibit 2, these short-term investments are shown to have increased by $838,237. This increase represents 36.71% of the *net* increase in the total assets. Together with the increase in cash we have 85.5% of the *net* increase in the total assets.

TEMPORARILY RESTRICTED PLEDGES RECEIVABLE

In Exhibit 1 of Chapter 15, *temporarily restricted* pledges receivable cover several types of pledges receivable. According to the Notes to the

Financial Statements, pledges receivable cover unrestricted pledges receivable as well as pledges receivable restricted for operating and pledges receivable restricted for capital purposes. A discussion of the reporting rules that require *unrestricted* pledges receivable to be reported in the *temporarily restricted* category was provided in the previous chapter.

In Exhibit 1 of this chapter, *temporarily restricted* pledges receivables are separated into two categories: (a) unrestricted and restricted gifts pledged for operating purposes, and (b) restricted gifts pledged for capital acquisitions. The pledges receivables that are unrestricted or restricted for operating purposes show an increase of $218,327 in Exhibit 2. Pledges restricted for capital acquisition show an increase of $84,000. Pledges receivable for operating purposes *drop* as a proportion of total assets from *18.5%* at June 30, 19X1 to *17.02%* at June 30, 19X2. Pledges receivable for capital acquisition show a *rise* as a proportion of total assets from *1.11%* at June 30, 19X1 to *1.54%* at June 30, 19X2.

Exhibit 2 of this chapter shows the same disparate behavior for these two categories of pledges. Both categories of pledges receivable show increases. The difference is that pledges receivable for operating purposes, show an increase of *9.56%*, but *lag* the overall *net* increase in the total assets at *19.91%*. The significance and meaning of this lagging increase in pledges receivable for operating purposes requires an examination and explanation by management of the NPO.

Permanent Endowment

Endowment also shows a lagging growth relative to total assets. Is such a lag something to be concerned about, or is it something that management of the NPO does not consider a negative change between the two fiscal years?

Endowment is held in the form of investments. The growth in endowment is partially the result of contributions to endowment and partially the result of changes in the value of endowment investments. Investment income from endowment investments is available in the form of unrestricted resources to be used for operating purposes. Total return on endowment investments includes both changes in the value of endowment and investment income from endowment investments. Total return on endowment investments is disclosed in Note I of the Notes to the Financial Statements in Exhibit 10 of Chapter 15.

Total return on endowment investments can be estimated approximately by an external user of financial statements by calculating it as a proportion of the average balance of endowment investments. The average balance of endowment investment for 19X2 is about $4,628,000, total return is $443,000, so that the rate of return is *approximately 9.57%*. The percentage increase shown in Exhibit 2 of this chapter for endowment investments is 9.79%. The two percentages are deceptively close because contributions to endowment were relatively close in value to investment income distributed for operating purposes.

A judgment as to the performance of endowment investment would not only have to take account of return but also the risk associated with the endowment portfolio. *SFAS No. 117* requires a disclosure with respect to investments. The *illustrative* disclosure in *SFAS No. 117* discusses Board of Trustee policy as well as legal requirements with respect to maintaining the purchasing power value of endowment as well as distribution policies with respect to total return on endowment investments. Judgments concerning an evaluation of the risk of investment portfolios whether for endowment purposes or other purposes are not an illustrated disclosure. Such judgments would provide useful information to external users but do not seem to be required disclosures in the not-for-profit area.

It is generally understood that appropriately diversified investment portfolios are an accepted way of reducing risk. This is brought about by selecting individual securities whose returns tend to be negatively correlated and whose individual risks evaluations fall within acceptable ranges of risk for the trustees of the NPO.

FIXED ASSETS

Exhibit 1 reveals that fixed assets dropped from *29.66%* of total assets at the end of fiscal year 19X1 to *22.2%* of total assets at the end of the current fiscal year. Exhibit 2 shows the drop to be not only relative to total assets, but also a drop in absolute terms by *$347,971*. That decrease may confront us and also management with certain difficulties of interpretation. As a start, fixed assets are carried on the books at historical cost. Second, fixed assets are subject to reductions due to depreciation estimates. To understand the drop, both management and outside users of the financial statements would need information on such matters as changes in the capacity of fixed assets and changes in the utilization of fixed assets. The change in value reported for the fixed assets is by itself only a starting point for further analysis. Nevertheless, the analyses of Exhibits 1 and 2 do provide a starting point for further investigation and analysis for external users of financial statements.

LIABILITIES AND EQUITIES—CAPITAL STRUCTURE

Exhibits 1 and 2 show that reliance on long-term debt financing has decreased so that equity as a proportion of total assets has risen over the course of the current fiscal year. While total assets rose by *19.91%*, long-term debt fell by *13.16%*.

Financing of significant additions to fixed assets tends to be linked to the use of long-term debt. This relationship between fixed assets acquisition and long-term debt financing opens up an important area of inquiry for the external user. An important issue for the external analyst would be management's plans with respect to fixed asset needs and use of long-term debt to finance these needs.

TRENDS IN COMMON SIZE ANALYSIS AND ANALYSIS OF CHANGES

The analysis carried out up to this point has concentrated on the current and prior fiscal years. The usefulness of the analysis can be extended if certain relationships in the composition of the assets, liabilities and equities tend to show some stability over time. This means that the analysis might be extended to take account of perhaps the past three to five years of recent historical experience. Using data from the past five or more years may also provide some insight into trends. A caution is in order, however; the study of these past trends is to be understood as a guide to the future only if you judge that there is sufficient stability in relationships being studied to warrant the use of such past data.

INDUSTRY SPECIFIC DATA

Analysis of financial statements requires not only relevant trend data, but also relevant industry specific data. There are a great variety of services provided by not-for-profit organizations. Funding and financing arrangements come in a variety of forms for not-for-profit organizations. The nature of the funding and financing arrangements for the "health" industry can differ greatly from that for the "education" industry as well as that for "health and welfare" organizations.

If you visualize not-for-profit activities in industry-specific terms similar to that for business entities, then you require industry-specific data for financial statement analysis.

ANALYSIS OF LIQUIDITY AND UTILIZATION

Common size analysis and an analysis of changes in the Statement of Financial Position are a starting point for a closer look at particular characteristics of individual types of assets and liabilities. Asset liquidity and asset utilization are characteristics of central interest to external users of financial statements.

Liquidity refers to the nearness that an asset is to cash. The more easily an asset is converted to cash with minimal cost or loss upon conversion, the more liquid is that asset. The more liquid an asset, the lower the level of risk of loss upon conversion. Asset utilization refers to the efficiency with which particular types of assets are used in the operating activities of the entity. Are certain assets being held in excess relative to the optimal levels for those assets?

The external user has some tools that serve as a starting point for judging liquidity and asset utilization.

CURRENT RATIO

The *current ratio* is one of the frequently used measures of liquidity. The *current ratio* is simply the ratio of the current assets to the current liabilities. Current assets are those assets that management expects will be converted to cash and cash equivalents over the normal operating cycle or one year, whichever is later. Similarly, current liabilities would be those liabilities that are expected to be repaid through the use of cash or cash equivalents over the normal operating cycle or one year, whichever is later. The current ratio is a measure of the degree to which current assets might be converted to cash to meet current liabilities.

In the *illustrative* example, the current unrestricted assets of the NPO are composed of cash and cash equivalents, accounts receivable, investment income receivable, inventories of supplies, and prepaid expenses. Current unrestricted liabilities are composed of accounts payable, prepaid services and the current installment of the mortgage note payable.

Exhibit 1 of Chapter 15 provides *illustrative* information on the current unrestricted assets and liabilities of the NPO. Using the *illustrative* data from

Exhibit 1 of the previous chapter, one can calculate a *current ratio* for the current unrestricted assets and liabilities of the NPO as of the end of the current and prior fiscal years, as follows:

		19X2	19X1
Current Unrestricted Assets	=	$2,317,207	$1,323,321
Current Unrestricted Liabilities		$855,880	$699,858
Current Ratio for Unrestricted Current Assets and Liabilities	=	2.71	1.89

The current ratio for 19X2 is significantly above that for 19X1. We already know that cash and cash equivalents increased significantly between 19X1 and 19X2.

The current ratios along with the composition of the current unrestricted assets provide an initial liquidity profile for these types of assets and liabilities. The use of industry-specific ratios would also sharpen the financial analysis.

TEMPORARILY RESTRICTED ASSETS AND THE CURRENT RATIO

The calculation of the current ratio has used the current unrestricted assets and liabilities. However, there are temporarily restricted assets that are expected to be realized in the form of cash over the normal operating cycle or one year, whichever comes later. These temporarily restricted assets have not been taken into account in calculating the current ratios for unrestricted current assets. The most important of these temporarily restricted assets are Pledges Receivable arising from gifts to finance operating activities. There are two types of Pledges Receivable: (a) unconditional and unrestricted Pledges Receivable, and (b) Pledges Receivable temporarily restricted for operating purposes. In addition to Pledges Receivable, there are Grants Receivable that are temporarily restricted to financing particular operating activities.

Temporarily restricted Pledges Receivable in Exhibit 1 of Chapter 15 shows the following breakdown at June 30, 19X2 and 19X1:

	19X2	19X1
Pledges Receivable	$2,551,822	$2,249,494
Less: Pledges Receivable, Temporarily Restricted for Capital Acquisition	212,000	128,000

Unrestricted and Temporarily Restricted Pledges Receivable for Operations	2,339,822	2,121,494
Temporarily Restricted Grants Receivable	<u>79,972</u>	<u>55,022</u>
Current Temporarily Restricted Assets	<u>$2,419,794</u>	<u>$2,176,516</u>

The breakdown in the composition of the temporarily restricted Pledges Receivable is available from information provided in Notes F and G of the Notes to the Financial Statements.

Using these figures, you arrive at alternative calculations for the current ratios at June 30, 19X2 and 19X1 of:

		19X2	19X1
Current Unrestricted Assets + Current Assets Temporarily <u>Restricted for Operations</u>	=	$2,317,207 + $2,419,794	$1,323,321 + $2,176,516
Current Unrestricted Liabilities		$855,880	$699,858
Current Ratio for Unrestricted Assets + Current Temporarily Restricted Assets for Operations and Current Liabilities	=	5.53	5.00

The inclusion of the current assets temporarily restricted for operating activities has a significant impact on the value of the current ratio. The nature of the restrictions that apply to pledges receivable would determine the degree to which the alternative ratios are appropriate. You should also understand that the major portion of pledges receivable are unrestricted despite the manner of their reporting. This information is provided to us in the Notes to the Financial Statements. The analysis of the liquidity of particular assets that enter into the calculation of the current ratio will be discussed subsequently.

LIMITATIONS OF THE CURRENT RATIO

The current ratio is a very limited measure of liquidity and the degree to which current assets can be used to pay off current liabilities. There are limitations to the use of the current ratio as a precise indicator of liquidity.

Generally speaking, unless an entity is ready to close its doors, it cannot simply convert its current assets to cash to pay its current liabilities immediately. It is likely that current assets are largely required for current operations. Of course, there may be excess amounts of current assets available to pay off current liabilities without jeopardizing the need of current assets for operating activities.

You should also note that management must forecast which assets will be converted to cash and which liabilities will be repaid through the use of cash over the normal operating cycle or one year, whichever is later. Thus, the measures of current assets and current liabilities may have a significant subjective component, based on management judgments and forecasts.

The current assets are not usually uniformly liquid and comparably convertible to cash. Certainly, Inventories of Supplies are less liquid than Accounts Receivable. Prepaid expenses are not a liquid asset as such, but are included in the current assets because such prepayments conserve cash in the future.

An alternative calculation of the current ratio was provided using pledges and grants receivable that were classified as temporarily restricted in the Statement of Financial Position. The liquidity of Pledges Receivable would differ somewhat from the liquidity of Accounts Receivable or Grants Receivable. The alternative calculation of the current ratio adds an additional dimension to the problem of uniformity of liquidity among the current assets.

The valuation of current assets and liabilities also enters into the calculation of the current ratio. Different measures of the value of these assets and liabilities are used for reporting purposes. Current market value as well as historical cost are typical methods of valuing the current assets and current liabilities. The actual market value to be recovered in cash form upon the liquidation of such assets could differ significantly from the values shown on the books and in the financial statements. Rapid versus orderly liquidation of assets can have a significant impact on cash realized from their sale.

The financial risk associated with certain of the current assets is not apparent directly from the calculation of the current ratio. For example, the concentration or diversification of Accounts Receivable or Pledges Receivable is not apparent from the disclosure provided. However, it is a requirement of financial reporting of business entities that such disclosures be made when material. The reduction of receivables through the use of allowances for uncollectibles is considered an appropriate approach to accounting for collection risk. Whether a particular not-for-profit entity provides for an adequate allowance for uncollectibles and for financial risk must be judged separately.

Current ratios generally are calculated using annual data. Seasonality in cash flows also affects liquidity. As a result, the effect of seasonality on liquidity will not be revealed through the use of the current ratio.

USING THE ACID-TEST OR QUICK RATIO

One of the limitations noted in the use of the current ratio is the lack of uniformity of liquidity of the current assets. An alternative ratio is the *Quick* or *Acid-Test* ratio. In place of the current assets are the *quick* assets. The *quick* unrestricted assets generally exclude inventories of supplies and prepaid expenses. The *quick* unrestricted assets are composed of cash and cash equivalents, accounts receivable, and investment income receivable.

		19X2	19X1
Quick Unrestricted Assets	=	$1,795,738	$700,248
Current Unrestricted Liabilities		$ 855,880	$699,858
Acid-Test or Quick Ratio	=	2.10	1.00

The exclusion of inventory of supplies and prepaid expenses results in significantly lower quick ratios than the initial current ratios calculated earlier. The increase in liquidity between 19X1 and 19X2 is even more apparent than for the initial calculation of the current ratio. The increase in cash and cash equivalents between 19X1 and 19X2 has an even more dominant affect on the quick ratio than on the current ratio.

ACCOUNTS RECEIVABLE AND THE TURNOVER RATIO

We turn from an examination of liquidity in terms of the current and quick assets to a closer look at the liquidity of the most important of the *unrestricted* current assets, accounts receivable.

One measure of the liquidity of accounts receivable is the average accounts receivable turnover ratio. Note that accounts receivable is measured net of uncollectible accounts. The average net accounts receivable turnover ratio is the number of times the average net accounts receivable "turns over" relative to the sales on credit that generate net accounts receivable. In the case of the NPO, the measure of sales on credit is in terms of "fees for services on credit."

Note also that if accounts receivable is to be measured net of uncollectible accounts, then sales on credit must also be measured net of uncollectible accounts. Normally, uncollectible accounts are treated as an expense in the statement that reports on operating activities. However, for purposes of measuring the turnover of net accounts receivable, the provision for bad debts expense is treated as a reduction of revenues from fees for services on credit.

Accounts Receivable and Revenues from Fees for Services are measured in different ways. Revenue from Fees for Services takes place over a period of time. Accounts Receivable are measured as an amount on a particular date. The ratio of Revenues from Fees for Services to Accounts Receivable assumes that both variables are measured in the same way. Average Accounts Receivable is an attempt to measure Accounts Receivable in the same way as Revenues from Fees for Services.

Using the *illustrative* data from the financial statements in Exhibits 1 and 15, and from Note B in Exhibit 3 (all in Chapter 15), the average accounts receivable turnover ratio is calculated as follows:

$$\frac{\text{Revenues from fees for services}}{\text{Average Net Accounts Receivable}} = \frac{\$2,991,495 - \$35,000}{\$430,673}$$

(Net of Estimated Provision for Bad Debts)

Average Net Accounts Receivable Turnover = 6.86 times

Given the Revenues from Fees for Services, the average Accounts Receivable balance is extended and collected almost *seven times* over the course of the year between June 30, 19X1 and June 30, 19X2.

Is this an appropriate turnover rate? Industry specific data would provide a benchmark against which to judge a turnover ratio for a particular not-for-profit organization. We will turn next to an alternative manner of measuring the rapidity with which accounts receivable is collected.

ACCOUNTS RECEIVABLE AND THE COLLECTION PERIOD

An alternative measure of how rapidly Accounts Receivable is collected is the Collection Period for the *ending* accounts receivable stated in terms of days. To calculate the collection period in days requires that annual revenues from fees for services be converted to daily revenues from fees for services.

How many days should be assumed for the calculation of daily revenues from fees for services? That depends on how services are delivered. Are they delivered every day of the year? If the answer is yes, then the number of days to be used will equal the number of days in that year. The number of days would be 365 or 366.

If services are delivered during a five-day workweek, then the number of days that year in five-day workweeks should be used. The number of days would be 52 weeks times 5 days per week which equals 260 days.

For our illustration, we shall assume that services were provided every day of the year, i.e., 365 days. The average daily net revenues from fees for services is calculated as follows:

$$\frac{\text{Revenues from fees for services net of estimated uncollectibles}}{\text{Number of days of services}} \quad = \quad \frac{\$2,991,495 - \$35,000}{365}$$

Average daily revenues from
fees for services net of
estimated uncollectibles   =   \$8,100/day

Using the average daily revenues from fees for services, the collection period for the ending accounts receivable is calculated as follows:

$$\frac{\text{Ending net accounts receivable}}{\begin{array}{l}\text{Average daily revenues from}\\\text{fees for services net of}\\\text{estimated uncollectibles}\end{array}} \quad = \quad \frac{\$415,467}{\$8,100/\text{day}}$$

Collection period for
ending net accounts receivable   =   51.29 days

ALTERNATIVE COLLECTION PERIODS

An alternative calculation for the collection period would be for the average Accounts Receivable. That collection period would be calculated as follows:

Average net accounts receivable   = $430,673

Average daily revenues from $8,100/day
fees for services net of estimated
uncollectibles

Collection period for average
net accounts receivable   =   53.17 days

Note that the accounts receivable turnover ratio times the collection period for the average Accounts Receivable would be equal to the number of days of services.

Number of Days of Services	=	(Turnover Ratio)	times	(Collection Period for Average Accounts Receivable)
365	=	6.8648	×	53.1695

In the illustrative example, the collection period for the ending accounts receivable has improved somewhat over that for the average accounts receivable by dropping from approximately 53 to 51 days.

You can carry the comparative analysis further by calculating the collection period for the beginning accounts receivable. In order to do this, you need information on the prior year's revenues from fees for services as well as the prior year's number of days of services. Let's assume that for 19X1, revenues from fees for services were $2,750,000 and that days of services were again 365 so that daily revenues were equal to $7,534.

Beginning net accounts receivable   = $445,879

Average daily revenues from fees $7,534/day
for services for 19X1 net of
estimated uncollectibles

Collection period for beginning
net accounts receivable   =   59.18 days

The improvement in the collection period between the beginning of the fiscal year of approximately 59 days to 51 days at the end of the fiscal year is quite significant. It is better than a 15% improvement.

Industry specific data would be helpful in determining an appropriate collection period against which to judge the collection period calculated in our illustrative example.

Aging and Size Distribution of Accounts Receivable

Analysis required for the management of the collection of accounts receivable calls for far more than the calculation of turnover ratios and collection periods. These calculations are for external users of financial statements. These simple calculations provide a quick overall impression of the current status of accounts receivable.

Management of accounts receivable requires pinpoint information. Whose accounts are the oldest? Of the oldest accounts, which are the largest still outstanding? The answer to these questions requires further analysis of the accounts receivable. The analysis required would be both a time distribution and a size distribution of accounts receivable.

The time distribution would be the standard "aging" of accounts receivable. Accounts receivable are analyzed and classified by billing period. The usual billing period is monthly. How many billing periods has a particular account receivable remained outstanding and unpaid? The aging analysis is performed and a schedule or report is prepared to answer this question.

The aging schedule or report would be prepared using the following format:

			Balances		
Customers' or Clients'			Days Past Due		
Accounts Receivable	Balances	Current	0–30	31–60	61–90	Over 90

The aging or time distribution report would be first prepared with the customers or clients of the NPO listed in alphabetical order. The same report could then be sorted by the size of the balances outstanding. The sorting would be done for each of the time distribution categories. The end result would be a separate schedule that shows both the oldest and largest accounts receivable by age.

Pledges Receivable and Turnover

Turnover ratios can be calculated for Pledges Receivable just as for Accounts Receivable. The turnover ratio would be calculated as the ratio of contributions from pledges for reporting purposes divided by average pledges receivable for reporting purposes.

The figure for unconditional and unrestricted gross contributions from pledges for operating purposes for 19X2 is provided explicitly in Note L of the Notes to the Financial Statements in Exhibit 16 of Chapter 15. This amount for gross contributions is given at $9,911,407. We require the amount for net contributions to take account of the reduction for estimated uncollectible contributions. The amount of the estimate for uncollectible, unconditional and unrestricted pledges is given at $350,000 in Note G in Exhibit 8 of Chapter 15. The amount of net unconditional and unrestricted contributions is thus $9,561,407.

The amount for average of unconditional and unrestricted pledges receivable net of uncollectibles can be calculated from the information in Note G.

Average Net Pledges Receivable = $$\frac{\$1,834,624 + \$2,113,325}{2}$$

Average Net Pledges Receivable = $1,973,975

The calculation of the turnover ratio is as follows:

Net Contributions for Operating
Purposes from Pledges = $9,561,407
Average Net Pledges Receivable $1,973,975

Pledges Receivable Turnover Ratio = 4.84

The turnover ratio of unconditional and unrestricted, average, net Pledges Receivable for operating purposes is significantly lower than the turnover ratio for average Accounts Receivable.

PLEDGES RECEIVABLE—DEFINING THE COLLECTION PERIOD

The lower turnover ratio for pledges receivable means a longer collection period. The collection period for accounts receivable is expressed in days. Days are used because these are related to the manner of delivering services that for our *illustrative* NPO, are on a daily basis. In contrast, pledges do not seem to have a "natural" period for activity. Therefore, the choice of measuring the collection period for pledges would be a matter of judgment for the management of a not-for-profit organization. It would also depend on the "collection cycle" for pledges. Are outstanding and unpaid pledges billed on a monthly or some other basis? We shall assume the monthly billing cycle to be the "natural" period for the measurement of the collection period for Pledges Receivable.

PLEDGES RECEIVABLE-CALCULATING THE COLLECTION PERIOD

You need to calculate the monthly contributions before calculating the collection period. That calculation is as follows:

Contributions for operating purposes
net of estimated uncollectibles   = $9,911,407–$350,000
Number of billing cycles   12

Average billed monthly contributions
for operating purposes net of
estimated uncollectibles   = $796,784/month

Using the average billed monthly contributions for operating purposes net of uncollectibles, the collection period for the ending pledges receivable is calculated as follows:

Ending net pledges receivable   = $2,113,325
Average billed monthly contributions $796,784/month
for operating purposes net of estimated
uncollectibles

Collection period for Net Pledges
Receivable for Operating Purposes   =   2.65 Months

AGING AND SIZE DISTRIBUTION OF PLEDGES RECEIVABLE

Does the collection period for pledges fall short of expectations and collection effort? Are there any industry norms against which to judge the NPO's effectiveness in collecting its pledges? Both a time distribution and size distribution of pledges receivable should be prepared similar to the time and size distribution schedules prepared for accounts receivable.

ANALYSIS OF OTHER RECEIVABLES

Other pledges and grants receivable would be analyzed in the same manner as illustrated already for accounts and pledges receivable. External users could calculate turnover ratios and collection periods. Those responsible for managing the collection of pledges and grants receivable would receive time and size distribution information.

INVENTORY OF SUPPLIES AND THE TURNOVER RATIO

In the case of the inventory of supplies, the analysis is focused on efficiency of usage and not on liquidity. Turnover ratio in the case of inventory of supplies is a measure of how efficiently supplies are used and whether excess inventory is being held relative to usage.

The average inventory turnover usage ratio is the ratio of the "annual total supplies expense" to the "average total inventory of supplies." The *illustrative* data for calculating the average total inventory of supplies is found in Exhibit 1 of Chapter 15.

$$\text{Average Inventory of Supplies} = \frac{\$360,648 + \$408,616}{2}$$

Average Inventory of Supplies   = $384,632

The *illustrative* data for the annual total supplies expense is from Note N of the Notes to the Financial Statements in Exhibit 18 of Chapter 15. The data in that note provide the following information on supplies expense:

Program A	$ 42,268
Program B	184,170
Program C	95,397
Management & General	19,418
Fund-Raising	22,784
Total	$364,037

Given the above information, the average inventory turnover usage ratio can be calculated as follows:

$$\frac{\text{Annual total supplies expense}}{\text{Average total inventory of supplies}} = \frac{\$364,037}{\$384,632}$$

Average inventory turnover usage ratio   =   0.95

The turnover ratio appears to be quite low. Inventory of supplies appears to be in excess and is not being used efficiently. The next stage of analysis is quite appropriate.

INVENTORY OF SUPPLIES AND AVAILABLE DAYS OF USE

At what rate are supplies being used? How rapidly would the current level of use of supplies deplete the inventory of supplies? The calculation of the "available days of use of the ending inventory of supplies" will help answer these questions.

First, it is necessary to calculate the average daily total supplies expense. To calculate this average, you must understand the number of days that involve using supplies. In other words, what are the workdays for the various programs and support services that require supplies? Are supplies used every day of the year by a particular program? The appropriate number of days for that program would be 365 or 366. If supplies are only used during five-day workdays, for that program the appropriate number of days would be 260. For purposes of the *illustration*, the number of days of use of supplies for the programs and supporting activities is calculated as a weighted average of 348.68 days over the course of a year.

Annual total supplies expenses	=	$364,037
Average number of days of supplies' use		348.68
Average daily total supplies expense	=	$1,044/day

The available days of use of the ending inventory of supplies is calculated as follows:

Ending total inventory of supplies	=	$360,648
Average daily total supplies expense		$1,044/day
Available days of use of the ending inventory of supplies	=	345 days

Given the weighted average of 348.68 days of use of supplies over the course of the year, the ending inventory has supplies in stock for a full year. The level of inventory of supplies is excessive and requires close management attention.

ANALYSIS OF THE STATEMENT OF ACTIVITY

ANALYSIS OF ACTIVITIES—BUDGET VS. ACTUAL

The Statement of Activities reports on the operations of the NPO in terms of the actual revenues and expenses resulting from operations. Note that revenues are quite broadly defined by the FASB to include both traditional revenue items arising from exchange transactions and support in the form of contributions and grants that do not involve exchanges. However, the external user is handicapped in understanding management decisions that have shaped the operating results reported in the income statement. There is no requirement by the FASB that NPOs report on the plans and budgets that reflect the management decisions that affected critically on operating activities. The Statement of Activities is an incomplete report from the point of view of the external user of financial statements.

To remedy the incompleteness of the Statement of Activities for the external user, we provide an analysis of activities for 19X2 in terms of a budget versus actual *illustrative* statement. *This is not a required statement for external reporting.* It is illustrative of what is normally available to the managers of an NPO. Exhibit 3 presents an "Analysis of Activities—Budget vs. Actual."

The budget called for a surplus from operating activities of $1,214,259 while the actual surplus is reported at $822,956. The bottom line shows an unfavorable variance of almost $400,000. A significant portion of that shortfall is due to the fact that the annual campaign fell short of its goal by more than $450,000. This shortfall was not reflected by reductions in the level of spending: rather, the actual surplus absorbed the difference.

We are dealing with an NPO that normally provides socially valuable and necessary services. We are assuming that our NPO's activities are recognized as qualifying under the provisions of tax law to benefit contributors. Contributors may or may not have expected their contributions and gifts would finance not only the socially necessary services of our NPO, but also generate a surplus. A surplus that is unanticipated is different from one that is planned. Trustee policy with respect to explaining the nature of surpluses would be appropriate. How and when this is done is a matter of judgment.

The external user and financial analyst would certainly find the information in the analysis in Exhibit 3 quite useful. But again note that it is not a required statement. Clearly, the information in Exhibit 3 is directed at the managers of the NPO. Analysis of variances of individual revenue and expense items would be the responsibility of individual managers.

ADDITIONAL ANALYSIS OF OPERATING ACTIVITIES

Exhibit 3 reports on expenses in a programmatic fashion. A detailed analysis of the individual items in Exhibit 3 would also call for a detailed review of expenses both in terms of program and in terms of object of expense. Exhibit 4 presents a common size analysis of actual expenses by object of expenses. Since we have reached the budget versus actual stage, Exhibit 5 presents budgeted expenses by object of expenses. Exhibit 6 presents a common size analysis of the budgeted expenses by object of expense. Exhibit 7 presents the variances that result from a comparison of individual actual expense items with their budget counterparts.

EXHIBIT 3

NPO Organization

Analysis of Activities -- Budget and Actual

Year Ended June 30, 19X2

	Actual Amounts	Actual Percent	Budget Amounts	Budget Percent	Variances Favorable (Unfavorable)
Changes in unrestricted net assets:					
Revenues and gains:					
Contributions (Note L)	$9,282,706	63.52%	$9,750,000	65.02%	($467,294)
Fees for services	2,991,495	20.47%	3,000,000	20.01%	(8,505)
Income on long-term investments	312,003	2.13%	350,000	2.33%	(37,997)
Income on short-term investments	24,276	0.17%	20,000	0.13%	4,276
Gain on sales of fixed assets	25,094	0.17%			25,094
Total unrestricted support, revenues, and gains	12,635,574	86.46%	13,120,000	87.50%	(484,426)
Net assets released from restrictions:					
Satisfaction of program restrictions	499,956	3.42%	475,000	3.17%	24,956
Satisfaction of equipment acquisition restrictions	1,161,763	7.95%	1,100,000	7.34%	61,763
Expiration of time restrictions	316,870	2.17%	300,000	2.00%	16,870
Net assets released from restrictions	1,978,589	13.54%	1,875,000	12.50%	103,589
Total unrestricted support, revenues, and other gains	14,614,163	100.00%	14,995,000	100.00%	(380,837)
Expenses:					
Program A	1,929,613	13.20%	1,800,000	12.00%	(129,613)
Program B	6,688,427	45.77%	6,800,000	45.35%	111,573
Program C	3,034,131	20.76%	3,100,000	20.67%	65,869
Management & General	555,677	3.80%	530,000	3.53%	(25,677)
Fund-Raising	354,421	2.43%	330,000	2.20%	(24,421)
Depreciation	937,589	6.42%	940,000	6.27%	2,411
Interest expense on line of credit	13,607	0.09%	8,000	0.05%	(5,607)
Provision for uncollectible accounts	35,000	0.24%	30,000	0.20%	(5,000)
Total expenses before interest on long-term debt	13,548,466	92.71%	13,538,000	90.28%	(10,466)

EXHIBIT 3, continued

Excess (deficiency) of support and revenue over expenses before interest on long-term debt	1,065,697	7.29%	1,457,000	9.72%	(391,303)
Interest expense on long-term debt	242,741	1.66%	242,741	1.62%	0
Increase in unrestricted net assets	822,956	5.63%	1,214,259	8.10%	(391,303)
Temporarily restricted net assets:					
Contributions for capital purposes	2,084,000	14.26%	2,500,000	16.67%	(416,000)
Contributions for operating purposes	535,198	3.66%	500,000	3.33%	35,198
Grants for operating purposes	524,905	3.59%	500,000	3.33%	24,905
Investment income for capital purposes	15,886	0.11%	20,000	0.13%	(4,114)
Net assets released from restrictions	(1,978,589)	-13.54%	(1,875,000)	-12.50%	(103,589)
	1,181,399	8.08%	1,645,000	10.97%	(463,601)
Permanently restricted net assets:					
Contributions	311,923	2.13%	400,000	2.67%	(88,077)
Investment income on endowment	18,944	0.13%	20,000	0.13%	(1,056)
Net realized and unrealized gains on long-term investments	125,000	0.86%			125,000
	455,867	3.12%	420,000	2.80%	35,867
Increase in net assets	2,460,223		3,279,259		(819,036)
Net assets, 7/1/19x1	8,239,664		8,239,664		0
Net assets, 6/30/19x2	$10,699,887		$11,518,923		($819,036)

EXHIBIT 4

Common Size Analysis of Expenses--By Object Classification --Programs A, B, C, Management and General, and Fund-Raising

Expense Object Classifications	Program A	Program B	Program C	Management & General	Fund Raising	Total
Salaries	56.76%	57.97%	58.24%	60.33%	53.57%	57.83%
Employee benefits	10.92%	11.16%	11.21%	11.61%	10.31%	11.13%
Payroll Taxes	4.35%	4.44%	4.46%	4.62%	4.10%	4.43%
Personnel Expenses	72.03%	73.57%	73.90%	76.56%	67.99%	73.39%
Professional fees	2.16%	3.62%	0.00%	5.77%	0.00%	2.52%
Contractual services	1.08%	2.49%	1.82%	0.00%	0.00%	1.93%
Facilities rents	3.05%	2.46%	0.00%	2.85%	0.00%	1.91%
Insurance	0.48%	0.51%	0.53%	2.30%	0.00%	0.57%
Utilities	0.95%	1.38%	1.24%	1.35%	0.00%	1.24%
Telephone	1.33%	0.80%	1.04%	1.85%	10.00%	1.24%
Heating	2.38%	2.17%	2.29%	2.32%	0.00%	2.18%
Equipment rentals	2.88%	3.19%	0.88%	0.00%	0.00%	2.35%
Maintanance and repairs	1.05%	1.55%	0.47%	1.35%	0.00%	1.16%
Project materials	1.96%	0.00%	6.18%	0.00%	0.00%	1.79%
Supplies	2.19%	2.75%	3.14%	3.49%	6.43%	2.90%
Printing and publications	0.29%	0.43%	1.65%	0.58%	10.71%	1.00%
Postage and shipping	1.24%	2.10%	1.27%	0.58%	4.87%	1.78%
Conference and meetings	1.85%	1.30%	2.18%	0.63%	0.00%	1.53%
Travel	0.71%	1.23%	3.29%	0.29%	0.00%	1.57%
Assistance to clients	4.19%	0.00%	0.00%	0.00%	0.00%	0.64%
Miscellaneous	0.19%	0.43%	0.11%	0.09%	0.00%	0.29%
Other than Personnel Expenses	27.97%	26.43%	26.10%	23.44%	32.01%	26.61%
Total Program & Supporting Activities Expenses	100.00%	100.00%	100.00%	100.00%	100.00%	100.00%

Note: Depreciation Expense, Provision for Bad Debts and Interest Expense are not included.

EXHIBIT 5

**Budgeted Expenses--By Object Classification --Programs A, B, C,
Management and General, and Fund-Raising**

Expense Object Classifications	Program A	Program B	Program C	Management & General	Fund-Raising	Totals
Salaries	$1,024,771	$3,975,781	$1,797,817	$318,028	$178,119	$7,294,517
Employee benefits	197,217	765,197	346,030	61,202	34,283	1,403,930
Payroll Taxes	78,511	304,622	137,753	24,364	13,648	558,898
	1,300,500	5,045,600	2,281,600	403,595	226,050	9,257,345
Professional fees	45,000	244,800	0	31,800	0	321,600
Contractual services	18,000	170,000	62,000	0	0	250,000
Facilities rents	54,000	170,000	0	15,900	0	239,900
Insurance	9,000	34,000	15,500	13,250	0	71,750
Utilities	18,000	102,000	38,750	6,890	0	165,640
Telephone	22,500	61,200	31,000	10,070	33,000	157,770
Heating	36,000	136,000	69,750	12,190	0	253,940
Equipment rentals	54,000	204,000	27,900	0	0	285,900
Maintenance and repairs	18,000	102,000	15,500	7,420	0	142,920
Projects materials	36,000	0	186,000	0	0	222,000
Supplies	36,000	170,000	93,000	17,225	19,800	336,025
Printing and publications	5,400	34,000	54,250	3,180	33,000	129,830
Postage and shipping	22,500	136,000	38,750	3,180	16,500	216,930
Conference and meetings	27,000	81,600	69,750	3,180	0	181,530
Travel	13,500	74,800	100,750	1,590	0	190,640
Assitance to clients	81,000	0	0	0	0	81,000
Miscellaneous	3,600	34,000	15,500	530	1,650	55,280
Other than Personnel Expenses	499,500	1,754,400	818,400	126,405	103,950	3,302,655
Total Program & Supporting Activities Expenses	$1,800,000	$6,800,000	$3,100,000	$530,000	$330,000	$12,560,000

Note: Depreciation Expense, Provision for Bad Debts and Interest Expense are not included.

EXHIBIT 6

Common Size Analysis of Budgeted Expenses--By Object Classification --Programs A, B, C,
Management and General, and Fund-Raising

Expense Object Classifications	Program A	Program B	Program C	Management & General	Fund-Raising	Total
Salaries	56.93%	58.47%	57.99%	60.01%	53.98%	58.08%
Employee benefits	10.96%	11.25%	11.16%	11.55%	10.39%	11.18%
Payroll Taxes	4.36%	4.48%	4.44%	4.60%	4.14%	4.45%
Personnel Expenses	72.25%	74.20%	73.60%	76.15%	68.51%	73.70%
Professional fees	2.50%	3.60%	0.00%	6.00%	0.00%	2.56%
Contractual services	1.00%	2.50%	2.00%	0.00%	0.00%	1.99%
Facilities rents	3.00%	2.50%	0.00%	3.00%	0.00%	1.91%
Insurance	0.50%	0.50%	0.50%	2.50%	0.00%	0.57%
Utilities	1.00%	1.50%	1.25%	1.30%	0.00%	1.32%
Telephone	1.25%	0.90%	1.00%	1.90%	0.00%	1.26%
Heating	2.00%	2.00%	2.25%	2.30%	10.00%	2.02%
Equipment rentals	3.00%	3.00%	0.90%	0.00%	0.00%	2.28%
Maintenance and repairs	1.00%	1.50%	0.50%	1.40%	0.00%	1.14%
Projects materials	2.00%	0.00%	6.00%	0.00%	0.00%	1.77%
Supplies	2.00%	2.50%	3.00%	3.25%	6.00%	2.68%
Printing and publications	0.30%	0.50%	1.75%	0.60%	10.00%	1.03%
Postage and shipping	1.25%	2.00%	1.25%	0.60%	5.00%	1.73%
Conference and meetings	1.50%	1.20%	2.25%	0.60%	0.00%	1.45%
Travel	0.75%	1.10%	3.25%	0.30%	0.00%	1.52%
Assistance to clients	4.50%	0.00%	0.00%	0.00%	0.00%	0.64%
Miscellaneous	0.20%	0.50%	0.50%	0.10%	0.50%	0.44%
Other than Personnel Expenses	27.75%	25.80%	26.40%	23.85%	31.50%	26.30%
Total Program & Supporting Activities Expenses	100.00%	100.00%	100.00%	100.00%	100.00%	100.00%

Note: Depreciation Expense, Provision for Bad Debts and Interest Expense are not included.

EXHIBIT 7

Variance Analysis of Budgeted vs. Actual Expenses--By Object Classification -- Programs A, B, C, Management and General, and Fund-Raising

Expense Object Classifications	Program A	Program B	Program C	Management & General	Fund- Raising	Total
Salaries	($70,415)	$98,432	$30,882	($17,195)	($11,749)	$29,955
Employee benefits	(13,558)	18,978	5,973	(3,314)	(2,258)	5,821
Payroll taxes	(5,397)	7,555	2,378	(1,319)	(899)	2,317
Personnel Expenses	(89,369)	124,965	39,232	(21,827)	(14,906)	38,094
Professional fees	3,279	2,466	0	(258)	0	5,486
Contractual services	(2,861)	3,274	6,672	0	0	7,085
Facilities rents	(4,807)	5,213	0	54	0	459
Insurance	(189)	73	(563)	480	0	(198)
Utilities	(377)	9,913	1,270	(590)	0	10,215
Telephone	(3,228)	7,886	(591)	(189)	(2,442)	(1,437)
Heating	(9,943)	(9,401)	143	(687)	0	(19,887)
Equipment rentals	(1,499)	(9,258)	1,128	0	0	(9,629)
Maintenance and repairs	(2,215)	(1,719)	1,222	(60)	0	(2,773)
Projects materials	(1,765)	0	(1,402)	0	0	(3,167)
Supplies	(6,268)	(14,170)	(2,397)	(2,193)	(2,984)	(28,012)
Printing and publications	(113)	4,920	4,276	(26)	4,973	4,084
Postage and shipping	(1,390)	(4,554)	288	(26)	(765)	(6,448)
Conferences and meetings	(8,744)	(5,640)	3,713	(346)	0	(11,018)
Travel	(283)	(7,594)	802	(13)	0	(7,087)
Assistance to clients	140	0	0	0	0	140
Miscellaneous	21	5,199	12,075	4	1,650	18,949
Other than Personnel Expenses	(40,243)	(13,392)	26,637	(3,850)	(9,514)	(40,364)
Total Program & Supporting Activities Expenses	($129,613)	$111,573	$65,869	($25,678)	($24,421)	($2,270)

Note: Depreciation Expense, Provision for Bad Debts and Interest Expense are not included.

STATEMENT OF CASH FLOWS

The Statement of Cash Flows was analyzed and dissected in great detail in Chapter 15. The basic relationships between cash flows and the items in the other financial statements have also been discussed in the previous chapter so that there is no need to repeat this discussion. Instead, the Statement of Cash Flows will be used to analyze circumstances of financial stress.

FINANCIAL STRESS

The *illustrative* NPO we have discussed has areas that require management attention. However, from the *illustrative* data presented, the issues are not life threatening for the NPO. We turn next to coping with the serious circumstances of financial stress.

In the case of the *illustrative* NPO, the Statement of Cash Flows (Exhibit 29 of Chapter 15) reveals that cash inflows from operations exceeded outflows for the current fiscal year by over $800,000. Cash flows from financing activities exceeded outflows from investing activities by another $300,000. By the end of the fiscal year cash balances had risen from an initial amount of $233,422 to an ending balance of $1,363,238.

Again, using the Statement of Cash Flows, we see that total cash outflows from operations were $12,500,000 before any consideration for interest expense. Average monthly cash outflows were around $1,041,600 per month. Total cash inflows from operations operating sources—such as contributions, grants and revenues from fees—were about $13,100,000. Average cash inflows are about $1,091,600 per month. There was a basic cash surplus of about $50,000 per month from these operating inflows and outflows to give an annual cash surplus of $600,000.

The potential surplus of $600,000 became the reported surplus of about $821,000. This increase of $221,000 is the result, in part, because of investment income of $300,000, interest income of $24,250, and cash released for equipment acquisitions of $153,600 for additional total inflows of about $477,850. Additional outflows were for long-term interest at $242,750 and short-term interest at $13,600 for a total of $256,350. Net additional cash inflows were about $221,000. Thus, we can identify the sources and uses of cash that resulted in the $821,000 cash surplus from operations.

Financial difficulties can arise when cash outflows from operations exceed cash inflows. Suppose circumstances in the following year for our *illustrative* NPO were less favorable. Rather than benefiting from cash inflows of

$50,000 per month from operations from such sources as contributions, grants, and revenues from fees, let's assume there were cash outflows of $150,000 per month so that operating sources such as contributions, revenues from fees, and grants generated a cash deficit of $1,800,000 for the year. Let's also assume this deficit was reduced by $150,000 because of cash inflows from investment income sources exceeded cash outflows for interest expense. The net cash inflow from operations would be $1,650,000.

Let's also assume that cash from financing sources just balanced cash flows into investments. The overall impact of these inflows and outflows of cash would be a cash reduction of $1,650,000 of the beginning balance for next year, which falls from a positive figure of about $1,363,000 to a potential negative balance of about $287,000. This is the potential negative balance before borrowing to maintain the minimum desired positive balance of $200,000.

The overall drop in cash during the year of $1,650,000 meant that there was an average monthly net cash outflow of $137,500. The initial positive balance of $1,363,000 was able to absorb the average monthly negative cash flow for a number of months. Actually, the initial cash balance of $1,363,000 overstates the available cash balance since our *illustrative* NPO desired a minimum cash balance of $200,000. Therefore, the cash balance available to absorb the negative cash flows was $1,163,000. At a net outflows of $137,500, there were some eight plus months of cash available to absorb these negative cash flows.

The potential negative cash position would have been recognized if the annual fund-raising campaign was carefully monitored. At the end of that campaign, the shortfall of contributions coupled with forecasted outflows from operations should have provided the first signs of an impending cash squeeze.

The shortfall in the annual campaign would have translated itself into a reduced level of cash inflows from contributions. Exhibit 23 of Chapter 15 provides a portrait of cash inflows from contributions over the course of the fiscal year. The effect of the shortfall is felt in a major way as early as the beginning of December since major cash inflows from contributions tend to begin in November.

RESPONSES TO FINANCIAL STRESS—THE INFLOWS SIDE

The tables in Exhibits 23 through 28 of Chapter 15 show historical cash inflows and outflows. A similar set of tables showing forecasted cash inflows and outflows is especially useful during periods of financial stress.

Actions must be taken either to increase inflows from various sources or decrease outflows or some combination thereof. This is fairly obvious. The key is early recognition of the extent of the negative cash outflow. Cash forecasts are a valuable tool in providing the needed early warning to detect financial distress.

INCREASING PLEDGED SUPPORT

Up-to-date information on current cash inflows and updated cash forecasts of inflows will focus attention on which sources of cash are falling short. During 19X2, pledges for operating purposes generated cash contributions of $9,600,000 out of $13,100,000 of cash from contributions, grants, and revenues from fees. Contributions generated about 73.3% of cash from these three major sources. Clearly, the Director of Fund-Raising would be responsible for providing an analysis of the factors that led to a less successful annual campaign for 19X3 than anticipated.

Some issues to be explored:

❐ Is the shortfall due to reductions in gift-giving by major donors or is it a general reduction across all classes of donors?

❐ Are general economic conditions more difficult? If so, what effect on gift-giving should have been anticipated due to generally reduced economic circumstances?

❐ Have there been changes in the tax laws that have made gift-giving less attractive for major contributors?

❐ Are the social services provided through the major programs of the NPO viewed with the same degree of social importance by our donors?

❐ Were there any aspects of the annual campaign judged to be less effective than the prior year?

INCREASING FEES FOR SERVICES

Cash generated from fees for services provided through Program B amounted to $3,000,000 in 19X2. Expenses directly identified with Program B amounted to $6,690,000. Expenses are not actually on a cash basis. Though not presented earlier, the actual cash outflows during 19X2 associated with Program B expenses were $6,600,000. The difference between expenses as reported in the Statement of Activities and cash expenses for Program B is $90,000. The real difference between the two figures has to do with changes in prepaid expenses, inventory of supplies and accounts payable associated with Program B activities. Generally, those sorts of details on a program-by-program basis would not necessarily be easily available from the accounting records of a particular not-for-profit organization.

Ultimately, what we are looking for is the gap between cash inflows from revenues from fees for services of Program B and cash outflows for expenses resulting from the activities of Program B. On a cash basis the gap is $3,600,000 for 19X2. The reported gap in the Statement of Activities is expenses of $6,690,000 less revenues from fees of about $2,990,000, equal to a gap of $3,700,000. The short-term cash gap is $3,600,000. The longer term cash gap is measured by the amounts in the Statement of Activities at $3,700,000. A short-fall in the annual campaign means that a lower level of contributions is available to close the gap between revenues from fees and expenses for Program B. As a result you must explore the possibility of increasing revenues from fees if the level of services of Program B is to be maintained.

Increasing fees excessively must be avoided if the charitable purpose of the program would be violated and unnecessary hardships would be placed upon the beneficiaries of the services. In the case of Program B, it is assumed that fees for services are paid directly by the beneficiaries of the services of that program. It was not made explicit, but the beneficiaries receive other types of social support that help defray their costs of Program B. Nevertheless, it is also assumed that fees for services would only cover part of the costs of Program B. Fees covered about 45% of the expenses of Program B during 19X2.

INCREASING GRANTS

Program A is partially supported by grants. Cash from grants for Program A is $500,000. Program A expenses reported in the Statement of Activities are $1,929,600. Cash outflows generated by expenses of Program A are about $2,000,200. The short-term cash gap is about $1,500,200. Support from grants in the Statement of Activities is also reported at $500,000. The longer term gap is $1,879,600. However the gap is measured, contributions available to close the gap between inflows and outflows have been reduced significantly. This suggests that greater attention must be paid to the possibility of increasing support from grants.

❏ Has the search for public and private grants been adequate?

❏ Have references such as the *Foundation Directory* been fully utilized?

❏ Have the right foundations been selected based on the nonprofit's activities? Does a foundation's philosophy and objectives match that of the nonprofit entity?

❏ Did the selected foundations require matching funds?

❏ Were applications to foundations carefully prepared with all relevant and necessary details included? Were uses of funds described adequately and as required?

❏ Were applications filed by due dates specified by the foundation? (Failure to file by due dates usually elicits automatic rejection.)

BORROWING

Where financial stress is expected to be short-term, there is also the possibility of borrowing to bridge the gap created by the temporary shortfall in contributions or other sources of cash inflows. This would permit services to continue at current levels for the various programs so that activities may be focused on obtaining increased support from contributors and granting agencies for the programs of the NPO for 19X3 and into the future.

Issues to be considered:

❏ Would borrowing unduly increase the NPO's debt burden?

❏ Is careful planning and forecasting being done to ensure the debt can be repaid?

❏ Is long-term borrowing generally being used in a growth circumstance? Such borrowing is generally inappropriate when extreme and extended financial distress is present.

❏ Collateralized loans that require property as security are generally used where lenders perceive greater risk or when borrowers wish to take advantage of lower interest rates than they would otherwise be able to obtain.

INVESTMENTS

The NPO has long-term investments in an endowment. Investment income from the endowment is unrestricted and available for financing operating activities.

Issues to be considered:

❑ What is the volatility of the securities in the portfolio?

❑ Is the portfolio considered adequately diversified? Is there an appropriate selection of securities whose returns are negatively correlated?

❑ Is total return on the portfolio considered adequate given the risk judged to be associated with the portfolio?

❑ Is there confidence in the investment advisers who provide guidance?

RESPONSES ON THE OUTFLOW SIDE

During times of financial stress, costs associated with programs and supporting activities are generally examined more closely to determine if reductions are possible without impairing services.

The reduction of costs is generally the less desirable and more difficult option for a not-for-profit entity than increasing inflows from various sources of cash. Cost reductions may only be possible through the reduction of vital social services. These are the same vital services that have induced contributed support.

Issues to be considered:

❑ Is it possible to rank program activities in order of social importance?

❑ If services must be reduced, lower priority programs would be reduced first.

❑ What effect would reducing program activities have on donors' willingness to contribute? Would it increase or decrease their support?

❑ How important are the services of volunteers? What would be the effect on volunteer services of reductions in program activities?

❐ For specific expenses such as fuel cost, have such costs been analyzed and various options considered, such as lowering costs by modifying the use of cars or trucks?

❐ Would the replacement of obsolete equipment or other assets result in cost reductions?

❐ Are there inactive assets that cause unnecessary maintenance costs?

❐ Have the latest technologies been explored for cost-reduction possibilities?

❐ Have cost reductions impaired necessary maintenance activities? Inadequate maintenance will be reflected in higher costs in the future.

❐ Have cost reductions impaired staff training programs and impaired staff productivity resulting in offsetting cost increases or losses in cost reductions?

❐ Are the costs of supporting activities—such as management & general and fund-raising—excessive?

The issues noted are suggestive of the items that need to be investigated, analyzed and acted upon.

INDICATORS OF POTENTIAL FAILURE

We turn from financial stress to the more serious circumstance of potential bankruptcy.

A nonprofit organization may experience financial stress so severe and so extended over time that it may be forced into bankruptcy. Signs of potential failure must be identified and corrected on a timely basis. "Red flags" must be recognized. A nonprofit that may appear at one time to have been financially strong may lose its financial viability if:

❐ Continued and extensive cash outflows have exceeded cash inflows without adequate trustee and management attention and response.

❐ Excessive debt levels have been incurred that generate burdensome levels of debt service to repay principal and pay interest.

❏ Understated and unreported liabilities have created unanticipated burdens.

❏ Underinsurance against known risks of loss that can be insured against has created unmanageable losses.

❏ Potential legal exposure was not recognized with resulting costs and losses that could not be managed effectively.

❏ Fund-raising activities have not generated the level of support for the level of expenditures required to maintain program activities.

❏ Operating costs have not been adequately controlled.

These are a sample of the signs and circumstances that could result in financial stress sufficiently severe as to bring about bankruptcy.

Some of the ways to manage extreme financial stress are listed below. The relevance of various methods to deal with financial stress and bankruptcy depends upon particular circumstances confronting the NPO. These include:

❏ Avoid debt levels and debt service that cannot be justified by financial circumstances and burdensome debt service.

❏ When debt is justified, arrange for manageable repayment schedules with staggered or installment payments on debt so that payments do not become due all at once.

❏ Choose maturity lengths of debt carefully considering financial circumstances. Lengthen the maturity dates of debt when necessary.

❏ Avoid the "balloon effect" when all debt comes due at one time.

❏ Take careful note of loan restrictions that the nonprofit may end up violating. Note how violations of such restrictions can be overcome with minimal damage. Avoid restrictions that pose special financial dangers.

❏ Plan and forecast financing needs carefully and continually so as to anticipate future financing needs and to minimize the cost of debt.

❏ Use a "hedging" approach to finance by matching the maturity dates of debt to the maturity dates of assets.

❐ Assure the adequacy of insurance coverage so as to minimize the dangers of predictable losses that may be economically insured against.

❐ Make necessary expenditures for viability and growth, such as research and development for those not-for-profits that are involved in research and development activities.

❐ Attempt to use current and proven development in technology that will result in the delivery of better and increased services through quality improvement or cost reductions.

❐ Avoid services that involve particular "problem" areas with which the NPO has insufficient knowledge and expertise.

❐ Avoid long-term, fixed-fee contracts where cost trends appear to be downward.

❐ Improve communication.

❐ Do not extend service activities if financial circumstances will not support such extensions.

❐ Develop and maintain open lines of credit with financial institutions.

❐ Obtain appropriate legal counsel to avoid possible litigation and losses from litigation.

❐ In times of extreme financial distress it may be necessary to seek a merger arrangement with an appropriate NPO counterpart where both entities might benefit from such an arrangement.

Again, the above methods of dealing with financial stress and extreme financial stress that may lead to bankruptcy are a starting point for analyzing and dealing with the problems. The trustees and managers must adapt, build upon, and add to the various suggested methods in the light of the particular circumstances with which they must cope.

MAINTAINING THE FLOW OF INFORMATION

Financial statement analysis by external users and financial analysis by managers and trustees can provide a valuable flow of information in the planning and control of the activities of the NPO. This provides a valuable set of tools from which to start and maintain an analysis to manage effectively the activities of the NPO.

Glossary of Budgeting Terms

ADMINISTRATIVE BUDGET   Formal and comprehensive financial plan through which management of an organization may control day-to-day business affairs and activities.

ALLOTMENT   Part of an appropriation that may be encumbered or expended during an allotment period, which is usually a period of time less than one fiscal year. Bi-monthly and quarterly allotment periods are most common.

ANALYSIS OF VARIANCES   Analysis and investigation of causes for variances between standard costs and actual costs; also called variance analysis. A variance is considered favorable if actual costs are less than standard costs; it is unfavorable if actual costs exceed standard costs. Unfavorable variances are the ones that need further investigation for their causes. Analysis of variances reveals the causes of these deviations. This feedback aids in planning future goals, controlling costs, evaluating performance, and taking corrective action. Management by exception is based on the analysis of variances and attention is given to only the variances that require remedial actions.

ANNUAL BUDGET   Budget prepared for a calendar or fiscal year. See also Long Range Budget.

BANKRUPTCY   Situation in which an entity's liabilities exceed the fair value of its assets.

BOND FUND   Fund established for the receipt and distribution of monies received from the issuance of a bond for a large nonprofit entity.

BONDED DEBT SERVICE   Expenses incurred for interest and redemption of bonds.

BREAK-EVEN ANALYSIS   Branch of *Cost-Volume-Revenue (CVR) analysis* that determines the break-even sales, which is the level of activity where total costs equal total revenue. See also Cost-Volume-Revenue Analysis.

BUDGET   Quantitative plan of financial operation consisting of an estimate of proposed revenue and expenditures for a specified time period and purpose. The budget expresses the organizational goals in terms of specific financial and operating objectives. Advantages of budget preparation are planning, communicating entity-wide goals to subunits, fostering cooperation among departments, control by evaluating actual figures to budget figures, and revealing the interrelationship of one function to another. See also Master Budget.

BUDGETARY ACCOUNTABILITY   Process of recording budgetary amounts in the accounts of a fund. Recording the balances has a dual effect. The control aspect of the budgetary function is stressed and recognition is given to the legal foundations of the budget.

BUDGET CONTROL   Budgetary actions carried out according to a budget plan. Through the use of a budget as a standard, an organization ensures that managers are implementing its plans and objectives and their activities are appraised by comparing their actual performance against budgeted performance. Budgets are used as a basis for rewarding or punishing them, or perhaps for modifying future budgets and plans. Budget cuts should be in the areas of least importance and/or having the least severe consequences (e.g., on quality of service performed). Spending and time limits may be placed on specific costs. What effect do budget cuts have on the scope, volume, or character of a program, on fund raising, or membership?

BUDGET VARIANCE   Any difference between a budgeted figure and an actual figure.

BUDGETING MODELS   Mathematical models that generate a profit-planning budget. The models help managers and budget analysts answer a variety of what-if questions. The resultant calculations provide a basis for choice among alternatives under conditions of uncertainty. Budgeting models are usually quantitative and computer-based. There are primarily two approaches to modeling: simulation and optimization. See also Financial Models; Simulation Models.

CAPITAL BUDGET   Budget or plan of proposed acquisitions and replacements of long-term assets and their financing. A capital budget is developed using a variety of capital budgeting techniques such as the payback method, the net present value (NPV) method, or the internal rate of return (IRR) method. See also Capital Budgeting.

CAPITAL BUDGETING   Process of making long-term planning decisions for capital investments. There are typically two types of investment decisions: (1) Selecting new facilities or expanding existing facilities. Examples include: (a) investments in long-term assets such as property, plant, and equipment; and (b) resource commitments in the form of new product development, market research, refunding of long-term debt, introduction of a computer, etc. (2) Replacing existing facilities with new facilities. Examples include replacing a manual bookkeeping system with a computerized system and replacing inefficient equipment with one that is newer.

CAPITAL EXPENDITURE BUDGET   Budget plan prepared for individual capital expenditure projects. The time span of this budget depends upon the project. Capital expenditures to be budgeted include replacement, acquisition, or construction of equipment. See also Capital Budgeting.

CAPITAL PROJECTS FUND   Fund that accounts for financial resources to be used for the acquisition or construction of capital facilities.

CAPITAL RATIONING   Problem of selecting the mix of acceptable projects that provide the highest overall net present value (NPV) where an entity has a limit on the budget for capital spending. The profitability index is used widely in ranking projects competing for limited funds.

CASH BUDGET   Budget for cash planning and control presenting expected cash inflow and outflow for a designated time period. The cash budget helps management keep cash balances in reasonable relationship to its needs. It aids in avoiding idle cash and possible cash shortages.

COLA   Cost of living allowance.

COLLEGE FUNDS   Funds set up for college and university accounting. It consists of current funds, loan funds, endowment funds, annuity and life funds, agency funds, and plant funds.

COMPREHENSIVE BUDGET   See Master Budget.

CONTINGENCY PLANNING   Adding a contingency account as a final budget item for unexpected occurrences such as a revenue shortfall.

CONTINUOUS BUDGET   Annual budget that continues to the earliest one month or period and adds the most recent one month or period, so that a twelve-month or other periodic forecast is always available.

CONTROL CONCEPT   Concept that ensures actions are carried out or implemented according to a plan or goal.

COST-BENEFIT ANALYSIS   Analysis to determine whether the favorable results of an alternative are sufficient to justify the cost of taking that alternative. This analysis is widely used in connection with capital expenditure projects.

COST CONTROL   Steps taken by management to assure that the cost objectives set down in the planning stage are attained, and to assure that all segments of the organization function in a manner consistent with its policies. For effective cost control, most organizations use standard cost systems, in which the actual costs are compared against standard costs for performance evaluation and the deviations are investigated for remedial actions. Cost control is also concerned with feedback that might change any or all of the future plans, the service method, or both.

COST EFFECTIVE   Among decision alternatives, the one whose cost is lower than its benefit. The most cost-effective program would be the one whose cost-benefit ratio is the lowest among various programs competing for a given amount of funds. See also Cost-Benefit Analysis.

COST-VOLUME FORMULA   Cost function in the form of

$$Y = a + bX$$

where Y = semivariable (or mixed) costs to be broken up

X = any given measure of activity such as volume and labor hours

a = fixed cost component

b = variable rate per unit of X

The formula is used for cost prediction and flexible budgeting purposes.

COST-VOLUME-REVENUE (CVR) ANALYSIS Analysis that deals with how revenue and costs change with a change in volume. More specifically, it looks at the effects on surplus or deficit of changes in such factors as variable costs, fixed costs, fees, volume, and mix of services rendered. By studying the relationships of costs, revenue and activity, an entity is better able to cope with many planning decisions.

DECISION SUPPORT SYSTEM (DSS) Branch of the broadly defined Management Information System (MIS). It is an information system that provides answers to problems and that integrates the decision maker into the system as a component. The system utilizes such quantitative techniques as regression and financial planning modeling. DSS software furnishes support to the manager in the decision-making process.

DEFICIT Excess of liabilities over assets.

DEFICIT SPENDING Excess of actual expenditures over actual revenue, also called an operating deficit.

DISCOUNTED CASH FLOW (DCF) TECHNIQUES Methods of selecting and ranking investment proposals such as the net present value (NPV) and internal rate of return (IRR) methods where time value of money is taken into account.

DOWNGRADING Same level of service or comparable results are sought through less expensive or time consuming ways.

DSS See Decision Support System.

ENCUMBRANCES Obligations in the form of purchase orders, contracts, and other commitments reserved for a specific purpose.

EXPENDITURES   Amounts paid or liabilities incurred for all purposes.

FAVORABLE VARIANCE   Excess of standard (or budgeted) costs over actual costs. See also Variance.

FINANCIAL MODELS   Functional branch of a general planning model. It is essentially used to generate pro forma financial statements and financial ratios. A financial model is a mathematical model describing the interrelationships among financial variables of the entity. It is the basic tool for budgeting and budget planning. Also, it is used for risk analysis and what-if experiments. Many financial models are built using special modeling languages such as *IFPS/Plus* or spreadsheet programs such as *Lotus 1-2-3*.

FINANCIAL PROJECTION   Essential element of planning that is the basis for budgeting activities and estimating future financing needs of an entity. Financial projections (forecasts) begin with forecasting sales and their related expenses.

FIXED BUDGET   See Static Budget.

FLASH REPORT   Report that provides the highlights of key information promptly to the responsible manager. An example is an exception report such as performance reports that highlight favorable or unfavorable variances. A flash report allows managers to take corrective action for an unfavorable variance.

FLEXIBLE (VARIABLE) BUDGET   Budget based on different levels of activity. It is an extremely useful tool for comparing the actual cost incurred to the cost allowable for the activity level achieved. It is dynamic in nature rather than static.

FLEXIBLE BUDGET FORMULA   See Cost-Volume Formula.

FORECAST   1. Projection or an estimate of revenue, income, or costs. 2. Projection of future financial position and operating results of an organization. See also Financial Projection.

FTE   Full-time equivalent. For example, FTE may express the salary of a social worker employed 2 days in a 5-day work week. The FTE is .40 (2/5) multiplied by 40 hours, or 16 hours.

FUND   Fiscal and accounting entity with a self-balancing set of accounts recording cash and other financial resources, together with related liabilities and residual balances, and changes therein.

FUND ACCOUNTING   System used by nonprofit organizations. Since there is no profit motive, accountability is measured instead of profitability.

GOAL SEEKING   Situation where a manager wishes to determine what change would have to take place in the value of a specified variable in a specified time period to achieve a specified value for another variable.

INCOME   Revenue and nonrevenue receipts.

INCREMENTAL BUDGET   Budget in which next year's budget will differ little from this year's budget and line item adjustments are made on a straight percentage basis.

INTERNAL RATE OF RETURN (IRR)   Rate earned on a proposal. It is the rate of interest that equates the initial investment (I) with the present value (PV) of future cash inflows.

LINE ITEM BUDGET   Budget typically used by nonprofit entities in which budgeted financial statement elements are grouped by administrative entities and object. These budget item groups are usually presented in an incremental fashion that is in comparison to previous periods.

LONG-RANGE BUDGET   Projections that cover more than one fiscal year; also called strategic budgeting. The five-year budget plan is the most commonly used in practice. See also Annual Budget.

MANAGEMENT BY EXCEPTION   Management concept or policy by which management devotes its time to investigating only those situations in which actual results differ significantly from planned results. The idea is that management should spend its valuable time concentrating on the more important items (such as the shaping of the entity's future strategic course).

MANAGEMENT BY OBJECTIVE (MBO)   System of performance appraisal having the following characteristics: (1) It is a formal system in that each manager is required to take certain prescribed actions and to complete certain written documents; and (2) the manager and subordinates discuss the subordinate's job description, agree to short-term performance targets, discuss the progress made towards meeting these targets, and periodically evaluate the performance and provide the feedback.

MANAGEMENT CONTROL SYSTEM   System under which managers assure that resources are obtained and used effectively and efficiently in the accomplishment of the organization's goals.

MANAGEMENT INFORMATION SYSTEM (MIS)   Computer-based or manual system that transforms data into information useful in the support of decision-making.

MASTER (COMPREHENSIVE) BUDGET   Plan of activities expressed in monetary terms of the assets, liabilities, revenues, and costs that will be involved in carrying out the plans. Simply put, a master budget is a set of projected or planned financial statements.

MODELING LANGUAGES   Usually English-like programming languages that are used to solve a specific task and generate various reports based on the solution and analysis. For example, financial planning modeling languages such as IFPS (Integrated Financial Planning System) are computer software packages that help financial planners develop a financial model in English terms (not requiring any computer programming knowledge on his/her part), perform various analyses such as what-if analysis, and further generate pro forma financial reports.

NET PRESENT VALUE METHOD   Method widely used for evaluating investment projects. Under the net present value method, the present value (PV) of all cash inflows from the project is compared against the initial investment (I).

NET PRESENT VALUE (NPV)   Difference between the present value (PV) of cash inflows generated by the project and the amount of the initial investment (I).

NONREVENUE RECEIPTS   Receipts of money in exchange for property of the entity or for which the entity incurs an obligation.

OBJECT   As used in an expenditure classification, a term that applies to the article purchased or the service obtained.

OBJECTIVES   Expected accomplishments. For example, budget objectives should be specific, attainable, challenging, measurable, documented, flexible, up-to-date, and timely.

OPERATIONAL (OPERATING) BUDGET   Budget that embraces the effects of operating decisions. It contains forecasts of revenue and costs.

PERFORMANCE REPORT   Medium to short-range report, highlighting the performance of individuals or departments within the organization. It is typical of the type incorporated by a program planning budgeting system (PPBS) but without references to long-range goals. It includes effectiveness measures and evaluation by program, service, or activity. An example is appraising fund raising by specifying donations obtained, call frequency, and dollar amount of contributions per hour spent.

PLANNING   Selection of short- and long-term objectives and the drawing up of tactical and strategic plans to achieve those objectives. In planning, managers outline the steps to be taken in moving the organization toward its objectives. After deciding on a set of strategies to be followed, the organization needs more specific plans, such as locations, methods of financing, hours of operations, etc. As these plans are made, they will be communicated throughout the organization. When implemented, the plans will serve to coordinate, or meld together, the efforts of all parts of the organization toward the entity's objectives.

PROFITABILITY INDEX   Ratio of the total present value (PV) of future cash inflows to the initial investment (I).

PROGRAM   Group of related activities that consists of a unique combination of objects that operate together to achieve common goals.

PROGRAM-PLANNING-BUDGETING SYSTEM (PPBS) Planning-oriented approach to developing a program budget. A program budget is a budget wherein expenditures are based primarily on programs of work and secondarily on character and object. It is a transitional type of budget between the traditional character and object budget, on the one hand, and the performance budget on the other. The major contribution of PPBS lies in the planning process, i.e., the process of making program policy decisions that lead to a specific budget and specific multi-year plans.

PROJECTED (BUDGETED) FUND STATEMENT Schedule for expected assets, liabilities, and net assets (fund balance). It projects an entity's financial position as of the end of the budgeting year. Reasons for preparing a budgeted balance sheet follow: (1) discloses unfavorable financial condition that management may want to avoid; (2) serves as a final check on the mathematical accuracy of all other budgets; and (3) highlights future resources and obligations.

PROJECTED (BUDGETED) STATEMENT OF INCOME AND EXPENDITURES Summary of various component projections of income and expenditures for the budget period. It indicates the expected surplus or deficit for the period.

RESPONSIBILITY ACCOUNTING Collection, summarization, and reporting of financial information about various decision centers (responsibility centers) throughout an organization.

RESPONSIBILITY CENTER Unit in the organization that has control over costs, revenues, or investment funds. For accounting purposes, responsibility centers are classified as cost centers, revenue centers, profit centers, and investment centers, depending on what each center is responsible for.

RESTRICTED REVENUE Monies that are received with some strings attached.

REVENUE Addition to assets for which no obligations are incurred.

REVENUE BUDGET Operating plan for a period expressed in terms of activity volume and fees for each class of service. Preparation of a revenue budget is the starting point in budgeting since revenue influences nearly all other items.

REVENUE FORECASTING Projection or prediction of future revenue. It is the foundation for the quantification of the entire business plan and a master budget. Revenue forecasts serve as a basis for planning.

SENSITIVITY ANALYSIS Form of simulation that enables decision makers to experiment with decision alternatives and possibilities using a what-if approach. The manager might wish to evaluate alternative policies and assumptions about the external environment by asking a series of what-if questions. See also Simulation.

SIMULATION   Attempt to represent a real-life system via a model to determine how a change in one or more variables affects the rest of the system, also called what-if analysis. See also Financial Models; Simulation Models.

SIMULATION MODELS   What-if models that attempt to simulate the effects of alternative management policies and assumptions about the entity's external environment. They are basically a tool for management's laboratory. For example, the financial effect of a change in expected contributions on the nonprofit entity may be seen.

SITE-ORIENTED BUDGETING   Budgeting method in which greater emphasis is placed on differences among sites such as schools rather than among programs.

STATIC (FIXED) BUDGET   Budget based on one level of activity (e.g., one particular service-volume).

STRATEGIC PLANNING   Implementation of an organization's objectives. Strategic planning decisions will have long-term effects on the organization while operational decisions are day-to-day in nature.

TEMPLATE   Worksheet or computer program that includes the relevant formulas for a particular application but not the data. It is a blank worksheet that we save and fill in the data as needed for a future forecasting and budgeting application.

TRANSFER   Interfund payments or receipts not chargeable to expenditures or credited to income.

UNAPPROPRIATED FUND BALANCE   Portion of a fund balance not segregated for specific purposes.

UNENCUMBERED BALANCE   Portion of an appropriation or allotment not yet expended or obligated.

UNRESTRICTED REVENUE   Monies where the grantor has tied no strings on how the money may be spent.

VARIABLE BUDGET   See Flexible Budget.

VARIANCE   Difference of revenues and costs from planned amounts. One of the most important phases of responsibility accounting is establishing standards in costs and revenues, and establishing performance by comparing actual amounts with the standard amounts. The differences (variances) are calculated for each responsibility center, analyzed, and unfavorable variances are investigated for possible remedial action.

WHAT-IF ANALYSIS (SCENARIOS)   See Simulation.

ZERO-BASE BUDGETING   Planning and budgeting tool that uses cost/benefit analysis of projects and functions to improve resource allocation in an organization. Traditional budgeting tends to concentrate on the incremental change from the previous year. It assumes that the previous year's activities and programs are essential and must be continued. Under zero-base budgeting, however, cost and benefit estimates are built from scratch, from the zero level, and must be justified.

Index